SOUNDS
Unlikely
ℰ Music in Birmingham ℭ

SOUNDS *Unlikely*

ဢ Music in Birmingham ෆ

Margaret Handford

BREWIN BOOKS

First edition published by
the Birmingham and Midland Institute 1992

This revised and expanded edition
first published 2006 by Brewin Books,
56 Alcester Road, Studley, Warwickshire, B80 7LG

www.brewinbooks.com

© Margaret Handford 1992 and 2006

All rights reserved

ISBN 1 85858 287 3

The moral right of the author has been asserted

A Cataloguing in Publication Record
for this title is available from the British Library

Typeset in Bembo
Printed in Great Britain by
Cromwell Press Ltd.

Contents

List of Illustrations..vii
Acknowledgements x
Foreword by Sakari Oramo...xii
Introduction..xiii

PART ONE: 1392-1900..1
1 Six centuries ago..2
2 Some evidence for medieval music in Birmingham................7
3 The town grows 1700-1768..12
4 Not to be written on the back.....................................29
   of a postage stamp 1740-1800
5 From Music Meeting to Musical Festival.........................46
   with a portrait gallery of stars 1768-1834
6 What else?..72
7 After the building of the Town Hall..............................82
8 Costa, Stockley and 'this wonderful choir'....................104
9 Costa's reign. The Birmingham Musical Festivals 1849-1882.....109
10 A Boa Constrictor? 1834-1880..................................120
11 The Harrison Concerts. Another gallery of celebrities.......137
12 Some Birmingham musical personalities......................147
13 Musical Education. The establishment.........................153
   of the Midland Institute School of Music
14 Nineteenth century church music in Birmingham.............161
15 By the people, for the people...................................165
16 Stockley's Orchestra 1873-1897.................................167
17 Chamber Music...173
18 Hans Richter. The Twilight of the Gods.......................175
   The Musical Festivals 1885-1912

PART TWO: THE TWENTIETH CENTURY..................................183
  19 Introducing the twentieth century......................................184
  20 Phase One: Birmingham Musical Festival – Cause of death.................189
  21 Elgar and Birmingham..195
  22 Halford's concerts..206
  23 An Orchestral Medley..214
  24 The Choral craze..225
  25 A miscellany 1900-1920..232
  26 Granville Bantock – larger than life..................................240
  27 Phase Two: A City Orchestra – the new musical flagship.................246
  28 Again, what else?...284
  29 Phase Three: Transformation – the Rattle effect.......................314

APPENDICES
  1. Office holders in the musical world in Birmingham.............331
  2. Biographical notes on some of the people mentioned............334
      in the text 1834-1992

Bibliography..342

Index...346

List of Illustrations

Birmingham, 1656 (Dugdale Antiquities of Warwickshire)..3
Westley's East Prospect of Birmingham, 1732...13
The Plan of Birmingham, surveyed in the year 1731 by Mr. Westley......................14
Blue Coat School, Birmingham...16
    The following four illustrations are reproduced by courtesy of the Birmingham Library Services, Local Studies and History:
        Title page of one of Michael Broome's Birmingham Publications, 1744...........17
        From *A Collection of Twenty-four Psalm-tunes*,.......................................18
            by Michael Broome, Birmingham 1744
        From *A Collection of Psalm-tunes in IV parts*,..19
            Michael Broome, Birmingham 1760
        St. Bartholomew's Church, Birmingham..21
James Kempson..28
Vauxhall Gardens...33
John Freeth and his friends by Eckstein..41
The tune of *A Warwickshire Lad*..43
Angelica Catalani, 1780-1849..56
John Braham, tenor, 1774-1856..62
Robert Lindley, 1776-1855..64
    (Reproduced with the permission of the *National Portrait Gallery*)
Theatre Royal, New Street, Birmingham, exterior view...................................74
Theatre Royal, New Street, Birmingham, interior view....................................75
Joseph Moore, 1766-1849..85
Interior of the Birmingham Town Hall as it appeared in 1846...........................86
A Concert scene, 1840 – (Source Unknown)..87
Hanover Square Concert Rooms, 1843...88
    (Reproduced with acknowledgements to the
    London Illustrated News Picture Library)
Clara Novello, 1818-1908...91
Birmingham Musical Festival, 1834. A Grand Selection of Sacred Music...............92
    to be performed in the New Town Hall on Tuesday Morning
    the Seventh of October

Birmingham Musical Festival, 1834. First Miscellaneous Concert..........................92
  to be performed in the New Town Hall on
  Tuesday Evening the Seventh of October.
Felix Mendelssohn, 1809-47 (Reproduced with acknowledgements.....................94
  to the *London Illustrated News Picture Library*)
William Pountney, chorus bass and Festival commentator, 1846-1897.....................95
Mario Giovanni Matteo, Cavaliere di Candia, 1810-1883..96
  (Reproduced by kind permission of the *Royal College of Music*)
Giulia Grisi, 1811-1869..97
Charles Lockey, 1820-1901. First tenor in *Elijah*..102
Michele Costa, 1808-84 (Michael Costa in 1872)...110
Gounod's sketch for the arrangement of choir and orchestra...............................115
  for *The Redemption* (Birmingham Musical Festival 1882)
Sims Reeves and Catherine Hayes in *Lucia di Lammermoor* 1846.........................126
Alfred Mellon, 1820-1867...127
Adelina Patti, 1843-1919..139
The Joachim Quartet, 1888 (Joachim, Louis Ries, Ludwig Straus and Piatti)..........140
Clara Schumann, 1819-1896...141
Wilma Norman-Neruda, Lady Hallé, 1839-1911...141
  leading a quartet 'At the Monday Pops'
Clara Butt, contralto, 1873-1936..146
F. Edward Bache...150
The Three B's – B sharp, B flat and B natural..150
  (Bülow, Buonamici and Walter Bache)
Sarah Ann Glover, 1785-1867..155
John Curwen, 1816-1880...156
The original Birmingham and Midland Institute, Paradise Street..........................160
William Stockley, 1830-1919..172
Hans Richter, 1843-1916..176
Henry J. Wood, 1869-1944...180
Birmingham Town Hall ca. 1905..181
Edward Elgar in 1900...198
Muriel Foster, mezzo - soprano, 1877-1937...199
Mason College, Edmund Street, before 1886...203
  (Later the University of Birmingham. This is
  where the present Central Library now stands).
Halford and Halford's Orchestra with Kreisler as soloist..210
  Kreisler's last concert with them was on
  7th November 1905 in the Town Hall
Granville Bantock..242

Very sincere thanks must go to the City of Birmingham Symphony Orchestra for making available from its archive the following photographs of its conductors, also to the named photographers for giving permission for their use:

Appleby Matthews..249
Adrian Boult (photograph by Constantine)...251
Leslie Heward...257
George Weldon...262
Rudolf Schwarz..266
Harold Gray (photograph by Constantine)..270
Hugo Rignold and the CBSO rehearsing in Nottingham....................272
Louis Frémaux at the Town Hall in rehearsal with the CBSO............277
    (photograph by Alan Wood)
G. D. Cunningham, Birmingham City Organist and.................................290
    Festival Choral Society Conductor
George Thalben-Ball...299
Simon Rattle in the recording studio...320
Simon Rattle and the CBSO in rehearsal...322
    (photograph by Alan Wood)
The audience of tomorrow: Rattle meeting children after a..............323
    CBSO family concert
Sakari Oramo...325
Simon Halsey (photograph by Alan Wood)..326
Symphony Hall...330

Acknowledgements

The author's thanks must go first to Patrick Baird and all the staff of the Birmingham Central Library's Local Studies and Archives Departments, where many valuable printed records relating to the city's music are held. He and all the staff there are always ready to help the honest enquirer and to point out other lines of enquiry. I would also like to acknowledge the ever pertinent and prompt guidance of the late Ian Ledsham, formerly Music Librarian at the University of Birmingham, as well as that of the current library staff member, Greg McKernon, who has given some exceedingly useful practical help. Kind permission to study Midland Institute School of Music registers was also granted by the Librarian at Birmingham Conservatoire, Robert Allan, and is much appreciated, and the Honorary Secretary of the Birmingham Conservatoire Association, John Smith, has also most helpfully furnished material which the author might not otherwise have come across.

Further permission willingly given by a number of organisations, to reproduce photographs and documents in their possession, must also be acknowledged with gratitude. Full details of these are given in the list of illustrations.

The author also very much appreciates encouragement given by the late Jo Hunt, formerly Administrator of the Birmingham and Midland Institute, and the historical material provided by the late Dr. Percy Young, the music historian and author, whose kindly interest is gratefully remembered. Nor must she forget Dr. Lawrence Snell who conducted the Local History course for Birmingham University Extramural Department which initially launched these enquiries.

Three people in particular have spent significant amounts of time in assisting the final stages of the production of this book. The author is most grateful to Michael Jones for sharing with her some of his encyclopedic knowledge of Birmingham residents who were, or are, composers and for allowing her to use some of it. Very special thanks must also certainly be expressed to Beresford King-Smith, the City of Birmingham Symphony Orchestra's Archivist, for his continued practical help and guidance; also to Christopher Morley, Music Critic of the Birmingham Post. All three have been prepared to spend time in reading and commenting on the script, though it must be emphasised that the author takes full responsibility for the final version. The writer is also indebted to Fathers Petroc Howell and Brian Doolan for information about the history of the music at St. Chad's Cathedral, to Margery Elliott for the use of Edwin Elliott's reminiscences about the choirs he joined and to Janet Waterhouse for allowing her to inspect J. F. Waterhouse's music reviews for the *Birmingham Post*.

Finally, a great debt of appreciation is owed to the writer's husband for his constant encouragement - and tolerance. This book is dedicated to him and to the family, particularly to one of our sons, John, who suggested the title 'Sounds Unlikely', and to his son David, who spent many hours scanning text and organising it on computer, ready for revision and correction. The title was intended to reflect the unfairly low expectations outsiders often seem to have had of Birmingham's artistic life, especially during the twentieth century - something that Brummies themselves were often guilty of before the 1980 'Rattle' watershed, - and also the surprise expressed by many at finding how far back this history reaches. It is hoped therefore that the following pages will remind all Birmingham's citizens of their rich heritage, and place in their true setting the more recent exciting and prestigious developments connected with the new Symphony Hall, Sir Simon Rattle, the city orchestra and other outstanding new musical enterprises.

Foreword

When I came to Birmingham in the mid-1990s to conduct the CBSO for the first time, I was well aware that the city had a lively musical scene beyond its world-famous orchestra. But over the course of my eight years here as Music Director I have become ever more aware not only of the exciting present but also of the distinguished past: the Triennial Festivals, the English Choral tradition, the contribution of the Churches and the educational institutions, and the many composers who have lived and worked here. All these stories and more are covered most fascinatingly by Margaret Handford in the following pages, and it is with some pride that I see the future activities of the CBSO, Symphony Hall, BCMG, Ex Cathedra, the Conservatoire and Universities, as well as the thriving amateur sector taking these great traditions forward. A strong musical future for this great city now sounds *most* likely!

Sakari Oramo, Music Director, CBSO
Birmingham, August 2006

Introduction

Not a place to promise much…

Many readers will be familiar with Jane Austen's *Emma*, written in 1815, in which the social-climbing Mrs. Elton speaks of an equally upstart family of her acquaintance who give themselves airs. She says of them: 'How they got their fortune nobody knows. They came from Birmingham which is not a place to promise much. One has not great hopes from Birmingham. I always say there is something direful in the sound'.

The writer must confess to rather similar expectations of Birmingham's *music* on moving to the city in 1961. This was in spite of favourable comments made by an elderly relative about the fame of Birmingham's Festival Chorus in the nineteenth and early twentieth centuries. In the event there were some pleasant surprises, with much more music-making than expected, some of it of a high standard, though not so high as after 1980 when the young Simon Rattle arrived in the city. Then, indeed, attitudes to the city did change.

It has to be admitted that Birmingham has at times been very good at neglecting and even burying its past, although things are now rather different. Intrigued by what lay behind the industrial facade, the writer attended a local history course at the Central Library in the 1970's. The class first learned to identify and use the available resources and were then encouraged to write something up on a subject chosen in consultation with the tutor. Urged by him to make the history of music in Birmingham the subject of my own research, it was soon a matter of being totally intrigued, not to say 'hooked' by the material uncovered.

Initially, this was put into public lecture form, only for it to be suggested along the way that it would be a good idea to expand the talks into a book. So the first, much shorter edition of the book came into being and the writer was later honoured by being asked to contribute the article on Birmingham to the second edition of the *New Grove Dictionary of Music and Musicians*, then edited by the late Stanley Sadie. This new and enlarged edition of my first book is intended for the general reader with an intelligent interest in history in all its aspects and in music as part of that. Some long-standing residents, as well as relative newcomers to the city, may well be surprised at what they discover. It is hoped that it will also be of interest to musicians and music historians.

PART ONE
1392 - 1900

Chapter 1

Six centuries ago

In 1392, some of the town's most prominent and well-to-do citizens were granted a licence to found a Gild and perpetual brotherhood of the Holy Cross for men and women in Birmingham. The Gild had its own hall and undertook some charitable work and certain public responsibilities, but from the point of view of this book, the most significant thing it did was to maintain chantry priests at St. Martin's to sing masses, and an organist who lived in a house by the church. This state of affairs lasted until 1536, when Henry VIII confiscated the funds which had been donated for the maintenance of the chantries. This was followed in 1547 by his son Edward VI's appropriation of the assets of the Gilds.

All this seems dim and distant to us now, six centuries later, but the facts are incontrovertible and of some musical significance. The Gild included leading citizens among its members throughout its one hundred and fifty years of existence, and music, along with its various social and practical activities, was a central and well-funded part of its purpose.

Before looking at the documents which provide the evidence for the foregoing statements, and considering their musical implications in more detail, perhaps we should try to fill in the general medieval background. Given that Birmingham has lost crucial documents which would have given us some specific facts about its early music, it is necessary to look at documents about music from other places in the kingdom at that period and try to draw some inferences from those. The reader is therefore asked to allow for the fact that the following section will deal less with documented facts and events, and more with a certain amount of explanation and extrapolation.

General Medieval Background
At the time of the Domesday Survey, which William the Conqueror ordered in 1086, Birmingham was about one and a quarter miles by three-quarters of a mile in area, and nestled among trees on the slope running up Digbeth to St. Martin's Church. Running across and beneath Digbeth was the River Rea (pronounced 'Ray'), then a free-flowing stream, rather liable to flood. It is very hard for us to imagine it all, but a drawing made in 1656 and found in Dugdale's *Antiquities of Warwickshire,* at least has the merit of helping us to visualise Birmingham as a parish and small town, separate

Chapter 1 - Six centuries ago

Birmingham, 1656 (Dugdale Antiquities of Warwickshire).

from its neighbours. The neighbours are now absorbed into Birmingham's inner city areas and suburbs of course. At any rate, here it is.

It is fair to assume, from other evidence, that while it seems to have increased in size, the town did not greatly change its overall shape during the 600 years after the conquest. Houses would be fewer and possibly smaller earlier on, and the lesser streets perhaps laid out differently, but basically Birmingham grew round Digbeth, St. Martin's Church and the V-shaped fork into High Street and New Street at the top of the hill.

Birmingham - a small but successful market-town

People often make the mistake of thinking that because Birmingham before the middle of the sixteenth century looks very small compared to the present city, it was of minimal importance. To put this into perspective we should first remind ourselves that at the same period London itself only extended from the Tower to Temple Bar, and North of the river as far as Moorgate and Cripplegate. It had 35,000 inhabitants as against Birmingham's 2,000 or 3,000, a proportion of ten or twelve to one, something of the same order as at present, though Birmingham's relative importance is, admittedly, far greater now.

The evidence

What Birmingham's importance was at that time can best be estimated by looking at the following chart. This summarises some of the facts about this medieval market-town. It is derived from the *Victoria County History. A History of the County of Warwick* (Volume VII. *Birmingham*).

3

BIRMINGHAM 1166-1400 Main Source: *Victoria County History:* Warwickshire

1166 (Confirmed 1189)	Grant for weekly market on Thursdays. (possibly only confirming existing situation)
1250	Annual 4-day fair at Ascensiontide approved. (Calendar of Charter Rolls. Membrane 13)
1275	Representatives of town's burgesses summoned to Parliament.
1322	Birmingham wool merchants at a council at York. Walter de Clodeshales, William de Mercer described as 'majores mercatores lanarium'.
1327	Sir William de Bermingham (Bremycham) summoned to Upper House of Parliament.
1327 1332	Levy records show town of Birmingham was paying more in taxation to crown than neighbouring settlements.
1340	Birmingham and Stratford third among Warwickshire towns whose merchants paid a levy on goods sold. Only Coventry ahead of them.
1400	A second fair granted, at Michaelmas (September). The *two* fairs survived to 1851. In 1875 'pleasure fairs' stopped.

Birmingham and some of its leading citizens, 1166-1400
(Majores mercatores lanarium - major merchants of wool)

We know also that one wool merchant, John atte Holte, had a substantial trading connection with the continent of Europe, and that European weavers settled in Birmingham. An earlier writer on Birmingham commented that the town was 'always in close touch with all the leading movements of national life', and this does seem to be a fair assessment.[1]

Birmingham's rather poor agricultural land stimulated trade, since it was not possible to depend entirely on the fruits of cultivation, and this tendency was encouraged by the Lords of the Manor, the de Berminghams, to whom the town owes a debt of gratitude. Subsequent independence of action, and successful industrial and commercial enterprises, were to no small extent the end result of the de Bermingham's policies.

Even in the medieval period, Birmingham's market was frequented by Welsh cattle drovers and by corn merchants, and by 1500 the Birmingham fairs which were trade fairs were selling pottery, iron and tin goods, salt and sugar, and a range of imported goods such as spice, almonds, oranges, soap and paper.[2] Well-to-do families are known to have done some of their purchasing here and, in general, Birmingham emerges as a busy market town and trading centre, already ahead of its neighbours, with some substantial wool merchants and an enterprising manorial family. Birmingham also elected a bailiff and an under-bailiff. These officials controlled matters connected with orderly market trading and selected jurors.

The musical implications

Rather typical of Birmingham, unfortunately, the bailiffs' accounts, along with the Court Rolls (manor records), have not survived. These might well have revealed, for example, whether or not Birmingham's officials spent any money on a town musician or musicians. Coventry certainly had its paid waits who, for a few years after their establishment around 1423, may very probably have been allowed to come and play in Birmingham. There is evidence that the Coventry Waits had trumpets, pipes, drums, a dulcimer, viols and organs, and wore coarse red woollen coats as part of their livery. They would probably sound the night watch to show all was well, play fanfares for the arrival of distinguished strangers, and provide music at banquets, weddings, and at the mystery plays. Soon after their establishment, however, they were confined by the Coventry authorities to playing within a 10-mile radius of the City, implying that until then they had been travelling much further afield and so – perhaps – as far as Birmingham. Other evidence, from 1571, shows that Liverpool on the other hand had one solitary bagpiper as town musician, but because of the lack of records, we can never know for certain whether or not the Birmingham bailiffs ever went in for the same kind of expenditure, and employed an official town musician or musicians. It seems highly probable that they did.

What is more certain is that itinerant or travelling ballad-singers, both male and female, and also minstrels, singly or in groups, would have put Birmingham with its market and fairs on their regular 'touring circuit' of market-towns, giving the town some musical input, even if the quality varied greatly. Some minstrels were little better than beggars, hence the need to establish official waits, but many must have provided genuine entertainment.

As to the ballad singers, we know from various descriptions that they usually employed the raucous tones now associated with an auctioneer at a cattle-sale. This is quite a skilled business, in fact, since the voice must not only carry, it must carry the words clearly as well. It must also be supported by the right breath control, or the voice will simply not survive when used constantly in that way, particularly in the open air. What did they sing about? Contemporary events and universally shared experiences, such as an unhappy love affair, or a harsh, over-demanding master, figured largely in their ballads. It is said that John Aubrey's nurse (John Aubrey was born in 1626) had a collection of ballads which provided a history of England from the Conquest to Charles I, and a ballad by Thomas Deloney about the Spanish Armada appeared in print immediately after that event and has survived.

Occasionally, singers indulged in political and social agitation, and some people would have liked to ban them, both for their strident voices and for their critical opinions. Nevertheless, they were undoubtedly popular and persisted until an impersonal and overcrowded industrialised society, and cheap daily newspapers, put them out of business.

Like the minstrels, who would probably accompany themselves, the ballad-singers would vary tremendously. Some were little better than a distraction, enabling pick-pockets to operate among the listeners. Some devised tunes memorable enough to have 'caught on' and gone into general circulation and would probably accompany themselves on an instrument. The best tunes might end up in print, because they were popular and would sell, others travelled so widely that they eventually acquired many local or regional variants. Others, again, were printed first, as with Deloney's Armada ballad, and then went out into the streets.

Some tunes found their way into church services and there they were expected to be sung with the 'high, sweet and strong' voice urged by authorities on choral singing, from Isidore of Seville, in the sixth century, onwards. We shall try to assess what happened in Birmingham's parish church in the next chapter.

In general, then, a tune was part of a musical coinage which passed from hand to hand, so to speak, the temporary owner making what use of it he wanted. Certainly Birmingham would be part of this system, hearing from the ballad singers old and new tunes, often conveying the latest news, the place being, as usual, 'in on the act'. And if you were a respectable singer or minstrel, where better to offer your services than in an inn or inn-yard in a busy market-town such as Birmingham?

---

1. William Moughton: *The Story of Birmingham's Growth Interwoven with the Growth of the Nation.*
2. Marie B. Rowlands: *The West Midlands from AD 1000.*

Chapter 2

Some evidence for medieval music in Birmingham

The chantries and the Guild of the Holy Cross 1392

So far we have been speculating, but what is certain is that there were a number of chantry priests in Birmingham in this period, appointed to sing divine service in St. Martin's Church and, what is of more significance, there was also a paid organist for whom the town's Guild actually went to the trouble of providing a house.

A chantry is an endowment which was made by a well-to-do patron, to pay a priest or priests to say or sing mass at an altar every day, in order to pray for the well-being of the soul of the patron in the after-life. In an age of belief, the welfare of the soul after death was as important a matter then as providing life-insurance for one's dependents today. This was a concern brought to the forefront of everyone's mind by the Black Death in 1348 and 1349, a particularly lethal outbreak of the plague which wiped out whole villages and was followed up by further epidemics later in the same century. This made people even more painfully aware of their own mortality and in this, as in other things, Birmingham fully participated in a contemporary trend.

In 1330 Walter de Clodeshales of Saltley, no doubt he who attended the York Wool Council in 1322, (see chart, chapter one), had put aside lands and rents to maintain a priest to sing mass daily in St. Martin's Church. In 1347 Richard Clodshall (sic) presumably Walter's son, founded a chantry for two priests to 'minister and synge masse and other divine service' within the parish church of Birmingham. Then in 1392, John Coleshill, John Goldsmith and William atte Slowe were licensed to found a gild in honour of the Holy Cross and they too endowed a chantry in St. Martin's Church (Calendar of Patent Rolls 1391-6. 137 and 138. Public Record Office).

The Guild of the Holy Cross in Birmingham seems to have been a semi-social and semi-religious foundation which carried out public works such as the repair of roads and bridges, not least the one over the River Rea, maintained a chiming clock and undertook works of charity for the relief of the poor and bereaved. It had a Guild Hall at the St. Martin's end of New Street, which was primarily for the sociable use of Guild members, and was later to become the King Edward Grammar School. The Guild's chantry in St. Martin's also found 'certyne priests to syng divyne service in the parsshe churche' and it was the Guild members who paid the organist whom they housed. So we seem to have here at least five priests involved as well as an official organist, not an insignificant establishment for that time.

Birmingham's Guild and chantry documents
Documents have survived which provide us with this information. These are chantry certificates made at the command of Henry VIII in the 1530s, at the time of the dissolution of the monasteries. This was of course long after the actual establishment of the chantries themselves, but at the time when Henry wanted a complete inventory of the lands and goods the church owned in order to appropriate them.

To quote from a transcription of one of the relevant documents: 'The said Gild was founded by Thomas Sheldon and other in the sixteenth year of King Edward the Second,[1] to find certain priests to *sing divine service* (author's italics) in the parish church aforesaid for ever, and to pray for the souls of the same founders. And in the same town of Birmingham (Byrmyngham) there be two thousand houselyng people (communicants), and at Easter time all the priests of the same Gild, and divers (various) others be not sufficient to minister the sacraments and sacramentals unto the said people found assisted and supplied by the said Gild in money, bread, drink, coals; and when any of them die they be buried very respectably at the cost and charge of the same Gild, and dirge and mass, according to the constitution of the same Gild; and there hath been no lands nor tenements sold since the time before limited, and the inventory of the goods and ornaments to the same belonging hereafter doth appear...' Yet another manuscript reveals details about the organist at St. Martin's. To quote: 'Fee for William Booth (Bothe) the organ player of the aforesaid church (St. Martin's, Birmingham) with 10 shillings for the rent of a tenement next to the same church held for life 73s 4d per annum'.

It is sometimes pointed out that chantry priests could be lazy and were not necessarily good singers. One can understand that where founders were dead or absent for any other reason, this could well be the case, particularly in small villages. In Birmingham, however, where the Clodshall family lived in the town, and the Guild of the Holy Cross paid a number of priests, housed an organist and maintained a guild hall, it seems much more likely that a decent level of competence would be expected. For the sake of their own dignity in the eyes of the citizens of the town, and as a matter of obtaining value for money, the Guild is likely to have insisted that the service it paid the priests to sing should be carried out in a seemly manner and that the organist should be worth the cost of his accommodation. The Guild is known to have devoted more money to its chantries and priests than to its charitable activities incidentally.[2]

It is unfortunately impossible to learn precisely what music they may have sung and played in Birmingham. Many churchwardens' accounts elsewhere do reveal

Chapter 2 - Some evidence for medieval music in Birmingham

payments for the purchase of music books for the services, some types of which are known to have been distributed quite widely in the more inhabited places between 1480 and 1547. Sadly, St. Martin's Churchwardens' Accounts were bombed and burnt at the church in the Second World War so that again the town has lost documents which other towns still have and which could have told us a great deal. There might, for example, have been a list of the copies of music which they owned, as has St. Peter's Church in Wolverhampton. In any case, lack of evidence certainly does not prove that things did not happen and the band of chantry priests and the organists at St. Martin's cannot have been maintained for nothing. The priests and organist which we do know were paid for, provided a small body of people sufficient to accompany the mass on Sunday and, no doubt, carols at festival times for example. If they were skilled, there were enough of them to be able to use the practice of *faux bourdon* or 'false bass', thought by some authorities to be a method of improvising a second and perhaps a third part, to combine with the plainsong chants or tunes, according to certain known customs; rather as jazz-musicians do today, though in a totally different style! There is uncertainty about this, but a competent Guild organist could also have written out certain items for the priests to learn, which he would accompany on the organ. Perhaps too, on the secular front, these musicians, along with minstrels and others, provided entertainment for Guild members in the Guild Hall? Guilds usually had their regular festivities, pageants and processions.

An organ-builder in Birmingham
To return to the Guild organists, who might with some justice be regarded as Birmingham's earliest official organists so to speak, it is interesting to note that someone was actually making organs in Birmingham by 1500. Yet again, typically, it is not from any Birmingham record that we find that out. It is the Halesowen Churchwardens' Accounts for 1503-1504 which give us the following entries:

> itm payed for rep'elyng the organs to ye organmacar of Bremycham Xs
> itm for beryng ye organs to Bremycham and whom a geyn vjd
> In modern terms, ten shillings (50p) and sixpence (2½p)

Since metal had begun to replace wool as Birmingham's economic mainstay by the late fifteenth century, should we be surprised at this information? Who better than a skilled metal-worker with a pair of keen ears and access to a supply of tin to shape and fashion organ pipes? This is the first of several notable examples we have in Birmingham of that fruitful combination of science and art which increasingly, since the Industrial Revolution, so many people have preferred to disregard, alienated perhaps by the ugliness it brought in its train.

After the Reformation

After the mid-1530s, the chantry priests at St. Martin's disappeared, the parish priest became a rector and the sung mass was replaced by the metrical psalm. Mid-sixteenth century Protestant writers all over Europe were busy turning the psalms into verses which would fit tunes that ordinary people in the congregations, unable to read music, could learn to sing.

As to the organist, we can only assume that his house was appropriated and the organ at St. Martins, as in so many other churches, dismantled. We do happen to know that the church had to 'put up an organ' in 1725, so the earlier one had obviously disappeared.

In 1547, according to Conrad Gill's *History of Birmingham*, the Commissioners of Gilds described the town as 'a very mete place and one of the fairest and most profitable towns to the King's Highness in all the shire'. Gill also tells us that to William Smith, forty years later, it was 'a proper town with a high spyre steeple'. Then in 1586, William Camden's survey of England speaks of the noise and activity of Birmingham, describing it as 'swarming with inhabitants and echoing with the noise of anvils'. One can only assume that with active enterprising citizens some, at least, would be making their own music, in spite of the loss of the Guild, its organist and the organ in St. Martin's Church.

A further shred of evidence

The absence of fuller Birmingham records for the town's earlier music is certainly unfortunate. We do however have a tiny glimpse of some musical activity in the seventeenth century town, gleaned serendipitously by Dr. Percy Young from a family's petty-cash book. The Shuttleworths of Gawthorpe Hall, near Burnley in Lancashire, travelled to London in 1609, apparently making two overnight stops on the way; one in Birmingham and one in Aylesbury. The entries in their accounts book read: 'To music at Birmingham, two shillings' and 'To music at Aylesbury 2d'. So either the minstrel in Birmingham was better than the one in Aylesbury or, alternatively, in Birmingham there was a band of minstrels! From what we know of what was paid at that period to court violinists for attending at royal events, it seems to the writer that in Birmingham there was most probably a band of musicians. In any case, could the obviously active and enterprising citizens of the town have been exempt from the natural human tendency to make music and some of it, by the law of averages, to a very good standard?

During the period of the Civil War, when 80 houses in the town were burned down by Prince Rupert's troops, the dearth of musical evidence is complete. Only one ballad, and that without a tune, could be found by this author in the local archives. Nevertheless, in spite of the Civil War, Birmingham's population grew inexorably from about two or three thousand in 1600 to about fifteen thousand in

1700. An iron master like John Jennens for example, well-established in the town by 1653, grew rich and prospered mightily, as did others on a smaller scale. His musical connections will become clear in the next chapter.

Some theatrical music in the town?
After the Civil War, only London theatres were re-licensed, but travelling theatrical companies, or drolls, continued to visit provincial towns, setting up temporary stages and offering favourite comic or tragic scenes from Shakespeare, or plays of their own making. These were usually well-laced with songs. It is fair to surmise that Birmingham with its market, its fair and its inn-yards would be on their touring circuit. No doubt, as has been said, standards of performance would vary!

So Birmingham has been unfortunate (or perhaps careless!) in that written records which other towns possess, it does not. It is certain from the few which have survived that Birmingham was a busy trading centre and, behind the scanty records, what we do have is the shadowy picture of a place with skilled artisans and active, intelligent leading citizens. Could such a place possibly have been silent, musically speaking, in times when there was no electronically-produced music and people made their own entertainments? Would not a few of them at least have been highly skilled musicians? A speech of Mr. Gladstone's at a much later date, in 1873, is relevant on this point. In it he said "It is not likely we shall be rated by posterity as highly as we have rated ourselves... It is an insufferable arrogance for men in any particular age to assume airs of immeasurable superiority over men of former ages".[3]

This above all is the idea borne in on the mind by a close acquaintance with this town's musical past. We should not assume that all musicians of past ages were less able than those of today, simply because their instruments and their printing of music were less sophisticated. Moreover, if we compare music with another human skill, that of navigation, can we honestly claim that today's merchant seamen are better navigators than the Viking mariners who successfully set their unaided courses across the wild waters between Scandinavia and the continent of America? In any case, it may be repeated that the law of averages suggests that some at least of the town's musicians would have been very competent. The case rests.

---

1. This should be Richard II as the year was 1392.
2. Conrad Gill: *History of Birmingham*.
3. Quoted by Charles Lunn in his open letter *Musical Education* (Birmingham 1881).

Chapter 3

The town grows
1700-1768

The building of St. Philip's Church and its important musical outcome

From now onwards in this account, we have an ever-increasing mass of firm and precise evidence about music in Birmingham. After 1700 it became obvious that a second church was needed to minister to the growing population, especially the part of it living in the new area which had sprung up to the West of the original town. Land was given by Robert Phillips in 1705, the building began in 1711 and the church was dedicated, with its founder in mind, to St Philip. By the time it was consecrated in 1715, it had been provided with a fine organ, built by one whose name was variously spelt as Schwarbrick or Swarbrick (originally Schwarbruch). The instrument then stood at the West end of the church, being moved to its present position, to the North of the chancel, in 1883. Schwarbruch had been employed by the great organ-builder Renatus Harris and, after moving to Warwick, was involved in either the building or the repair of a number of Midland organs, as for example at Coventry (St Michael's), Warwick, Uppingham and Worcester Cathedral. He repaired the St. Philip's organ in 1734 for the sum of £30 (about £900 in to-day's values), and again in 1748, for £50. In 1777 Snetzler, who built the organ used for the first performance of Handel's *Messiah* in Dublin in 1741, restored and enlarged the St. Philip's instrument.

The fine new church, with its fine new organ, was a magnet which was to attract some very gifted and enterprising musicians to the town, and this, in turn, played an important part in the development of the musical life of Birmingham. One wonders how much they, (that is Robert Phillips and the church's designer, Thomas Archer) were spurred on by the rebuilding of St. Paul's Cathedral in London, after the Great Fire in 1666. St.Paul's, started by Wren in 1672, was only completed in 1717. The dominance of St. Philip's in Westley's *East Prospect of Birmingham,* 1732, which depicts the church as towering over the town in a way which is quite out of proportion to the reality, suggests that they all had some such grand parallel in mind.

One wonders, also, how much some of the townspeople at that time were conscious of there being something of a re-establishment of an older order. Family memories might still have reached back as far as the 'Romish' services at St. Martin's

Chapter 3 - The town grows 1700-1768

Westley's East Prospect of Birmingham, 1732.

before Good Queen Bess's time. In any case the first of the 'new' generation of organists was Barnabas Gunn, who was at St. Philip's from 1715 to 1730, and he was typical of the calibre of musician associated with the growing town in the eighteenth century. He is thought to have been born in Birmingham and it would be very interesting to know where he had been trained for he seems to have been particularly noted for his ability to extemporise. Here is an area for some further research into local records, but Gunn seems to have left St. Philip's in 1733 when he was appointed as organist at Gloucester Cathedral. He then published *Two Cantatas and Six Songs* in 1736, with Handel and most of the principal musicians of the day among the 464 subscribers, pledging themselves to buy a copy. He also seems to have produced some sonatas for harpsichord, and there were in addition two sets of solos, one for 'cello and the other for violin and 'cello, published in London and Birmingham respectively. He left Gloucester Cathedral in 1740, presumably to return to Birmingham. Like his successors, (and like organists today!) Gunn needed to earn a good part of his living from some other activity, and at his death on 6th February 1753, he was described as organist of two churches (St. Philip's and St. Martin's) and Post-Master of the town.

A new organ for St. Martin's Church
It is not surprising to discover that all this spurred the original parish, St. Martin's, into activity. Some parts of the St. Martin's Churchwardens Accounts are fortunately preserved in the Town Book, held at the Birmingham Central Library. The relevant entry reads as follows:

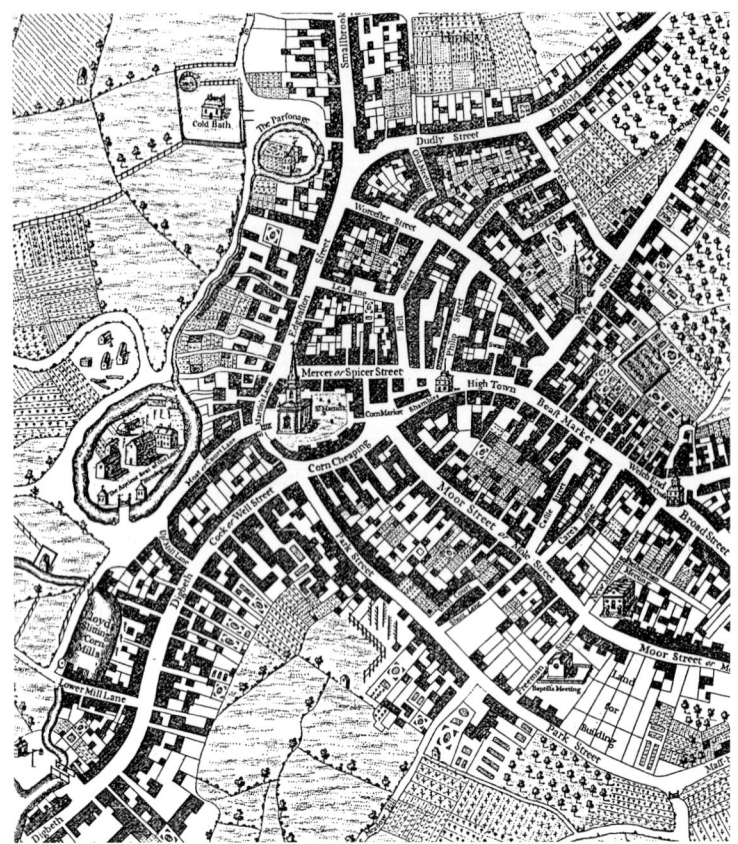

The Plan of Birmingham, surveyed in the year 1731 by Mr. Westley.

'We the Minister, Churchwardens and Inhabitants within the Parish of St. Martin's Birmingham being desirous to put up an organ in the said Parish Church have at a vestry called for this purpose unanimously agreed to raise the sum of 3001 (£300) and upwards for completing the same, and for ourselves, and in behalf of the rest of the Parishioners have hereunto sett our hands this 17th day of May Anno Dom' 1725'.

This was signed by the rector, Tho. Groom(?), the Churchwardens, Tho. Wood, Joshua Lowe and twelve parishioners.

Barnabas Gunn's other musical activities
To return to Barnabas Gunn we find that, again like his successors at St. Philip's, he had an entrepreneurial spirit. He promoted 'musical entertainments' (as they were described), at the Apollo pleasure-gardens and at Mr. Sawyer's 'great room' at the

Moor Street Theatre. More of these venues later, but meanwhile disabuse yourself immediately of the idea that these were modest affairs, promoting local amateurs. Gunn brought celebrities to Birmingham, people associated with the already-established Three Choirs Festivals and with the much older Chapel Royal at Windsor. This we learn from *Aris's Birmingham Gazette,* the early Birmingham newspaper, set up in 1743.

One final reference to Barnabas Gunn should be made in connection with an 'Evening of Entertainment' arranged for his benefit, and that of another musician, Dr. Heighington, in the early days at Moor Street Theatre. These benefit concerts were a feature of the Birmingham theatrical and concert scene; a way of supplementing the always variable and sometimes very poor income earned in these spheres. In the days before Social Security payments and pensions, this was for some the only way of achieving some savings for 'a rainy day' or a nest egg for retirement.

Michael Broome

An outsider attracted to Birmingham by the new church was Michael Broome (1700-75) who came as Clerk to St. Philip's probably sometime before 1733. His origins may well have been in the Chilterns for he had published a collection of music for use in churches in 1725, in which several tunes are named after places in Buckinghamshire and Oxfordshire. One by Broome himself is called 'Wendover'. This particular collection was issued under the names of Michael and John Broome, but we do not hear much more of John. Michael, however, also had an East Anglian connection, and later in 1741, one John Buckenham was to acknowledge that 'a considerable part' of the psalmody of Norfolk and Suffolk at that time had been 'introduced into those counties by Mr. Joseph Needham and Mr. Michael Broom (sic), ingenious teachers of the same'. This opinion is taken from the preface to John Buckenham's own *The Psalm-singer's devout exercise* (1741).[1]

Broome's duties at St. Philip's Church, Birmingham, from 1733 onwards, included leading and training the adult male singers, some of whom were paid. The melody line, or treble part, was provided by the boys and girls of the Blue Coat School, a charity school established in 1724 to care for, and train up, orphans or destitute children in some useful trade. The school was built at a right angle to the church.

From records relating to the Blue Coat School [2] it appears that the Master and Mistress were to take the children to church twice every Sunday, and the boys only, on Wednesday and Friday. Among items of expenditure recorded much later, in 1783, there are payments to 'Mr. Clark', organist, for teaching the children to sing the hymns £1.1s.0d' (that is, £1.05p). The same amount was paid him for 'teaching them to chant, and his attendance at St. Philip's, June the 5th'. Mr. Kempson, on the other hand, of whom we shall hear a great deal more, was paid only 15s (75p) for the same duties, presumably because he was only a chorister at St. Philips, and not

Blue Coat School, Birmingham.

the organist. Interestingly a Mr. Probin was also paid similarly for 'assisting the children to sing the hymns at the chapels'. The Probin family supplied a succession of good musicians in Birmingham over many years, not least later on as horn players.

To return to Michael Broome, however, he earned more fame at the time from the collection of psalm-tunes and anthems he printed. These were distributed all over the Midlands, by the men who, every week, carried the newly established *Aris's Birmingham Gazette* to centres like Coventry, Northampton and Stamford, as well as round Birmingham itself. Broome's business premises were in Litchfield Street at first, but were moved to Colmore Row when the business prospered. Nevertheless, like Gunn, Broome also needed two occupations, both as a music publisher and distributor, as well as being Clerk at St. Philip's.

Michael Broome's Birmingham publications

A Choice collection of Sixteen Excellent Psalm-Tunes. Birmingham 1733
Michael Broome's Collection of Church Music. Birmingham ca. 1733
A Choice Collection of Twenty-four Psalm-Tunes in Four Parts. Birmingham 1744
A Collection of Twenty-Eight Psalm-Tunes in Four Parts. Birmingham 1753
A Choice Collection of Eleven Anthems. Birmingham 1754
Choice Collection of Twenty-Four Psalm-Tunes. Birmingham 1756
Divine Harmony: being a collection of Twelve Anthems. Birmingham 1758
A Collection of Psalm Tunes in IV Parts. Birmingham 1760.

Chapter 3 - The town grows 1700-1768

We notice that Broome must have supplemented his income still further by teaching 'young gentlemen' to sing the tunes he published (See 1744, title page).

Why was there such a demand for these publications? To answer this we must go back to the Reformation and recall the popularity of the metrical psalms which were introduced then, giving the generality of the people a chance to sing in their own language, as opposed to standing and listening to the priests, and possibly a choir, chanting the words of the service in Latin. In due time, however, the situation deteriorated. Increasingly ill-educated and ill-paid parish clerks attempted to lead the congregation, a task not made easier if the clerk's voice was swamped by the higher voices of the women and children. This led in turn to ever slower speeds, and a general chaos of sound associated with some parish church singing in the seventeenth century. The number of tunes used dwindled, many were forgotten and in some churches the singing died out altogether. As the new urban churches were built, early in the eighteenth century, the installation of an organ re-established the organist's control over the performance of church music. Allied to this was the desire for a greater variety of psalm-tunes for the congregations and some simple, straightforward anthems in English, for the choirs which were also being re-established. As early as 1671 John Playford's *Whole Book of Psalms* had been a pioneer in this field, Playford being Clerk at the Temple Church in London. From about 1700 onwards, there was a sudden increase in demand for this publication so that others, seeing a growing market, jumped in to satisfy it. Prominent and important in this number was Michael Broome, and once again we see an ample demonstration of the point made in the first chapter of this book, that Birmingham usually managed to get itself into the mainstream of contemporary developments, sooner or later. Indeed it was helping to pioneer a new one as a closer examination of the contents of two of Broome's books will show.

In the 1744 collection there is a setting of Psalm 42 (As pants the Hart for cooling Streams), to the tune we know today as 'Oh God our help in ages past', namely 'St. Ann'. The tune is in the top line, or treble part, and this is significant.

Title Page of one of Michael Broome's Birmingham Publications 1744 (These publications are held in the Birmingham Central Library).

From a collection of twenty-four Psalm-tunes, by Michael Broome, Birmingham 1744.

To us now this seems the obvious and natural place for it; but it was not always so. If we look at Broome's 1760 Collection we shall begin to see what the significance of this is. The St. Ann tune appears again, set to different words, those of Psalm 111 (Songs of immortal praise belong). This time the tune is in the third line from the top, that is, in the tenor part (see opposite). Although this is the later collection, it is in fact in an older style, with the higher male voices singing the tune; a relic, in fact, of the days when the priests led the singing. It is ironic that this collection was for the use of dissenting meeting houses, who are thus clinging to a style which had its roots in what they would probably have dubbed a Romish practice, had they realised its source! Both the Roman Catholic church and the Puritans, of course, joined in their disapproval of female dominance, and the *castrato* singer of that era was also, in part at least, a way of avoiding any danger of petticoat government in music!

Be that as it may, the tendency for the highest voice to dominate was irresistible, for musical as well as social reasons. Musically, the melody in the top line provides a great deal more choice and variety for anyone attempting to harmonise, or put chords to, a tune. This had long been realised by composers of 'art' music. Promoting it in church was only bringing the singing of ordinary congregations more up to date. Socially, the presence of children from charity foundations in church choirs also re-inforced this musical trend, and the use of Blue Coat School children in Birmingham to sing the tunes, with their treble (soprano) voices, was typical. Since someone was paid to teach them the *tunes*, then that is what they sang when they went to church. The adult men of the choir who were also trained - and some of them paid - provided the lower parts and the congregation usually sang with the children. This would no doubt play a crucial part in Broome's promotion of treble predominance in most of his Birmingham editions, except where otherwise requested.

Chapter 3 - The town grows 1700-1768

Broome also published other people's work, such as a folio of songs 'with symphonies' by John Barker. Barker, thirty years Broome's junior was, in about 1720, a chorister at the Chapel Royal. This was in the time of Dr. Croft, of the family of Croft Castle, near Ludlow. Barker eventually became organist at Holy Trinity Church, Coventry. Above all, Broome collaborated with James Kempson in a project which was to have a profound affect on Birmingham's musical life, for his tombstone in St. Philip's churchyard is inscribed: 'To the Memory of Michael Broome, Late Clerk of St. Philip's and Father of the Musical Society of this Town'.

From A Collection of Psalm-tunes in IV parts, Michael Broome, Birmingham 1760.

Before describing the momentous development connected with this 'Musical Society', however, it should be pointed out that James Kempson also published church music a generation after Michael Broome. His connection with the church will become clear in due course, but these were his Birmingham publications.

Church Music by James Kempson published in Birmingham

Collection of 21 Psalm Tunes 1770
A Collection of Psalm Tunes in Four Parts 1775
Choice Collection of Thirteen Anthems 1780

In addition, an announcement in Aris's *Gazette* on 6th December 1784 shows that Kempson published eight anthems for three and four voices 'adapted for the use of country choirs'. He was, it continued, 'ready to deliver them from his house at 51 Great Charles Street'. This would no doubt then be a small but pleasant residence in eighteenth century style, one street away from open fields!

Another Birmingham musician worth a mention is Joseph Harris. Born here in humble circumstances, he went in about 1745 to Magdalen College, Oxford, as an organist, matriculating in 1773. A number of his compositions were performed while he was in Oxford. He returned to Birmingham, becoming organist at St. Martin's Church in 1787. He is thought to be the composer of a one-act pastoral called *Menalcas,* but this is not proven.

19

The Musical and Amicable Society in the cherry orchard

What, then, was the Musical Society of this Town, referred to on Michael Broome's tombstone? The full title of the organisation was the 'Musical and Amicable Society', and it was formed in the following way.

The account given of this is based on an article by E. Edwards, written just before the Birmingham Musical Festival of 1882.[3] In this article Edwards explains that he has access to some private documents which enable him to give authentic details of the origins of this very significant musical society. Edwards' own words explain the situation very clearly.

'For some years after the opening of St. Philips Church (1715), the choir was in the habit of meeting in the large room at Cooke's for practice. Amongst them was a young man named James Kempson, a musical enthusiast and a performer of no mean order. Some time after St. Bartholomew's Chapel was opened, Kempson took the lead in the choir there and afterwards the two choirs met at Cooke's for joint practice, a custom which was continued for some years. In 1762, the numbers of musicians meeting there was very large and in that year they resolved to form themselves into a Society or Club. It was settled that it should be called the "Musical and Amicable Society" and under its rules subscriptions were collected to build up a fund for assisting members who might, in case of illness or otherwise, require aid. It met at Cooke's at short intervals for practice and recreation. A printed code of rules was issued'. The seventeenth rule is interesting in that it reveals that 'the performance shall begin at half an hour past Seven 'clock, or sooner if possible, and end by Ten, when the reckoning shall be discharged'. No smoking was to be allowed during the performance - which implies that it was allowed during the break in rehearsal, and before and after it!

The cover of the rule book depicted four gentlemen in periwigs and cocked hats, arranged around a circular tripod table, singing a glee, the conductor beating time with his finger. This scene was surrounded with an elaborate rococo design. As to the recreation mentioned, drinking (and smoking) obviously played a part in this, for on the table was a decanter and a wine glass and a banner above their heads is inscribed with these lines:

> To our Musical Club Here's long life and Prosperity
> May it flourish with us, and on to posterity
> May Concord and Harmony always abound
> And divisions here only in Music be found.
> May the Catch and Glass go about and about
> And another succeed to the Bottle that's out.

Two questions will no doubt have come into the reader's mind in all of this. Where was 'Cooke's' and where was St. Bartholomew's Chapel, where Kempson

Chapter 3 - The town grows 1700-1768

St. Bartholomew's Church, Birmingham.

went to lead the choir? Cooke's Coffee House (to give it its full title) was a pleasant dwelling-house, converted into a tavern, situated in the cherry orchard which extended from what is now Bull Street into Cherry Street and Cannon Street. The last two streets were laid out soon after the building of St. Philip's Church and it was at their junction that Cooke's tavern was situated. It was known then as 'Cooke's, in the Cherry Orchard' and according to the parish ratings books, Joseph Cooke occupied it from 1756 to 1777. A large room at the back of Cooke's ran as far as what is now Corporation Street. A hearth was unearthed there at the time of the creation of Corporation Street, in Victorian times. In this large room, presumably, the men of the two church choirs, from St. Philip's and St. Bartholomew's, met.

As to St. Bartholomew's Chapel, it was a Church of England foundation built in Masshouse Lane in 1749. It was mainly funded by the Jennens family who were descended from the prosperous ironmaster, John Jennens, whom we met at the end of chapter 2. The current head of the family had evidently married a woman who was herself wealthy, and it was £1,000 of Mrs. Jennens' own money which helped to build the new church, the rest being raised by public subscription. Charles Jennens, who selected and compiled the words for Handel's oratorios, *Saul, Belshazzar* and

Messiah was a member of the same family. This fact demonstrates yet again Birmingham's continuing connections with the wider world generally, through its trading associations; and not least with the wider world of music.

To sum up, the men of St. Philip's had met regularly and informally to rehearse and be sociable, possibly from the 1730s or even earlier, and James Kempson, already mentioned, was eventually among their number. Kempson was born in 1742, so is not likely to have been an active member of the adult choir until the 1760s. When he became Clerk at St. Bartholomew's, where he would probably also be assistant organist, he added his choristers to the number already meeting at Cooke's tavern; and as we have seen was then instrumental in establishing, in 1762, the formal Musical and Amicable Society, with its own rules and orders.

In that same year something had happened which, indirectly, was to add very considerably to the Musical and Amicable Society's activities and responsibilities. The Seven Years' War had ostensibly come to an end, but very hostile relations between this country and America persisted, adversely affecting Birmingham's trade and manufactures. In addition, poor roads and the high price of horse-feed made transport of goods both difficult and expensive. The town suffered a decline in trade, and many families had to reduce their expenditure very drastically.

Ever aware of life around him, James Kempson proposed that a Music Meeting in aid of 'aged and distressed housekeepers' be held at St. Bartholomew's Chapel, Masshouse Lane, on Christmas Day, 1766. The intention seems to have been to pay money to very poor householders for essential household commodities, particularly bread, the elderly and unsupported receiving special attention. In proposing this, Kempson must have been mindful of two factors which were likely to make such a venture successful. He must have been conscious, first of all, of the charitable purpose of the Three Choirs Festivals, held in turn at Worcester, Gloucester and Hereford Cathedrals, and begun in 1724, possibly earlier. He may also already have been involved in the oratorios given in Birmingham itself, and perhaps we should pause for a moment in our account of Kempson's activities, to discover when and how these had been presented.

The first known Oratorio performances in the town
The earliest reference so far found to the giving of oratorios in Birmingham dates from 1740. In his book, *Birmingham Theatres, Concert and Music Halls,* Victor Price tells us that the Moor Street Theatre, a converted building, opened in that year with the performance of 'an Oratorio with Vocal and Instrumental Music', for the benefit of Mr. Gunn and another composer, Dr. Heighington already referred to in the paragraph on Gunn's other activities. Jumping forward a little, there is evidence of oratorios presented in the New Theatre, in King Street, by Richard Hobbs, Organist of St. Martin's Church, in 1759 and 1760. These oratorio presentations were given on three successive days, in either

Chapter 3 - The town grows 1700-1768

September or October, and employed approximately 24 chorus singers, 40 instrumentalists and a select band of well-known oratorio vocal soloists. Hobbs conducted – from the organ presumably – and also played organ solos. Presumably too, he would use a portable chamber organ. In the 1759 event, in the year of Handel's death, that master's music naturally dominated the programmes, but Boyce was allowed a little look-in, in the shape of his oratorio *Solomon*. In 1760, also at the New Theatre, a Miss Young was a soloist. This may have been Isabella Young, junior, a niece of Thomas Arne's wife, Cecilia Young, since the older generation of ladies in the family were by then singing under their married names. This was probably, by the way, the same Miss Young who sang at Duddeston, or Vauxhall Gardens, in Birmingham in the same year, 1760, and again in 1761. Balls were also arranged as an added attraction. In any case, we find *Aris's Gazette* in September 1760 reporting that these performances were 'honour'd with very polite Audiences, and received the greatest Applause'.

Another name which crops up in this connection is that of Capell Bond, the organist, of Coventry. He too had been organising the performances of oratorios, in Coventry, and, as with Hobb's presentations in Birmingham, these also seem to date from 1759. The spur in both cases must surely have been the death of Handel on the 14th April of that year.

No further announcements regarding full-scale three-day oratorio sessions appeared in the Gazette until 1767, but the citizens of Birmingham were not completely deprived of their ration of Purcell and Handel, for in July of 1762 the Treaty of Paris was signed, thus ending the Seven Years War, and in May of that year the coming of peace was,

'...celebrated in Birmingham in the usual manner; and at St. Bartholomew's Chapel was performed the late famous Mr. Henry Purcell's Te Deum, Jubilate, and celebrated Coronation Anthem; also the late Mr. Handel's celebrated Coronation Anthem: The Vocal Part by a Society belonging to the Chapel, accompanied with Instruments by Gentlemen Whose Abilities rendered the Performance compleat. The whole conducted by Mr. Richard Hobbs'. *Aris's Birmingham Gazette* July 1762.

As this was at St. Bartholomew's then Kempson would probably have trained and led the choir.

Another announcement in *Aris's Birmingham Gazette* reveals that 'Mr. Bond', Capell Bond of Coventry that is, was eventually to make an appearance on Birmingham's oratorio scene, and on 5th October 1767 he announced three days of oratorios on the 21st, 22nd and 23rd of the same month. The singers were to be Miss Thomas, Messrs. Norris, Matthews, Price, Saville, etc, the principal 'Instrumentals' Messrs. Adcock, Miller, Lates and others, and the whole performance to be conducted by 'Mr. Capell Bond, Organist, of Coventry'. We know from this announcement that Bond's organist was Richard Hobbs, evidence that Bond and Hobbs, had decided to unite their efforts. They were obviously wise to combine and not to compete, for their offerings attracted large audiences.

It is clear, then, that an interest in oratorio, particularly Handel's, was present in Birmingham and indeed a verse was written to celebrate the fact.

ON THE REVIVAL OF THE ORATORIOS IN BIRMINGHAM

> In other Towns whilst Oratorios please,
> Shall we in gloomy Silence spend our Days?
> Nor taste of those Enjoyments that impart
> Melodious Sounds to captivate the Heart?
> Sons of Apollo, who the Name revere
> Of Handel, and his Memory hold dear,
> Let not the circling Seasons pass unsung;
> And whilst you've power to charm the list'ning throng
> Bid dulness fly, nor let it e'er be said,
> Where Arts are cherished, Music droops its Head.

Aris's Birmingham Gazette, 19th October 1767.

The last two lines, incidentally, address the very problem which has already been mentioned in these pages. The 'Arts', namely pursuits followed by 'artisans' or craftsmen, were thought by some to be incompatible with music. It is part of the purpose of this account to show that they are not in the least incompatible, and that Birmingham's musical history, when examined carefully, proves the point.

James Kempson and a Music Meeting in aid of the poor, at St Bartholomew's Church 1766

To return to Kempson. The scene was set then, and when the hardship following the end of the Seven Years' War, already referred to, was at its worst, it occurred to Kempson that it would be possible to exploit this interest in oratorio, in order to raise money for the benefit of those hardest hit by the trade recession. Christmas Day, 1766, was chosen as an appropriate occasion, and the first Music Meeting to be held in Birmingham, *in aid of charity*, took place. This was to be at St. Bartholomew's Chapel, Masshouse Lane. How was it achieved? Kempson called together members of the Musical and Amicable Society and proposed that a special section should be set up, with the aim of performing for charity. It was called the 'Chappell Society'. Some boy singers were brought in and Kempson was to be paid a small sum for training them. Otherwise most of the performers gave their services; apart, that is, from one or two adult members of St. Philip's Choir, who refused to sing without some remuneration! On the day itself, a collection was made at the doors, and afterwards the profit was used to distribute bread to the neediest of the 'aged and distressed housekeepers'. In fact, it was left to the discretion of the individual distributors to select those they personally knew to be in the worst circumstances.

The success of this first James Kempson Christmas Festival was not in doubt, and people immediately began to talk about the next one. In fact the one-day Christmas festival continued at St. Bartholomew's for just over seventy years, until 1838, still administered by the Chappell Society which itself survived until 1847.

What was performed at what can fairly be claimed as Birmingham's first music meeting held with a charitable purpose? No details have so far been discovered, but we can derive a clear idea of these Christmas Festivals from some later 'programmes' which have survived. The one from 1777 shows that the music was an integral part of the Christmas morning and evening services. To take just the morning service, the 'overture' was Purcell's *Te Deum* and *Jubilate,* obviously favourite pieces. This music had been given at the Treaty of Paris celebrations at St. Bartholomew's in 1762, and a simplified version of it appears in one of Broome's Birmingham publications. After the prayers, the Hundredth Psalm was sung, with instrumental accompaniment, and following the communion service itself, a Christmas anthem by our old friend 'Mr. C. Bond' was performed. After the sermon, and as a grand *finale,* Handel came into his own with the coronation anthem, *Zadok the Priest and Nathan the Prophet anointed Solomon King* and the *Hallelujah* chorus. Exuberant sounds to speed the congregation homewards on a Christmas Day!

The First Birmingham Music Meeting in aid of the General Hospital

We have already seen how Capell Bond and Richard Hobbs, after what seems to have been a seven-year gap, re-instated their three-day programme of oratorios in 1767, the year following Kempson's first Christmas Festival. Immediately after that, in October 1767, there was an announcement in the Birmingham Gazette revealing that they intended to have these 'Performances continued annually for the Benefit of a Public Charity'. How much were they influenced in this by Kempson's success at St. Bartholomew's the previous Christmas? We do not know for certain of course, nor do we know whether they had any particular charity in mind when they made their announcement. What is clear is that Hobbs and Kempson must have collaborated in 1762, as did Bond and Hobbs in 1767. However, Edwards' account of things [4] makes it quite clear that he believes that it was Kempson who first mooted the idea of a music meeting, specifically to assist in the completion of the General Hospital, now left half-built for lack of funds. According to Edwards, Kempson suggested to some friends of his on the Hospital Board, that large-scale musical performances, 'upon similar principles to those at St. Bartholomew's', might bring in a useful sum of money. The suggestion was accepted and an announcement by a committee for the first music meeting in aid of the General Hospital, given verbatim, speaks for itself:

'...And for the Benefit of this Public Charity, on Wednesday, Thursday, and Friday, the 7th, 8th, and 9th of September the Oratorios of Il Penseroso etc, Alexander's Feast, and the Messiah will be performed here. The Oratorios of Il Penseroso etc, and Alexander's Feast, will be at the Theatre in King-Street, on the Wednesday and Thursday Evenings. On the Thursday Morning, at Eleven O'Clock, will be performed in St. Philip's, Church, Mr. Handel's Te Deum and Jubilate, with the Coronation and other anthems, and the Messiah on Friday Morning at the same place... The best Vocal and Instrumental Performers will be engaged on this Occasion, the further Particulars of which will be inserted in a future Advertisement'.

On 5th September 1768 the *Gazette* adds:

'The Principal Vocal parts will be performed by Mrs. Pinto, Mr. Norris, Mr. Matthews, Mr. Price etc. Instrumental by Messrs. Pinto, Miller, Adcock, Jenkins, Park, Lates, Hobbs, Clark, Chew etc, etc.

The Oratorios will be conducted by Mr. Capell Bond of Coventry, and the Performers are desired to attend the Rehearsal on Tuesday the 6th Inst, at 9 o'Clock in the morning.

Tickets at 5s each to be had at the Swan, Castle, Hen and Chickens, Dolphin and the Red Lion Inns, Cooke's Coffee-House, and Duddeston Hall; of Miss Jefferies's, Mrs. Tildesley's, Miss Matthews', Miss Mallett's, Mr. Chawner's, and of Pearson and Aris, Printers.

The Music at the Church on Thursday Morning is to be opened with a Trumpet Concerto by Mr. Bond'.

(The name Hobbs in the list of instrumentalists above is presumably Richard Hobbs, Organist at St. Martin's Church).

And just to show that nothing changes, the *Gazette* appends the following note:

'N.B. Ladies and Gentlemen are desired to order their Servants to drive their Carriages down Peck-Lane and up King-Street, as they go to and from the Playhouse: the Streets will be lighted from the Playhouse to the Ball room'.

This is the same one-way system, in and out of New Street, which applied there for a number of years until 1991!

On 12th September 1768, the *Gazette* recorded the music played and where, and says that it was given to 'a brilliant and Crowded Audience'. On the Thursday morning (Sept. 8) a collection was made 'which the Countesses of Dartmouth and Aylesford very obligingly stood to receive at the door'. In general the 'Concourse of Nobility and Gentry from this and the neighbouring counties gave the whole a most Splendid Appearance, and at the same time showed their Desire to concur with the Inhabitants of this Place in support of a Charity so beneficial and extensive'.

Did the enterprise succeed in the way James Kempson had hoped? It did; and today we can only look on, amazed and rather envious, when we read that the money taken over three days was £800 (about £26,000 in to-day's values); and the net profit, which was presented to the hospital, was £299, equivalent to £10,000.

Notice, too, that Capell Bond was the conductor and James Kempson trained the choir. In this three-day oratorio event, all those who had already been presenting oratorios in Birmingham seem, once again, to have combined their efforts. In addition they were meeting an increasing popular demand, and thus had the basis for a new, strong growth, well-rooted in local soil. As to the performers generally, we should further bear in mind that the chorus numbered about 45, the men's voices of the Musical and Amicable Society and of the Chappell Society, both of which would include counter-tenors by-the-way, being joined by some women singers from Lancashire, who mainly contributed the soprano parts. The *Gazette's* claim that the best vocal and instrumental performers were engaged is perfectly just, and a study of some of them will be made in the chapter about the early Music Meetings and Festivals, 1768-1834, entitled '*A portrait gallery of stars*'. The orchestra, or band, about 25 in number, were mostly leading virtuosi, working mainly in London. The style of playing would be Italianate and Handelian, with most performers decorating melodies with trills and runs; supposedly extemporised, but often written down beforehand, sometimes by another musician altogether.

Some reasons for the Music Meeting's success

Why did the 'brilliant and crowded audience', the 'concourse of nobility and gentry' come from this 'and neighbouring counties' to join Birmingham in this musical and charitable exercise? To answer this, we have to imagine ourselves in a world without recorded music of any kind and where the only concerted music to be heard by most people was at the local parish church. Public concerts of a professional standard were being given in London from the mid-eighteenth century, and the Chapel Royal and a few cathedrals continued to attract gifted singers. One can understand the very great pleasure that an eighteenth century provincial audience would have in hearing, for the first time, a body of seventy or more trained singer and players, in Handel's noble and uplifting music, Surely the 'tingle factor' must have been operating overtime!

We should not forget, either, that sense of responsibility for the less fortunate now beginning to stir on a corporate scale. The preacher, John Wesley, was making many aware of the degraded physical and moral state of some of their fellow citizens. The congregations he organised themselves became an influence for good in society, and were actively benevolent. They were also especially noted for hearty singing, and many hymns were composed for them. The churches established charity schools for the children of the poor, and voluntary hospitals were being built even if, as in Birmingham, with some difficulty. Some of this effort was practical and utilitarian, but most of the people involved were sincerely altruistic in what they did. To go to the Music Meetings was to assist good causes, and the rapidly growing middle class was pleased to join with the aristocracy in events which were not only in elegant taste but also benevolent in intent. There were some dissenting voices, of course, but more of these in a later chapter.

As for the social dimension, a short passage in the novel *Wives and Daughters,* published much later in 1863, by Elizabeth Gaskell, (one of whose daughters had piano lessons from Charles Hallé incidentally), gives us a vivid little picture of the 'festival fever' which prevailed around the time of these great events. It must surely be valid generally, for in 1778 at the time of the second Music Meeting in aid of the General Hospital in Birmingham, the *Gazette* announced on 31st August 1778 that lodgings had already been engaged for many 'genteel families', and visitors to the meeting were expected to be very numerous. It was an event which obviously took the place of the later annual holiday, in that it provided communal excitement and a late summer festival before nights grew too dark and roads too difficult. The passage from *Wives and Daughters* tells us that, in imitation of greater cities with their festivals, Mrs. Gaskell's 'Hollingford', with two other small towns, takes it in turns to organise an annual ball for the benefit of the county hospital. The anticipation is described like this,

James Kempson.

'It was a fine time for hospitality, and every house of any pretension was as full as it could hold, and flys were engaged long months before'.

A fly was a one-horse, covered carriage available for hire - an 18th century taxi!

Before going on to describe the evolution of the first Birmingham Music Meeting into the firmly-established, premier Festival it soon became, we should look at what else the town was providing musically, and who and what the customers were who enjoyed the fare regularly on offer in the ever-growing town.

---

1. Nicholas Temperley: *The Music of the English Parish Church.*
2. *Short account of the Charity School in St. Philip's Church Yard in Birmingham from its institution in 1724 to 1806.* (Printed by T. Chapman, 76 Bull Street).
3. E. Edwards: *Some Account of the origin of the Musical Festival and of James Kempson the Originator.* Article in Birmingham Institutions, Birmingham Central Library.
4. E. Edwards: op. cit.

Chapter 4

Not to be written on the back of a postage stamp 1740-1800

Another misconception about Birmingham's musical past is that once the 'Triennial Festivals' have been described, that is virtually the end of the story and the rest can be written 'on the back of a postage stamp'. It is hoped that this chapter will go some way to exploding that myth.

The previous chapter ended with a reference to the novelist Elizabeth Gaskell and, rather happily, she provides a link with some of the people who lived in Birmingham in the late eighteenth century; contributing so greatly to its prosperity and well-being, and to the high level of its social and cultural life. She was connected by marriage to Josiah Wedgwood, and was an admirer of the courageous and enquiring spirit of Erasmus Darwin's grandson, Charles Darwin, whom she met several times. In Rome, in 1857, incidentally, the young Birmingham musician Edward Bache was part of her circle of friends - more of him in a later chapter. The names of Josiah Wedgwood and Erasmus Darwin lead us straight to the Lunar Society which met from about 1765 onwards and for a few years into the nineteenth century, very often at Matthew Boulton's home, Soho House, in Handsworth. This was an informal society with no constitution and with no minutes or records of its meetings, which gathered in turn at the houses of its members. The meetings were held at the time of the full moon, to assist negotiation of the bad roads, hence the name Lunar Society. The group met to share ideas, especially scientific ones. Discoveries and inventions and their wider application in manufacturing, or in the home, loomed large in their discussions, but frequently one member would render a practical service to another; as when Wedgwood made chemical apparatus for Priestley, and Erasmus Darwin amputated Wedgwood's badly infected leg, thereby prolonging his life.

It was Matthew Boulton, however, who more than anyone was the leading spirit of the Society, no small tribute to his abilities if one considers who the other members were. As well Josiah Wedgwood, Erasmus Darwin and Boulton's partner, the illustrious James Watt, there were Joseph Priestley, William Small, James Keir, Samuel Galton, Richard Edgeworth, Thomas Day, William Withering (of digitalis fame) and three or four others. The list of achievements is considerable and amazingly wide-ranging and it is gratifying to learn that Boulton, Galton, Keir, Priestley, Small, Watt and Withering were all resident in areas now occupied by the present city centre or its inner suburbs. Of these, Boulton, Galton and Small were elected to the General Hospital Committee on 24th December 1765. This was the committee which accepted Kempson's suggestion that a Music Meeting should be held in aid of the General Hospital building fund. Boulton himself, the great pioneer of mass-production methods, is known to have been a keen music-lover as was his chief designer, John Southern, and Boulton took an active part in the promotion of concerts in Birmingham. This was in addition to his connection with the Festivals and will be described in the chapter headed *'What else?'*. Less well-known is the fact that James Watt was not only an engineer but also a maker of optical and musical instruments. He made organs, violins and guitars; another very obvious connection between engineering and music.

The Pleasure Gardens
What musical entertainment was available in the growing town for Lunar Society members, their wives, families, employees and associates?

In the summer months they appear to have attended Birmingham's pleasure gardens 'in their thousands', strolling in delightful surroundings, taking some refreshments and listening to the popular music of the day. The music we are alluding to was by Handel and Arne, both English of course; one by adoption the other by birth, (Handel died in 1759 and Arne in 1778). One can only wonder what would happen today if thousands of 'Brummies,' strolling in the grounds of Aston Hall, were to be offered the music of Benjamin Britten and Michael Tippett, who in terms of dates would be the nearest modern equivalents. Such music would hardly be regarded as 'entertainment' and would more often than not be met with incomprehension or even, one fears, hostility. Here again it ill behoves us to assume 'airs of immeasurable superiority' over our forbears. Nor can we do other than look with horror at what has happened to the sylvan spots which were once Birmingham's pleasure gardens.

There were three of them; the Vauxhall, the Apollo and the Strawberry Gardens and only the last has escaped the process of industrialisation. The Vauxhall Gardens were at Duddeston Hall, an area subsequently and until recently occupied by the Saltley railway sidings. The Apollo Gardens were in Moseley Street, just off Deritend, now also a built-up inner city area. The Strawberry Gardens were at Wyddrington, Church Road, Edgbaston, where a hall of residence now stands. Birmingham University students can still enjoy the tree-shaded, rural aspect of this still very pleasant tract of land. Occasional announcements in the *Birmingham Gazette,* spanning just over a hundred years, from 1748 to 1850, give us glimpses of these places of popular relaxation. The earliest so far discovered by the writer is dated 9th May 1748. Again the flavour of these eighteenth century gardens comes over to us most effectively in the original words.

Chapter 4 - Not to be written on the back of a postage stamp 1740-1800

'Whereas the Performance of Music and Fire-Works at Bridgman's Gardens, at the Apollo at Aston, near Birmingham, was to have been on Thursday last, but the Inclemency of the Weather preventing 'tis postpon'd to next Thursday Evening, when a grand Trio of Mr. Handel's out of Acis and Galatea, and that favourite Duet of Arne's call'd Damon and Cloe, will be perform'd by Mr. Bridgman, and a Gentleman of the Town'.

There is only one trio in *Acis and Galatea,* composed in 1718, and that is 'The flocks shall leave the mountains', and a very charming piece it is. The song by Mr. Arne was the eighteenth and last in a second set of *Entire New Songs and Ballads Perform'd at Vaux-Hall Gardens,* printed in London in 1746 and originally intended for London's Vauxhall Gardens. The two sets were each called a *Volume of Lyric Harmony.* The song 'Damon and Cloe' (there is no 'h' in the lady's name) was for two voices, two violins and either 'cello or, more usually, harpsichord. Again, one can see from the score why the song was popular. Presumably these two items were highlights in an extended programme of music, which may well have exploited other theatre music of the time. More of that shortly.

In 1763 the Apollo's bigger rival, Birmingham Vauxhall Gardens, changed hands and the advertisement in *Aris's Gazette* on 23rd May of that year gives us a description of their attractions.

'To be Lett, and entered upon immediately DUDDESTON HALL commonly called VAUXHALL, near Birmingham in the County of Warwick, being a large House, with necessary Out-Buildings, and large genteel Pleasure Garden, neatly laid out and planted, with a large Bowling-Green; it lies within Half a Mile of Birmingham, and greatly resorted to by the Inhabitants thereof, as well as from other places, being used in the Public Way, and in the Summer Season is a Concert every other week. There is a Close Cock Pit. The Place is well known to most Travellers...'

We see from the *Gazette,* however, that the civilised elegance of a stroll in the gardens, and the concerts of music by Handel, Arne and others, were not all that was on offer and the baser part of human nature was, as ever, in evidence. Cock-fighting was still unashamedly popular and the movement against it, begun in the 1770s, did not succeed in having it made illegal until 1849.

It is obvious from a number of announcements in *Aris's Gazette* that pleasure gardens were considered to be appropriate places for benefit concerts of the type described in the last chapter. Money was raised in this way for a number of named musicians and also, in August 1778 for example, for the benefit of the waiters at Vauxhall.

To complete our picture of these places of open-air leisure and recreation, a description of the Apollo Gardens in the *Gazette* of 12th March 1787 is informative. We learn that they were situated in a new street called Moseley Street in the hamlet of Deritend. To arrive at the 'lovely, sequestered and elegant' place it was then possible to take a pleasure boat on the Rea, rowing up-river under Deritend, Bradford Street and Cheapside bridges, between field paths 'gay with wild flowers'. The river Rea was not then the poor, culverted trickle it is today. J. T. Bunce in his book written in 1899 and entitled *Birmingham Sixty Years Ago* [1] describes Vauxhall Gardens as having winding, shady walks, wide lawns, arbours for the serving of refreshments and, at night, lines of oil lamps with coloured glass. He reports that 'Entertainments, musical and otherwise were attended by thousands of people', among them, no doubt, visitors to the Birmingham Festivals.

Vauxhall seems to have had a slight edge over the Apollo, and to complete this brief outline of a hundred years of activity, it may be appropriate to quote from one of John Freeth's ballads, entitled *Invitation to VAUXHALL GARDENS*. Freeth, the Birmingham ballad-maker, will have a section to himself at the end of this chapter, but these verses are taken from the collection *The Political Songster,* published in 1790.[2]

> When the Evening is fine, how enlivening the scene,
> The Walks to parade, or to trip o'er the green;
> No troubles to harass, no fears to alarm,
> The mind sits at ease, when there's Music to charm,
> Then quickly away, to the regions resort,
> Which pleasure makes choice of for keeping her court
>
> The TRADESMAN who's got a few moments to spare,
> Finds leave a refreshment to solace his care,
> The ARTIST will often his labour throw by,
> The sweet rural pasture awhile to enjoy;
> For genius whose sons oft incline to be gay,
> Would droop if there was not a season to play.
>
> When all appears charming and grac'd with the Fair,
> What Gardens for splendor with these can compare;
> When nature embellish'd with choice strokes of art,
> The mind to regale does her beauties impart,
> And mirth and good fellowship keep up the ball,
> What more would the heart wish to find at VAUXHALL

NOTES TO THE ABOVE:
A. Tradesman and Artist would be craftsman and artisan today, that is skilled engineering craftsmen.
B. The era of the pleasure garden came to an end in 1850 when Vauxhall Gardens were finally closed.

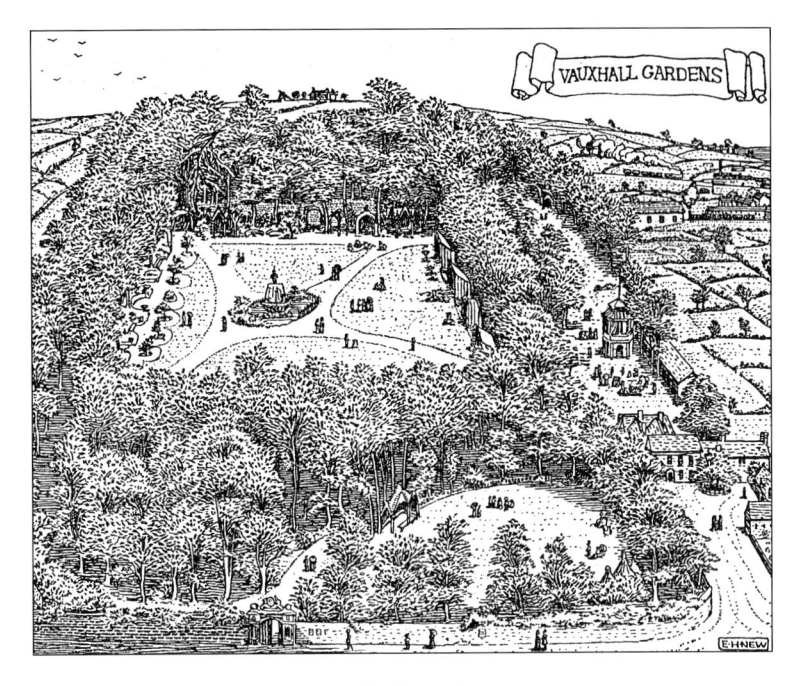

Chapter 4 - Not to be written on the back of a postage stamp 1740-1800

Vauxhall Gardens.

The Ball

As we know, a ball was often an added attraction when musical events were organised and one was always to be an important feature of the Birmingham Music Meetings, later Musical Festivals, in aid of the General Hospital. The earliest reference to dancing so far found is again in a number of *Aris's Gazette,* the one on 25th April 1748. It was placed in the paper by Mr. Harry Barton of Smallbrook Street and offers dancing tuition, but especially 'classes teaching French Dances to children'. He intends to start the classes on 2nd May, continuing them on 'the same day of the week as the late Mrs. Eades did'. One wonders when Mrs. Eades began her classes. It could have been as early as 1730 or even 1720.

The dance music played at the balls was fairly rumbustious, usually an arrangement of some well-known tune, perhaps a folk-tune or a ballad or something current in the theatre at the time. Balls were not just adjuncts to other events, however, but were important events in the social calendar in their own right, as we saw from the Gaskell quotation from *Wives and Daughters.* Even then, however, when the dancers sat to recuperate from their exertions they expected to be entertained by music of a higher order than the rumpty-tumpty tunes they had just been dancing to. Announcements in *Aris's Gazette* often name the musicians who are to provide this added inducement to attend the ball. On 26th August 1784, for example, at Mr. Fletcher's Annual

33

Concert and Ball, the band of performers included, as singers, James Kempson and members of the Probin family, with others. Kempson and the Probins, we have already met and know of their musicianship. Among the instrumentalists was a Mr. Valentine. Could he be the father (or other relation) of Thomas Valentine (1790-1878), music teacher and glee composer in Birmingham at a later period?[3]

The star of the show on this occasion, however, was the noted 'Miss Field', a soprano very well known on the London theatre scene. She it was for whom Thomas Linley wrote additional Ariel songs for a revival of *The Tempest,* mainly with Arne's music, in 1778. Known especially for her *coloratura* style of singing, her performance of the florid 'O bid your faithful Ariel fly' would no doubt be worth hearing. It could well have been this, or another of the Ariel songs, which refreshed the Birmingham dancers during the interval of Mr. Fletcher's ball at 'The Hotel'. William Fletcher was a music-seller and publisher, with premises in Bull Street. Balls are frequently announced in the *Gazette* not only as taking place in Birmingham, but in surrounding towns like Sutton Coldfield, Lichfield, Stourbridge and Stratford and at some of these, Birmingham musicians played an important part. On 10th November 1783, the musical entertainment during a ball at the Town Hall, Sutton Coldfield, was 'under the direction of Mr. Clark, Organist in Birmingham'. This was Jeremiah Clark who was organist at St. Philip's Church from 1765 to 1803 and subsequently organist at Worcester Cathedral for a short period.[4] One of the singers at Sutton in 1783 was Mr. Saville, good enough to be asked to perform at the Birmingham Festivals in 1787 and 1790. All these folk were competent musicians.

The Theatre

We have already seen how songs and arias from contemporary stage works were used as single items in other musical entertainments, elsewhere than in the theatre. The reverse process also occurred and folk-songs, other already well-known melodies or specially composed tunes in the popular style, found their way into theatres. These were duly fitted with new words, harmonised, arranged and strung together into a complete theatrical presentation. Usually librettists wrote a new text based on an older play or on some classical theme or stage situation, and composers used and re-used their own and other people's music, to fit the dialogue and verses. This patch-work approach is a particular characteristic of the eighteenth-century stage.

Two main factors account for this. It was very much according to the taste of the times not to want an uninterrupted flow of words, especially if these dealt seriously with serious matters. Government ministers were very happy to encourage this trend since it avoided dangerous political comment in very unstable times. They were quite content that audiences should hear about rustic village characters, often aristocrats in disguise, or mythical personages, suitably removed from the real world of changing dynasties and power complexes. All the better if it was garnished by music which

Chapter 4 - Not to be written on the back of a postage stamp 1740-1800

would, so to speak, 'trip it... On the light fantastic toe'.[5] The play-and-music mixture was also very much encouraged across the Channel, but in any case the tendency had been indirectly reinforced in England as a consequence of the closing of theatres during the Commonwealth period. This had not been because of an objection to stage plays as such, but mainly to the lewd life-style of theatre people. The only way to circumvent the ban was to advertise a concert of music which was charged for, and then present a stage piece between the two 'acts' of the concert, theoretically free of charge and therefore not legally a public presentation. We shall find miscellaneous concerts given at some of the earlier Birmingham Festivals divided into 'acts' rather than parts, incidentally.

Cromwell's election as Protector in 1649 had brought some relaxation of attitude, since he liked music, and masques and other musical entertainments were encouraged. Hostility to the play, pure and simple, was thus increased and sometimes play-readings had to be resorted to by those who still wanted a straight play. Any dramatic presentation attempted had to be short anyway, in case of the arrival of Puritan soldiery. After the restoration, London theatres were re-licensed and plays could be given again, but this only extended to named theatres and not to the theatre in general. In any case, for all the causes outlined, the trend away from the straight play proper was the order of the day, and theatres built after 1660 followed this fashion. Both the Italian Opera and the 'mixed-media' pieces were all the rage and in fact it was a great time for theatre building after the Restoration. Drury Lane was built by Wren, in 1672, and Betterton's smaller theatre in Lincoln's Inn Fields followed in 1695. In Birmingham the earliest recorded theatre, opened in 1740, was in Moor Street, but this was not purpose-built and not licensed. Whether there had been earlier theatres in the town is at present difficult to tell, but it seems very unlikely that there would have been a purpose-built, permanent one and the town would probably have had to rely on the visits of the 'strollers' or travelling theatre companies, who, according to William Hutton (1723-1813), Birmingham's first resident chronicler, would set up in what was little more than a shed where Temple Street now is. He further reports that by 1730, stage presentations were given a 'superior home' in a sort of stable in Castle Street![6] The Moor Street theatre sounds impressive by comparison and it was joined in 1751 by the first purpose-built theatre, namely 'The Theatre', in King Street. The second purpose-built theatre was the handsome Theatre Royal in New Street, opened in 1774. This was not licensed until 1807. There was yet another theatre in Smallbrook Street functioning from as early as 1747.

Let us then examine some samples of what was produced on Birmingham stages from 1740 onwards. An early example dates from 1744 when a 'Company of Comedians' from London presented an evening of drama and music on 29th August at 7 p.m. Boxes were 2/6 (two shillings and sixpence, now 12½p) and the pit and the balconies 2/- (two shillings, now 10p). *The Tempest* subtitled *The Enchanted Island* was to be given 'as altered by Mr. Dryden and Sir William Davenant' and the proceedings were to conclude with a grand masque entitled *Neptune and Amphitrite*. The version of *The Tempest* referred to was no doubt the operatic adaptation made by Dryden and D'Avenant in 1670 from the Shakespeare play. Characters were added to the cast, including a boy who had never seen a girl and a sister for Miranda. Dryden made much of the sexual innocence of these three who only knew life on 'The Enchanted Isle'. Three years after this version, Thomas Shadwell derived an opera from *The Tempest*, also called *The Enchanted Isle*. Later, in David Garrick's time, Thomas Arne set the Ceres, Iris and Juno masque in Act 4 to music, also Dryden and Shadwell's un-Shakespearian *Neptune and Amphitrite* masque of Act 5. This is the masque advertised in the *Gazette*, given below as it appeared in the announcement, and it is certain that the version seen and heard in Birmingham in 1744 was a recent one. The music is of a high quality according to Roger Fiske.[7]

At the same theatre in Moor Street, a Concert of Vocal and Instrumental Music was advertised on 4th August 1746. The announcement reads as follows:

'Between the two parts of the concert will be presented (Gratis) a Comedy called THE MISER. After this will be added an opera call'd 'The Mock Doctor' or 'The Dumb Lady Cured'.

Again, the performance is to start at 'exactly 7 o'clock'.

In fact *The Miser* was written by John Thurmond with music by Richard Jones. A sequel to *Dr. Faustus,* this piece was given nineteen performances at Lincoln's Inn Theatre in London. Some of Jones's music has survived and includes an *allegro* movement in the style of Handel, an *adagio* and some dances, including a statue dance. The coming-alive of statues continued to be a popular stage device in pantomime, well after Shakespeare's serious use of it in A *Winter's Tale*. The 'opera' included in the other part of the entertainment at Moor Street in 1746, namely *The Mock Doctor* or *The Dumb Lady Cured,* was an adaptation made in 1732 by Henry Fielding, the author of Tom Jones, of Molière's *Le Médecin Malgré Lui*.[8] It had first been presented at the Drury Lane theatre in London in 1732. A rather shadowy character, possibly German, called Seedo, probably arranged all the music for this opera, contributing three out of the total of ten songs himself. Like the composer Gerald Finzi in our own century, he was a foreigner who could express himself easily in the English style. The other seven or so songs in *The Mock Doctor* had been contributed by Henry Carey.

We have news of the theatre in Smallbrook Street in June 1747, when Congreve's *Love for Love* was played. This was part of a six-week programme given by a visiting company and again, to circumvent the law, singing and dancing was given between the acts of the play; and it would be for that the theatre patrons would ostensibly pay. In June of the same year, incidentally, *Hamlet* was given at Moor Street and on the same night, *Othello* at Smallbrook Street.

Chapter 4 - Not to be written on the back of a postage stamp 1740-1800

Much later, in September 1770 there was a performance at the Theatre in King Street for the benefit of the General Hospital. *The Jealous Wife* and *The Padlock* were on the bill, the latter being classed as a comic opera, with music by Charles Dibdin. This was first performed at Drury Lane, before the King of Denmark, and the date of the London performance was 10th October 1768, a day which made Dibdin's name and fame. *The Padlock* was thus only two years old when it came to Birmingham, still a smash-hit. Several of the players were leading singers from Drury Lane and we know that, in general, the larger provincial centres had orchestral resources and could have hired music parts from London if they wished; but it seems more likely that, in some productions, local players would supplement the orchestra of the visiting company, who would bring the instrumental parts with them. It is difficult to be sure about this. Certainly, 'the best performers of this town' were supplying the instrumental accompaniment at the theatre in 1769, for the Garrick-Shakespeare celebrations (see section on Ballads, below).

We come now to the New Street theatre in 1778. On Monday 17th August for one night only, by permission of the magistrates and with the consent of the proprietors, *The Duenna* or *The Double Elopement* is to be played. Added to this was *All the World's a stage*. In *The Duenna* the songs are Scotch and in 1775, the younger Thomas Linley harmonised and orchestrated them in the *galant* style of J. C. Bach and Mozart. On arriving in Birmingham this piece was only three years old and from the cast-list printed in the *Gazette* it seems that some noted London singers were taking part in this production, among them Mrs. Smith and Mr. Shuter. The unlikeable Mr. Theodore Smith published some Vauxhall Songs in 1769, to be sung by his wife; and from 1772 Mrs. Smith, who was a great beauty, sang at Drury Lane. Mr. Shuter had sung in London for the older Thomas Linley, in Linley's opera *The Royal Merchant* (1767).

Another theatrical event perhaps worth mentioning was the presentation of *The Maid of the Mill* at the Theatre in New Street in April 1784. This opera had first been performed at Covent Garden in 1765 and was composed by Samuel Arnold with words by Isaac Bickerstaffe. The piece was in imitation of Arne's *Love in a Village* but does not borrow from it, and is in a much more sophisticated, *galant* style. Arnold attempted a complete edition of Handel's works later but, in this opera, he himself wrote some pleasing music. There were as usual borrowings, supposedly from Pergolesi, Vinci, Hasse and J. C. Bach, but these did nothing but add to the success of the work, since it toured the world, and was presented in New York in 1769 and St. Petersburg in 1772.[9] Drury Lane had staged it from 1769. The piece was advertised in Birmingham as being 'given by their MAJESTIES SERVANTS'. A ballet, a bassoon concerto played by the Mr. Shaw who performed at Mr. Fletcher's Annual Ball that same year, and a farce called *The Irish Widow* were all added to the evening's entertainment!

At the grass roots

We have firm evidence therefore of the visits of noted London performers to Birmingham's theatres, but it is also clear that there were keen and excellent musicians in the town itself. Indeed, there must have been enough of them, both amateur and professional, to warrant the establishment of a home-based series of subscription concerts, as well as a number of businesses selling copies of music and musical instruments. First the concerts. What did Birmingham's musical calendar look like in the middle part of the eighteenth century? The theatrical presentations, often consisting of three or four different programmes played in turn, were given in the town from June to August. The pleasure gardens provided outdoor musical entertainment for most of the late Spring and Summer months. In 1759 and 1760, as we have seen, there was a tentative beginning of what was to be a mighty growth, when an early autumn feast of oratorios, lasting for three days, was tried; and in the Winter, the musical scene was not necessarily deserted. In October 1758 for example, a series of fortnightly Thursday evening concerts was announced, with a ball after the first, third, sixth and ninth concerts. The concerts were to continue all through the winter months and were held in Mr. Sawyer's room in The Square. The subscriptions were taken by Mr. Eversmann, undoubtedly he who was organist at St. Philip's from about 1735 to 1765. Strangers could be introduced by a subscriber for five shillings (5/- now 25p) on a ball night, or for half a crown (two shillings and sixpence, 2/6d now 12½p) on other nights. A special attraction at the first concert were the French Horns employed by the Earl of Plymouth, musicians who had also performed at Duddeston, or Vaux-Hall, Gardens the previous August. Eversmann's concerts seem to have continued and there was certainly a series in 1762, but in 1764 it was announced that he was ill and that there would be a benefit concert for him. He also advertised a chamber organ for sale, perhaps his own. Unhappily, he died the following year.

In the 1780s, the Dilettanti Musical Society seems to have taken over Eversmann's role to some extent. They arranged concerts at 'The Hotel' and brought in well-known singers to contribute to concerts of vocal and instrumental music. Announcements are to be found in the *Gazette* on 18th November 1780 and on 21st June 1784, but these apparently relate to single concerts and not to a series. Mr. Fletcher, who has already been mentioned, appears to have been the organiser.

As to the music-sellers, here more than ever, *Aris's Birmingham Gazette* is the obvious place to find their advertisements, and these reveal a surprising amount of this kind of activity. Only a selection of items can be given, but the *Birmingham Gazette* of 25th September 1758 advertised a collection of all the new songs sung by 'choice spirits', at Vauxhall, Ranelagh, Marybone (sic) Gardens and the Theatres, and at Sadler's Wells. They were printed by J. Staples in the Royal Exchange, Cornhill, and sold by most booksellers both in town and country, including

Chapter 4 - Not to be written on the back of a postage stamp 1740-1800

obviously the town of Birmingham and its surrounding area. Later, a *Gazette* for 30th November 1778 tells us that William Hall of the Music Ware Room at 'Hotel', Birmingham, was selling Handel songs, and overtures for the harpsichord. He also sold the harpsichords on which to play them, together with 'organs, piano-fortes and spinnets (sic)'. In December 1777 we meet Jeremiah Clark (sic) 'Organist in Birmingham' once more, now inviting subscribers to assist in the publication of *Six Sonatas* for the harpsichord or 'piano forte', with accompaniments for violins and violoncello. Following suit again, intentionally or otherwise, we find on 31st August 1778, 'Joseph Harris Mus. Bac, (c1745-1814) organist of St. Martin's', whom we met in the last chapter, appealing for subscribers to assist in the publication of twelve songs. By 1783 there were enough musically interested people in the area to warrant the following advertisement on 10th November. Addressed to 'Lovers of Music', it is an announcement of the first number of 'The New Musical Magazine'. This is to appear monthly, at the beginning of the month, priced one shilling and sixpence (1/6d or 7½p). It is to include a –

'Complete library of vocal and Instrumental Music... comprehending the entire works of Handel, Arne and other celebrated modern composers with all the most favourite serious and comic Operas, Entertainments, Odes, Oratorios and copious and pleasing selections of the best Overtures, Concertos, Sonatas, Lessons, Cantatas, Songs, Canzonettes, Canons, Catches and Glees. The whole accompanied with a Universal Dictionary of Music comprising not only a familiar explanation of every word used in this Divine Science but even the true principles of the Science itself; including the Rules for Composition and Instruction for Playing on every Instrument, together with the lives of the celebrated Musicians and Composers etc, etc, etc. And the General History of Music with the present state of the Science in Italy, France, Germany and Great Britain.

The First and Second Numbers of this valuable Work will contain, besides two sheets of elegant and interesting letter(?) the entire opera of Artaxerxes, which alone sells for HALF A GUINEA.

London: Printed for Harrison and Co., No. 18 Paternoster Row; sold by Pearson and Rollson, Printers, Birmingham, and all other Booksellers in Great Britain and Ireland'.

NOTES TO THE ABOVE:
A. By the time of this announcement, the star of Arne's *Artaxerxes,* Mrs. Pinto, née Charlotte Brent, had already sung in Birmingham, at the 1768 Music Meeting.
B. Half a guinea was ten shillings and sixpence (10/6d or 52½p).
C. Harrison, the above printer, was related to Percy Harrison who promoted the nineteenth century celebrity concerts. (Chapter 11).

In 1784, a Michael Woodward advertised himself as a maker of organs, harpsichords and 'Forti Pianos' a further indication of a market for music in Birmingham. It is noteworthy, too, that on 7th June 1784, Number V (five) of the *Beauties of Music and Poetry* was published to commemorate Handel's Grand Jubilee, that is, the twenty-fifth anniversary of his death. This is very likely to have been available through Birmingham's music sellers, who can hardly be supposed to have missed such a business opportunity. It is interesting, and surely significant, that this volume contained Handel songs, particularly associating them with named singers, who were then invited to the Birmingham Music Meetings, later Festivals, in aid of the General Hospital. Miss Abrams came in 1784 and 1790, for example, Mr. Harrison in 1787 and Madame Mara herself, no less, in 1790 and 1796. These singers will be portrayed in the next chapter.

Ballads
Emerging onto the streets for a moment, we can be sure that the ballad-singers and other open-air entertainers still appeared, but their days were numbered. After the arrival of daily newspapers, the ballad singer's role as a purveyor of, and commentator on, the events of the day and on life in general, was undermined. In general, better organised public entertainment was increasingly on offer as we have seen, both indoors and outdoors, and was no longer just for the wealthy. One result was that a number of rather superior balladeers went indoors and upmarket. Birmingham's John Freeth was probably the best of the type, certainly more sophisticated than Sheffield's Joseph Mather, for example, and we have already encountered one of Freeth's ballads earlier in the chapter, on the subject of Vauxhall Gardens. John Freeth lived from 1730 to 1808 and was for forty years the proprietor of a coffee-house and tavern at the corner of Lease Lane and Bell Street, in an area cleared when New Street station was built. He was described by the Gentleman's Magazine for October 1808, in what was obviously an obituary, as 'a facetious bard of nature', but his own description of what he did, in an introduction to his first printed collection of ballads in 1790, cannot be bettered.

The full title of this was, as we may remind ourselves, *The Political Songster* or, a *Touch on the Times on Various Subjects and Adapted to Common Tunes.* It was printed in Birmingham 'for the author' and 'sold by all the booksellers', and it had a healthy subscription list of well over 350, drawn largely from Birmingham and the Midlands, but also from London, Manchester and, even, Ireland. Freeth explains himself as follows:

'It is a very common, and not an untrue saying, that every man has his hobby-horse. Sometimes indeed it is a profitable one, more frequently it is otherwise. My hobby-horse and practice for thirty years past have been, to write songs upon the occurrence of remarkable events, and nature having supplied me with a voice somewhat suitable to my stile *(sic)* of composition, to sing them also, while their subjects were fresh upon every man's mind; and being a Publican this faculty, or rather knack of singing my own songs, has been profitable to me; it has in an evening

Chapter 4 - Not to be written on the back of a postage stamp 1740-1800

crowded my house with customers, and led me to friendships I might not otherwise have experienced. Success naturally encouraged me to pursue the trade of *ballad making,* for without it, it is not probable I should have written a tenth part of what this Volume contains.

My songs are principally adapted to the particular times in which they were written. I now lament I did not go more upon general topics, but engaged in many contested elections...'

John Freeth's inner circle, pictured below, was sometimes called *The Jacobins* or *The Twelve Apostles.* They had a rival Tory establishment in Peck Lane, off New Street, and no love was lost between the members of the two houses who were even known to come to blows occasionally.

Freeth is, in 1790, regretting his partisanship, being in his mature and wiser years convinced that 'the contest of most politicians is only for power and for favours'. Nevertheless, *The Political Songster*, on sale at three shillings and sixpence (3/6d or 17½p), about £5 now, was produced in response to many requests from 'travellers in the mercantile line from every county, who pay me such frequent and friendly visits'.

It is obvious, then, that Freeth of Birmingham had nation-wide fame and his tavern was a port-of-call for many who came to the town to do business. He also seems to have had 'attention and respect from personages of the first rank in life' and he indulges in a little name dropping, mentioning the Duke of Norfolk and the Earls Stapleford and Stanhope. In the final paragraph of this introduction he refers to friends that he, in turn, has visited.

John Freeth and his Friends by Eckstein.

'My numerous friends in and near my native town, the respectable companies I have so often met at the annual festival at Droitwich, High-Wycomb, Coventry and Stratford, and my hearty and cheerful companions at Worcester, Alcester, Evesham, Waltham, etc, are all entitled to my best thanks'.

He tells them that he can no longer invent new ballads, but hopes they will be satisfied if he simply sings the old ones.

There were others who tried their hand at ballad-making, but none of them have made the mark which Freeth did. Some of the tunes Freeth used can be identified and one of them, *The Warwickshire Lad,* neatly demonstrates the mongrel nature of the musical and theatrical arts at that period. The tune was used by Charles Dibdin for David Garrick's *A Warwickshire Lad,* written in 1769 for the bicentenary celebration of Shakespeare's birth. The opening of Birmingham's first canal in the same year was naturally marked by a new Freeth ballad. As was the custom of the day, he used the 'Dibdin' tune for his own words, extolling the superior virtues of Birmingham as opposed to Stratford-upon-Avon. Whether Dibdin had used an existing traditional song or whether it was a *pastiche* is hard to tell, but it is still alive and well, which perhaps suggests the first alternative, a popular tune. At any rate, it can be heard to this day ringing out from the chimes at St. Marys Church, Warwick, four times every Friday; that is three-hourly, on the hour, between 9 a.m. and 6 p.m.

How did Freeth hear the tune? He got about, as we have seen, and could have visited Stratford for the Shakespeare jollifications, but it was not necessary for him to have done that, for Birmingham was to see a version of the Garrick show. Stratford's Shakespeare Jubilee celebrations took place on 6th, 7th and 8th September 1769 and Birmingham followed suit on 5th October. The Gazette for September 25th had this announcement:

SHAKESPEARE - FOR ONE NIGHT ONLY

'At the Theatre in King Street, Birmingham, on Thursday, October 5, will be performed a Concert of Vocal and Instrumental Music, in Three Acts. To consist of all the Songs, Glees, Catches and Roundelays lately performed at Stratford Jubilee, with the Ode written by David Garrick, Esq., in Honour of Shakespeare - The Vocal Parts by Mr. Parsons and Others, the Instrumental by the best Performers of this Town, and from Gloucester, Worcester, and Lichfield, etc. - The speaking of the Recitative Parts of the Ode will be humbly attempted by a Gentleman of this Town. - Also a New Occasional Prologue, and other Particulars, which will be expressed in a future Advertisement, and in the Bills of the Day'.

This Birmingham performance could well have been far better than the Stratford one, which had been turned into a humiliating failure by heavy rain.

Here is the tune A *Warwickshire Lad* with the words of its first verse. There are five other verses.

Chapter 4 - Not to be written on the back of a postage stamp 1740-1800

This day for our new navigation,
We banish all care and vexation,
The sight of the barges each honest heart glads
And the merriest of mortals are Birmingham lads,
Birmingham lads, jovial blades,
And the merriest of mortals are Birmingham lads.

The tune of A Warwickshire Lad.

Folk song

In fact we see in John Freeth's ballad-singing activities exactly the kind of thing which was going to be an increasing threat to the existence of true folk-song in England. True folk music arose spontaneously, and circulated naturally, being passed aurally from person to person. A folk tune was rather like a coin which passed from hand to hand, each individual making what use they wished of it. Tunes, unlike coins, change slightly as they circulate, however, and it is that natural and spontaneous flexibility which is the essence of the true folk song. Undoubtedly Warwickshire had its share of folk tunes. Until the coming of the canals and the building of factories in Birmingham, from the 1780s onwards, the countryside with its farms was still no more than a mile or so away from the centre of the town. The songs sung by the small farmers and cottagers, the ploughmen and the milk-maids, must still have been familiar to the residents of Birmingham who may well have sung these tunes about the streets and in the small work places.

By the middle of the eighteenth century however, there were already theatres in the town, as we have seen, which used tunes like the Warwickshire Lad in their shows. Certainly this preserved them to some extent but this process also 'fixed' them, by removing much of their essential freedom and flexibility. From now on they would be arranged by some trained musician in a formal setting. With increasing industrialisation, work places were indoors and often noisy. Music became more organised, heard mainly after work and in situations such as the theatre, music hall, concert hall or church. In the home too, printed sheet music was increasingly used.

Folk song is a huge subject in its own right. Much research has been done on it but here it is only possible to draw the reader's attention to relevant books which are listed in the bibliography.

Bells
Accessible to all, and free of charge, were the church bells. St. Martin's, again not wishing to be left behind by the 'upstart' parish of St. Philips, began to add to its peal of bells from 1725 onwards, until an agreement had to be reached between the two churches in 1737, not to sound their bells at the same time. This must surely pull the present-day reader up with a jolt. The implication that the buildings between the two churches were small enough and few enough, and the streets quiet enough, to be able to hear not just one ring of bells, but both, needs a few moments for thought, and a big effort of imagination. In general the bells were rung to celebrate many public occasions, as well as to call people to worship, and announcements appear in *Aris's Gazette* either recording the occasion, or notifying the public of what is intended. A very early *Gazette* entry on 16th November 1741 reports that Admiral Vernon's birthday was marked with 'the clamming of the bells', bonfires and, it may be added, more liquid forms of greeting. The Admiral Vernon here so enthusiastically saluted was he who had captured Portobello from the Spanish two years before, in 1739, thereby becoming a national hero. He was also to play an important part in staving off any possible French assistance for the Jacobite rebellion in 1745.

While still on the subject of bells which obviously played a far more important part in life than they do now, J. T. Bunce in his *Birmingham Sixty Years Ago,* reports that in 1730, or earlier, a bell foundry was established at Good Knave's End, better known now as Chad Valley, in Harborne. The proprietor, named Smith, seems to have specialised in casting church bells, many of which were still hanging in the towers of Midland churches when Bunce wrote in 1899. They evidently had a fine, clear tone.

Birmingham by 1800
To sum up, Birmingham by the end of the eighteenth century was a lively, active town of 30,000 inhabitants, about one thirtieth of it present size. Some of these former inhabitants are now household names. It could boast of pleasure gardens and

Chapter 4 - Not to be written on the back of a postage stamp 1740-1800

theatres, oratorios and organists on a scale which we may well envy. Its three theatres would be the equivalent of ninety to-day and even if one only counts the purpose-built one, that would still imply thirty theatres, had the number increased in proportion to the rise in population. Birmingham was already hosting important Music Meetings - (from 1790, called Festivals) - in aid of its new hospital, bringing more leading musicians to the town. Yet in spite of this, it was still a pleasant place, and its town houses still had gardens as they had had earlier in the century. All of this we can derive merely from the notices in its weekly newspaper, and from programmes which have survived, but it seems best to let a contemporary observer have the last word. William Hutton, approaching Birmingham for the first time in 1741, tells us that 'St. Philip's Church appeared first, uncrowded with houses, (for there were none to the North, New Hall excepted) untarnished with smoke and illuminated with a Western sun. It appeared in all the pride of modern architecture. I was charmed with its beauty and thought it then, as I do now, the credit of the place'. Hutton was equally impressed with the vivacity of the people, their alertness and sense of purpose. He wrote that 'Every man seemed to know what he was about'.

1. J. T. Bunce: *Birmingham Sixty Years Ago*, (Compiled from notes written for the Birmingham Weekly Post 1899, and based on personal recollections).
2. *The Political SONGSTER or a Touch on the Times on Various Subjects* and adapted to common tunes. (Printed by Thomas Pearson).
3. See chapter 6, *What else?*
4. Not the Jeremiah Clark who wrote what was often thought to be Purcell's *Trumpet Voluntary.*
5. Milton: *L'Allegro.*
6. William Hutton: *History of Birmingham* (Birmingham 1780).
7, 8 and 9. Roger Fiske: *English Theatre Music in the Eighteenth Century* Oxford 1986.

Chapter 5

From Music Meeting to Musical Festival, with a portrait gallery of stars 1768-1834

The genesis of the First Music Meeting in aid of Birmingham's General Hospital, and its success in raising funds, was described in chapter three. By 1778 building had again been halted for lack of money. This time it was the choir of another new church, St. Paul's, Hockley, which James Kempson called on to assist in putting on the second Music Meeting for the hospital. The foundation stone of St. Paul's had been laid in 1777 and Kempson was offered the post of clerk and choirmaster there. According to Edwards (op. cit.) it was a deputation consisting of James Kempson and some of the singers from St. Paul's Church which proposed this second meeting to the Hospital Board, the profits to be shared between the hospital and St. Paul's. In passing it should be mentioned that a Music Meeting on the same early-Autumn three-day pattern, had been arranged in 1774 to assist the completion of St. Mary's Chapel in Whittall Street, near where St. Chad's Cathedral and the Dental Hospital now are.

Returning to the 1778 music meeting, once again the atmosphere of it comes over to us most vividly in the words of the *Gazette's* reporters, writing in the paper on 27th July and 31st August 1778:

Birmingham 27th July 1778

'Oratorios - On Wednesday, Thursday, and Friday, the 2nd, 3rd, and 4th of September next, will be performed, for the Benefit of St. Paul's Chapel and the General Hospital.

At St. Philip's Church, on Wednesday Morning, in the Course of the Service, Handel's Grand Dettingen Te Deum, Jubilate, and Dr. Boyce's Anthem, to conclude with Handel's Coronation Anthem. In the Evening, at the Theatre, in New Street, A grand Miscellaneous Concert, consisting of Select Vocal and Instrumental Pieces, by the principal performers.

On Thursday Morning, at St. Philip's, the Oratorio of Judas Maccabaeus; and in the Evening, at the Theatre, the Serenata of Acis and Galatea. Between the parts will be introduced some favourite Pieces.

Chapter 5 - From Music Meeting to Musical Festival, with a portrait gallery of stars

On Friday Morning, at St. Philip's, the Sacred Oratorio of Messiah; and in the Evening at the Theatre, a grand Miscellaneous Concert, consisting of several capital Pieces, by the principal Performers.

Principal Vocal Performers, Miss Mahon, Miss Salmon, Messrs. Norris, Matthews, Price and Salmon.

Principal Instrumental Performers, Messrs. Crammer, Carvetto, Park, Ashley, Storacci, Jenkins and Mahon. And other Parts of the Band, which will be very full, by the most approved Performers, and the celebrated Women Chorus Singers from Lancashire'.

The Performers are desired to be in Birmingham in Time to rehearse on Monday Morning'.

31st August 1778

'The Appearance of Company at the approaching Musical Entertainments, which begin on Wednesday next, is expected to be both numerous and respectable, lodgings we are informed being already engaged for many genteel Families; and we have Reason to believe the Performance will be such as cannot fail giving universal Satisfaction, no Pains nor Expence (sic) having been regarded in selecting the most approved Performers, both Vocal and Instrumental. Amongst the former, Miss Mahon's distinguished Merit deserves particular Notice; she having received, at the last Encoenia at Oxford, and other polite Places, the highest Approbation of her Judgement and Execution. - Of the Instrumental, it may be thought sufficient to observe, that Mr. Crammer, the first Violin, has directed, for a considerable Time, with singular Honour and Ability, the most complete Band in the Kingdom, to perhaps one of the most Brilliant Audiences in Europe. - On the Clarionett, Mr. Mahon is said to have peculiar Excellence, and to stand unequalled by any Competitor. In short, the Band, which is exceedingly full, is composed of Performers of great Eminence in the Parts in which they are severally meant to appear; and the superior Powers of many, it is presumed, must be fresh in the Recollection of those who had the Pleasure of hearing them on a former similar Occasion in this Town'.

On 7th September, the *Gazette* reports that the music was performed to 'a crowded and respectable Company with universal approbation'. Readers were informed that an excellent sermon was preached pointing out 'the Necessity of a liberal and public-spirited Support of the Objects under Consideration'. In fact 'the produce of the several Entertainments' was £800, equivalent now to £26,000. The sum of £199, or about £6,500 today, was reserved for the General Hospital.

The above accounts give a good summary of the essential ingredients of the music meetings. The love of Handel's music was a vital part of the mixture. It fostered in an amazingly large proportion of the population a positive passion for choral music and for singing in choirs, which persisted well on into the twentieth century. The opportunity to meet and socialise with friends and acquaintances, to share in the enjoyment of music and the support of a worthy cause, alluded to in chapter 3, was another. Last but by no means least was the chance these meetings offered to Birmingham's citizens to hear some of the most brilliant performers of the day, singers and instrumentalists alike. The people who came here were crowd-pullers, and a good part of this chapter will be devoted to describing the talents which lay behind the names listed in the programmes and newspaper reports. The Gazette's comments about their abilities are not exaggerated. It is only the wording that is a little quaint.

Before embarking on our survey of Festival stars, however, there are perhaps two other aspects of this review of the early Music Meetings and Musical Festivals to be considered.

To begin with, it may help if a summary of the dates and titles is given in a formal list, together with the amounts of money raised.

Music Meetings for the benefit of the General Hospital

	Presidents	Receipts	Profits
1768	No president	£800	£299
1778	No president	£800	£170
1780	No president	?	?
1784	Viscount Dudley & Ward	£1325	£703

The 1784 Meeting was modelled on the Westminster Abbey Commemoration of the 25th Anniversary of Handel's death.

After this Music Meeting the Hospital Trustees agreed to hold the event every three years.

	President	Receipts	Profits
1787	Earl of Aylesford	£1980	£964

Birmingham Musical Festivals for the benefit of the General Hospital

	Presidents	Receipts	Profits
1790	Viscount Dudley & Ward	£1965	£958
–	No Festival in 1793 because the theatre had been burnt down, a common occurrence in those days.		
1796	Earl of Aylesford	£2044	£897

Chapter 5 - From Music Meeting to Musical Festival, with a portrait gallery of stars

(Cont.)	Presidents	Receipts	Profits
1799	Earl of Warwick (Joseph Moore directed the Festivals from now until 1849)	£2544	£1470
1802	Earl of Dartmouth	£3820	£2380
1805	Earl of Aylesford	£4222	£2202
1808	Lord Guernsey	£5511	£3257
1811	Earl of Bradford	£6680	£3629
1814	Earl of Plymouth	£7124	£3111
1817	Earl of Warwick	£8746	£4296
1820	Earl of Dartmouth	£9483	£5001
1823	The Earl Talbot	£10859	£5806
1826	The Earl Howe	£9760	£4592
1829	Earl of Bradford	£9604	£3806

(The next festival was delayed until 1834 when the Town Hall was ready)

* The 1780 Music Meeting was certainly organised for the benefit of The General Hospital. Who the organisers were is not at present clear.

The total of the profits is approximately £43,500, which to-day would be about £1,130,000, in other words over a million pounds. This was an astonishing feat for a three-day event and Birmingham obviously took great pride in it. A note, in ink, in a surviving programme for 1808, compares the £5,000 raised by Birmingham's Musical Festival, that year, giving a net profit of £3,257, with the net profits of £2,000 in Liverpool and £10,000 in London's Westminster Abbey. The provincial towns and cities raised, proportionately to their size, more money than London and, of these, Birmingham was pre-eminently successful in achieving the charitable purpose of the Festivals. The practical involvement of members of the Midland aristocracy gave a lead. Many of them were keen music lovers and there was, for example, a family connection between Handel's librettist Charles Jennens and the Earls of Aylesford. The Earl of Plymouth's horn-players we have also met (page 38).

The Programmes 1768-1834

A second point which should be made concerns the content of the programmes. It is not quite fair to dismiss them as 'all Handel' and nothing else, as is so often done. This was (almost) true at first, certainly, and Handel's oratorios monopolised the morning concerts at St. Philip's. *Messiah, Judas Maccabaeus, L'Allegro ed Il Penseroso, Acis and Galatea, Israel in Egypt* and *Esther* were all given in full, with *L'Allegro* and *Acis* declining somewhat in popularity as tastes changed. *Goliath* was also once given in full, at the New Street Theatre on Thursday evening 23rd September 1784. Sections and individual recitatives and arias were also taken from other Handel oratorios, such as *Joshua, Jephtha, Saul, Samson* and *Solomon,* and inserted into miscellaneous programmes; some sacred, some secular. If, however, one had attended some of these Grand Miscellaneous Concerts (as they were called), in the evenings, with a little care, one could almost have avoided Handel, even in the early days of the Music Meetings. As early as 1780, Abel's *Sixth Symphony* was played and the Friday evening concert in 1784 began with a Haydn overture and went on to exploit the exceptional abilities of the performers, with Mr. Parke, Mr. Crosdil, Mr. Mahon and Mr. Wilton displaying their virtuosity in solos and concertos on the oboe, 'cello, clarinet and violin respectively. Wilbye's madrigal, *Flora gave me fairest flowers* was included, also two Purcell choruses, a piece called *Hark the Lark* by Dr. Cooke and a final air and chorus from Boyce's *Solomon*. Especially interesting for local people was the inclusion of a glee called *Come shepherds* by a Mr. Cunningham, to commemorate the Halesowen poet, William Shenstone (1714-63). An Oxford alumnus and a writer admired by Johnson, Shenstone lived at The Leasowes, at the top of Mucklow Hill, Halesowen and designed a famous garden there, overstretching his means in the process. Only two Handel arias seem to have crept into that particular programme!

The influence of Joseph Moore
The tendency towards a better balance and a wider choice of composer was undoubtedly encouraged by Joseph Moore who was, as we would describe him today, an early 'artistic director' of the Birmingham Musical Festival; this from 1802 to 1849. He may well have had support and encouragement not only from his friend Matthew Boulton, but also from the brilliant violinist who was to lead the orchestra at very many Festival events from 1778, namely Wilhelm Cramer. Often called 'Mr. Crammer' in the *Gazette,* and even in the programmes, Cramer played a Corelli concerto in 1787 and a piece by Geminiani in 1796. The Italian Geminiani had settled in England in 1714, and it was he who helped to restore Handel to the Elector of Hanover's favour, when that prince became George I of England. Geminiani was himself a composer of some merit, though never equal to Tartini or Corelli. His main contribution to music was his book, *The Art of Playing on the Violin*. This handed down Corelli's teaching and made the playing of Corelli's music, sometimes found very difficult by other violinists, more effective. The way to hold both instrument and bow, the use of the shift of position in the left hand, and the technique of double-stopping, were all described in what was the first book of its kind published in this country.

As a pupil of Stamitz and a member of the famous Mannheim orchestra, Wilhelm Cramer must have been more than ready to co-operate with Moore's advocacy of the music of composers other than Handel, great master though Handel was. In 1802, Mozart's overture to *The Magic Flute* was played, but English composers were not neglected and the names of Purcell and Boyce feature fairly often, also occasionally

Chapter 5 - From Music Meeting to Musical Festival, with a portrait gallery of stars

those of Crotch and Croft. Vocal pieces by William Shield and Samuel Arnold also got a look in, as did some by the Italian contemporaries, Guglielmi and Paisiello. Haydn's pupil, Pleyel, was represented in 1802 by a *Grand Concertante* (sic), still in manuscript, for violin, tenor (viola), 'cello, oboe, bassoon and flute obbligato. The performers were Cramer, J. Lindley, R. Lindley, Erskine, Holmes and Ashe. More details will be given about these men and about Joseph Moore in due course. Also in that year two harpists, the Misses Cantelo, contributed as duettists, one of them also accompanying the singer Madame Dusseck in a vocal piece.

In 1805, Moore again secured the services of Mrs. Billington, who had sung at the 1787 Music Meeting. Part one of Haydn's *Creation*, first performed in Vienna in 1798, was given an important place in the 1805 programme, and Mrs. Billington must therefore have sung the aria 'With verdure clad' and also in the chorus 'The marvellous work behold amazed'. In 1808, she sang Purcell's *Mad Bess*, which continued to appear in Birmingham Musical Festival programmes until 1912.

In 1811, both a Beethoven Symphony and a Haydn Symphony were played - at the Theatre in fact - but in the casual manner of the time neither keys nor numbers are given! This was virtually contemporary music - of the greatest kind.

In 1814, the frost scene from Purcell's *King Arthur* was in the programme and Mozart's *Jupiter Symphony* (no. 41 in C major K551) was given in 1817, as was another Haydn Symphony, labelled in the programme as 'number 10'. This was very probably one of the 'Paris' symphonies, no. 86 in D major, composed in 1786. For an explanation of this discrepancy in numbering, please see chapter 16, footnote 2. In addition a 'Grand Symphony' by Beethoven, again at the theatre, was performed. Perhaps this means the Fifth Symphony, composed between 1804 and 1808, but this is really only speculation. In 1817, Mozart's *Requiem* was introduced; but not until 1820, apparently, was it given with the proper complement of wind instruments 'as its great author designed'.[1] Other items on a smaller scale included such pieces as a Marenzio madrigal on the one hand, and Pepusch's cantata *Alexis* on the other; the same Dr. Pepusch who chose and arranged the music for Gay's *Beggar's Opera*. The great contemporary continental composers were being increasingly represented. In 1817, Purcell and Boyce are still in evidence, but the Hallelujah from Beethoven's *Mount of Olives* was also performed. Composed in 1803 and revised in 1804, it became a popular festival item for some years.

In 1820, another Haydn symphony was played. Named as 'number 7', it was in fact no. 97 in C major, composed in 1792 (again, please see chapter 16, footnote 2). Beethoven's Second Symphony was also played in 1820, and Weber's Overture to *Der Freischütz*, written in 1821, was played in Birmingham in 1826. Rossini was quite often represented by arias and overtures, such as the one to the opera *Tancredi*, written in 1813.

Meanwhile, a popular performer at the Birmingham Musical Festivals was the tenor John Braham. He began his visits in 1802, and brought with him pieces of his own composition. There seems to have been a selection of songs taken from *The Cabinet* (1802), a second-rate opera by someone else for which he, wisely, insisted on re-writing those numbers he himself sang. They were in the English theatre music style and entitled, for example, 'Ah, could I hope my fair to see', and 'No more by sorrow chafed'. In a more heroic vein were his own pieces *Abercrombie* and *The Death of Nelson,* which he sang in Birmingham in 1811, and 1817. The effect of these pieces apparently depended mainly on Braham himself being there to sing them. Obviously a man with a strong personality, like many tenors!

Naturally, Handel continued to have an honoured and vital place in Musical Festival programmes well on into the nineteenth century, but after Costa's retirement as conductor in 1873, Handel was represented mainly by the Thursday morning performance of *Messiah*. This was a feature which had been established by 1805, certainly, and continued until 1906. The Wednesday to Friday three-day pattern, used until 1817, was expanded to four when Joseph Moore persuaded the hospital trustees to agree to Tuesday as the opening day; this from 1820 onwards.

The Performers 1768-1834
Mention has already been made in passing of Mrs. Billington and John Braham, soprano and tenor respectively, and it is time to enquire further into the personalities behind these and other names appearing in Festival programmes at this period. A portrait gallery of the vocalists and leading instrumentalists, and some account of the choirs and the conductors, will occupy the next part of this chapter.

First the singers. From the beginning, they were all competent and some were of a very high calibre indeed; noted not just in London but increasingly, as time went on, on the continent of Europe also. There were, in addition, intriguing personal and family connections between some of those who belonged to the late eighteenth-century musical establishment. An example was Mrs. Pinto who came with her husband, the violinist Thomas Pinto, to the first Music Meeting in 1768.

Star singers at the Festivals,
Charlotte Brent, Mrs. Pinto ca. 1735-1802,
Birmingham Musical Festival 1768
A Soprano, perhaps better known under her maiden name of Charlotte Brent, she was both pupil and mistress of the composer Thomas Arne, for whom he had written the extremely demanding part of Mandane in his opera *Artaxerxes,* in 1762. She had supplanted Arne's unhappy wife, Cecilia Young, in that philandering gentleman's affections. Mrs. Arne was herself a fine singer in her youth, chosen by Handel for two of his operas, and one of her nieces was a visitor to the pleasure gardens and the theatre here in Birmingham. Mrs. Arne's rival, Charlotte Brent, less patient and forgiving than the long-suffering wife, deserted Arne in 1766 and married Thomas

Chapter 5 - From Music Meeting to Musical Festival, with a portrait gallery of stars

Pinto, when she was 33, and Pinto 52. Arne was furious, but we can feel little sympathy for him since it was certainly a case of the biter bit! We have a number of clear descriptions of Charlotte Pinto's voice, including some lines by a contemporary theatrical commentator, Hugh Kelly.[2] He said that her voice,

'Melts the whole breast divinely while it storms,
Pains with delight, and wounds us as it charms'.

Apparently she decorated the vocal line in moderation. She created an enthusiastic *furore* as Polly in *The Beggar's Opera* at Covent Garden in October 1759 and her peerless singing made a fortune for that theatre. David Garrick had rejected her for Drury Lane and lived to rue his mistake. Arne wrote *Thomas and Sally* in 1760 to exploit Miss Brent's superlative gifts and *Artaxerxes* and the part of Mandane, already mentioned, came two years later. This called for scintillating singing associated in our day with, for example, Joan Sutherland. Such was the brilliance of the earliest visitors to Birmingham's Music Meetings and Musical Festivals.

Elizabeth Billington, 1765-1818
Birmingham Musical Festivals 1787, 1805, 1808
In the next generation of sopranos was Elizabeth Billington, possibly one of the best *coloratura* singers there has ever been. In youth she was sufficiently capable as a pianist to play a piano concerto in public, and is known to have had harpsichord lessons from the 'London' Bach, Johann Christian, already mentioned in connection with the programmes (above). Lord Mount-Edgcumbe, a connoisseur of the singers of the day, noted that as a young singer, Mrs. Billington was 'pretty, has a delightful fresh voice of very high compass... in its very high tones it resembles a flute or flageolet. Its agility was very great and everything she sung was executed in the neatest manner and with utmost precision'. A description by Dr. Charles Burney also sheds a clear light on her vocal powers. He wrote that 'the natural tone of her voice is exquisitely sweet, her knowledge of music so considerable, her shake so true and her closes and embellishments so various and her expression so grateful, that nothing but envy and apathy can hear her without delight'. She could reach with ease the F in alt which so embarrassingly eluded Florence Foster Jenkins in her recorded attempt at the Queen of the Night's 'revenge' aria, from Mozart's *The Magic Flute*. Many older readers particularly will no doubt have heard this record at some time, although it is still revived for our amusement from time to time. Very few of even the best singers can take these high F's successfully, so that Mrs. Billington's voice was obviously exceptional. One has only to look to Mandane's aria, 'A Soldier Tir'd' from Arne's *Artaxerxes* which she, as well as Charlotte Brent, used to sing, to realise this.

Like Mrs. Pinto she was not an especially good actress, although she was probably adequate for the stylised parts prevalent at the time, but whatever else she was, she was apparently a very conscientious worker. Her career fell into two parts, separated by her flight to Italy in 1794. This was because a very damaging account of her disgraceful private life was published. Perhaps what could be tolerated in a man was not acceptable in a woman, although she does seem to have damaged her reputation still more by being disagreeable at times. Perhaps it was that which people did not like and could not readily forgive. She was a great success in Italy, however, where she was patronised by Sir William and Lady Hamilton. She ventured to return to England in 1801, when the scandal had died down, her vocal reputation enhanced by her European experience. Her visits to Birmingham in 1787, 1805, and 1808, belong, therefore, to both periods of her life. After Italy, Elizabeth Billington was considerably stouter, but also more likeable. We have a local comment on her voice, interestingly, and William Pountney, who was from 1846 to 1897 a festival chorus bass, and also on one occasion a soloist, said that many referred to the 'brilliant sweetness of her voice'.

Gertrud Elizabeth Mara (née Schmeling), 1749-1833.
Birmingham Musical Festival, 1790 and 1796.

In Madame Mara's case we have a singer with some training abroad as well as in London, though her teachers in London could hardly have been more distinguished. Born Gertrude Schmeling in Kassel in 1749, she toured the provinces of Britain, also the Continent, as a child violinist in an endeavour to keep her improvident, violin-maker father out of debtors' prisons. She had some vocal training in London from Paradisi, or Paradies, a pupil of Porpora and then in Leipzig from J. A. Hiller, a musical editor scholar and composer, founder of German *Singspiele*. (This was a mixture of songs and dialogue based on English ballad opera). Again we are in debt to Charles Burney for a description of Mara's singing, her powers being truly astonishing according to his account. Less happily, she often had to sing music which turned the voice into a mere instrument for executing clever vocal 'stunts'. Burney postulated that if she were to go to Italy she would probably not meet with any singer who was fundamentally any better than herself but 'by adopting the peculiar excellencies of many performers, of different schools and talents, her style... would be an aggregate of all that is exquisite and beautiful'. Mara herself was plain, and her English atrocious, facts which in themselves emphasise the compensatory power of her beautiful voice.

In 1771, she was introduced to Frederick the Great who took her into his service, at the Berlin Opera. From then on she was to all intents and purposes, a prisoner. Mara's husband was a 'cellist, also with a royal master; the Emperor's brother. When Mara wished to accept an invitation to sing elsewhere, Frederick would put her husband in jail, or send him off to do a stint in a regimental band, as a drummer! Perhaps the couple's real offence, in the first place, was to have married without the Emperor's permission. In 1780, after an 'illness', Mara was prescribed a cure abroad and by this means got away from Frederick's court. Soon after, Frederick's own interest in music-making waned and he released her from her contract.

The Maras came to London and in 1786, Madame Mara made her stage debut in the title role of *Didone abbandonata*, (Dido abandoned), a *pastiche*. She dominated the Handel-Haydn oratorio scene until, after 1802, she settled in Russia.

Birmingham was fortunate to obtain her services quite early in her reign, that is in 1790, and again in 1796. The reader will remember that the Birmingham Musical Festival presidents in those years were The Viscount Dudley and Ward and the Earl of Aylesford. An invitation sent under the patronage of these English aristocrats must have reassured a lady who had been in an Emperor's service, and secured her presence in this town. In any case the whole provincial festival movement was gathering momentum and importance, and was to provide many notable musicians with a regular source of income at least until the First World War. Birmingham was in the vanguard of this movement, and in 1823, even the monarch sensed the popular mood, and from that year the King, or Queen, was always the Musical Festival's chief patron.

To return to Madame Mara, she was noted for a magnificent and beautiful voice of even tone, with a high compass, from G below middle C to E in alt, or E above high C. She stressed the force and meaning of the words, which compensated somewhat for her poor acting; which was not even as good as Mrs. Pinto's and Mrs. Billington's - but surely this was irrelevant in all three cases? They came to Birmingham to sing oratorio and isolated songs and arias. The voice was all, and superlative voices were what the town got.

Some other British women singers at the Music Meetings

Two other women singers from the early days of the Music Meeting were Miss Mahon and Mrs. Wrighten. Miss Mahon (Mrs. Ambrose) was a soprano principal with Madame Mara and Mrs. Billington at Westminster Abbey in 1784, when the great celebration to mark the twenty-fifth anniversary of Handel's death took place. There were also some very distinguished instrumentalists in this Irish family, and they will be introduced later in this chapter. Miss Mahon (Mrs. Ambrose) sang at the Birmingham Music Meetings in 1778 and 1780. One of her sisters, Mrs. Second, came in 1796; and later, in 1817 and 1829, Birmingham was visited by a niece of the Mahons through her mother, the singer Mrs. Salmon. Earlier members of the Salmon family itself had also visited the town, in 1778.

Mrs. Elizabeth Wrighten who sang in Birmingham in 1774 and 1780 was another noted singer from the London stage. She was married to the Drury Lane prompter, but left her husband in 1787, fled to America and thereby deprived this town of any further enjoyment of her talent.

Angelica Catalani 1780-1849, Birmingham Festivals 1811, 1814, 1823, Theatre Royal New Street from 1807 to 1828

Catalani was probably the starriest of all the divas who came to Birmingham, with the possible exception of Adelina Patti. Billed, probably at the suggestion of her husband, as the 'prima cantatrice del mondo' ('the world's top singer', in modern parlance) there was justification for this claim. Catalani not only had a splendid voice, she was also handsome as we can see for ourselves from her picture (opposite). Her voice was brilliant but the purity of her perfect intonation was thrilling in itself. She could execute with absolute accuracy the most difficult embellishment of the

Angelica Catalani 1780-1849.

vocal line, and she had a perfect trill. Being human, she was not entirely without fault, and there was an awkward break between the middle register and the high notes of her voice, with some weaker notes at the top of the stave (say, F and G, an octave and a half above middle C). She was certainly not intellectual and made no attempt to remedy this deficiency by general reading. Occasionally, she could seem impassive in her singing, but some observers attributed this to nervousness, having seen her tremble like a leaf before going on to the stage or platform. She was always magnificently dressed and a pleasure to look at, and the voice itself stifled most criticism. Again we are indebted to Lord Mount-Edgcumbe's *Musical Reminiscences* for a brief description of her voice which was, he said, 'of a most uncommon quality, and capable of exertions almost supernatural'. It had, he added 'a volume and strength that are quite surprising; while its agility in divisions, running up and down the scale in semitones, and its compass in jumping two octaves at once, are equally astonishing'. Even Stendhal the French writer, a critical listener, described her voice as 'filling the soul with a kind of astonished wonder, as though it beheld a miracle'.

Mount-Edgcumbe nevertheless criticised her want of taste in overloading melodies with trills, runs, leaps and other decorative devices. What she did would probably have been too much of a good thing, even at the height of the baroque era, but the early nineteenth century taste for emotion and lyricism brought different ideas about what singing should be like. Catalani's style was beginning to sound pointlessly flowery.

All the same, Catalani brought in the patrons, both in the theatre and at the Festivals, and another glance at the table of receipts at the beginning of this chapter will show notable rises in the 'Catalani years', 1811, 1814, and 1823, and a slight falling-off in 1826, after her departure. A singer who could help the Hospital trustees to a profit at each of 'her' festivals in the order of four or five thousand pounds (£85,000 to £105,000 now) proved thereby her enormous popularity.

Although born in Italy, Catalani worked for some time at the King's Theatre in London, eventually retiring to Paris. She came regularly to the Theatre Royal in Birmingham between 1807 and 1828, so that she already had a following in the town when booked for the Festivals. At first her English was shaky, and the following is an attempt to render her version of *God save the King,* as she sang it at some of the festivals, including Birmingham's.

O Lord avar God arais
Schaeter is enemies
And mece them fol.
Confound tear politekse
Frostrere tear nevise trex
On George avar hopes we fix
God save te Kin.

This is quoted in William Pountney's *History of the Festival*. In justice to Catalani, it must be said that she did work to improve her English, apparently with some success. [3] In general, too, Pountney is full of the praise he had heard of her, saying that her voice was 'of purest quality' with a compass of nearly three octaves. It was so powerful that 'no band could overwhelm its tones. Her singing created a sensation like no one had ever made before. She had one peculiar undulating tone - said to be higher than the highest note on the piano'. Music critics called it a double *falsetto* and she seems to have been the only one ever to use this note, employing it to thrilling effect.

In spite of her defects she was, as Pountney confirms, a great favourite of the British public. People seem to have been fond of her, in an exasperated sort of way, a response, perhaps, to a certain naivety in her character, but also, surely, to that in her nature which made her a generous benefactor to others in the last years of her life. Her personality comes over even now. Were she to be reincarnated and suddenly appear before us, we can only think that we would like her and be as thrilled by the sheer power and purity of her voice as her contemporaries were.

Kitty Stephens, (1794-1882), Birmingham Festivals, 1814-1826

The appealing Catherine Stephens was the first lady of the English operatic stage in her day, and from 1813 to 1835 a favourite at the major concerts and festivals. She had a rich and powerful soprano voice, marred by rather poor diction, which did not, however, prevent her from profoundly moving her hearers, especially in such arias as 'Angels ever bright and fair', from Handel's *Theodora*. She was one of those theatre ladies who married into the aristocracy. After retirement in 1838, at the age of 44, she became the wife of the 80-year-old Earl of Essex. Polly *(The Beggar's Opera)*, Donna Anna *(Don Giovanni)* and the Countess *(Marriage of Figaro)* were her best roles. She sang at Birmingham's Theatre Royal several times.

Mary Ann Paton, (1802-1864), Birmingham Musical Festival, 1826, 1829
At the time of her Birmingham appearances Miss Paton was still Lady Lennox, the wife of Sir William Pitt Lennox; another singer who married into the aristocracy. Unfortunately the marriage did not last and Miss Paton later married Joseph Wood, a tenor, with whom she found happiness. She was considered by no less a person than the composer Weber as 'a singer of the very first rank'. She sang Reiza in the first production of his opera *Oberon,* at Covent Garden in April, 1826. Fresh from this success, she came to Birmingham.

Born in Edinburgh, she was a member of a very gifted family of Scottish musicians and could play the harp, the piano and the violin as a small child. As an adult singer, she both looked and sounded beautiful.

Maria Malibran (Garcia), (1808-36), and the Garcia family. Birmingham Musical Festival, 1829
Malibran on the other hand was born into a family some of whose members were themselves to become the aristocrats and arbiters of the vocal world. She was the daughter of the famous tenor, Manuel Garcia. Her mother was also a singer. Garcia was the first Almaviva in Rossini's *The Barber of Seville.* Six of the Garcia children distinguished themselves as singers, three of them outstandingly so. These last were Maria Malibran Garcia herself, Pauline Viardot Garcia and the younger Manuel Garcia. Manuel, junior, was probably the most famous vocal teacher of the nineteenth century, and both he and his sister Pauline Viardot were noted for formulating vocal principles for the demands composer were making of singers. Jenny Lind and the baritone Charles Santley were among Manuel Garcia's most outstanding pupils. Pauline Viardot's influence as a teacher was also considerable, although this waned in her later years.

Maria Malibran, however, seems to have needed all her father's sometimes harshly-exercised training to discipline a wayward mezzo-soprano voice. She succeeded brilliantly in achieving this, but was apparently very occasionally in danger of overdoing her acting; there was some disagreement on this point. Many argued that all she did in the way of stage business and stage movement was always justified. Ernest Legouvé, the critic, who with Scribe was author of *Adriana Lecouvreur,* said that until he had heard Malibran, music had been an amiable art, all graciousness and spirit. After Malibran, it became 'the purest and most dramatic expression of poetry,

Chapter 5 - From Music Meeting to Musical Festival, with a portrait gallery of stars

of love and of pain. A new world was revealed to me'. She was one of those singers who, like Maria Callas in our own time, took the art of singing a step, or several steps, forward. Like Callas too, Malibran wrestled with an imperfect vocal instrument, but Malibran's battle with her voice was well-directed, as well as unremitting. The gruelling training which her father had imposed on her, and which she had readily accepted, came to fruition in her brilliant success on both sides of the Atlantic. She made her operatic debut in London on 7th June 1825, when she sang Rosina in *The Barber of Seville*. In New York she sang in the same opera, also in *Otello, La Donna del Lago, Cenerentola, Semiramide, Don Giovanni, Romeo and Juliet* and *Il Turco in Italia*. During that season, 1825-26, she had her eighteenth birthday. In 1829, she returned to London, this time as a great star. In that same year she came to Birmingham. It will be noticed that from that time onwards, America was ever more frequently on the star singer's touring circuit. Happily, Birmingham was to remain an important link in that chain for many years to come.

Malibran married a worthless Frenchman; and left him. She had a son, by a noted Belgian violinist; then married him. Headstrong and courageous, she died at the early age of 28, after a riding accident. She had insisted on singing at the Manchester Festival, (1836), in spite of what must have been severe internal injuries. Nine days later she was dead. H.F. Chorley, the librettist said of her that she 'passed over the stage like a meteor, as an apparition of wonder rather than as one who, on her departure, left her mantle behind her for others to take up and wear'. Her brother and sister, Manuel Garcia and Pauline Viardot, by contrast, lived to a great old age; Manuel to 101 and Pauline Viardot to 88. They died in 1906 and 1910 respectively. Viardot came to the three Festivals between 1852 and 1858.

Festival Personalities in general - singers, instrumentalists, conductors

Let no-one think therefore that the leading singers named in the Music Meeting and Musical Festival programmes were anything but the very best the world could then offer. It was like having Kirsten Flagstad, Birgit Nilsson, Maria Callas, and Joan Sutherland coming to Birmingham, not once but twice or more each, not just to the Festivals but to the town's theatre as well. The presence of the great prima donnas of the era (1768-1834) played a very important part in establishing Birmingham as the premier provincial festival; along with the enthusiastic interest and generosity of the audiences it should be said. The touring circuit of the singing stars in those days included not just the capital cities but also the major towns of Europe. As we saw, America began to be included in this in the 1820s and, as the circuit widened to encompass the whole globe so, eventually, Birmingham was excluded from it. Patti's last visit here was in 1907, a date which, in some ways, marked the end of Birmingham's front-rank place in the world of music for many years to come.

Notable Festival Gentlemen

As to the gentlemen visitors to the Festivals, one suspects that the pulling power of some of the instrumentalists may have been as great, or greater, than that of many of the male singers. The Cramers, violinists, both father and son, Robert Lindley, the 'cellist, John Mahon, the clarinettist, the oboist, John Parke and Andrew Ashe the flautist – all of them were *virtuosi* whose names were given great prominence in early festival announcements in the *Gazette*, and were obviously expected to be a great attraction.

The male vocal soloists at the festivals of this period were mainly skilled church, oratorio and concert singers. They performed with a high degree of musicianship, taste and artistry, though not always possessing powerful voices. Such were Samuel Harrison (1787), Mr. Saville (1787, 1790) whom we met at Sutton Coldfield Town Hall in 1783, also Thomas Norris (1768, 1778, 1790), Charles Knyvett, senior (1790) and the trio of Charles Knyvett, junior, presumably an alto like his father (1811-29), Thomas Vaughan, tenor (1811-40) and Thomas Bellamy, bass (1811-34). The dates given in brackets are those of the Birmingham Festivals at which they performed. All were highly musical and stylish vocalists, coming from the Chapel Royal, from St. Paul's, London, or from the Vocal Concerts or the 'Concert of Antient Music' as it was styled. Indeed Harrison and Knyvett senior, themselves established the Vocal Concerts. A number of these singers were also minor composers, so that their embellishments of vocal lines are likely to have been musically more appropriate than was the case with some other singers.

Musical clans

Two members of the Knyvett family were mentioned in the previous paragraph, but a third, Charles senior's other son, William, not only came as a singer, in 1814, but was also the Festival Conductor between 1834 and 1846. The tenor Thomas Vaughan, mentioned above, was married to Miss Tennant who sang here in 1802, and the Knyvett family also forged a link, by marriage, to another English musical clan, when William Knyvett married Deborah Travis. Born near Oldham, Deborah Travis was the niece of Mrs. Travis, one of the Lancashire chorus singers engaged at the Concert of Ancient Music. Deborah herself sang in the chorus in 1813, but so impressed the powers-that-were that she was given a place as an articled pupil to Thomas Greatorex, himself conductor at the Birmingham Festival in 1805 and between 1814-1829. She was soon established as a much-admired singer in oratorio, especially in Handel's music, and sang as a principal at every Birmingham Festival between 1820 and 1843. Between 1820 and 1829 she appeared as Miss Travis, afterwards as Mrs. Knyvett.

The Reinholds

Among other gentlemen singers of particular interest is Frederick Charles Reinhold (1737-1815), the bass. Also a Chapel Royal product, he soon distinguished himself on the London stage, but his greatest claim to fame, perhaps, is that his father, Henry Theodore (1690-1751) sang with Handel's company from 1736. From 1743, all Handel's bass roles were written for Reinhold senior, a genuine bass, admired for his character as well for his voice. Some of Arne's Vauxhall Songs were also written with Reinhold senior in mind. The son, Frederick Charles, seems to have inherited the same rich bass voice and was one of the principal singers at the 1784 Handel commemoration in Westminster Abbey. He came to Birmingham in 1790, and took part in *Acis and Galatea* among other things. Reinhold junior was heard, therefore, in the bass aria 'O ruddier than the cherry' an item which would be eagerly anticipated. He retired from professional life soon afterwards.

Michael Kelly, (1762-1826), Birmingham Musical Festival, 1796

Our next singer is connected with Mozart, no less. Michael Kelly the Irish tenor, who studied and sang in Italy and Vienna, was on 1st May 1786 the first to sing the parts of Don Curzio and Don Basilio in Mozart's *Marriage of Figaro.*

His was not the most beautiful of tenor voices but he impressed people by the stylishness of his singing and particularly by the fact that all his high notes were true tenor notes. Many operatic tenors in those days, when the really important roles had been written for women or for *castrati,* used the *falsetto* voice for the high notes. The best tenor voices at that time were in fact to be heard in the churches and at concerts, where there was not the need to develop a large and robust sound.

When Kelly came to Birmingham in 1796, he was 33 years of age and the leading tenor at the King's Theatre, London. He certainly sang the tenor warhorse, 'Sound an Alarm' from Handel's *Judas Maccabaeus* on that occasion. After this, he spent more time in theatre management than in singing. He also published his somewhat unreliable memoirs in 1826.

John Braham, (1774-1856), Birmingham Musical Festivals, 1802, 1808-34, 1840

Born in London, of Jewish parentage, Braham's name was originally Abraham. Left an orphan early in childhood, he was rescued from what might have been a poverty-stricken life by his voice. After lessons from a Jewish singer, he appeared at Covent Garden Theatre in 1787, as Master Braham. He created a very great impression with his youthful treble in our old favourite 'A Soldier Tir'd', Mandane's aria in Arne's *Artaxerxes.* From then on Braham's life was dedicated to singing. He progressed steadily, giving concerts and being engaged by Stephen Storace for the Drury Lane Theatre. This led to an affair with Storace's sister, Nancy, friend of Michael Kelly, and the first Susanna in *Figaro.* Nancy had a son by Braham. The two toured in Italy in 1798 and 1799, Braham returning to Covent Garden in 1801. It was then that he seized London by storm and never ceased to create a sensation whenever he sang.

John Braham, tenor 1774-1856.

John Braham, all five-foot-three of him, played a very important part in establishing the link between the tenor voice and the leading male role in opera. He sang in Italian opera at the King's Theatre in London and then, for the Lyceum theatre, himself wrote the opera *The Americans* (1811), from which his famous party-piece 'The Death of Nelson' was taken. In opera and in the concert hall he had no rival, and his many appearances in Birmingham, at both the festivals and in the theatre, are evidence of his great popularity. He had a splendid voice with ringing high notes, and could confidently execute very florid music. A good musician he could display excellent taste and great depth of emotion. This, and his excellent diction, were a cover for his deficiencies as an actor. Occasionally tempted into playing to the gallery, however, especially when singing what should have been a simple ballad, he would 'do a Catalani' and use too much florid display. This sometimes verged on vulgarity.

In total, his voice, his imagination and the force of his personality carried all before them, especially when he sang Handel. These must have powerful indeed, for there are a number of things about Braham which cannot have been very likeable. Invited to sing Sir Huon in the first performance of Weber's *Oberon,* in London, in 1826, Braham insisted on the composer making alterations to the part, the better to suit his own voice. Then we learn from Leigh Hunt that our tenor would indulge in the 'loud-soft' style of singing, singing words like 'love' and peace' very quietly, and bursting out in a triumphant roar at 'hate', 'war or 'glory'. In most other singers this would have been ridiculous, but Braham seems to have got away with it. Or perhaps it was the touch of vulgarity in the taste of the day, of which more in due course. Finally when Braham left Nancy Storace, her own career suffered. He married and had a large family. Nancy, on the other hand, was either ignored or belittled, for perhaps no-one wanted to offend the great tenor of the day by making a fuss of his

Chapter 5 - From Music Meeting to Musical Festival, with a portrait gallery of stars

discarded mistress. Nevertheless, she died a rich woman, having contributed greatly to the art of singing in comic opera, and having been well rewarded in the process.

Again we see that Birmingham was host to a great star on many occasions and the ticket prices were not inflated when he sang, as they would be today for Pavarotti or Domingo for example. Braham did earn a great deal of money, but not so much that a place like Birmingham, with only 100,000 inhabitants - a tenth of its present size - could not afford him.

Postscript

On a note of slightly black comedy, we can perhaps point to an occasion when Birmingham did first what another place did later. If Manchester finished off poor Malibran, nine days after the 1836 festival, Birmingham had already pre-empted the Northern city. The tenor, Thomas Norris, sang at the 1790 Birmingham festival and died only ten days later. He was taken to Himley Hall the house of that year's festival president, Lord Dudley, and there he breathed his last, at the age of 49. For some, the festivals could obviously be pretty lethal experiences!

More about the instrumentalists

In general, the leading players were quite as brilliant and distinguished as the singers who came to Birmingham between the first music meeting in aid of the General Hospital and the building of Birmingham's splendid classical Roman Town Hall. Thomas Pinto, the violinist, has already been mentioned in connection with his appearance with his wife Charlotte Brent, at the Musical Festival in 1768. A very fine player, he fled the London scene when some doubtful financial speculations failed. His place as leader of the festival bands was then taken by Wilhelm Cramer (1745-99) whose name appears in the list of performers in the announcement of the 1778 Music Meeting, given at the beginning of this chapter. Born in Mannheim, the son of Jacob Cramer, one of the famous Mannheim orchestra's violinists, he became a pupil of the composer-conductor Stamitz and entered the Mannheim orchestra himself. Technically brilliant, as well a expressive in his playing, Cramer brought his gifts and his experience to London in 1772 quickly becoming a leading violinist. He was leader of the King's Band, the Opera Orchestra, the Ancient Concert (1780-89) and the Professional Concerts, all in London. He also led the band at the Handel Commemoration in Westminster Abbey in 1784. Wilhelm Cramer came to Birmingham in 1778, 1780 1784 and 1787, appearing as a soloist as well as a leader. He must have brought a more disciplined idea of orchestral playing with him from Mannheim, but it seems unlikely that he would have been able to insist on the uniform bowing associated with that orchestra, and apply it to the *ad hoc* bands gathered for festivals. Only in the 1880s, with Richter' arrival, was that finally achieved, More about platform organisation and orchestral discipline later.

There were family relationships among the festival players as well as among the singers, and Wilhelm had two sons who each took an important part in Birmingham Musical Festivals. The second son, Franz (1771-1848), was a leading violinist in each festival from 1805 to 1843, and the eldest son, Johann Baptist, was solo pianist in Birmingham in 1826. Franz became Master of the King's Music in the early part of Victoria's reign. He died in 1848.

Cellists and Double Bassists
The 'cellists who came to Birmingham were also the leading players of the day. Cervetto (called 'Carvetto' by *Aris's Gazette),* John Crosdil and the Yorkshireman Robert Lindley, all came to the town between 1778 and 1834. It was Crosdil, the Englishman, who seems to have been the fiery *virtuoso.* He was principal 'cellist at the 1784 Westminster Abbey Handel commemoration. James Cervetto the younger, on the other hand, had the more beautiful tone and sensitive phrasing. Crosdil came to Birmingham in 1780, 1784 and 1787, Cervetto having deputised for him in 1778.

Probably the most famous of the 'cellists, Robert Lindley was born in Rotherham and seems to have arrived at the Birmingham Festivals by 1802, via leading positions at the opera and all the usual prestigious concerts in London. He was heard at the age of 16 by Cervetto who gave him some free lessons, and his career progressed from then on. His reign as leading 'cellist in London lasted from 1794 to 1851, a phenomenal fifty-seven years; and his visits to the Birmingham Musical Festivals more or less coincided with that period. The very relaxed attitude to the arrangement of players is revealed if we remember that Lindley always shared a desk with Dragonetti, the double bass player, also a regular visitor to Birmingham. Even more amazingly, Dragonetti's dog Carlo, often sat between them!

Robert Lindley 1776-1855
(Reproduced with the permission of the National Portrait Gallery).

Chapter 5 - From Music Meeting to Musical Festival, with a portrait gallery of stars

Much earlier, in 1778, a Mr. Storacci was listed among the performers for the Music Meeting. This seems likely to have been Stephen Storace, senior, a Neapolitan who settled in this country in about 1750. He married the daughter of the proprietor of Marylebone Gardens, John Trusler, and translated Italian opera into English for use at the Gardens. He played the double bass at the King's Theatre, London, and it must surely have been in his capacity as a bass player that he came to Birmingham. He is listed among the instrumentalists, but no precise information is given in the programme as to which instrument he played. Stephen Storace was the father of Stephen, the English theatre composer, and of Nancy whose happy link with Mozart, and the less happy one with John Braham, we have considered.

The Mahons - and other woodwind players
Yet another family of musicians, of Irish origin in this case, were the Mahons. As with the Garcia family, both the women and the men distinguished themselves. Two daughters and a niece who sang in Birmingham (Mrs. Ambrose, Mrs. Second, Mrs. Salmon) we have already met. The Mr. Mahon who was such a frequent visitor to the Birmingham Musical Festival must surely have been John Mahon, rather than his brother William. Both were clarinettists and one can only wish that the newspaper announcements and programmes of that day had vouchsafed more details and included christian names or initials. Occasionally there is a helpful initial, but not in this case, and we have to do some detective work to decide which 'Mr. Mahon' is meant. John (c1746-1834) is known to have been a regular provincial festival player and, more particularly, concerto soloist. 'Our' Mr. Mahon certainly played a clarionet (sic) concerto at the 1784 Music Meeting. William (?1750-1816) on the other hand was the Philharmonic Society Orchestra's first clarinettist, and seems to have worked mainly in the south of England. He was also an oboist and violinist, and it was as a violinist that he led the festival orchestra at Salisbury for thirty years.

To the writer it seems very much more likely, given what is known of the brothers' other activities, that it was John Mahon who came to Birmingham. In any case, the town would have had the services of a first rate clarinettist and, here again, we have yet another example of Birmingham's contact with a new development. Whatever the origins of the clarinet, it was not used as a concert instrument until the mid-1750s. Arne, for example, had used clarinets in *Thomas and Sally* and *Artaxerxes,* but the instrument's intonation was faulty and not until Mozart showed what an expressive musical instrument it could be, did brilliant players arise who stimulated the improvements in the mechanism. The Mahon brothers and Thomas Willmann were the leading English *virtuosi,* and at least two of these men were regular visitors to Birmingham.

Many clarinettists were originally oboists and we have already mentioned John Parke who certainly appeared here in 1768, 1778 and 1784, possibly after that. He seems to have been replaced as first oboe as early as 1769 by Erskine, who reigned

65

from then on. Erskine himself moved to second place when Griesbach became first oboe in 1814. The skill of Erskine and Griesbach is not in doubt, but John Parke, and his brother William, also an oboe player, are the most interesting to us now. They were noteworthy for being the first Englishmen to cultivate the new, sweeter and more expressive tone of oboe playing, as opposed to the strident sound prevalent up to the 1760s. It was one of Frederick the Great's bandsmen, J.G. Fischer, who had first brought this style to Britain. Here is yet another new development which Birmingham was privileged to enjoy, and again we find, in general, that some of the best musical talent then available anywhere was to be found among the players at our Musical Festivals. By 1814, incidentally, the total number on hand was 82, in other words a band the size of a modern symphony orchestra. For the initiated, the strings were 16.16.14.6.6, with double woodwind, 3 horns, 3 trombones, harp and timpani.

The Chorus
The chorus was at the heart of the Festival movement in eighteenth and nineteenth century England. The growth of choral singing matched the growth of the population generally and the clustering of communities into growing towns. Added to this, singing was relatively cheap. Even if a choral society subscription had to be paid it was not like having to buy an expensive instrument. Add to this again the evangelical fervour arising from the spread of Wesleyan Methodism and non-conformity generally, and one can see why the communal singing of oratorios was embraced so enthusiastically in places like Birmingham.

More specifically, Birmingham's Music Meetings in aid of the General Hospital had come about in the first place because the gentlemen of the Musical and Amicable Society, formed from adult male members of St. Philip's and St. Bartholomew's choirs, had provided a ready made chorus for early oratorio performances. As we have seen in chapter 3, a branch of the Musical and Amicable, calling itself the Chappell Society, was formed specifically to sing at Music Meetings which were in aid of some charity. Together with the noted women singers from Lancashire, the first 'festival' chorus was about 45-strong. Within Birmingham itself a larger chorus was developed as time went on and in 1808 the 'Choral Society of the Town' was being thanked by the General Hospital trustees for its services in aid of hospital funds. In 1811, it was referred to as the Birmingham Oratorio Choral Society. Its conductor was Samuel Buggins, obviously a fine singer himself, since he was a treble soloist at the festival in 1808, and an adult soloist in 1814. The Oratorio Choral Society continued until the establishment of the Birmingham Festival Choral Society in 1845, the latter still in existence to-day. The Birmingham choir was augmented for the festivals by members of other singing bodies, namely the Concert of Ancient Music, the Vocal Concerts, the Philharmonic Society and the Italian Opera.

Chapter 5 - From Music Meeting to Musical Festival, with a portrait gallery of stars

Tastes were changing, as we are seeing. What this meant as far as the festival chorus was concerned was that it grew larger and by 1834, the end of our present period, it numbered 184 singers, about two thirds of them from Birmingham itself. The other third came from London, Manchester, Liverpool, from Oxford, the Three Choirs cities and from as far afield as Norwich and Canterbury. Many of these were professional choralists, known by name, as was Mrs. Travis whom we have met. The Birmingham Festival was part of a national network, and many chorus members would arrive thoroughly versed in what they had to sing, partly because they were competent musicians and could read music well, and partly because they had rehearsed or sung items in the programme many times, either in London or at some other festival.

The Conductors
How did the conductors control two or three hundred skilled musicians, both vocal and instrumental, many of whom must have had strong ideas of their own about how things should be performed? In the early days of the festivals, the conventions of baroque performance would be well-understood by all, and that would aid cohesion of effect. The conductor was not a conductor in the modern sense, standing in a position of total command where all could see him, and wielding a baton. He conducted the performance from the harpsichord, later the piano; or from the organ. Since he was sitting down and not visible to everyone, a co-ordinating beat was conveyed to some of the players by the first violinist. In such a situation, both conductor and violinist would need to understand one another completely and in the case of the provincial festivals, it would obviously help a great deal if both of them belonged to the same London-based musical establishment. In any case the musical forces in Birmingham were small enough initially, with 25 players and a chorus of 45, to work well under the direction of the Coventry-based Capell Bond. The numbers of players and singers involved increased enormously as the nineteenth century progressed, a factor which contributed to the coming of the single conductor, controlling the whole proceedings, as we shall see.

Thomas Greatorex, 1758-1831
Thomas Greatorex took over in 1796 and was conductor until 1829, except for the years 1808 and 1811. He had all the right connections and experience to give him the necessary authority for his task. Born near Chesterfield in 1758, Thomas Greatorex was the son of Anthony Greatorex of Riber Hall, Matlock. His upper class background gave him great confidence and he was able to converse with people of the highest rank, evidently with ease. He was taken into the musical service of the Earl of Sandwich, who was another example of the type of aristocrat devoted to organising the performance of oratorio, in this case in his own home. When the

Concert of Ancient Music was established in 1776, Greatorex sang in the chorus. He then became organist at Carlisle Cathedral (where a later Birmingham Town Hall organist was to come from) afterwards travelling on the continent where he made a favourable impression on the Young Pretender, Bonnie Prince Charlie, then exiled in Rome. On his return to London he established a successful teaching practice there, and was the obvious and unchallenged candidate 'for the position of conductor' of the Concert of Ancient Music in 1793. He joined Messrs. Knyvett, Harrison and Bartleman (all three visitors to Birmingham) in establishing the Vocal Concerts in London in 1792, and in 1819 became organist of Westminster Abbey. He conducted the York and Derby Festivals, as well as Birmingham's, and was an arranger and composer for both concert organisations with which he worked in London. He was, furthermore, skilled in mathematics, astronomy and natural science and was a Fellow of the Royal Society. In other words he was a fine product of the eighteenth century enlightenment. He had all the right qualifications and knew all the right people to make a success of conducting Birmingham's Musical Festivals. He knew the chorus people, the solo instrumentalists and the solo singers, and had the strong intellectual and musical gifts to control and co-ordinate their efforts. He was honoured by burial in Westminster Abbey.

William Croft and Samuel Wesley

The two breaks in Greatorex's reign in Birmingham came in 1808 and 1811, when the conductors were Dr. William Crotch and Mr. Samuel Wesley respectively. In 1808, Crotch introduced Mozart's anachronistic and un-baroque accompaniments for Handel's *Messiah*. This is something which may well have been a turning point, some may think for the worse, in the way Handel's music in particular, and baroque music in general, was to be performed in the future. Crotch had a strong team to accompany. It included Mrs. Billington and John Braham, as well as the bass player, Anfossi, and all the usual leading instrumentalists.

As one would expect, Samuel Wesley (1766-1837) made some very individual contributions to the 1811 Festival. He was, of course, the nephew of the great evangelist and preacher, John Wesley, and son of John's devoted brother Charles. Samuel Wesley was a considerable, though now neglected, composer and the organ concerto he played on St. Philip's organ would almost certainly have been one of his own (he wrote eleven). His gift for extemporization on the organ was said to be unequalled at that time and Birmingham was privileged to hear him in that role also. He managed to squeeze a Bach item into the programme. True, it was only the oboe and bassoon 'Concertante', but could this have been the Concerto for two oboes, bassoon, strings and continuo (BWV 1066) by J. S. Bach, written between 1724 and 1725? Perhaps we shall never know for certain if the composer of this 'Concertante' was J. S. Bach or his youngest son, J. C. Bach, the so-called English Bach. What is

Chapter 5 - From Music Meeting to Musical Festival, with a portrait gallery of stars

certain is that, along with William Shield and one or two other musicians, Wesley was an enthusiastic advocate of J. S. Bach's music, editing some of it for publication in this country – which might argue for father Bach being the composer. Interestingly, according to Wesley's own account, it was George Pinto, grandson of our old friend Thomas Pinto the violinist, who first introduced him to J. S. Bach's music. Wesley, was a passionate convert and for him J. S. Bach was a superhuman genius whom he called 'Saint Sebastian', 'Our Apollo' and other devotional names. He needed to go a little 'over the top', as we would say, to combat the immovable worship of Handel, but Bach's devotees were certain that 'Bach's grand, truly Protestant, robust and erudite genius', as Hegel termed it, had at least as much to offer the British public as Handel's.[4] Sadly for many years it was only the organists who were persuaded, and it was to be a long time before the general public in Birmingham could appreciate Bach's major choral works, as we shall discover.

One would have given a great deal to have heard Wesley's improvisations at St. Philip's on that Friday morning in October, 1811. There seems to have been only the one visit. Wesley's health was poor following a bad fall, involving a head injury, and he certainly did not come to another Birmingham Festival in a professional capacity.

Festival Footnotes

On a more mundane level we have some glimpses of the arrangements made by the many unpaid festival organisers for the greater comfort of audiences. The one-way system for carriages, introduced in 1768, was mentioned in the introduction to Birmingham's first charitable Music Meeting. Later in the early years of the nineteenth century, the festival programmes reveal that assemblies were held at the Shakespear (sic) Assembly Rooms each evening after the concert, and that in the day, substantial 'ordinaries', including malt liquor, were available at the two principal inns, the Shakespeare and the Stork, for five shillings (25p) a head. This would be about £5.00 in today's values. An 'ordinary' was simply a standard menu provided by an inn, at a fixed price. The festival committees seem to have come to an arrangement with the inns which was aimed at precluding any exploitation of festival visitors. It was also arranged that no more than ninepence a head (9d or approximately 3p) should be charged for tea at the balls, or assemblies. This would mean about 60p today. It is plain that people did not then expect such a high profit margin as they do now.

A register of lodgings for visiting families was kept at the office of the *Birmingham Gazette* and many a conveyance must have arrived in Birmingham loaded with huge portmanteaux, for here was an opportunity to display the latest in one's wardrobe. That this caused considerable inconvenience at times is shown by an occasional appeal to the ladies who attended the performances to abandon hoops or later, in 1820, bonnets, either because of the room they occupied or the way they deprived others of a clear view. 'The ladies' do seem to have complied, it should be said, and wore caps at concerts, instead of bonnets, from then on! This is just as well, since St. Philip's and the Theatre were always filled to capacity according to contemporary reports. For example, we learn from William Pountney that the doors of St. Philip's Church were opened on the Tuesday morning, 7th October, in 1823 at 9 o'clock, and the church was full long before eleven, when the service was due to start. Tickets cost 10/- (50p) and £1 (St.Philip's), or 7/- and 14/- (Theatre). A complete set of programmes is preserved in the Local Studies and History Department of Birmingham Central Library.

William Pountney's *History of the Festivals*
Programme notes and press reviews on the other hand, were a thing of the future and belong to the later part of the Town Hall era. For the earlier festivals we have to rely on sporadic sources for comments about performances. William Pountney, a chorus bass whom we have met commenting on Catalani's English pronunciation, did a hand-written account of all that he could himself recollect. He also includes what are evidently the reminiscences of others, given to him when young. From Pountney we learn that the chanting of the psalms at the opening service in St. Philip's, in 1820, created a most striking effect. The singers were divided into two choirs, each consisting of sixty-five selected voices, which sang the verse of the psalms alternately. They came together for the *Gloria* at the end, thrilling everyone. Some of the soloists also contributed to the singing at these opening services. The sources of the London contingent, which Pountney gives, have already been listed in the paragraphs above entitled 'The Chorus'. In the orchestra, the violin and viola players he tells us came from the King's Concert, the Philharmonic Society and the King's Theatre. In addition, four were from as far away as the Paris Conservatoire, while from nearer to home came 'the leaders of concerts in various large towns in the Kingdom'. According to Pountney's testimony, the greatest credit was due to Thomas Munden for his training of the choir and to 'Mr. Greatorex' for his skill and judgement as conductor.

Pountney also reveals that some of the performers made donations to the Musical Festival Funds. In 1820, for example, our old friends Mrs. Salmon and Kitty Stephens each gave twenty pounds (£20, or £500 to-day), Vaughan, Bellamy and Greatorex giving ten pounds (£10) each. They could no doubt afford to be generous, but at least some of them made the gesture. About the lighter side of the Festival, Pountney tells us that for the grand ball, the theatre pit was boarded over, the stage cleared and a capacious assembly room thus formed. A French band 'as employed at noble balls in London and at Almack's club' provided the music for dancing. And just to show that the festival fringe is not a new phenomenon, in 1823 a balloonist named Sadler took advantage of the large number of people in the town and ascended from The Crescent, watched, so Pountney says, by 100,000 people. This should have taken place on the Saturday at the end of the festival week but, because of unsuitable weather, was postponed until Monday. The Crescent was behind (to the North of) the present indoor arena of the International Convention Centre.

Progress at St. Martin's Church
Once again we find Birmingham's original parish church, St. Martin's, initially first in the field, only making further progress by following where the newer St. Philip's, and other churches, are leading. We saw that Richard Hobbs, an earlier organist at St. Martin's, organised three-day oratorio festivals at 'the New Theatre', in 1759 and 1760. His efforts, combined with those of Broome (St. Philip's), Kempson, (St. Bartholomew's and St. Paul's) and Bond (St. Michael's, Coventry), were instrumental in leading up to the establishment in 1768 of what were to become the Birmingham Musical Festivals. These, of course, were held at St. Philip's in the morning, not at St. Martin's, and at the theatre in the evenings. In spite of Bond's early efforts, it is somewhat later in the day that some 'Selections of Sacred Music' were performed at St. Martin's, in 1822, 1825 and 1828. The organist concerned was Thomas Munden, of whom more in due course. The composers represented in 1822 were Palestrina, Handel, Pergolesi and Attwood, the last-named a pupil of Mozart and the composer of a fine anthem for George IV's recent coronation, in 1820. In 1825 it was the music of Gibbons, Handel, Boyce and Beethoven which was performed and in 1828, that of Attwood, Crotch, Handel and Mozart. Among the soloists we see some names made familiar to us by Musical Festival programmes; those of the most famous (and expensive) do not appear. These performances were all held on a Sunday, in the manner of James Kempson's original Music Meeting in Aid of Aged and Distressed Housekeepers at St. Bartholomew's, in 1766.

1. Comment from William Pountney: *History of the Festivals*. 1899 (in manuscript) Birmingham Local Archives Department, Central Library.
2. Hugh Kelly: *Thespis*. Quoted in Roger Fiske op. cit.
3. Aris's *Birmingham Gazette*, 4 March 1822. Report of Catalani concert at the theatre.
4. Quoted from Emery, Wolff and Temperley: *Johann Sebastian Bach* (Article in The New Grove Dictionary of Music and Musicians. First edition).

Chapter 6

What else?

The theatre

The theatre continued to be a source of music in Birmingham, not only because of the popular mixed music and drama formula, already described, but also because the New Street Theatre was, in effect, the town's only large concert hall. The period of the French Revolution and the Napoleonic Wars, between 1789 and 1815, was not an easy one, and the theatre did not escape the consequences of shortages, poor trade and very high taxation. In addition, as we have noted, tastes were changing and managers had to find new ways of pulling in the patrons. This was exacerbated in towns like Birmingham by the arrival of thousands of people seeking work at the new 'manufactories' being built. Some of these, freed from the constraints of rural life, had different ideas about what they wanted to see at the theatre. The pastoral, aristocratic elegance of the eighteenth century English stage was passing in any case, but some tawdry and debased imitations of it persisted, and there were many repetitions of the most sensational stock characters and situations. The words and music to go with them, too, had neither the grace nor skill of Garrick and Sheridan, or of Dibdin, Storace, Arne and Shield. The end result was really in the realm of music hall or pantomime. Other shows were empty spectacles, consisting of unconnected scenes and recitations, the more pathetic or melodramatic the better. Birmingham's new audience obviously liked to 'oo' and 'ah' over impressive effects. The loudest 'oo's' must surely have been reserved for a show called 'La Guillotine', presented at the theatre in April 1793. A gentleman, 'present at the fatal period', examined the real guillotine and constructed a stage model of it. This was taken round to English theatres and the beheading of the 'late unhappy King of France' was enacted, with a life-size model. As the notice in *Aris's Birmingham Gazette* described it: 'the Head is severed from the Body by a tremendous fall of the Axe, and the Illusion is complete'. Many a sympathetic tear must have been shed at our New Street Theatre! – or would there have been cheers? And one can only wonder what music was played to accompany the lugubrious production.

We are not entirely surprised to learn that the theatre managers of the period had trouble with unruly behaviour from rowdies. Missiles were sometimes thrown at the stage, for no apparent reason, and paying patrons would sometimes arrive to find their seats occupied by ruffians. No doubt, in many case, drunkenness was the cause.

Probably not unconnected with these disturbances is the fact that in 1793 the Theatre Royal was maliciously burnt down. It was, however, quickly rebuilt. This is interesting in view of the difficulties the General Hospital Trustees had in completing their building. By that time, William Macready (M'Cready in old programmes) was lessee and manager of the theatre. His management lasted for twenty years from 1792 to 1812 and during his reign two important theatrical developments were germinating, which would appeal to Birmingham's 'other' audience, the one which supported the Musical Festivals. On the one hand, Shakespeare plays were gradually restored to their original form, and in this Macready's son, William Charles, played an extremely important part. In 1810, Macready junior made his debut in Birmingham in *Romeo and Juliet,* with great success. From 1837 onwards he was the leading Shakespearian actor and producer on the London stage. Mrs. Siddons, Edmund Kean, Fanny and Charles Kemble also trod the New Street Theatre's boards. Kean, too, brought Shakespeare to Birmingham and we find him, as well as the younger Macready, presenting the Bard's plays in the 1822 and 1823 seasons respectively.

The eighteenth century theatrical pieces still lingered on, however, and on 22nd June 1819 the *Gazette* announced the first appearance in Birmingham of a Mr. Paul Bedford, 'a great bass singer from the Theatre Royal, Drury Lane'. He was to appear in 'the musical farce of The Quaker'. As was quite usual at that time, the composer's name was omitted; perhaps on the assumption that everyone knew it anyway; or perhaps because they were primarily interested in the leading singer. The piece was a rather undistinguished one by Charles Dibdin, in fact, and had had a *coloratura* aria added to it by Thomas Linley, in 1777, for Mrs. Wrighten to sing; she who sang in oratorios in Birmingham in 1774 and at the Music Meeting of 1780. Paul Bedford revisited Birmingham, certainly in 1838, when he sang at Vauxhall Gardens, 'then in their splendour', and in 1840 when he again appeared at the theatre.

The other development was in the realm of Italian opera. This was to become very popular. Full-scale productions of complete operas do not seem to have arrived in Birmingham until the French wars were over, but in November 1827, Italian operas were being offered 'at theatre prices'. Increasingly, from then on, complete operas were presented on a regular basis, by visiting companies. The *Barber of Seville,* for example, was given in 1833.

The taste for Italian opera must surely have been kindled by the appearances of Catalini and Braham at the Theatre, 'in concert' as we would say. Catalini's visits to the Theatre Royal drew rapturous applause and *Aris's Gazette* in 1809 speaks of her,

'extraordinary powers of voice, and wonderful flexibility in executing her bravura songs, the richness of tone and the beautiful, pathetic and exquisite manner of her singing 'O questa l'anima', and other pieces, produced sensations of the liveliest interest in the audience and called forth the greatest bursts of applause ever witnessed

Theatre Royal, New Street, Birmingham, exterior view.

in the Theatre... she possesses the finest combination of talents, as a singer, ever heard in this country'.

The aria mentioned, 'O questa l'anima' from *Lauso e Lidia* by an immediate predecessor of Rossini, Simone Mayr (1763-1845), was a pretty, short aria, popular enough to be sung about the streets.

Braham too contributed five nights of singing in 1830 and 1831, and in 1832 an overwhelming sensation was created in Birmingham by the appearance of the violinist Paganini. Hotels and lodgings, stabling and coach-houses overflowed with the huge number of equipages. Paganini was evidently intending to entertain the citizens of Birmingham and district with his violinistic stunt of playing the melodies on one string with the left-hand, *pizzicato* accompaniment on the others with the right. It seems a pity that he felt it necessary to play down to the sensationalist spirit of that over-romantic, melodramatic age. He was certainly a good enough player to have captivated and impressed them all without resorting to tricks.

In a sense, the appearance of such stars in solo performances at the theatre could be described as Birmingham's first organised celebrity concerts, which perhaps began with Elizabeth Billington's visits to the New Street Theatre in 1802. This singer had inspired an adulatory verse dedicated to the 'Vocal Enchantress', from Joseph Weston of Solihull. It was published in the *Gazette* on 2nd August of that year.

Chapter 6 - What else?

Theatre Royal, New Street, Birmingham, interior view.

The theatre certainly had a band of musicians and some of these were local people. Some visiting companies would bring their own instrumentalists for the summer season, June to September, but we know from announcements in the *Gazette* that the management were able to draw on a reserve of talent more readily to hand. There are a number of Birmingham families which provided musicians for the town over several generations. Such were the Probins, the Priestleys, the Hydes and the Simms. Later there were others, but at present we are only speaking of the 1768-1834 period. Their names crop up in programmes and a special study of these families alone would be an interesting one.

One of Birmingham's Musical Families and other matters

Perhaps we may mention the Simms family in a little more detail at this point, although they are mainly known as organists. John Simms, who was in fact a violinist as well as an organist, was born in Stourbridge in 1744. He was also a musical instrument-maker. He worked to improve the construction of various instruments. and was an early maker of that unusual instrument, the upright harpsichord or clavicytherium. He had eight sons, six of them organists, in Bromsgrove, Stourbridge, Handsworth and elsewhere. One of the most relevant from our point of view was Bishop Simms, organist of St. Mary's Chapel, and also St. Philip's Church, in Birmingham, from 1803 to 1829. He was succeeded at St. Philip's by his nephew,

Henry, who held the post for forty-two years (1829-71). Another was Samuel Simms, a great grandson of John, whose Birmingham Glee Union contributed noted singers to the Festival choruses in the last quarter of the nineteenth century. Another grandson of John, Edward Simms, was organist at St. Michael's Parish Church, Coventry. He gave George Eliot music lessons and is mentioned in her novel *Middlemarch*.

Another possible family connection might be one between the Valentine who was an instrumentalist at one of Mr. Fletcher's Annual Concerts in 1784 and the Thomas Valentine (1790-1878) who composed glees for Birmingham's St. Cecilia Club, in the early 1820s - another 'non-festival' activity at the period. One of Valentine's glees, 'When from the skies divine Cecilia came' merits inclusion in a collection called *The English Glee,* edited by Percy M. Young. Valentine Road, in Kings Heath is named after the composer. It may be added that the formation of glee-clubs, between 1750 and 1850 approximately, is yet another manifestation of the passion for communal singing evinced by our predecessors.

Other concerts, often in aid of charity, were given at the theatre, so that all in all there were opportunities to hear music in Birmingham in the times between the three-yearly Musical Festivals. One man who thought there were not enough, was Matthew Boulton.

Concerts
A whole series of private concerts came about through a casual conversation between Matthew Boulton and Joseph Moore. Boulton's connection with the Lunar Society has already been described. A pioneer in the mass-production of coins and high-quality, silver-plated goods, he attracted world-wide attention. Kings, princes and ambassadors were to be seen driving up what is now Soho Road to his Soho works, near Handsworth. Boulton's interest in music has already been mentioned; nor are we surprised to learn that the meeting with Joseph Moore just referred to, was to do with the setting-up of a charitable dispensary for the poor. Boulton coincidentally happened to mention that he thought there was not enough music-making in the town and urged Moore to do something about it, saying that he wanted to get professionals and amateurs together to 'raise some good music'.

Joseph Moore was a die-sinker, and, like Boulton, a living refutation of the idea that industry and culture do not mix. Born in Little Shelsley, Worcestershire, in 1766, Moore was sent to Birmingham in 1781 to learn the trade of die-sinking, eventually becoming a partner in a business involved in the button trade. His role in ensuring the continued success of the Musical Festivals all through a very difficult time in this country's history will be discussed in the next chapter. The Private Concerts at Styles Hotel, later Dee's Hotel, for which Moore and Boulton were stewards, employed an orchestra. They were also, in effect, promoting contemporary composers. And what contemporary composers! Programmes reveal Mozart's overture to *The Marriage of Figaro* being given in 1819, Beethoven's overture *Prometheus* in 1820 - during the composer's lifetime - and Mozart's overture to *La Clemenza di Tito* in 1821. In 1820, Mrs. Salmon (niece of the Mahons) and Garcia himself were soloists in this series.

By 1829 the room was becoming too crowded for comfort and this circumstance, taken together with the fact that, otherwise, the theatre provided the only large space for concerts, was an argument Moore was to use in persuading the Town Commissioners to build the Town Hall. The Private Concerts survived Boulton's death in 1809 and went on until Moore's own death in 1849 - a run of fifty years. Other private concerts were announced in *Aris's Birmingham Gazette* from time to time, such as a new series in 1819. From their announcement it is obvious that they too are intending to invite some of the singers and players associated with the Musical Festivals.

There does however, seem to have been something of a lapse in this type of performance during the period immediately following the French Revolution in the early years of the nineteenth century, and something of a lessening of taste and discretion. One can see why Matthew Boulton spoke as he did in 1799 about raising some good music in the town - 'in the town' that is, as opposed to that which they were just hearing every three years, from visitors at the Festivals. The gradual widening of horizons certainly needed encouraging at that point. A small indication of the good effect that Moore and Boulton's efforts had, however, is the fact that, by 1829, it was possible for a Memorial Concert for Beethoven to be held in St. Philip's Church on 6th October 1829. This was directed by Ignaz Seyfried (1776-1841), composer and conductor and a pupil of Haydn. One of the works played seems to have been a Beethoven *Equali* for four trombones, arranged as a *Miserere* and set to English words. A contemporary comment says - that 'the music is in the peculiar style of this great composer, and its solemnity and beauty were elevated to an almost overpowering height by a double choir of trombones'. Whatever we may think of this type of arrangement, at least Beethoven was being played and honoured in Birmingham only a year after his death.

View and Review. Grand Pause

It is time to stop for a moment to take stock. We have seen that long before 1834, Birmingham had been a busy and ever-growing market town. In the last quarter of the eighteenth century the seeds of industrialisation were sown by townsmen who were brilliantly innovative in their thinking and capable of carrying out the practical enterprises which embodied their thought. They and their associates and employees, and the families of both, together with visiting friends and relatives, provided an enthusiastic audience for festivals of music which had the double purpose of enjoying the best music then available anywhere, supporting a good cause at the same time.

This they did generously, as the profits accruing from early Music Meetings and Music Festivals testify. It may be argued that such patrons could afford to be generous and in some senses that was true. Compared to agricultural workers, on anything from half-a-crown (two shillings and sixpence or 12½p) to ten shillings (50p) a week, and the industrial worker, with perhaps £1 a week, the gentlemen on even the smallest allowance or annuity of, say, £300 per annum (about £6 a week), was comparatively affluent. The professional and business classes expected to be open handed when it came to assisting those in real need, because of poverty, illness or a too-large family. Poor law relief was actively distributed in Birmingham, and music meetings in aid of charity were a natural expression of this same attitude of mind. This was also part and parcel of the growing social conscience following the evangelical revival already referred to, which demanded a more personal and individual commitment to Christian beliefs about love of God and neighbour and a more practical, down-to-earth application of them.

Nevertheless, some strict souls objected to the very idea of the festivals. In *Aris's Birmingham Gazette* of 5th October 1829 a piece was published deploring the distribution of a circular entitled 'Considerations on the Musical Festival. Freely transmitted through the Post-Office'. This had appeared at the end of the week before the festival, which was arranged that year for 6th to 9th October. The Gazette deplored the timing of this, since it gave no chance for anyone wishing to refute the arguments in the circular any chance to undo its effects. Among these could have been a reduction in support for the festival and, more particularly, in the size of the donation to the General Hospital. A fortnight later the author, Joseph Sturge, a Quaker, came out into the open. The timing of the circular, he said was due to force of circumstance rather than to deliberate planning, but he reiterates his view that there are 'serious evils connected with the Oratorio' and that many excellent people give the festivals their support because they have not seriously thought about the objections to them. He simply wished to bring the issue before 'the Christian Community of Birmingham', to use his own words.

One can perhaps understand the problem. Oratorios were originally composed for presentation in Church and were developed as bearers of Christian teaching, much as the miracle plays had been earlier. To present them in a theatre, associated with what some would consider to be the razzmatazz of star performers and high box office takings, was for some people quite unacceptable. Even when performed at St. Philip's, a non-religious and mercenary aura surrounded them, not really justified by the worthy cause they were intended to assist.

So ran the Quaker argument, though Sturge carefully disassociated his fellow Friends from his circular. The argument did not prevail, however, and one can only think that from an entirely musical point of view, let alone the charitable one, this was fortunate.

To sum up, we have firm evidence that after 1715, when St. Philip's Church was consecrated, Birmingham citizens could hear some first-rate music, played by highly competent people, and that, increasingly during the eighteenth century, the town enjoyed some of the best offerings which London could provide - perhaps a year or two behind the capital, but what of that? Surely the Musical Festivals must be regarded as establishing a regular, solid core to this musical activity, a consequence of, and a further stimulus to, the musical life of the town. From 1787, the year of Mrs. Billington's first visit and 1790, that of Madame Mara, Birmingham heard with increasing frequency, and not just at the festivals, but also at the theatre and the pleasure gardens, the very best that could be heard anywhere at that time.

In reviewing the town's musical history to this point we may perhaps defend the notion that the potential for this eighteenth century flowering was there long before this, and that the earlier citizens of Birmingham had made provision for music to be heard in St. Martin's Church and in the Guild hall. In the end, however, it comes down to the fact that men and women over the centuries have, with Joseph Addison, thought 'Music the greatest good that mortals know, And all of heaven we have below' (*A song for St. Cecilia's Day*). Nowadays we would have to add; 'it depends on what sort of music you are talking about'.

Some general history
Finally let us remember that this was a town, still not incorporated as a borough. The population is estimated to have been about 73,000 in 1801 and 142,000 for Birmingham and Aston in 1831. Edgbaston and 'the Quinton', Northfield and Yardley were still well out in the country, the rural scene reaching in as far as Harborne Hill, Five Ways, Sherlock Street and Balsall Heath Road. Doctors and lawyers lived in the middle of the town, in Temple Row, Colmore Row, New Street, Bennett's Hill and Waterloo Street. Many of the houses in these same central streets still had gardens. The area of unacceptably poor housing was small by later, nineteenth century standards although, sadly, it was already growing. No-one 'commuted' in the modern sense, and in the industrial work-place, mainly then in the Masshouse Lane area, masters and men sometimes worked at the same bench and called one another by their christian names. Skilled mechanics could set up in business on their own, becoming employers in their turn. As we have seen, Joseph Moore, the festival organiser, did just that and he was only one of dozens.

Before the coming of the railway, in 1837, well-to-do families used their carriages; while others, less well-off, went on horse-back or hired a post-chaise, with four horses and a postilion, from the Hen and Chickens in New Street. This had stables, a brewhouse, a bowling green and large rooms for meetings - and for music. Another eight or nine inns also had large yards and ample stabling. Businessmen met for a cooked mid-day dinner (an 'ordinary' in fact) and for talk and company in the evening in the taverns. One of these had been John Freeth's coffee-house, whose ballad-singing owner has already been described. Farmers' wagons and carriers' carts still bumped along the roads approaching Birmingham from all points of the compass, their occupants perhaps singing their folk songs as they went. The River Rea still harboured trout and occasionally, as in 1839, made a nuisance of itself by flooding, rendering parts of Moseley Street, Deritend and Rea Street impassable for hours.

The lack of borough status did not hinder the establishment of a number of highly significant and enduring scientific, medical and artistic institutions at this period. An Academy of Arts was established in 1817, with Benjamin West, then president of the Royal Academy, as one of the teachers of painting. This Birmingham Academy also included a Department of Anatomy. In the same year the Orthopaedic Hospital (the Institution for Bodily Deformity) was established, and in 1823 various musical performances were given to assist the School for the Deaf and Dumb at Edgbaston, opened in 1814. The Eye Hospital was opened in 1823 and, in 1828, the intention of founding a Medical School was announced. From the latter, both Queen's College, (in Paradise Street from 1833), and the Queen's Hospital, (until recently the Birmingham Accident Hospital), evolved. In the following decade, in 1842, the Lying-in Hospital, was established. The Royal Society of Arts was founded in 1821, its museum opening the following year. Some eight years after that, in 1830, new buildings for King Edward's School were proposed. In 1831 came Birmingham's Law Society Library and soon after 1800 a scheme for Botanical Gardens was mooted, though not carried out until 1832. In that year, warm support for the great Reform Bill was much in evidence in the town, various large meetings being held, one at Mr. Dee's Royal Hotel - an indication it may be said of the size of the room in which Boulton and Moore's private concerts were held. A hymn was especially composed to mark the passing of the Reform Act, incidentally.

What a list of achievements for the town, with only a tenth of its present population and half the size of present-day Wolverhampton! Remember too that it was situated in a country whose population was then only of the order of 15 million, as opposed to today's 60 million. Again we are reminded that we have no grounds for belittling the accomplishments of our ancestors.

We leave the revolutionary 1768-1834 period with Birmingham's music in remarkably good shape, considering all the vicissitudes stemming from industrialisation and from the French Revolution and Napoleonic wars. The Musical Festivals were undoubtedly the main focus of the town's musical life, but they did not crush every other musical enterprise. On the contrary, they engendered a desire to hear more music, more often, and on a regular basis. They taught people what the best music and the best performance of it were like. Nor should we be superior about the choice of music for the festivals themselves. Anyone attending just one of them was presented with a revelatory compendium of musical styles, ranging from the

Chapter 6 - What else?

sixteenth century to their own remarkable period, with Haydn living until 1809 and Beethoven until 1827. If festival buffs were also 'into Handel' in a big way who can blame them. One can think of many worse things to be 'into' than the joy and nobility of Handel's music. If, too, some favourite masterpieces, such as Hadyn's *Creation* and Mozart's *Jupiter Symphony* came up rather often in festival programmes, we are again in no position to criticise. We, too, without even having to stir from our homes, do exactly the same thing when we wear out a favourite recording or choose the same CD many times. Let us therefore salute all that had been achieved by our Birmingham predecessors, when travel, before the coming of railways, was slow, uncomfortable and often risky, and when folk usually had to accomplish their life's work in many fewer years than most of us are granted today.

Chapter 7

After the building of the Town Hall

It is particularly appropriate to start a new chapter at this point, in 1834, when Birmingham's Town Hall was opened. Nationally, the Reform Bill of 1832 ushered in (by the establishment of a wider, male franchise) an age of very gradually increasing democracy. Growing care and concern through Factory Acts and other measures for the safety and welfare of every citizen, no matter how humble, very slowly followed. Prosperity created by industrial production did not keep pace with the huge growth of population, however, and the time-lag created much hardship and poverty. The final phase of the process of enclosing common land, while bringing better food production had also put many country people out of work. These flooded into the towns to seek employment in the new industries, increasing further the difficulties of places like Birmingham. The town was on the brink of a troubled period. Added to this, the growing burden of overseas territories, which expected to be defended and serviced by the Mother Country, prevented the lowering of taxation, which continued its inexorable rise. Generally, it was a time of huge social upheaval, with new opportunities opening up for some and a slither down the social scale for others. Initially, none of this affected the Musical Festivals, but it did have a somewhat depressing effect on the rest of Birmingham's musical life during the middle years of the nineteenth century. Ultimately it was to affect the festivals too. How it did so will be discussed in a later chapter.

The crucial role of Joseph Moore. The Town Hall
Let us look first at how the Town Hall came to be built. We have already learned that Boulton and Moore's Private Concerts Society was finding its accommodation at Mr. Dee's Royal Hotel too small, and that the New Street Theatre, was in effect, Birmingham's only large concert room. The increasingly popular festivals filled both theatre and church to overflowing. This was far from ideal from anyone's point of view. Since Birmingham hosted many of the musical promotions then on offer in London and drew a large number of musicians from the same sources, it was but a small step to think in terms of a hall in Birmingham which would match the capital's Hanover Square Rooms, home to all the leading London concert-giving bodies from

1775 onwards. It was a step which a number of people, including Joseph Moore, eventually took. He had hoped that when, in 1825, the ecclesiastical authorities planned the new church of St. Peter, in Dale End, they would make it large enough to house the festival events which Moore was already envisaging. The ecclesiastical authorities had other ideas on the subject, however, and Moore turned instead to the Town Commissioners for support. Here he was successful. The town had taken some pride in the part it had played in the moves towards political reform, and a place for large meetings would obviously be a great asset. Large crowds could be accommodated with less fear of unruly jostling because of shortage of space, and prestigious speakers could be invited. Festivals also brought valuable trade to Birmingham's inn-keepers and landladies, providers of transport and printers of programmes. The greater the number of visitors the better it would be. In 1828 the Birmingham Improvement Act made provision for the building of a Market Hall, a Corn Exchange and a Town Hall. It was also agreed 'that the said Town Hall and its appurtenances shall also, for the space of six weeks before the day appointed for any Musical Festival to be from time to time held in the said town, be under the control of the Governors of the General Hospital and the said Governors shall have the power to put up an organ in the said Town Hall, the property of which organ shall be vested solely in them'. The ownership of the Town Hall organ was in fact retained by the General Hospital Governors until the 1920s, either 1922 or 1924.

From the first, Moore urged a really large hall, to be 'the double cube of 70', in other words 70 feet high by 70 feet wide by 140 feet long. The final measurements ended up in fact as 65, 65 and 145 respectively. Moore then betook himself to the Continent to view the 'great room in Amsterdam' and make enquires about other European halls. Returning to Birmingham, he showed his plan to members of the hospital committee and to the Town Commissioners. Confident of support, he also urged a canvas of the townspeople, asking for signatures approving his plan. A general meeting of the rate-payers was called and Moore's proposition was agreed. Eventually, after some delays, a site was found, Let us, once more, have the *Birmingham Gazette's* words on the matter, from its issue on 16th August 1830.

'At a numerous meeting of the Commissioners of the Street Act on Tuesday last, specially convened, it was unanimously determined that the intended Town Hall should be erected in Paradise-Street. This very desirable site, so well calculated to give a good architectural finish to Newstreet, has, we understand, been contracted for and obtained by the Commissioners at a fair and reasonable price; and there is now every prospect that the work will proceed without further interruption'.

Also, 'to prevent the erection of any nuisance in the immediate neighbourhood', the Commissioners bought the reversion of the property behind the future Town Hall, in Edmund Street and Congreve Street.

A detailed plan for the hall from the architects Hansom and Welch of Liverpool was accepted, and the building we know today came into being. It was this Hansom who also patented the eponymous Hansom cab by the way. Built of Anglesey marble, the exterior design of the Town Hall was based on the Temple of Castor and Pollux in the Forum, in Rome. As a result of all the attendant expenditure, the senior partner of the firm of architects, Mr. Welch, and two other men who had also advanced money for the building of the hall, suffered serious financial loss, totalling £6,410, over half of this being Welch's money. There does seem to have been an attempt to put this situation right. Annual Christmas Festivals were held in the Town Hall from 26th December 1834 onwards. For the morning performances, tickets were eight shillings (40p) in the gallery and five shillings (25p) on the ground floor and in the evening they were six shillings (30p) and three shillings and sixpence (17½p) respectively. The profits in 1834 were handed over to the Town Hall Committee to be used to repay £1,000 to Mr. Lloyd, one of the sureties concerned and to 'liquidate at the discretion of the Committee, such trade men's accounts as remain unpaid, from circumstances over which the Commissioners have no control'. What happened about Welch's money is not certain, but Hansom certainly lost all his.

The Town Hall organ
Meanwhile Moore went off on his travels again, this time to seek advice about a specification for a grand organ for the new hall, consulting both the Chevalier Neukomm and Mendelssohn in the process. The consequence was a fine William Hill organ, built for £3,000 (£85,000 today) which, when Neukomm himself eventually played it on 16th September 1834, surpassed all that generous man's highest expectations. The word generous is used advisedly and will be explained in due course. As to the vexed question of who was Birmingham's first Town Hall organist, perhaps a claim for Thomas Munden could be stated at this point. In his capacity as Chorus Master and Assistant Conductor for the 1834 Musical Festival, it was Munden who automatically presided at the organ, except when the Chevalier Neukomm was playing organ solos. The organ was first heard publicly on 29th August 1834. This seems to have been a choral rehearsal for the 130 Birmingham and Midland members of the festival choir, again with Munden at the organ. By 1840, George Hollins is Chorus Master and Munden Assistant Conductor. This presumably meant that Hollins 'presided at the organ' as Munden had previously done. Further, we learn from the *Birmingham Gazette* that when Marshal Soult visited the town's 'manufactories' in July 1838, an official reception was held for him at the Town Hall where 'very judiciously Mr. Hollins entertained the assemblage with an occasional performance on the organ'. When the Marshal himself arrived, Hollins evidently played some solos. Munden and Hollins could therefore be said to be *de facto* if not

de jure, the first Town Hall organists. Certainly John Stone, in an article on Birmingham in Hinrichsen's *Musical Year Book* 1945-6, lists Munden and Hollins as the first Town Hall organists, with the dates 1834-37 for Munden and 1837-41 for Hollins. The appointment of James Stimpson as official town organist in February 1841 seems less equivocal, however, though John Stone may well have possessed evidence for his assertions. His papers are, unfortunately, no longer available.

More about Moore and the prestige of the Festivals

Before embarking on our survey of the next notable events at the new hall, let us once again pause to consider just what it was that Joseph Moore had achieved in pressing so hard for a really commodious concert room. It cannot be emphasised sufficiently that long before 1834, Moore had already established the Birmingham's Musical Festivals on the international music scene. Our study of the Festival programmes up to this date has made this plain, but Moore's contemporaries were well aware of it, too, and as early as 1812, Moore was presented, by 'gentlemen of the town and neighbourhood with a silver vase and stand, and four silver dishes, in acknowledgement of his

Joseph Moore 1766-1849.

disinterested services'. For Moore received no payment for his festival labours, yet he had successfully increased the profit from the festivals, for the use of the hospital, to unprecedented levels. In his speech at this presentation, Dr. Outram, Rector of St. Philip's, paid tribute to the fact that Moore 'without any selfish end in view, without any other motive than that of compassion for the afflicted' had 'combined repeatedly the first musical talents' and 'harmonised the jarring interests that are, perhaps, inseparable from such combination of skill'. Perhaps more significantly for this study, the Rector adds that Moore had thus 'raised the Birmingham Festivals from the state of respectable country meetings to unrivalled, and what may justly be called *national* grandeur and celebrity'. Let us remind ourselves yet again that Outram was speaking in 1812 and, further, that the Festival was already enjoying gradually increasing ticket takings and thus profits for the General Hospital. It was well on the way to becoming what the conductor Costa was later to call the country's 'Festival number one'.

What the Rector said was simply the sober truth and the building of the Town Hall was a response to a pressing need for more space. It had not created that need. What it did do, however, was to encourage still more the passion for large scale choral works, and vigorous efforts had to be made later on to redress the balance and give more prominence to the orchestral repertoire. The hall also put Birmingham's Festival firmly ahead of every other Festival in having purpose-built premises. This was obviously a big 'plus point' for Moore in his negotiation with performers and, increasingly, composers, but his own personality seems to have been his best asset. His large generosity of spirit attracted all he met and it is noticeable that Mendelssohn always stayed with Moore during his visits to Birmingham. More of that shortly. Meanwhile let us remember that Moore started out as a mechanic and a craftsman, but by now we should not be surprised at this. We can place him, along with Kempson, in our pantheon of men without whom Birmingham's music would not have developed so strongly.

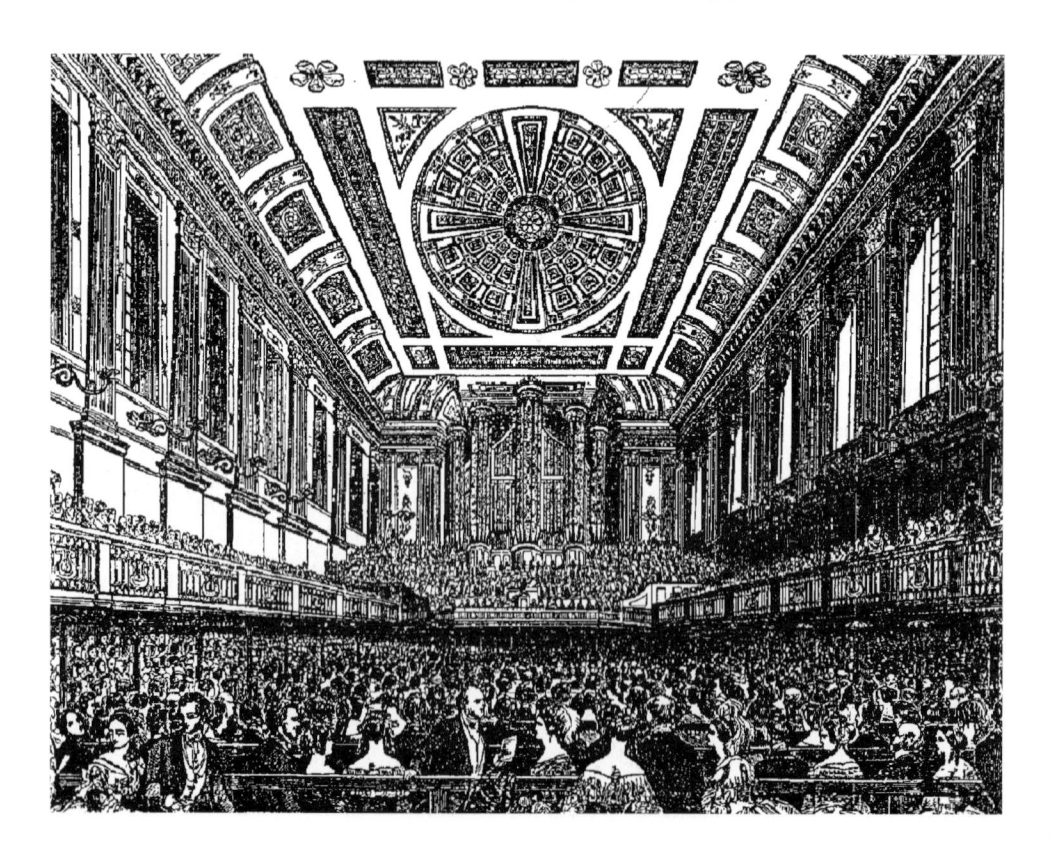

Interior of the Birmingham Town Hall as it appeared in 1846.

Chapter 7 - After the building of the Town Hall

The first Town Hall Birmingham Musical Festival, 1834
The Chorus and Orchestra

We have seen that already, by 1814, the chorus and orchestra had grown greatly, reaching something in the order of 120 and 80 respectively. Although the orchestra mainly consisted of visitors to the town, two-thirds of the chorus lived in Birmingham. In 1834 the equivalent choral and orchestral figures were 184 and 151. The limitation of space even on the Town Hall platform bears out the idea that, certainly as far as the bands were concerned, it was a matter of horses for courses. Instrumentalists from the Concert of Ancient Music, Vocal Concerts, Philharmonic Society and from the Italian Opera would each play the repertoire they knew best. Whatever the number of instrumentalists on the platform at any one time they would still be arranged in the old, chaotic way. It may even have been that some of the players stood, though this seems less likely when one considers the length of some of the performances, which could be three hours or more. The two illustrations (below) date from 1840 and 1843, and the judicious reader may like to form his or her own opinion as to which resembles the likely Birmingham situation most closely.

While on the subject of the arrangement of very large numbers of people on the Town Hall platform, perhaps we may further analyse the composition of both chorus and orchestra at this point. First, an analysis of the full chorus, totalling 184 singers excluding the semi-chorus, may best be tabulated as follows:

A Concert scene, 1840 - (Source Unknown).

Hanover Square Concert Rooms 1843 (Reproduced with acknowledgements to the London Illustrated News Picture Library).

Chorus in 1834	**From Birmingham**	**From elsewhere**
Trebles	34	15
Counter Tenors	24	16
Tenors	26	18
Basses	30	21
Total	114	70

NOTES TO THE ABOVE:
A. Counter Tenors are still being used (1834).
B. The seventy singers from elsewhere were provided as follows: London, 26; Leamington, 17; Liverpool, 12; Oxford, 3; Canterbury, 3; Manchester, 2; Worcester, 2; Lichfield, 2; Gloucester, 2 and Norwich, 1. Birmingham thus provided 67 per cent of the chorus.

The total number of orchestral players employed included 50 violins, 24 violas, 16 'cellos, 10 double basses, 4 flutes, 4 oboes, 4 clarinets, 4 bassoons, 8 horns, 6 trumpets, 8 trombones, 1 serpent, 2 ophicleides 1 corno di basetto (sic), 1 octave flute,

Chapter 7 - After the building of the Town Hall

1 harp, 1 double drums, 1 tower drums and organ. As has been pointed out, it is likely that two bands were involved here, one for St. Philip's and one for the theatre. Birmingham itself contributed 5 violinists (including a member of the Simms family), 5 violists, 2 'cellists, 1 double bass, 1 flute (Stanier) and judging by the names (Hyde and Probin) 1 trumpet and 2 horns, although the programme dries up in its details once it has reached the woodwind. At any rate, the total was about 17, and if we again remind ourselves that Birmingham was hardly more than a tenth of its present size, this would be the equivalent of 170 players today. Not a bad effort! The trouble was that these local players had no regular opportunity of rehearsing together simply as an orchestra. Many taught, and some played in the theatre orchestra mainly in the summer season, but neither of these activities fostered the qualities needed for front-rank players.

Perhaps a word should be said at this point about the unfamiliar instruments in the list above. The *corno di basetto*, more correctly *corno bassetto*, is a tenor clarinet which, since its appearance in about 1770, has been alternately in and out of fashion. The other two, the serpent and the ophicleide belong to an obsolete cornett and key-bugle class of instruments, which was like woodwind in that it achieved different pitches by stopping holes in a tube and like brass in that an important part of the sound-production stemmed from the player's lips vibrating against a cup-shaped mouthpiece, as in a trumpet. The serpent, its tube eight feet long and pressed up into a series of curves, (hence the name), was a transposing instrument, naturally in B flat. Notes lower than the fundamental could be coaxed out of it, as with the horn today. In the serpent, a scale was played by uncovering holes, as with a recorder, a second octave being sounded by overblowing. The ophicleide, on the other hand, belonged to the key-bugle class and it eventually replaced the serpent in reinforcing the bass line of the music. Handel used the serpent in his *Fireworks* music, as did Mendelssohn in *St. Paul* (1836). For *Elijah* in 1846, the ophicleide was used.

William Ponder, whose name we can see in the 1834 programme, was the leading player of the ophicleide from that time, until Gloucester did for him in 1841 what Birmingham and Manchester had done for Mr. Norris and Maria Malibran in 1790 and 1829, and killed him off in the middle of a Three Choirs Festival. These events were obviously extremely hazardous!

As to the 1834 festival itself, the patrons were King William IV and Queen Adelaide, together with the Duchess of Kent and her daughter Princess Victoria, the latter soon to be queen. The president that year was the current holder of the Aylesford title and the sixty vice-presidents included the Archbishop of York, the Duke of Sutherland, sundry Earls, Viscounts, Knights and mere Esquires, seventeen men in these last three categories being members of parliament. Many of these vice-presidents, it should be said, seem to have had a genuine interest in music.

The soloists, orchestral leaders and instrumental soloists were as follows.

Soloists. Birmingham Musical Festival 1834
Vocalists
Trebles: Madame Caradori, Madame Stockhausen, Mrs. Knyvett, Miss Clara Novello.
Tenors: Mr. Braham, Signor Curioni, Mr. Vaughan, Mr. Horncastle.
Counter-tenors: Mr. Hawkins, Mr. Terrail
Basses: Mr. Phillips, Mr. Machin, Mr. Bellamy, Mr. Taylor

Instrumental Performers
Leader of the morning performances: Mr. Cramer
Leaders of the evening performances: Messrs. Weichsel, Mori and Loder

Solo Instrumentalists
Piano-Forte: Mr. Moscheles
Violin: Mr. Mori
Violoncello: Mr. Lindley
Organ: Chevalier Neukomm
Harp: Mr. Stockhausen
Conductor: Mr. Knyvett
Chorus Master and Assistant Conductor: Mr. Munden

We can see some old friends in this list such as Braham, now 60, Vaughan, Bellamy, Cramer and Lindley. Once again we have evident relationships between performers, not just between Mr. and Mrs. Knyvett, whom we have met, but between the two Stockhausen's, singer and harpist, both German born. Margarete Stockhausen's soprano voice evidently lacked dramatic power, but her no-nonsense approach gained her friends, especially in England, and her thoroughly musicianly singing ensured repeated engagements at our provincial festivals. Caradori on the other hand, a contemporary and regarded by some as a rival of the late-lamented Malibran, was a highly-paid Italian soprano who had created the role of Giulietta in Bellini's *I Capuleti e i Montecchi* (The Capulets and Montagues). She was equally at home in concert, however, and a great favourite at the festivals as was, more deservedly, Miss Novello.

Born in 1818, Clara Novello, daughter of Vincent Novello the founder of the publishing house, began her public singing career at the age of 15, and went virtually straight into the front rank. She held her own, even at that age, with seasoned stars like Braham and Grisi, on occasions such as the Handel Commemoration in Westminster Abbey for example. She won high praise from the aged and discerning Lord Mount Edgcumbe who had been present at the first Handel Festival fifty years before, in 1784. Her charming nature and happy private life seem to have prevented her from being vain and bombastic about her gifts or about her privileged position

Chapter 7 - After the building of the Town Hall

as a member of an influential musical family. Her mother, Mary Novello, managed her career. When Clara retired in 1860, the representative of the *Musical Times* present at one of her final concerts at the Crystal Palace reported as follows:

'The Director having assigned to the members of the press, as usual, the upper gallery in the far off distance, we were enabled to give our undivided attention to Madame Clara Novello, who, if truth must be told, was the only singer whose voice could be heard to advantage in that position. In the upper gallery, choruses sound as if veiled, and the solo singers as if they were singing in the garden instead of within the building. Madame Novello's voice is the only one that can be said to reach the further end of the building in all its purity of tone, undiminished by the vast area through which it has to travel. The softest accents are heard with distinctness, and her voice stands out as the prominent and only voice of the oratorio'. *Musical Times* 1860.

Clara Novello 1818-1908.

It is clear that Clara Novello was not retiring because her voice was failing. It was quite obviously still at the zenith of its power, but at the age of 42 she had already had a public career of nearly thirty years and simply wanted to live quietly with her husband. Like Catalini before her, and Patti later, Clara Novello was one of those Italian-bred sopranos who could sing difficult arias in childhood, in Novello's case at the age of three. Catalini, whose voice attracted attention when she was 12 and whose public career began at 17, was almost a late-starter by comparison. More of Patti in the appropriate place, but for all three, singing was as natural as breathing.

Again, we have Birmingham attracting the newest vocal star to perform in the town, and Clara Novello at 16 was a bright attraction at the 1834 Festival, with no fear of her clear voice not being heard in the large new hall.

The 1834 Festival was an occasion of splendour, not least because of the elegant costumes of the ladies, shown to advantage by the new gas-lighting. There was also a wide selection of music on offer and programmes, copied from the originals, are shown below.

91

```
                    SCHEME.                                                    SCHEME.
                                                                                PART I.
                                                           CORONATION ANTHEM, Zadok the Priest  ...  ...  ...   HANDEL.
                                                           SONG, Miss CLARA NOVELLO, The Infant's Prayer  ...  ...  NOVELLO.
                    ACT I.                                 ANTHEM,
                                                           QUARTET. Mrs. KNYVETT, Messrs. HAWKINS, HORNCASTLE, and PHILLIPS, } CROFT and
                                                                   Sing unto God                                          } GREATOREX.
SYMPHONY PASTORALE     ....     ....     ....    ....   BEETHOVEN.  CHORUS, Cry aloud and shout
SONG, Mr. VAUGHAN, Forget me not  ....     ....    ....  MOZART.   RECIT. Mr. BRAHAM, O loss of sight  ...  ...  ...  (Samson.)
MADRIGAL, Full Choir, Sweet honey-sucking Bees  ....    JOHN WILBYE. AIR,     ditto,   Total eclipse!  ...  ...  ...  }HANDEL.
SCENA—Recit. Miss CLARA NOVELLO, In quali eccessi  } (Don Giovanni) CHORUS,           O first created beam
  Air,    ditto,   Mi tradi   ....     ....    } MOZART.  RECIT. Mr. PHILLIPS, And God said
"The Recollections of Ireland," FANTASIA, with Orchestral Accom- }   AIR,     ditto,   Now herein in fullest glory shone  ...
  paniments, GRAND PIANO FORTE—Mr. MOSCHELES  ....  } MOSCHELES. SESTET, Madame STOCKHAUSEN, Mrs. KNYVETT, Miss CLARA NOVELLO, Messrs. }
                                                              HORNCASTLE, BELLAMY, and MACHIN—and CHORUS, Et incarnatus est ... } HAYDN.
DUET, Madame STOCKHAUSEN and Mr. PHILLIPS, Calma, oh bella  ... } (Der Berggeist) CHORUS (SOLO, Mr. VAUGHAN), Glory to God ...  ...
                                                             } SPOHR.                (Introduced by Mr. Gauntner in his Oratorio of Judah.)
CANTATA, Mrs. KNYVETT, Mad Bess  ....     ....    ....   PURCELL.  RECIT. Madame CARADORI, Chi per pietà  ...  ...  ...  } BEETHOVEN.
FANTASIA, ORGAN, Chevalier NEUKOMM, "A Concert on a Lake," }  AIR,    ditto,    Ah! parlete                          } CIMAROSA.
  interrupted by a Thunder Storm                         } NEUKOMM.
                                                                      A SELECTION FROM MOUNT SINAI,
                                                                           BY THE CHEVALIER NEUKOMM.
                    ACT II.                                  INTRODUCTION.
                                                           RECIT. Mr. TAYLOR, And Moses spake and said,
OVERTURE (Anacreon)    ....     ....     ....    ....   CHERUBINI.  SEMI-CHORUS, He leveth his flock.
CAVATINA, Madame CARADORI, Come per me serena   ....     BELLINI.   AIR,    ditto,   I carried you upon eagles' wings.
SONG, Mr. BRAHAM, I've been toss'd among the wars  ....  NEUKOMM.   RECIT. Mr. BRAHAM, And on the third day.
FANTASIA, VIOLIN, Mr. MORI   ....    ....    ....   MORI.          CHORUS, I am the Lord thy God.
SONG, Mr. PHILLIPS, When forced from dear Hebe to go  ....  ARNE.   RECIT. Mrs. KNYVETT, According to the name, O God.
DUET, Madame CARADORI and Mr. BRAHAM, Oh! lovely maiden stay { (Azor & Zemira)  AIR,    ditto,    Holy and great is thy name.
                                                             } SPOHR.  CHORUS, Make a joyful noise to the Lord.
SONG, Madame STOCKHAUSEN, Let me wander not unseen                                      PART II.
  Or let the merry bells ring round    ....   } HANDEL.       THE LAST PART OF THE LAST JUDGMENT,
PRIZE GLEE, Miss C. NOVELLO, Messrs. HAWKINS, HORNCASTLE, and }                       BY SPOHR.
  TAYLOR, Old May Morning   ....     ....    ....    } NOVELLO.  RECIT. Mr. PHILLIPS, Thus saith the Lord.
FINALE—QUARTET. Messrs. TERRAIL, VAUGHAN, HORNCASTLE, and } (Maid Marian) DUET, Madame STOCKHAUSEN and Mr. VAUGHAN, Forsake me not.
  BELLAMY, and Chorus, Hart and hind  ....     ....  } BISHOP.   CHORUS, If with your whole hearts.
                                                           SOLO, Mr. BRAHAM, Jehovah now cometh to Judgment.
                                                           CHORUS, Destroyed is Babylon the mighty.
                                                           SYMPHONY.
                                                           SOLO, Mr. BRAHAM, It is ended!
                                                           QUARTET. Miss CLARA NOVELLO, Messrs. HAWKINS, HORNCASTLE, and TAYLOR, Blessed are the
                                                                   departed.
                                                           RECIT. Mr. PHILLIPS, I saw a new heaven.
                                                           SOLO, Mr. BRAHAM, Behold! I be soon shall come.
                                                           QUARTET. Miss CLARA NOVELLO, Messrs. TERRAIL, VAUGHAN, and BELLAMY, Then come, Lord
                                                                   Jesus.
                                                           CHORUS, Great and wonderful.
                                                           QUARTET. Miss CLARA NOVELLO, Messrs. TERRAIL, VAUGHAN, and BELLAMY, Who shall not fear
                                                                   thee.
                                                           CHORUS, Hallelujah.
                                                           AIR, Madame STOCKHAUSEN, Laudate Dominum   ...  ...  ...  MOZART.
                                                                   (Organ Obligato, Mr. NOVELLO.)
                                                           SONG, Mr. VAUGHAN, O Liberty  ...  ...  ...  ...  } HANDEL.
                                                                   (Violoncello Obligato, Mr. LINDLEY.)
                                                           RECIT. Mr. BRAHAM, Immortal Lord  ...  ...  ...  }
                                                           RECIT. Mr. MACHIN, He measured the waters
                                                           AIR,     ditto,    He layeth the beams
                                                           AIR, Madame CARADORI, Let the bright seraphims
                                                                   (Trumpet Obligato, Mr. HARPER.)
                                                           CHORUS, Let their celestial concerts all unite
                                                           RECIT. Mr. BRAHAM, And God said                    } (Creation)
                                                           RECIT. accompanied, In splendour bright           } HAYDN.
                                                           CHORUS,            The heavens are telling

           LEADER, Mr. WEICHSEL.                                           LEADER, Mr. CRAMER.
```

Left - Birmingham Musical Festival 1834. A Grand Selection of Sacred Music to be performed in the New Town Hall on Tuesday Morning the Seventh of October.

Right - Birmingham Musical Festival 1834. First Miscellaneous Concert to be performed in the New Town Hall on Tuesday Evening the Seventh of October.

As will be seen, Neukomm's compositions were given pride of place, his oratorio *David* being especially composed for that occasion. This was a greater *coup* for the town than we now appreciate, for the Austrian Neukomm, (1778-1858) was the composer of around a thousand works, and highly regarded by bodies like the Philharmonic Society in London. His *Mount Sinai* was a favourite at festivals in London and elsewhere, and his popularity during this festival earned him the popular nickname, 'King of Brummagen'. We have the testimony of one of Mendelssohn's letters for this. Neukomm's complete eclipse by Mendelssohn at the succeeding Musical Festivals, and his generous acceptance of the younger composer's success, are a tribute to the high nobility of character mentioned earlier. As a pupil of Haydn and a devotee of Palestrina's music, he had elevated models for his compositions. It would be interesting to know what a modern audience might make of Sigismund Neukomm's music and why it sank from sight after being so popular. Is it worthless, or simply forgotten?

Chapter 7 - After the building of the Town Hall

The Mendelssohn Years, The Birmingham Musical Festivals, 1837-46

So, in 1837, the Mendelssohn connection began which is, sadly, often all that some people know of Birmingham's musical history. The diligent reader, who has studied this present account of things so far, will be in a better position to evaluate the real importance of 'the Mendelssohn years'. The arrival of the romantic young Dr. Felix Mendelssohn Bartholdy was undoubtedly an exciting one, but no more so perhaps than the earlier arrivals of Catalani or John Braham, or that of Patti later on. Musically, it may not have been any more influential than the appearance of Moore in 1799, Costa in 1849 or Richter in 1885, as this book should make clear.

From the point of view of the financial benefit to the hospital, it must be said that the total receipts at Mendelssohn's first Festival in 1837 were down on those in 1834, and they fell even lower in 1843, with a rise in 1846, his last, but only to the 1840 level. Interestingly, and ominously too, in the long term, the net profits also fell from the highest yet in 1834, (approximately £5,500) to only £2,000 in 1837. They rose again in 1846 the year of *Elijah,* but, again, were no better than they had been in 1820 and 1823 – the years of Kitty Stephens, Madame Vestris, Mrs. Salmon, Messrs. Vaughan, Knyvett, Bellamy, Cramer and Greatorex on the one hand, and of Catalani on the other; the years when Moore introduced Mozart's *Requiem,* Beethoven's Symphonies and increasing amounts of Haydn's music. No doubt the 'hungry forties' were playing a part here but a fuller discussion of the financial factors affecting the festivals will be reserved until later.

In considering the purely musical aspects of Mendelssohn's importance or otherwise in Birmingham's musical history, we can perhaps argue as follows. Though *Elijah* is a fine work it is perhaps only because its popularity survived to a time within our own living memory that many have assigned it undue importance on our festival scene. It is not the greatest work ever performed at the town's Musical Festivals, nor necessarily the greatest to have been commissioned by the organiser - nor yet again the best of Mendelssohn himself. Is the importance often assigned to it still today partly because the phrase Mendelssohn's *Elijah* trips readily off the tongue, and the date and place of the premiere - Town Hall, 1846 - are easy to remember?

Let us take the Mendelssohn years for what they were; just one more peak - a musical Munrow - in a series of peaks which can be pointed out as having lent the Birmingham Musical Festivals lustre during their 146-year existence. The fact that it occurred roughly half way through their history does not make it the highest point, as though it were at the top of a sine curve, with everything before and after at a lower level. It was one of the high points, but not necessarily the highest. No doubt readers will want to judge for themselves after they have had the opportunity of comparing the festival programmes of later eras with those of the 'Mendelssohn period' which will now be summarised. For one outstanding local musician at least, namely Edward Bache, the non-Mendelssohn year, of 1855 yielded the 'perfect' festival, as we shall see - and this although he had played under Mendelssohn's baton in 1846.

In 1837, the Mendelssohn choral work featured was *St. Paul,* given on Wednesday, 20th September, in the morning. This was the work's fifth performance, not its first, since it had already been given in Düsseldorf and other places, including Liverpool (1836). Wagner, incidentally, thought *St. Paul* a witness to the flourishing state of the art of music, which created pride 'in the times in which we live'. Certainly, it is a work which was being performed until the first part of this century. It was Mendelssohn's Piano Concerto in D minor which was his new work, composed especially for Birmingham, and played by the composer at the Thursday evening Grand Miscellaneous Concert (1837). In that same festival week, he also conducted his own *Midsummer Night's Dream* overture (Tuesday evening), and played J. S. Bach's *Prelude and Fugue* in E flat (St. Ann) on the three-year-old Town Hall organ. This was the first time the Bach piece had appeared in a festival programme and, what is more, the duet and chorus from the end of Part One of Bach's *St. Matthew Passion,* listed in the programme as 'My Saviour now is taken', was also included at the same festival.

Felix Mendelssohn 1809-47.

Mendelssohn, like the Wesleys, Samuel and Samuel Sebastian, was a committed and enthusiastic ambassador of Bach's music and he had made a crucial contribution to the revived presentation of Bach's large-scale works, by means of a successful performance of the *St. Matthew Passion* in Berlin in 1829. Birmingham, like the rest of this country, was not yet ready for Bach and the German style, being wedded still to 'the Italian' as they termed it. Nevertheless, Birmingham's was the first festival to attempt some Bach choral music, something suggested by Mendelssohn. Moore and the Festival Committee should be given some credit for taking his advice, particularly as it had some interesting consequences.

First and foremost it stimulated imitation. Players from London and singers from all over the country, had taken part in the performance, which, for all that it was apparently rather laboured, had at least made a number of people aware of Bach's music. Added to this is the fact that we see Lord Burghersh's name in the list of Birmingham's festival vice-presidents. Later Earl of Westmoreland, this soldier, violinist and composer, was a founder and first President of the Royal Academy of Music in London. He was also a director, at that time, of the Concert of Ancient Music. It is surely significant that within six or seven months of the Birmingham performance, the Concert of Ancient Music

Chapter 7 - After the building of the Town Hall

and the Choral Harmonists' Society, in London, included Bach choral items in their programmes (April and May 1838). These were the Credo from *The First Grand Mass* (surely the *B minor Mass?*) and an extract from the *Magnificat*.

An eagerly anticipated feature of the 1837 festival was an improvisation on the new organ by Mendelssohn. This seems to have occasioned a little disappointment in some quarters, however, for the chorus bass singer William Pountney, in his reminiscences of the festivals, wrote in the following terms:

'The extempore performance of Mendelssohn on the organ, was rather an exhibition of the entire properties of the noble instrument before him than the entire resources which we have heard him pour out, in moments of happier inspiration'.

In other words, the music which came forth did not represent the Mendelssohn of the formally composed works.

William Pountney, chorus bass and Festival commentator, 1846-1897.

Nevertheless, both Mendelssohn and Birmingham were well pleased with one another and everyone anticipated further visits from the composer with lively pleasure.

Other Festival stars

What about the rest of the 1837 festival? Of the vocal stars, apart from Clara Novello, already described, Giulia Grisi and Signor Tamburini were undoubtedly the most interesting. Giulia Grisi and her husband, who was simply known as Signor Mario, more often just Mario, were the handsomest couple then appearing before the musical public. According to Mendelssohn himself they were also splendid singers.[1] Writing to his brother, he admired the way 'the Italians' simply strolled on to the stage and sang - and how!! All this without any fuss or pretension. Sadly, however, Grisi could be jealous and selfish and, at times, even ruthless. She would employ devious stratagems to prevent her husband from singing with another soprano, and managed to avert his appearances with Pauline Viardot Garcia in *La Sonnambula* in London in 1848. This, however, did not prevent her from appearing with the bass, Lablache, a frequent visitor to the English provincial festivals, including Birmingham's. Lablache himself came in 1840, with his son Frederick. Some enduring operatic roles were written for Grisi in the earlier part of her career. She sang the first Adalgisa in Bellini's *Norma,* in Milan in 1831, and the composer himself took an interest in her career. Her Norma on that occasion was the legendary Giuditta Pasta, and Grisi took over Pasta's roles in Rossini's *Semiramide* and Donizetti's *Anna Bolena* (1830), having sung lesser roles herself in the original casts. Rossini was also one of Grisi's advocates. With a better and more secure voice than either Pasta or Malibran, she was also a better actress and a more beautiful woman, being particularly good in Mozart roles such as Susanna and Pamina. Even Jenny Lind, not normally given to praising people, admired Grisi's acting. It must have been good!

In view of Grisi's known imperiousness, it is interesting to learn from Pountney's record that on leaving Birmingham, her carriage was on the receiving end of some stone-throwing. As it passed through the crowd of curious by-standers, the attitude of one of her man-servants was seen as too threatening, which provoked the missiles. Perhaps a case of 'like servant, like mistress' though one has some sympathy with his impatience as they faced the long coach journey back to London, with the prospect of travelling on to Paris after that.

Mario Giovanni Matteo, Cavaliere di Candia, 1810-1883.

Grisi's fellow-countryman Tamburini, along with Luigi Lablache, was a bass-baritone who played an important part in establishing a serious place for the bass voice in the nineteenth century repertoire, worthy of something more than comic *buffo* parts. You, dear reader, will not be surprised to learn that Tamburini, as with so many singers in this account, came from a musical family and that he played an instrument as a boy, and sang in an opera chorus at the age of twelve. His solo singing career began at 18, and nothing seems to have stood in the way, either of his highly-successful career as a solo vocalist, or his popularity with audiences. He was apparently as light and agile in his physical movements as he was skilled and accurate in florid singing. We know that he and Grisi had already sung together in a production of Rossini's *Semiramide* at the Théâtre-Italien in Paris in 1832, when Grisi made her debut in the name-part, and Tamburini sang Assur. Both came to Birmingham, therefore, bearing a seal of approval which had already been attached to them by Rossini himself. Tamburini was 37 in 1837, Grisi still only 26.

The 1840 festival was again a Mendelssohn occasion, the composer, referred to as Dr. Mendelssohn, being listed as playing Piano-Forte (sic) and Organ. The programmes as a whole may be summarised as follows:

Chapter 7 - After the building of the Town Hall

On Tuesday morning, 22nd September 1840, Handel's *Israel in Egypt* was performed. Included in the Miscellaneous Concert on the Tuesday evening were Beethoven's *Symphony* no. 8 in F, the vocal quintet from Mozart's *The Magic Flute* (Perché mentir non lice) and *Mad Tom* by Purcell, sung by the tenor, John Braham. This last item had also been given in 1834. The Wednesday morning Selection of Sacred Music consisted mainly of Handel's *Joshua* and Mendelssohn's cantata-symphony *Lobgesang* (The Hymn of Praise). The latter was a second performance, the first having taken place in Leipsig the previous June. This work did not reach London until three years later.

On Wednesday evening, at the Theatre Royal in New Street, excerpts from *La Gazza Ladra* (The Silken Ladder) by Rossini and from *La Prova* (The Rehearsal) by one F. Grecco, were performed by Madame Caradori-Allan, Signori Musatti and Lablache. The pianist was Thomas Munden, presumably directing the orchestra from the keyboard, with no need for extra assistance from the leader as would be the case with full choral or orchestral items in the Town Hall. On Thursday morning, as usual, *Messiah* was given, when Braham must have sung the aria 'Every Valley', no doubt a memorable experience. At the Thursday evening Miscellaneous Concert, Mozart's *Symphony* no. 39 in E flat was played, with excerpts from his opera *Così fan tutte* to follow, together with passages from Rossini's *The Barber of Seville* (1816), from Meyerbeer's *Robert le Diable* (1831) and from Spohr's *Azar and Zemira* (sic) (1819). Still faithful to Purcell, an item by him was included, while the violinist, Emiliani, contributed a piece of his own, which would no doubt be designed to show off his technical skill.

Finally, on Friday morning, the Selection of Sacred Music included excerpts from Handel's *Jephtha*, also Braham in 'Sound an alarm' from *Judas Maccabaeus*. Something we learn only from a pencilled note in the programme, preserved in our central Library, is that Mendelssohn again extemporised at the organ at that concert. Madame Caradori-Allan singing 'Let the bright seraphim' from Handel's *Samson*, with Thomas Harper playing the trumpet, two choral items by Mendelssohn and Mozart, an extract from Haydn's *The Creation* and a Handel coronation Anthem,

Giulia Grisi, 1811-1869.

which they named as 'God Save the King', brought this festival to a rousing close. This last item is more correctly known as *Zadok the Priest*.

The chorus and orchestra were constituted much as described in detail, for 1834. Some names are different, of course, and we see from the programme that the ophicleide player was now Mr. Thurstan of Birmingham, William Ponder, still alive at this point, being in charge of the 'monstre ophicleide', the contrabass version of that instrument.

The Birmingham violinists were Messrs. Mellon, Lyon, Simms, G. Hayward, Hawkes, Stannard, Evans and Fenney; eight violinists altogether. Again, given the tenfold increase in Birmingham's population since then, that would be the equivalent of 80 today. It is a much larger number than the town is usually given credit for. We can see, too, that H. Shargool of Birmingham has become co-principal viola player. The London based Robert Lindley and Thomas Willman are still principal 'cellist and clarinettist, respectively, but this was Willman's last visit to Birmingham. He died at the age of 57 two months later, on 28th November. Willman was admired even by the Belgian composer and writer, Fétis, an anglophobe, who was normally scathing about English instrumentalists. For those who are interested in technical details, Willman apparently played with the reed against the upper lip, using an English clarinet with thirteen keys. Among the chorus trebles we note the name of Master Freeth. A grandson of the balladeer?

For completeness, perhaps we should include the following details:

1840 Birmingham Musical Festival September 22-25
Principal Singers
Madame Dorus Gras, Madame Caradori-Allan, Mrs. Knyvett, Miss Birch, Miss Maria B. Hawes, Signor Luigi Lablache, Mr. Braham, Mr. H. Phillips, Signor Musatti, Mr. Vaughan, Mr. Machin, Signor F. Lablache, Mr. Pearsall, Mr. Young

Instrumental Performers
Leaders: Mr. Cramer and Mr. Loder
Violin: Signor Emiliani
Piano-Forte: Dr. Mendelssohn
Organ: Dr. Mendelssohn
Violoncello: Mr. Lindley
Conductor: Mr. Knyvett
Assistant conductor: Mr. Munden
Chorus Master: Mr. Hollins (who also played the organ)

As a postscript to this description of the 1840 festival, it may intrigue avid readers of nineteenth century novels to hear of an incident connected with George Eliot. She was very fond of music, as many readers will know, but at the 1840 Festival she was so extremely moved by what she heard that she gave way to hysterical sobs which seriously distracted the attention of those sitting near her.[2] This is interesting because we know that some audiences of the day would be fairly used to non-musical interruptions during performances. Some folk simply attended concerts because it was the fashionable thing to do and then stayed to gossip! This phenomenon seems to have been much worse in London than further North, however, and we derive the impression from various commentators, including Mendelssohn, that the majority of festival audiences listened with rapt attention, hence their demands for encores in what we would regard as the 'wrong' place. It seems likely that in Birmingham's Town Hall and Theatre Royal the presence of the Festival President, who literally presided and generally acted as master of ceremonies, must have restrained the loquacious and calmed the restless. It is perhaps significant that George Eliot's temporary lapse was worthy of comment and attracted attention in the Birmingham setting. There was some trouble at later festivals because of too many encores, but that will be described in the appropriate place. The players themselves were not blameless, however, and the 'cellist, Robert Lindley, was known to clown occasionally when on the platform.

The 1843 festival did not include Mendelssohn among its visitors and both gross receipts and net profits fell. The town had, by now, taken Mendelssohn to its heart and was evidently disappointed by his absence. A similar drop in takings occurred in 1849, after Mendelssohn's death, and subsequently the profits were only as low as that again in the years 1858, 1888 and suddenly, in the final year, 1912. A full list of takings at the festivals, 1834-1912, is given at the beginning of chapter 20.

Otherwise, there was no reason for audiences to fall off in 1843. Clara Novello and Signor Mario, himself, headed an excellent list of singers. Of course, Mario was replacing that old favourite John Braham and was, for Birmingham, still an unknown quantity. The list of visiting instrumentalists was also rather short and they seem to have relied on Samuel Sebastian Wesley (Dr. Wesley) as their main soloist. Many would remember his father, Samuel, conducting and playing at the 1811 festival. The programmes were much as before, with Mendelssohn represented *in absentia*, by *St. Paul* and his *Fingal's Cave* overture. Extracts from Mozart's *The Magic Flute, Così fan tutte* and *The Marriage of Figaro,* together with scenes from Rossini's *The Lady of the Lake* were given, along with solos and ensembles from Bellini, Donizetti and Cimarosa operas. Paisiello and Pergolesi, Beethoven and Hummel were represented, as of course were Handel and Haydn. Party-pieces included Clara Novello in Casta Diva (Bellini: *Norma),* Mario in Beethoven's *Adelaïde,* with orchestra, and Signor Fornasari in 'Non più andrai', from Mozart's *Figaro.* Nor were other composers neglected; as, for example, Palestrina and Cherubini and the Englishmen Croft, Attwood and Crotch.

In addition to all this, we learn that the orchestra contributed some of its best players to a band for the Festival ball. There were six first violins, four second violins, three violas, two 'cellos, three double basses, two flutes and two clarinets for that event.

So another Musical Festival has been reviewed and, during it, works of near contemporaries, Haydn, Mozart, Beethoven, Hummel, Bellini and Cherubini were played, as were those of true contemporaries such as Rossini (1792-1868) and Donizetti (1797-1848). Also represented was the Englishman, Attwood (1765-1838), now less well-known but highly regarded by his teacher, Mozart, and by Mendelssohn.

Another Mendelssohn commission

It was the obvious next step to take advantage of the established connection with Mendelssohn, and of the growing interest in contemporary music, and invite Mendelssohn himself to write a full-scale choral work for Birmingham. He had already given the town the first performance of his D minor *Piano Concerto,* so that it was no presumption on Moore's part to commission a full-length work from the composer. Thus it came about that Mendelssohn's *Elijah* was written for, and premiered at, the Birmingham Musical Festival of 1846, the best-known event of Birmingham's musical past, rightly or wrongly,

Before going into the details of this first performance, it should perhaps be mentioned that Mario and Grisi came together to this festival, and sang in Rossini's *Stabat Mater* with Staudigl, the first Elijah. Frederick Lablache, Luigi's elder son, was also on hand, as was a Miss Bassano who seems to have been a soprano and a connection of a Midlands family of musicians. More remarkably, Braham sang in the usual Thursday morning performance of *Messiah.* Already 69 years of age, Braham continued to sing in the oratorio and concert repertoire until 1852, when he was 75. The year 1846, however, was his last visit to a Birmingham Festival.

As to the programmes, they were designed on the usual lines, though the modern reader notes, with some pleasure and relief, that on the one hand, Beethoven's Symphony no. 7 in A was played and on the other, that the key is given, making identification certain. Also, this appears to be the first festival at which some of Verdi's music was performed, including a trio from the new opera *Ernani* (1844). The big point of interest must, of course, be our first hearing of Mendelssohn's *Elijah*.

Let us exercise our imaginations at this point and ask ourselves what the impact must have been on the audience at Birmingham's Town Hall, on that Wednesday morning of 26th August 1846. Here was a work which was in the romantic, heroic style of the day, yet linked by its subject to all that they were most familiar with; scenes from the Old Testament set to noble and dramatic music. We may perhaps note also that nineteenth century audiences seem to have felt uncomfortable with attempts to do the same for the New Testament; another factor perhaps in their resistance to Bach's *Passions.* This is not the place to analyse the reasons for this, historical, theological, artistic or otherwise, but it is perhaps something to be remarked in passing. At any rate, *Elijah* was a coming-together of all that the festival audiences loved best. They could relish, with Wagner, their pride in their own times, while enjoying something set firmly in a loved and respected tradition. They could also feel justifiable satisfaction in the fact that the composer had been prepared to write the work specially for Birmingham, and come himself to conduct it. If we add to this the fine voices of the soloists, all but one well-suited to the parts they took, and a chorus and orchestra intent on doing their best, thus delighting Mendelssohn; then, the wild applause, referred to by George Grove of dictionary fame is perfectly understandable. The audience's judgement appears to have been vindicated by the survival of the work, although Mendelssohn himself was not totally satisfied with what he had written and made a number of corrections before it went into print in 1847.

The composer's personal satisfaction with the performance was expressed in a letter to his brother as follows:

'No work of mine ever went so admirably at the first performance or was received with such enthusiasm both by musicians and the public as this. It was evident at the first rehearsal in London that they liked it... but I was far from anticipating that it would acquire such fresh vigour and impetus at the performance... During the whole two and a half hours it lasted, the large hall, with its two thousand people and the large orchestra, were so fully intent on the one object in question, that not the slightest sound was to be heard among the whole audience, so that I could sway at pleasure the enormous orchestra and choir, and also the organ accompaniments'.

The composer goes on to say that four numbers were encored and not one single mistake occurred in the first part, though there were some in the second part which he, however, considered trifling and unimportant.

Yet a writer in the then newly established music journal, *The Musical Times,* comments that even *Elijah,* which had the advantage of the composer conducting, was imperfectly given because of lack of rehearsal. He goes on to say that Beethoven's *Mass in D* was 'wretchedly mutilated', causing great disappointment, and urges future Festival committees to increase the number of rehearsals, thereby ensuring that people still want to go on attending the festival events. Who was right, the composer or the critic?

Perhaps there is truth in both reactions, after we have reminded ourselves that critics can sometimes be wrong, and composers, even the best, just pleased to hear a new work of theirs come 'off the page' for the first time. Nevertheless the level of performance does seem to have varied from work to work, within one festival, and the general problem which the critic identified, of lack of rehearsal, was appreciated in other quarters also. What happened to improve matters will be described in the next chapter. No doubt the journalist, whose duty was to keep a cool head, did not abandon himself to the fervent communal enthusiasm of the occasion, something Bernard Shaw wrote about much later, in 1889. Shaw had attended a performance of Handel's oratorio, *Alexander's Feast,* given in East London by the Handel Society of Bow. Afterwards, he wrote that 'the band reinforced by wind and organ, got through with a healthy roughness that refreshed me, and the choruses were capital'. All this though he was sitting on a cane-bottomed chair, without adequate room for his knees! If Shaw could feel like that about a rough-and-ready, semi-amateur affair, then the enthusiastic reception of *Elijah* is easy to explain, even if there were blemishes.

Something must also be allowed for the fact that people were obviously prepared to forgive lapses, just for the chance of hearing fine music, and if a work in an unfamiliar idiom, like the Bach and Beethoven items, defeated the performers initially, at least these same performers should be given credit for their open mindedness in attempting these works.

As to the first singer of the part of Elijah, Staudigl, we have a description of his voice in the *Memoirs of Hector Berlioz* translated by David Cairns and published in 1969. Berlioz speaks of a smooth voice, as sumptuous as velvet, suave yet powerful, with a huge range, an effortless flow of

Charles Lockey, 1820-1901. First tenor in Elijah.

tone, a quality of emotion in its timbre, yet able to execute fairly rapid runs without difficulty. About the soprano, Maria Caradori-Allan in the first performance of *Elijah* on the other hand, Mendelssohn had nothing good to say. In a letter to his brother he expressed his disgust at her pretentious and 'pretty' version of what he conceived of as a simple aria. She is elsewhere described as having an agreeable and unassuming manner, perfect for the concert room, so perhaps she was overcome by the presence of the composer and overdid things?

We know also from another part of the Mendelssohn letter just quoted that Charles Lockey's sweet tenor tone in 'If with all your hearts', from *Elijah*, so profoundly moved the composer that he had to make a great effort not to be quite carried away, and cease beating in time. And it is from Lockey that we have some very important information about Mendelssohn's *tempi*. An interesting article was published in the *Musical Times* of January 1902, a month after Lockey's death. Just before that a letter from Charles Stanford had appeared in *The Times* of 7th December 1901, four days after Lockey died. What we learn from these two sources is that Stanford visited Lockey especially to question the singer about the right speeds for Mendelssohn's music. Stanford's own faster-than-expected *tempi* had been challenged by an orchestra he was rehearsing for a performance of *Elijah*. Stanford pointed out to them that he was simply obeying the metronome marks but, in the intervening fifty years since Mendelssohn himself

Chapter 7 - After the building of the Town Hall

conducted it in Birmingham, *andantes* had been sentimentalised and the composer's fiery speeds reduced. Stanford therefore asked Lockey to hum some of the disputed numbers at Mendelssohn's speeds, as nearly as he could recall. In every case these coincided with the composer's metronome marks. Lockey further commented that Mendelssohn had emphasised that 'O rest in the Lord', sung by Maria Hawes at the first performance, should be sung quite simply and without dragging, and that the final Baal chorus and the aria 'Is not his word like a fire?' should go at 'a prodigious pace'. Stanford had already been told by his own father that 'Mendelssohn's conducting was like whipping cream'. It has to be said that 'O rest in the Lord' has quite often got the over-reverential treatment from many singers over the years!

The next paragraph of Stanford's letter is worth quoting in full,

'I then told Lockey of the modern fashion, beloved of solo tenors, of making a sweeping *portamento* at the return of the theme in 'If with all your hearts' and asked him if it was traditional. Lockey threw up his hands in horror at the idea and told me Mendelssohn impressed upon him again and again the vital importance of perfect simplicity in singing this air'.

We can only reflect that with numbers of a new work being taken as the composer intended 'at a prodigious pace', small wonder if there were some flaws at its first performance. The amazing thing is that hundreds of people, assembled for one week, could tackle such a long work at all, especially if we remember that they had to prepare it using hand-written copies and perform it by gaslight!

We are now almost at the end of the Joseph Moore years of the Birmingham Musical Festivals, effectively 1802 to 1849, and perhaps we should, even at this distance, salute him and pay tribute to his achievement, The miracle he worked was to make the festivals continue to be profitable while, at the same time, adding new and unfamiliar items amongst the old favourites, so extending the town's musical horizon. His was also a period where, as we have seen, Birmingham was quite often leading where others, even London, were to follow. Of course, Moore lived in an age when those who did have a good regular wage or income had more of it to spare, and there were far fewer competing entertainments, but that does not detract from the fact that he had great vision and the energy to put his ideas into practice successfully. We owe him a great deal of gratitude.

---

1. Mendelssohn: *Letters.* Copy held at Birmingham University Music Department Library.
2. J. W Cross: *George Eliot's Life.* London. 1885.

Chapter 8

Costa, Stockley and 'this wonderful choir'

The Birmingham Oratorio Choral Society was formed by the indefatigable Joseph Moore in 1808, and between 1811 and 1834, Samuel Buggins, and later Thomas Munden, had prepared the local oratorio singers for the festivals; Munden certainly from 1820. It must be said that they covered a large number of works in a concentrated period running up to the festivals themselves. Some of the music they would know very well but, as Moore continued his efforts to widen the repertoire, it became clear that the chorus, as well as the soloists, would have to tackle new works more often and, moreover, in an unfamiliar idiom. We have seen that they found the Bach and Beethoven items performed in the 1834-1846 period difficult, but it is amazing that they achieved as much as they did. As far as we can tell, they gave only occasional concerts between the festivals at this period, but things obviously needed to be put on a firmer footing, with regular rehearsals and concert-giving.

Again a simple table will best illustrate the evolving situation, after 1834, as regards the allocation of tasks related to training the chorus, and to the accompanying and conducting of the performances. Costa's influence can be clearly seen.

Trainers, organists and conductors at the Birmingham Musical Festivals. 1834-1882

Conductors:	1834-1846	William Knyvett
	1849-1882	Michael Costa
1834	Chorus-Master and Assistant Conductor	Thomas Munden
1837	Assistant Conductor	Thomas Munden
1840	Assistant Conductor	Thomas Munden
	Chorus-Master	George Hollins
1843	Assistant Organist	James Stimpson
	Assistant Conductor	Thomas Munden
1846	Sub-Conductor	Thomas Munden
	Chorus-Master	James Stimpson
1849	Chorus-Master	James Stimpson

Chapter 8 - Costa, Stockley and 'this wonderful choir'

NOTES TO THE ABOVE:
A. Stimpson was also listed among the four solo organists along with 'Dr. Wesley, Mr. E. Chipp and Mr. Simms'.
B. George Hollins was a member of a local family, his brother Peter being a sculptor who sculpted a bust of Mendelssohn.

1852	At the organ and Chorus Master	James Stimpson

PLEASE NOTE ALSO:
A. From 1849, there is no assistant conductor and from 1852-1870, Stimpson as organist and Costa as conductor, are the only people listed as responsible for the conduct of rehearsals and performances.
B. Up to 1852, the Chorus-Master had also been the festival organ accompanist.

1855-79	Organist	James Stimpson
	Chorus-Master and Conductor of the Birmingham Festival Chorus	William Stockley
	Conductor of the Birmingham Amateur Harmonic Association	A. J. Sutton

Costa - the conductor in charge

It is plain that there was still too much divided responsibility up to 1849, both in the preparation and in the execution of festival performances, particularly if we remember to add the orchestral leader, with his sub-conductor's function, to this list. Some of the section leaders too, such as Lindley and Harper, were stars in their own right. We can see what the Rector of St. Philip's meant in 1812, at the presentation to Joseph Moore, when he spoke of the need for Moore's skill in harmonising jarring interests. The result was that the total effect of some performances did not match the high level of skill and musicality to be found in individual players and singers. With the arrival of Michael Costa as festival conductor, things changed radically. Costa was a conductor in the new autocratic mode and he must have played a great part in setting higher standards at festival performances. It is clear that one firm hand was needed to guide these, now that such large numbers of people were involved. Long gone were the days of the orchestra of twenty-five players and a chorus of forty-five singers of the 1760s, 1770s and 1780s. Costa's new approach was also an encouragement to musicians to come to Birmingham and to stay here and work for the same idea. More will be said about Costa himself in the next chapter. Let us turn aside, then, and examine the contribution of another newcomer to Birmingham whose name appears in the above list, namely William Stockley who lived from 1829 to 1919.

Stockley and the Chorus
What was the situation as regards choral singing in the town at the time of Stockley's arrival, in 1850? The official Birmingham Oratorio Choral Society had been in existence from 1808 and gave some concerts for charity between the festivals. Due perhaps to economic hardships and social readjustments in the 1830s and on into the 'hungry forties', only a small amount of chorus singing was undertaken between the festivals. The population was growing apace however, and the pressure of this created an increasing demand for more, and better organised, permanent choirs. This included church choirs as we shall see. An attempt to rectify matters was made in 1840 when several small local choirs came together to form the Birmingham Musical Institute. This society gave three oratorio concerts a year during its brief existence but unfortunately, the choral section under Henry Simms, organist at St. Philip's Church, fell out with Thomas Munden's Oratorio Choral Society, and the Birmingham Musical Institute was wound up in 1844. The need for something new to take the place of both these bodies was urgent, and the Festival Choral Society was established in 1845. The choir practised at the house of James Stimpson, the festival organist, and was started off as a provident association for the assistance of members. This scheme did not work, but the Festival Committee seems to have kept the enterprise going until 1855, at which time it had seventy members. Stimpson resigned as conductor in 1855 and, according to Stockley, 'it was thought that the members would share the benefit fund (£500) and the Society be disbanded'. There was a majority in favour of its going on, however, which it did, under its own separate management and no longer that of the Festival Committee. They then invited William Stockley to be their new conductor and in doing so opened a new chapter of Birmingham's musical life. Apart from any consideration of standards, the number of members of the Festival Choral Society had increased to two hundred by 1859, from the rather shaky seventy in 1855.

We have Stockley's own account of the methods he used to achieve this result. Coming to Birmingham from Sevenoaks in Kent, in 1850, Stockley describes his high expectations of a town 'so noted for it musical gatherings' and with such 'a splendid reputation'. He goes on:

'Undoubtedly, these gatherings were the best of the kind in the whole musical world, for not only were the performances of the oratorios unequalled, but the Committee by their generous policy offered to the composers of all nations the opportunity of introducing their compositions to the world in a manner of exceptional excellence, thus giving to the town the honour of being the birthplace of some of the greatest works ever composed'.

About the quantity of music in Birmingham, between the festivals, Stockley confessed himself very disappointed, however. He set to work to do something about it, and was able to ride the tide of improving social conditions, after the 'hungry forties', and before the slump of the last part of the century. His active musical career in the town spanned the years 1850 to 1897, and he must be credited with an enormous three-fold contribution to Birmingham's musical life; in the choral sphere, at the festivals themselves and, even more significantly for the future, in the orchestral sphere. Stockley saw the importance of basing a healthy future for the festivals on a solid local foundation, with local people involved as much as possible in music-making all year round, every year.

The specific purpose of Stockley's move to Birmingham was to learn the business of a piano and music dealer, with Messrs. Sabin of Bull Street. He soon became organist at St. Stephen' Church and, having had choral training experience during his Sevenoaks days, his appointment as conductor of the ten year old Festival Choral Society, five years after his arrival in the town, is a measure of the mark he had already made for himself. His first concert with the Festival Choral Society was, of course, what Stockley described as *The Messiah,*[1] more correctly *Messiah*. The performance was given with local principals and organ accompaniment. The latter he describes as 'heavy work for Mr. Stimpson at the organ', and, as a consequence of his dissatisfaction, Stockley alarmed the Festival Choral Society committee considerably by suggesting that they should organise a regular orchestral band to accompany the choir's concerts, instead of relying entirely on the organ. This in 1856. Stockley carried his proposal by a majority of only four votes, but he goes on to say:

'On gaining my point I immediately set about the task of forming an orchestra, and as there were but few instrumentalists in the town, and those principally engaged at the Theatre Royal and the music hall, my task was a difficult one'.

Equally problematic, of course, was the question of finance, but Stockley was not one to let that defeat him. He therefore invited the leading musicians to a conference at Christ Church rooms. The Festival Choral Society had generously agreed to a proposal that the players should have two-thirds of the profit from an experimental first concert, the Society taking the remaining third. The players accepted this proposition, and loyally kept to the agreement for about two years. From about 1858 onwards they asked for a definite, pre-arranged fee, even if it were to be a very small one. This was done and everyone's faith was justified; for the enterprise prospered, and the fees were increased until they reached a satisfactory level. In Stockley's own words 'This record is given in justice to both instrumentalists and vocalists, upon whom, I consider, it reflects great honour'.

Not only was an orchestra now available for choral concerts, but the choir itself grew. The choice of works to be presented at the Festival Choral Society's own concerts became more adventurous and the soloists invited more prestigious. In these circumstances the choir was always at the peak of its condition, and thereby more able than ever to cope with any demands made of it at the festivals. Moreover, the number of visiting choralists, who had to be paid, was gradually reduced.

By 1861, indeed, the members of the town's Festival choir were publicly acknowledged as the finest choral singers in the land. In a piece on the Festival of that year, a report in *The Times* said: 'The Birmingham singers, covered with new laurels, have now a perfect right to regard themselves - until other competitors are found - as the Champion Choristers of England'. In 1879, no less a person than Saint-Saëns, in the town for a premiere of a work of his own, was to concur with this view. In a French newspaper this time, he wrote: 'I wish people who describe the English as unmusical could hear the Birmingham singers. This wonderful choir has everything: intonation, perfect timing and rhythm, finely shaded expression and a lovely sound. If people who sing like this are not musical, well, they certainly perform as if they were the finest musicians in the world'.

Can there be any doubt that, given their innate musicality in the first place, it was the regular training and the concert-giving, under Stockley's guidance, which had brought this chorus to this peak of achievement?

Stockley's input as far as Birmingham's music was concerned was three-fold, 'outward' to the festival and an ever more famous festival chorus, and 'inward' to an improving local concert scene. Perhaps his most enduring gift to the town, however, was his orchestra meeting regularly and giving a series of concerts between 1873 and 1897. This will be considered in a separate chapter.

It is to Costa, however, as well as to Joseph Moore before him, that credit must be given for the following comment by Lowell Mason, writing from New York in 1852: 'The Birmingham Festival seems to move the whole musical kingdom. It brings together the best talent that can be found and the works of the greatest masters are performed under circumstances more advantageous than are elsewhere to be found in the world'. Meanwhile, let us return to Costa and the festivals.

---

1. W. C. Stockley: *Fifty Years of Music in Birmingham* 1912.

Chapter 9

Costa's reign. The Birmingham Musical Festivals 1849–1882

Michael Costa, born in Naples on 4th February 1808, had as one of his teachers a fellow-Neapolitan, Niccolo Zingarelli. Zingarelli was a noted composer in his day, writing operas (many for La Scala, Milan), oratorios and cantatas. He wrote in what might be described as the serious Italian style, really preferring the composition of a mass to that of an opera. He was invited to write for the Birmingham Musical Festival in 1829 and produced a cantata called *Isaiah,* a setting of some verses from the book of that prophet in the Old Testament. Zingarelli was by then 80 years old and did not feel able to undertake either the journey or the conducting of his new work. Instead he sent his pupil, Michele Andrea Agniello Costa (1808-84), otherwise the future Sir Michael Costa. So Costa came and saw, but certainly did not conquer; at least not at first.

The intention was that the 21-year-old Italian should direct the first performance of *Isaiah,* but Greatorex and Cramer had other ideas. Costa's obituary in *The Musical Times* (June 1884) says that they 'elbowed him off', without explaining whether this was a literal or a metaphorical statement! At any rate, the Festival Committee offered to recompense the young man by inviting him to sing instead, and his name duly appeared in the programme as a tenor, where it can still be viewed by the interested enquirer. *The Musical Times* did not come into existence until 1844, but we do have some pungent comments from an earlier music journal, the *Harmonicon,* about the efforts of both Zingarelli and Costa. It described the cantata, as 'a heap of commonplace trash from the first note to the last', and the singer as so far 'below mediocrity' that 'had he remained but a few moments longer on the stage, he would have witnessed a storm compared to which the roarings of his own Vesuvius would have seemed but a murmur'.

This did not get rid of him, however! Costa must have known perfectly well that for centuries past, England had been a 'soft touch' a far as Italian musicians were concerned, and a happy hunting-ground for any of them wanting to earn far higher fees than they could possibly earn anywhere else in Europe. So the determined young man stayed on – in Birmingham. In his *Fifty Years of Music in Birmingham,* Stockley tells us that it was customary for the Italian vocalists at the festivals to attend, and take part in, the masses at St. Peter's Church, Broad Street, during the Sunday before the festival opened. Costa obviously made this same connection with St Peter's, with the result that he was invited to remain as choirmaster, which he did for several months. In 1830, however, he was engaged as *maestro al piano* at the King's Theatre in London where he obviously found his true *métier*. He improved the standard of performance there out of all recognition, and gained such a good reputation as a trainer and conductor of singers and players that in 1846 he became director of the Philharmonic Orchestra, and of the new Italian Opera at Covent Garden. In 1848, he was appointed as director of the Sacred Harmonic Society, and in 1849, twenty years after his first disastrous visit to the town, conductor of the Birmingham Musical Festivals.

Michele Costa, 1808-84 (Michael Costa in 1872).

There is no doubt that during Costa's 'reign' the standard of performance rose enormously. That Stockley also contributed to this is also not in doubt, but Costa's qualities were crucial in bringing everything together at the performances, in order to achieve some brilliant results. Some reactions to certain of 'his' festivals have come down to us as we have seen (page 108) and in 1855, for example, the highly gifted young Birmingham musician, Edward Bache, wrote some of the local critiques of the concerts, afterwards saying that this festival was so perfect that he did not wish to hear another.[1] These were tragically prophetic words in fact, for in 1858, exactly a week before the first day of the next festival, Bache died. He was only twenty-five. We shall consider Edward Bache's own career in another chapter.

Costa was, evidently, something of an autocrat, but this was a good thing in a situation where a huge number of gifted people came together in one place to perform music. As we have observed from the list at the beginning of chapter 8, Costa dispensed with the services of the old-style assistant conductor, and we know that he changed the role of the leader of the orchestra, who had been virtually a sub-conductor, or even co-conductor. This would have been a sweet revenge on Costa's side had Franz Cramer still been leader in 1849, but Cramer's last festival was in 1843, and he died in 1848. The reader will perhaps remember that Cramer was one of those who ousted Costa as a conductor in 1829. Costa brought a close colleague with him to Birmingham as orchestral leader, the Frenchman, Prosper Sainton. The two understood one another and worked agreeably together. Sainton was also a conductor himself, but in his role as leader he knew how to subordinate himself to the demands of his 'chief', for Costa conducted in the modern way, alone, at a desk, in front of the orchestra, so that everyone could see and obey him. The unanimity thus achieved eventually persuaded everyone of the benefit of this custom, especially where such large numbers were involved.

The idea of a conductor controlling an orchestra in the way that a pianist or organist controls an instrument was a foreign one, in every sense, to most people in this country, certainly up to the time of Spohr's visit to London in 1820. As late as 1843, at a Hanover Square concert in London, the conductor was in the back row of players, facing the audience. Costa certainly established the one-man, one-conductor regime in Birmingham; and as conductor of festivals in Bradford (1853) and Leeds (1874), and of the Sacred Harmonic Society's Handel festivals in London (1857-80), he played an extremely influential part in establishing it in the country at large. Of course there have been some conductors since then who have suffered from delusions of grandeur, seeing themselves as the *equal* co-partners of the composer, but the disadvantage is more than offset by the fidelity and subtlety of interpretation which can be achieved through good orchestral discipline, and conscientious orchestral training by one person. Again we have the *Musical Times* to thank for an appreciation of Costa's role in establishing this:

'He had what all conductors should possess, the secret of command. This it was which enabled him at the outset to reduce an English orchestra to order and discipline. Yet he did not bluster. A few quiet words and the matter in hand was settled without appeal... Under Costa's rule the orchestra became a model of punctuality and serious work; but the chief was rarely harsh and would always stand up for his men in times of emergency. He insisted on duty being done. In that respect he was a Wellington, but outside the demands of duty he knew how to be kind, and even indulgent. That he was absolutely loved by the orchestra cannot, perhaps, be said. He inspired respect and esteem, but also the fear with which a warmer feeling can hardly exist'. *Musical Times,* 1884.

Costa's Solo Singers
What were the festival programmes like during Costa's reign in Birmingham? As one would expect from a Neapolitan, he gave full reign to the vocal soloists in particular, who were encouraged to offer arias and ensembles from operas which demonstrated the most brilliant singers in some of the best samples of this nineteenth century Italian genre. Just to take a single instance, the soprano Therese Tietjens with the

tenor Mario and our own Charles Santley sang the trio 'Guai se ti sfugge' from Donizetti's *Lucrezia Borgia* in 1864.

In general many of the finest continental singers continued to come to Birmingham, gradually to be joined, once more, by a growing number of British singers with the same kind of audience-pulling power that Elizabeth Billington, Kitty Stephens and John Braham had exerted at the beginning of the century. Sims Reeves and Charles Santley were the most outstanding examples of this, but the contralto Janet Dolby (Madame Sainton Dolby) and the Scottish-born Janet Patey, née Whytok, along with others such as the tenor Edward Lloyd, made a solid and respected contribution to the re-emerging reputation of British singers.

As to the continental visitors, their names are a roll-call of all the most illustrious singers of the day. The great quartet, Grisi, Mario, Tamburini and Lablache, for whom Donizetti wrote *Don Pasquale,* we have already met, but they were succeeded by Clara Novello, Sontag, Alboni, Castellan, Pauline Viardot, Tietjens (already mentioned), Rudersdorff, Nilsson, Albani, and the great Queen of Song herself, Adeline Patti. The soloists were outstanding but what of the programmes for the 1855 festival; the one which so enraptured young Edward Bache?

The 1855 Festival
This included performances of Mozart's *Requiem,* Beethoven's *'Leonora'* overture - which one is not revealed - and the latter's Sixth Symphony *(The Pastoral)*. Indispensable to the proceedings, of course, were Mendelssohn's *Elijah* and Handel's *Messiah,* but the former's, Symphony no. 4, *The Italian,* and the latter's oratorio *Israel in Egypt* were thrown in for good measure. The usual display pieces for the vocal soloists were there in profusion, but what treats the audience must have had, with Giulia Grisi singing 'Casta Diva' from Bellini's *Norma* and Pauline Viardot in 'Wie nahte mir der Schlummer', from Weber's *Der Freischütz*. Interestingly, Purcell retained his small but secure place in the programmes, and the song with trumpet obbligato, 'To arms heroic prince', from *The Libertine,* was sung by Sims Reeves and Willoughby Weiss. The trumpet part must surely have been played, once again, by Thomas Harper. On that Wednesday evening, 29th August 1855, the audience enjoyed the services of contemporary equivalents of Sutherland, Caballé, Domingo and Pavarotti, all in the one programme!

Another strong characteristic of the Costa period in Birmingham was the continuing introduction of new works. Costa was a composer himself, and his own compositions figured prominently in the programmes, but he was generous enough not to oppose the presentation of other men's music, and a long list of compositions can be drawn up for the period of 'Costa's reign'. Indeed, a list is probably the best way of conveying to the reader, in a concise way, all the new pieces which Birmingham audiences were offered for their consideration and, we hope, enjoyment. First, Costa's own works.

Works by Michael Costa presented at the Birmingham Musical Festivals 1849-82

Date sonitum (Offertory for bass and choir, with Lablache as the bass)	1849
Oratorio: *Eli*	1855, 1858
The Dream – short cantata	1858
Oratorio: *Naaman*	1864, 1870

Also a small number of short items for solo voice, vocal ensemble and orchestra.

Other first performances at the Birmingham Musical Festivals 1849-82

S.S. Wesley:	*The Wilderness*	1852
Henry Leslie:	*Judith*	1858
Henry Smart:	*The Bride of Dunkerron (Part One)*	1864
Arthur Sullivan:	*Kenilworth*	1864
*Julius Benedict:	*St. Peter*	1870
John Francis Barnett:	*Paradise and the Peri* (Words by Thomas Moore)	1870
Ferdinand Hiller:	*Nala and Damayanti*	1870
F. Schira:	*The Lord of Burleigh*	1873
Alberto Randegger:	*Fridolin* (Libretto by Mme. Rudersdorff the singer)	1873
F.H. Cowen:	*The Corsair* (Dramatic Cantata)	1876
Louis Spohr:	*The Last Judgement*	1876
G.A. Macfarren:	*The Resurrection*	1876
Niels Gade:	*Zion*	1876
Niels Gade:	*The Crusaders*	1876
Max Bruch:	*The Lay of the Bell*	1879
Saint-Saëns:	*La Lyre et La Harpe*	1879
Niels Gade:	*Psyche*	1882
A.R. Gaul:	*The Holy City*	1882
Gounod:	*The Redemption*	1882

★ Weber's favourite pupil

In most cases, the composers conducted their own works, but where, occasionally, they did not feel competent to do so, the task was given to William Stockley, rather than to Costa, certainly from 1859. Costa refused to conduct any more first performances of other men's music after being criticised by one of the composers concerned. From what Stockley has written, Costa's decision was taken some time immediately before 1859 and one may speculate that the dissatisfaction was expressed by Henry Leslie with regard to Costa's direction of his oratorio *Judith*. Leslie was a noted choral conductor himself, and may have had strong ideas of his own. In any event these opportunities added immensely to Stockley's fund of experience as a conductor. He certainly conducted the first performance of A. R. Gaul's *The Holy City* for example. Some composers who did conduct their own works were, nevertheless, still very ready to enlist Stockley's advice and assistance at rehearsals. Such were Niels Gade and, later, Hubert Parry, who wanted guidance about *tempi*, especially in the choruses, since Stockley knew the Town Hall's acoustics better than they did. How wise they were!

A story is told by Stockley in connection with the first rehearsal for the premiere of the cantata, *The Crusaders,* by Denmark's Niels Gade, given in 1876. The performance was to be in an English translation, made for the festival. At the very opening of the work, the altos came in with the first vocal entry, crying 'hot rolls, hot rolls', while the rest of the choir collapsed in helpless merriment. When decorum was restored, they were able to discover that the composer had chosen the most unfortunate way of setting the line 'Hot rolls the sand-wave'. Not a very happy phrase anyway, you may think! Stockley rather quaintly goes on to explain that the chairman of the orchestra committee, Richard Peyton, decided that 'it would not be wise to risk a repetition of the fiasco in public', and had the 'Hot rolls' changed to 'Fierce flames' – 'as it stands, I suppose, to this day', Stockley adds.

Among the composers of new works listed above was G. A. Macfarren and it was evidence of a growing practice that he contributed an analytical programme note on Mendelssohn's *Italian Symphony* for one of the 1855 events. This had not been done before, but the analytical note was to become a much more common feature of later festival programmes. In 1882, for example, Joseph Bennett, librettist and music critic for *The Daily Telegraph,* contributed a note on Gounod's *The Redemption;* to which work we may now turn.

It is of some interest to know that Gounod sketched out his own plan for the arrangement of the choir and orchestra on the platform, for the first performance of *The Redemption.* One wonders how closely this plan could have been adhered to.

More intriguing, perhaps, is the fact that some very tough negotiating went on between Gounod and the Birmingham Festival Committee in relation to the completion and first performance of this work. Appalled by the idea of finding the £4,000 demanded by the composer, the committee entered into the following agreement. They bought the work outright from Gounod, paying him his preposterous £4,000 (now worth about £130,000) on 1st November 1881. They then treated with Messrs. Novello, the music publishers, who for the right of copyright and performances throughout the world, paid the Birmingham committee £3,250. So the festival got the work for £750 and an agreement from Gounod to conduct the first performance, or pay a penalty if he did not. The Novello connection, and the public interest taken in the business deal itself, ensured world-wide anticipation of the work's first performance. In the event, visitors from all over the country, and from Europe also, crowded into the Town Hall that Wednesday morning, 30th August 1882. The full rehearsal, before the

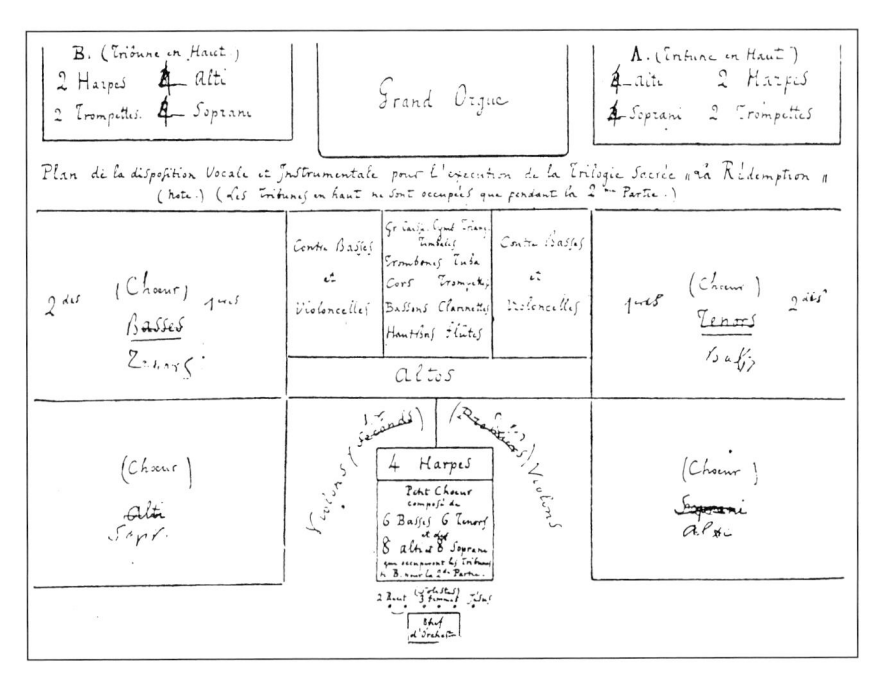

Chapter 9 - Costa's reign. The Birmingham Musical Festivals 1849-1882

Gounod's sketch for the arrangement of choir and orchestra for The Redemption (Birmingham Musical Festival 1882).

opening of the festival, was attended by an audience of the privileged, among whom was Cardinal Newman. The excitement generally was such that there was not even standing-room available in the Town Hall for the performance itself.

We are indebted to reports from various numbers of the *Musical Times* for these details about Gounod and his Birmingham Musical Festival commission. The same source tells us that 'it was felt on all hands that the oratorio was a great work... frequent and spontaneous applause testified to the fact'. The composer was indeed there to conduct, generally out-manoeuvred, in spite of his avarice, by Birmingham business acumen! Because of the huge success of *The Redemption*, Gounod might have done better to have given the Festival Committee the work and kept the copyright himself.

Music of Costa's era still heard today

What of the works presented during the Costa period which are still in today's church, concert hall and opera house repertoires? In the concert hall Costa's audiences did hear enduring masterpieces such as Mozart's *Ave Verum*, his Requiem and Mass in G, Beethoven's, *Pastoral Symphony, Emperor Concerto* (with Arabella Goddard as soloist), and Violin Sonatas in F and G (with Prosper Sainton

115

and Goddard), Mendelssohn's Second Piano Concerto and some of Berlioz' *Benvenuto Cellini* music for example. We still treasure these works today. In general, and taking all the programmes into account, it is the operatic music which has survived most successfully however. Most of the new oratorios and cantatas of Costa's day, particularly his own, have fallen by the wayside. Some of them were popular for a few years, but almost none got a second look-in at the Birmingham festivals, their places being taken by works from the latest 'contemporary' composers from whom, it was hoped, might come some masterpiece. It took until 1900 for that actually to happen.

There was one festival curiosity by an acknowledged master which is perhaps worth pointing out. This was the scriptural scene *The Holy Supper of the Apostles,* for men's voices and full orchestra, by Wagner. Stockley tells us how difficult this was, 'the greatest trial for a choir I have ever known'. The men are required to sing without accompaniment until the climax, at the finale. Costa considered this was impossible and wrote a 'cello accompaniment to keep the singers in tune, which helped but was not completely successful. When the whole orchestra did enter, however, the effect, according to Stockley, was 'truly stupendous and overwhelming. It must have electrified the audience as it certainly did me. I have never heard anything like it before or since'.

In a very brief footnote to this section it should perhaps be pointed out that no music by J. S. Bach was performed at this period.

The ballots

At the practical, grass-roots level, how would we have had to go about getting tickets, had we been present in Birmingham at Musical Festival time? Tickets were for secured and unsecured places and to obtain a secured ticket we would have had to pay our money and then wait for our place to be determined by ballot. Our name and the number of places we required would be written on a ticket with counterfoil, which was then placed in a wheel. Eight draws were held on the Friday and Saturday before the festival week, one for each performance. The ballot was held at the Blue Coat School, in St. Philip's Place until 1882, the end of the period we are considering. After that, other venues were used which will be detailed later. Secured places cost one guinea (£1.1s.0d or £1.05p) in the mornings, and fifteen shilling (15/- or 75p) in the evenings. One guinea and fifteen shillings would now be the equivalent of £30 and £22, so very similar to today's highest priced concert tickets. Unsecured places (ten and sixpence or 52½p, and eight shillings, 40p) were sold at the ticket office, Waterloo Rooms, Waterloo Street, where late applicants for secured places were also dealt with.

Let us remind ourselves at this point that Festival events gave audiences three hours of music, not two as is usually the case today. How do we know the concerts were so long? Well, even if we could not calculate their length from the list of items in the programmes, we should know from the railway time-tables. After 1837, the programmes included announcements from the railway companies involved – seven of them by 1861 – all offering special fares and midnight trains, from New Street and Snow Hill stations. These travelled as far as Shrewsbury, Macclesfield, Derby, Oxford and Gloucester, as well as to Midland towns like Lichfield, Kidderminster and Wolverhampton.

The encore nuisance
We learn from the 1852 programme, for example, that the evening concerts were arranged 'so that they may conclude soon after 11 p.m.' The same announcement goes on to ask that no encores should be demanded since the delay they caused meant that some patrons (those catching a midnight train for example) would have to leave before the end, while the rest – and more particularly the performers – would be so late to bed as to be scarcely rested before having to rise for the next morning's concert. The craze for encores had obviously begun to be a serious nuisance. It is as well to remind ourselves that these were not just calls for the addition of an extra item at the very end of a programme. Enthusiastic applause could – and did – lead to repetitions of whole arias in the middle of an oratorio for example or, worse, could bring the whole performance to a noisy and disagreeable halt. If a great singing star finally went off before the audience had had what it thought was a sufficient number of encores, the performers following after could and did have their efforts drowned in 'stamps, whistles and shouts'; or be driven from the platform entirely. This happened in Liverpool, Manchester and Leeds in 1875 and 1876, when the great tenor Sims Reeves had been singing; though this, it should be emphasised, was not at a festival.

As to Birmingham itself, some reports from the ever-informative *Musical Times* reveal that sometimes things were very unsatisfactory in this respect even here. At least the Musical Festival had a President who indicated with a wave if an encore was to be permitted. This prevented any possibility of the wild northern scenes described above, but the Festival Presidents themselves could be extremely insensitive. They were not musicians, of course, and, as aristocrats, obviously felt they were being extremely gracious to both performers and audience in indicating their permission for an encore.

The atmosphere at the festivals is well conveyed by the following extract from the *Musical Times* for October 1870. Benedict's oratorio *St. Peter* was being given its first performance in Birmingham that year, and the journal reports:

'The Soprano solos are the most attractive in the work, and the gracefully, melodious song, 'I mourn as a dove' producing so evident a sensation in the room that, had not the President given the signal for an encore, we believe that the delighted auditors would, in this instance, have taken the matter into their own hands'.

The soloist in that 'melodious song' was IIma de Murska incidentally, a Croatian soprano whose voice had a range of three octaves.

The next extract demonstrates the insensitivity referred to before:

'As usual the President (on this occasion the Marquis of Hertford) exercised his privilege of demanding encores, graciously selecting for repetition..... the Trio, 'Lift thine eyes' although the choir had actually commenced the following chorus. Comment upon this time-honoured absurdity is, we fear, useless'. *Musical Times* (Birmingham Festival 1876).

This latter example was a particularly inappropriate act, since the programmes 'earnestly requested' that there should not be 'any audible expression of applause' at the morning performances, because of the sacred music performed. Indeed, on this occasion, it was a trio from Mendelssohn's *Elijah,* sung that particular morning by Tietjens, Trebelli, and Janet Patey, soprano, mezzo-soprano and contralto respectively, which came in for this tactless treatment.

Sometimes, with a little innocent guile, performers did manage to dodge an encore, as happened at the 1873 festival. This was during the Thursday evening Grand Miscellaneous Concert, at the Theatre Royal, when Madame Albani had just sung 'Angels ever bright and fair' from Handel's *Theodora.*

'By a signal from the President, the air was encored, but Madame Albani, who had left the orchestra, *could* not see it, and Sir Michael Costa *did* not see it, consequently it was not repeated'. *Musical Times,* 1873.

Sims Reeves, himself so often encored, endeavoured to put an end to the practice by refusing to give encores. The mayhem this sometimes caused has been described, but a least the point was being made. Nevertheless, it took many years for the 'middle-of-a-performance' encore to die out. Its demise may be dated from the period immediately following the First World War, perhaps, from about 1920. As always, it seems to have been, in the main, a curse foisted on the long-suffering majority by an ignorant or over-excitable minority.

We may speculate about the level of compliance with another request to audience members to the effect that 'parties will remain uncovered during the whole of the Performance in the Hall'. In other words, gentlemen should remove their hats and ladies their bonnets.

The police were there to maintain free access to and from the hall, and stewards within the building wore a blue ribbon in their coats. Also in the programmes was a statement about the finance of the General Hospital and the number of in-patients and out-patients treated there in the previous year. In the 1861 programme for example, the 1860 figures were given and these included 12,383 accidents and 'urgent medical cases admitted without tickets'. The statement, signed by J. O. Mason, (James Oliver Mason, a founder member of the Birmingham and Midland Institute), Chairman of the Festival Committee, concludes as follows:

'The Festival Committee, deeply impressed with the extreme importance of maintaining this noble Hospital unfettered in its operations, and of enabling it to dispense in an enlarged manner the inestimable blessings of health to the sick and afflicted poor, earnestly appeal to the public, and invite their patronage and support on the occasion of the forthcoming Festival. They feel that the cause for which they are striving is good and great – that Hospitals are, of all charities, the most capable of affording relief, and least liable to abuse – and that there is none more worthy than the Birmingham General Hospital'.

What did specialist hospitals, like the Eye Hospital for example, think about that last statement one wonders?

Some comments on the 1858 Festival
Finally, for another contemporary impression of what the Festivals of this period were like we may perhaps quote once more from the *Musical Times*. In October 1858 the reviewer wrote as follows: 'The first morning performance opened with the National Anthem, the solo parts being sung by Madame Clara Novello in that brilliant and impressive style for which she has acquired so much celebrity. The oratorio was Mendelssohn's *Elijah*'. The journal names the other principal singers and continues: 'The execution as a whole was perfect. All the singers and instrumentalists exerted themselves with a spirit worthy of the immortal work, and complete success was the result of their exertions. Mr. Costa was the conductor, and Mr. Stimpson presided at the organ. The Town Hall was crammed to suffocation, and the *coup d'oeil* was grand in the extreme'.

At the miscellaneous Concert that evening, Handel's *Acis and Galatea* was given last. 'This arrangement was evidently putting the cart before the horse. The light introductory music of Verdi, Donizetti etc, seemed to have unsettled the audience, and they could not sufficiently devote their attention to the classical music of Handel, and many of the audience actually left before the conclusion of the serenata, and the noise materially marred the effect of the last chorus, 'Galatea dry thy tears'. According to the reviewer the rest of the Festival went extremely well, however, and he particularly praises the police and the organisers: 'The admirable and efficient arrangements of the police caused everything to pass off without the slightest confusion and no trouble was spared to make the Festival deserving of the highest patronage and to maintain for the town of Birmingham the distinction which has made it famous throughout Europe as the home of the grandest musical celebrations ever witnessed'.

---

1. Constance Bache: *Brother Musicians*. Reminiscences of Edward and Walter Bache. London. 1901.

Chapter 10

A Boa Constrictor? 1834-1880

Sullivan at Birmingham's Clef Club

Turning away from the festivals, let us look around and see what other music was being offered in the rapidly expanding town. The title of this chapter refers to some words used in a speech to the Clef Club in Birmingham, by Sir Arthur Sullivan of Gilbert and Sullivan fame. The Clef Club, formed in about 1881, met in Paradise Street. It was a society of local musicians working for better knowledge of music and better standards in its performances within Birmingham itself. It had 275 members, social and musical, some of whom gave concerts, mainly of chamber music. Many such societies came into being all over the country in the middle of the nineteenth century, partly as a reaction to the low state of indigenous British music. This anxiety was caused particularly by our lack of a front-rank composer and first-rate instrumentalists, and by what was coming to be condemned as the invasiveness of the 'musico-charitable' festivals, of which Birmingham's was the prime example. Sullivan was president of the Clef Club at the time of his speech and was, according to William Stockley, reviewing the progress of music in the city since he, Sir Arthur, was first associated with it in 1864, when his *Kenilworth* was premiered. His words were: 'When I first knew Birmingham it reminded me, in musical matters, of a huge boa constrictor that took an enormous gorge once in three years and fasted in the interim'. Sullivan was comparing the earlier time of the 1860s with the situation then, in the 1880s, when so much more was going on; thanks in no small measure to Stockley it has to be said.

Sullivan's boa constrictor gibe was not entirely a fair assessment even in 1864, however, nor before that if the truth were known. Quite a lot of musical activity was afoot of which the ill-informed outsider knew nothing. The remarkable thing was, perhaps, not that so little went on between the festivals (which was not altogether true), but that provincial towns could mount huge festivals in the first place. In 1864, Birmingham had only about 250,000 inhabitants, the size of Wolverhampton today.

The other problem, that of the invasion of the festivals by foreign composers and performers, only the choir being entirely British and local, was more intractable. The loss of confidence among British musicians cannot have been helped by another invasion, that of heavy industry, leading to rapidly expanding towns and the loss of huge tracts of the countryside. An enormous proportion of this small island was made ugly. Other countries were industrialised later, but with the same number of people,

Chapter 10 - A Boa Constrictor? 1834-1880

and much more space, could accommodate their industrial base less intrusively. It is no surprise to learn that when Wagner sailed into London, the banks of the Thames were for him the physical manifestation of the imaginary gloomy and stygian Niebelung of his *Ring Cycle* operas. Ultimately, original British creativity seems to have had to draw on, or retreat to, the British countryside for inspiration. Later on, Elgar's Worcestershire landscape was to be of crucial importance for his musical thinking; and the themes of Holst and Vaughan Williams were to owe much to their interest in traditional country tunes, whilst Delius and Walton actually escaped abroad, eschewing their industrial Yorkshire and Lancashire origins altogether. More recently, Britten and Tippett also moved back into the countryside to work, after excursions into metropolitan spheres. Much of the music of these composers is imbued with a certain sadness - for a way of life now destroyed?

Many people, even from earlier on in the nineteenth century, could see what was happening and were greatly concerned to try to counteract it by giving encouragement to British composers, by inviting them to compose for the Festivals. Sullivan's amusing comments about Birmingham's musical life are understandable, but the rest of this chapter will be concerned to show that there was still a desire to hear fine music on a regular basis in the town, in spite of all the overcrowding, and all the smoke, grime and noise with which people had to contend even if, so far, the best of such music was composed abroad.

The theatre
The theatre continued to be a regular source of music between the festivals, and the Town Hall was increasingly exploited for concerts all through the rest of the century. Only a few selected examples can be quoted, but here are some. First, the theatre. Rather interestingly, a late specimen of the 'Shakespeare-scenes-relieved-by-music' formula, so beloved of the eighteenth century, appears as late as 1836, this time in the form of an illustrated lecture. On 31st October the *Gazette* contains the following announcement:

'It will be observed that Mr. Pemberton, the well-known lecturer upon Shakespeare has kindly consented to perform the character of Macbeth at our Theatre on Friday evening next, in aid of the Building fund of the Mechanics Institution, and that to give the best effect to the celebrated choruses, a portion of the Choral Society have been engaged'.

Where did the 'celebrated choruses' come from? Well, Sir William D'Avenant (1606-68), said to have been Shakespeare's godson, did an adaptation of *Macbeth,* and several composers wrote incidental music for this version. These were Matthew Locke (c1630-70), Richard Leveridge (c1671-1758) John Eccles (c1672-1735) and Samuel Arnold (1740-1802). It seems to have been Leveridge's music which survived Garrick's restoration of the play to something like its proper form, in the middle of the eighteenth century, and this version was used until as late as 1875 or thereabouts.

As an aside, Charles Reece Pemberton (1790-1840), who gave this lecture, had been apprenticed to his uncle, a brass-founder in Livery Street. He ran away to sea and eventually became an actor, achieving fame, and being especially admired for his performance as Shylock. He lectured regularly at the Birmingham Mechanics Institute, and all over the country, delighting all his audiences.

Also at the theatre, Rossini's *Stabat Mater* was given in September, 1842, when Giovanni-Battista Rubini (1794-1854) made his farewell visit to the town. He had sung the leading tenor roles in the first performances of Bellini's *La Sonnambula* (1831) and *I Puritani* (1835), in Milan and Paris respectively. He was 'transformed into a tragedian by dint of being a sublime singer',[1] and if singing was Rubini's profession, then, by heaven, sing was what he did. He went early into an extremely affluent retirement, having put a little too much pressure on a rather vulnerable voice. Something of a Maria Callas in this perhaps? In any case, Birmingham had the opportunity of making its own judgement.

Concerts

Later that same month (the 23rd) three respected English festival singers, on their way to the Worcester Festival 'appeared in a concert for one night only', as a local paper worded it. These were the Misses Birch and Hawes and a Mr. Phillips who, after some research, we may be certain were Charlotte Birch, soprano, Maria Hawes, contralto and Henry Phillips, bass. All three sang at the Birmingham Festivals as we have seen, and it is interesting to learn that Charlotte Birch was a student at the Royal Academy of Music between 1831 and 1834, and that Henry Phillips taught singing in Birmingham for a few years, following his retirement in about 1863. The press reported that the house was crowded in every part for this Town Hall concert.

Franz Liszt in Birmingham

A particularly interesting connection with a renowned composer was made, briefly, when Liszt gave a piano recital at the old Royal Hotel on 26th November 1840. The concert was shared with John Orlando Parry, harpist and singer, and was part of a tour of all the main provincial cities of England, Ireland and Scotland organised for Liszt by Louis Lavenu, 'cellist and music publisher. Miss Louisa Bassano, with probable local connections, was also one of the concert party. In that same year, the journal *Musical World* described Liszt as the 'Polyphemus of the piano - the Aurora Borealis of Musical Effulgence - the Niagara of Thundering harmonies'.

From time to time certain individuals 'played impresario' and organised a celebrity concert at the Town Hall. Such was Mr. Pearsall, presumably the bass singer, who presented Caradori Allan, Signor Giubilei, Henry Phillips and the violinist, Alfred Mellon, on 24th September 1842. Pearsall himself took part in the concert, though in what capacity is not stated. At the theatre two months later, in November 1842, citizens of our town were able to enjoy the playing of the great pianist, Sigismond Thalberg (1812-71). He rivalled Liszt and many thought him as great. This rivalry engendered the same kind of partisanship as that between the devotees of Wagner and Brahms later in the century, with Fétis leading the Thalberg camp and Berlioz that of Liszt. Added to the attractions at this event was the presence of two members of the Ronconi family of singers. Giorgio Ronconi, baritone, and his wife, formerly Giovannina Giannoni, soprano, were not in the top flight of Italian singers. His voice had a limited range, was weak and often out of a tune, but his dramatic powers were such that he could be extremely persuasive as Iago or Figaro for example. His wife, who sang in London as Elguerra Ronconi, had only a limited success. It is noticeable that Ronconi appeared only once at a Birmingham Musical Festival, in 1858, though he was still singing at Covent Garden until 1866. His wife was never invited to a festival.

There is no doubt that our Festival Committee in those days was extremely discerning about singers and was in a position to be choosy. The Ronconis were only good enough to be a rather poor second in the bill to Thalberg and the announcement in the local press also makes it plain, by the way it is printed, that Ronconi was, correctly, rated above his wife.

Sims Reeves - a great British tenor

A singer who was not only destined to be in the very front rank in both opera and oratorio, but was also British, was the tenor Sims Reeves (1818-1900), he who hated encores. His first visit to our town was to the New Street Theatre in May 1843. The *Birmingham Gazette* reported that he was a vocalist of great promise, with a fine tenor voice and great purity of style. It criticised his diction, however, speaking of a 'deficiency in his articulation'. This was something he certainly remedied as time went on. At the time of this first visit to Birmingham, Reeves was a member of Macready's company at Drury Lane, singing as a second tenor in parts such as the First Warrior in Purcell's *King Arthur* and Ottokar in Weber's *Der Freischütz*. Almost immediately after this Birmingham visit, he went to Paris and then to Milan for further training, and by 1846 was able to take the part of Edgardo in Donizetti's *Lucia di Lammermoor* at La Scala itself, with great success. He sang the same part for Louis Jullien at Drury Lane on 6th December 1847, and from then on was universally acknowledged as an actor and singer of the first rank. So, of course, in 1849 he was invited to the Birmingham Musical Festival, and was a regular and extremely popular visitor to every festival after that, until 1873. By then, his growing habit of announcing his 'indisposition', not only just before, but sometimes in the middle of a concert, may well have deterred the festival committee from inviting him again. In any case he made difficulties about the pitch of the Town Hall organ, which he said was too high.

On one occasion, in the middle of a Gloucester Festival performance, in 1859, Reeves quietly disappeared and his place was very graciously and gracefully taken by Clara Novello, who sang an item from her own repertoire. We find this lady herself at our Theatre Royal in 1843. She had obviously stayed on in the town when the festival finished, (on Friday 22nd September), and was assisting at the opening of the theatre's 1843-44 season, on Saturday the 23rd by appearing in selections from Bellini's opera *Norma*. Three other festival singers, Elizabeth Rainforth, Signor Giubelei and Mr. H. Phillips, joined her. Three months later John Braham gave a concert at the Town Hall, with his sons Charles and Hamilton, and the following summer, 1844, saw the great violinist, Sivori, playing in the town. In August of that year Grisi, Mario, and Frederick Lablache joined with other festival singers in a Grand Concert, and this was presented by Mr. Machin, also a festival principal, who sang in the concert himself. A Grisi and Mario 'farewell' was also at the Town Hall, in 1853.

Grand Opera in Birmingham

In August 1826, the theatre manager put on Italian operas 'at theatre prices'. Five years later, in 1833, a Mr. and Mrs. Wood were presenting Rossini's *The Barber of Seville*. Scenes from Verdi's *A Masked Ball* in 1841 and from Bellini's *Norma* in 1842 kept this new trend going. On 30th August 1844, the theatre season opened with Balfe's *The Bohemian Girl*, first produced at Drury Lane only 9 months before, on 27th November 1843. From that point onwards, opera companies visited regularly and soloists went on giving occasional concerts, either at the Theatre Royal or the Town Hall. The hallmark of this period as far as music in the theatre was concerned was the grand opera of the Italian tradition of Rossini, Bellini, Donizetti and Verdi. As usual, Birmingham was 'in the swim', and anyone who attended all the productions brought to the Theatre Royal would gain an extremely good idea of the latest developments in this genre. They were hearing many of these pieces at the beginning of what was to be a long life; and most are still in the repertoire. Again, a table provides us with the clearest way of summarising what was on offer.

Opera performances in Birmingham, 1836-60, with a little-known Birmingham 'first'

Composer	Title of opera & date of first performance	Date of performances at Theatre Royal, Birmingham
Rossini	*Il barbiere di Siviglia* (1816)	1838, Aug 1857 (IC)
Bellini	*Norma* (Selections with Clara Novello) (1831)	Sept 1843

Opera performances in Birmingham, 1836-60, with a little-known Birmingham 'first' (Cont.)

Balfe	*The Bohemian Girl* (1843)	Aug 1844, 1852 (SR) Nov. 1858
Bellini	*Norma* (1831)	Jul 1845
Bellini	*La Sonnambula* (1831)	Sep 1845, Sep 1849 (IC/SR) 1852 (SR), Aug 1857 (IC). Nov. 1858
Donizetti	*Lucia di Lammermoor* (1835)	Sep 1849 (IC/SR), 1852 (SR), Aug 1857 (IC)
Bellini	*I Puritani* (1835)	Sep 1849 (IC/SR), 1852 (SR), Aug 1857 (IC)
Wallace	*Maritana* (D.L. 1845)	Mar 1850 (P & H), Nov. 1858
Verdi	*La Traviata* (1853)	Aug 1856, Nov. 1858
Donizetti	*La Figlia del Reggimento* (1840)	Aug 1856
Verdi	*Il Trovatore* (1853)	Mar 1857 (IC), Aug 1857 (IC), Sep 1858, Nov. 1858
Donizetti	*Don Pasquale* (1843)	Mar 1857 (IC)
Mozart	*Don Giovanni* (1787)	Mar 1857 (IC)
Donizetti	*La Favorita* (1840)	Aug 1857 (IC)
Donizetti	*L'Elisir d'Amore* (1832)	Aug 1857 (IC)
Rossini	*Elizabetta d'Inghilterra* (1814)	Aug 1858
Flotow	*Martha* (1847)	June 1859 Royal English Opera Company (Pyne & Harrison)
Balfe	*Rose of Castile* (1857)	"
Balfe	*Satanella* or *The Power of Love* (1858)	"
Bellini	*Sonnambula* (1831)	"
Verdi	*Il Trovatore* (1853)	"
Auber	*The Crown of Diamonds* (1841) (Les Diamants de la Couronne)	"

ABBREVIATIONS:

IC/SR - The Italian company run by Sims Reeves. IC - An Italian Company. SR - Sims Reeves Company. P&H - Pyne and Harrison Company. DL - Drury Lane Theatre

A high opinion of Catherine Hayes (below) was expressed by no less a person than Liszt who declared that he did not know of any voice more expressive than that of Catherine Hayes. A tribute indeed!

Verdi's *Macbeth* (unrevised version, 1847) 27th-30th Aug. 1860. First performance in this country. Given complete, with English words

This Birmingham performance was organised by the Ladies' Garibaldi Benevolent Association, for the wounded and orphans among Garibaldi's followers and for the

Sims Reeves and Catherine Hayes in Lucia di Lammermoor 1846.

Birmingham Hospitals. Garibaldi was the military figure in the campaign for the unification of Italy and its release from an oppressive Austrian domination. The dates of the earliest performances of Verdi's *Macbeth* are as follows: first performance 14th March 1847 in Florence, performances in Bologna, 1850 and possibly 1851, in New York 1850, Dublin 1859, and Birmingham, 1860. It was then revised for a Paris performance in 1865.

From 1849, some of the above performances in the above list were announced as being by 'An Italian Opera Company'. Sims Reeves and his wife, Emma Lucombe, came under that heading in July 1849, whereas Giulia Grisi, from Covent Garden, and the bass-baritone Edward Gassier, from Drury Lane, were engaged under the same title for March 1857. A different but equally well-known cast was involved in the August performance in that same year, again called 'an Italian Company'. The Royal Italian Opera in London was established at the rebuilt Covent Garden theatre in 1847. Companies visiting Birmingham often included Covent Garden singers but not exclusively so. The decision as to who was contracted to visit Birmingham would presumably be in the hands of the Theatre Royal manager, much as the Festival Committee decided who was invited to take part in the festivals.

Meanwhile, Mr. & Mrs. Sims Reeves and their colleagues had transformed themselves into the Grand Operatic Company for their visit to the town in 1853, and another company who came, as a company, was the Royal English Opera company, visiting in 1859. Formed in 1858 to attempt an escape from Italian domination, by promoting British operas, and Italian operas in English, this latter company was the brain child of Louisa Pyne the soprano and William Harrison the tenor. It performed at the Lyceum, Drury Lane and Covent Garden theatres, and obviously did some touring. The Pyne-Harrison partnership was dissolved in 1864, and in 1868 Louisa Pyne married Frank Bodda, a baritone who had sung in Birmingham with the Sims Reeves company in 1849. The orchestra of Pyne and Harrison's Royal English Opera Company was conducted by the admirable Alfred Mellon, regularly named as leader of the orchestra at the Theatre Royal, New Street, in the 1840s. More details are given about him in appendix number 2.

Alfred Mellon, 1820-1867.

Birmingham was also on the Carl Rosa company's touring list. This was a company established in 1873 which from 1875 onwards brought the best of recent operas, sung in English, so that all in all the town's opera buffs were able to be very well-acquainted with this repertoire, well sung.

To turn again to the Town Hall, among some notable musical occasions there, were several appearances of 'the Swedish nightingale', Jenny Lind. In 1846, although she had not sung at the Festival itself, she gave a concert in the Town Hall the day after it finished, on Saturday 29th August Later her visits were connected with fund-raising, for the Hebrew National School, on 9th September 1846, and then for the Queens Hospital (until recently the Accident Hospital in Bath Row) on 28th December 1848. This second concert raised £1,000. Jenny Lind also sang in a performance of *Elijah* in the town in February 1849 with 'tremendous success', but never took part in the festivals as such.

A Mendelssohn Memorial Concert and other events

The death of Mendelssohn was, understandably, felt very keenly by many in Birmingham, and a Mendelssohn Memorial Festival was held at the Town Hall (27th April 1848). *Elijah* was performed in the morning and *Walpurgis Nacht* in the evening. Then, between 1841 and 1855, before Stockley took over as conductor, the Birmingham Festival Choral Society was giving a regular series of concerts. The first subscription concert given by them was on 11th May 1841, at the Town Hall, and included Handel's *Judas Maccabaeus* and a piece by Palestrina 'generally admired at the preceding Music Festival'. This implies that the Festival Choral Society was functioning before its official establishment under that name, in 1845.

Other 'one-off', fully choral concerts, some at the Town Hall and some at the New Music Hall (where weekly miscellaneous concerts were also given) were often organised. Something altogether different at this period was a Steel and Rock Band, which (whatever it was) certainly bore absolutely no resemblance to anything bearing that title to-day.

Widening the audiences. Intellectual advancement and refinement for the people.
But we must return to Louis Jullien and his Promenade Concerts, a phenomenon which reached the unsuspecting town in September 1844. Jullien, who may perhaps be described as a composer of popular dances, was ignored and unappreciated when a student at the Paris Conservatoire. After leaving, things were not much better and he became insolvent. He naturally made a beeline for London, where foreign musicians always prospered, presenting himself as a conductor. He started some 'shilling concerts' at Drury Lane theatre which he called 'Concerts d'été' (Summer Concerts). These opened in June 1840. In January 1841 these became 'Concerts d'hiver' (Winter concerts) and were followed in 1842 by 'Concerts de Société' at the Lyceum (English Opera House). At one of these, Rossini's *Stabat Mater* was performed for the first time in this country. From December, 1842, this series became an annual one and lasted until 1859.

Jullien was a great showman and exploited those exhibitionist tendencies which the reticent English tended to expect of a Frenchman. He dressed the part, wearing a white waistcoat with coat thrown open to display the opulently embroidered shirt-front. Long wristbands were turned back over his cuffs, his raised head showing off his black hair and moustache. He used the baton with great magnificence of manner, always employing a jewelled one for Beethoven, and changing to a clean pair of kid gloves brought to him on a silver salver, to show his reverence for the great master. At the end of the performances he sank back into a sumptuous velvet chair. He took all his productions on tour, travelling as far as Scotland and Ireland and Birmingham was, of course, on Jullien's touring list.

To take a 'show' like that around the country must have been a huge undertaking in those days, for Jullien's Concerts de Société featured an orchestra of over ninety players and a chorus almost as numerous. He engaged the very best performers for these, and soloists of the greatest skill and virtuosity also took part. Furthermore, he included some more easily appreciated pieces in his programmes, not least the latest quadrille of his own; but he also presented classical music, thus helping to popularise it, which was one of his main aims. After he became more firmly established, he would include whole symphonies at his concerts, sometimes even two in one evening.

In 1848, Jullien again went bankrupt; hardly surprising in view of his extravagant way of doing things. His answer, characteristically, was to arrange something even more extravagant. From 1849, he organised the 'Concert monstre et Congrès musical', which involved four hundred instrumentalists, three separate choruses and three separate military bands. Jullien and his Monster Bands also visited Birmingham - but of course! Sadly a fire at Covent Garden Theatre in 1856 destroyed, along with everything else, the manuscripts of Jullien's most popular quadrilles. These were not in print. He also lost over £5,000 in another theatrical venture the following year and was imprisoned for debt in Paris in 1859, but released on bail. His farewell concert in Birmingham on 30th December 1858 was so successful it led to 'positively the last concert' on 25th January 1859. The soloists were the soprano Anna Bishop, a brilliant technician, and the prodigious violinist, Wieniavsky, of whom we shall hear more.

Jullien ended in a lunatic asylum near Paris. Before the Jullien Fund, set up to help him, could raise any money, he was dead. An early sample of what we now might call a brilliant public relations man, Jullien did arouse interest in, and enjoyment of, music of all types, from his own popular dances to the symphonies of Beethoven, whom he quite clearly genuinely reverenced.

The Monday Evening Concerts

Others too - if more earnestly and less flamboyantly - were concerned to bring good music to a much wider audience. In this sphere Birmingham seems to have had a fair claim to be the first in the field. *Aris's Birmingham Gazette,* dated 3rd December 1855, reveals that concerts of good music, with low ticket prices, had been held at the Town Hall on Monday evenings since 1844, the year of Jullien's first promenade concert in the town. So far as the present writer has been able to discover, these do really seem to have been the earliest of Monday Evening 'Pops'. The fifth edition of Grove's *Dictionary of Music and Musicians* contains an entry headed 'Popular Concerts'. The article speaks of 'This unique London institution more familiarly known as the Monday and Saturday "Pops"'. These, according to this same article, owed their origin to some miscellaneous concerts given in the early days of St. James's Hall, which stood on the site later occupied by the Piccadilly Hotel. St. James's Hall was built in 1858, well after the beginning of the Birmingham Monday Evening Concerts for work people. A little earlier than these London concerts, a similar enterprise had been started by the directors of the Lecture Hall in Greenwich. These are described in The *Musical Times* of January, 1847. It says that at Greenwich they engaged 'the most distinguished artists' and admitted the public at a very low price. The motives of the organisers are made clear from this quotation from their announcement:

'What provision do we find for the cheap and innocent amusement of the mass of the population of the Country? What sort of resources have they to call up the cheerfulness of their spirits, and chase away the cloud from their brow after the fatigue of a day's hard work, or the stupefying monotony of some sedentary occupation?' (Sir John Herschel).

It has not been possible so far to find out whether the concerts at Greenwich had started before 1847, but by 1852 and 1853 respectively, cheap but good 'concerts for the people' were being successfully presented in Bath and in Canterbury, both with the backing of the mayors and in the latter case the gentry and clergy as well.

The fact that all these enterprises are being written about in *The Musical Times* suggests a new phenomenon, dating apparently from between 1847 and 1853, and certainly well before the London 'Pops'. The Monday Evening Concerts beginning in Birmingham in 1844 could very well have been the first in the field. What was significant, however, was that here, the initiative came from the skilled and intelligent artisans themselves. From the item in the 1855 *Birmingham Gazette* already mentioned, comes the following quotation. It is from a report presented to the festival orchestral committee by the sub-committee charged with the management of the Monday Evening Concerts.

'In the year 1844 a Memorial, signed by a number of work people in the employ of several manufacturers, was addressed to the Trustees of the Organ, praying that a performance on that instrument might be given once a week for their special recreation. This was at once acceded to, and Monday evening was set apart for the purpose, at an admission fee of three pence each person. The free use of the Hall was granted by the then Commissioners and their resolution subsequently confirmed by the Town Council. It being found that the organ alone was too monotonous and too abstruse, in 1845 additions to the performances were made by the introduction of a choir, and afterwards principal singers and a pianist were added. The charge for admission to the side galleries and two front rows of the great gallery was then raised to sixpence, but to the other parts of the Hall it was continued at threepence. Up to the year 1852 the Concerts prospered, being regularly attended by an average number of persons of all classes; and after defraying the outlay attendant on the engagements, lighting, printing, and general management, providing for the expences (sic) connected with the organ, namely, tuning etc, there was usually a surplus, on the three years, ranging from £200 to £250, which was paid over with the Festival receipts to the Treasurers of the General Hospital. During the eleven years which have elapsed since their institution, frequent changes have necessarily taken place in the vocal staff of the Concerts, it being found that whenever a singer had established himself as a favorite (sic) with the audience, he was generally, from the success he had obtained, sure to be withdrawn to a different sphere of action, thereby causing much inconvenience in supplying the vacancy, and disappointment to the public. With regard to the class of music performed, the system laid down at the outset has been steadily pursued, and the selections, consisting of portions of oratorios, cantatas, glees, madrigals, duets, and soli pieces with chorus, have been kept up to pretty nearly the same standard throughout. With this view the schemes have usually been arranged from the

Chapter 10 - A Boa Constrictor? 1834-1880

compositions of the best writers and formed with the desire to raise the public taste to the appreciation and enjoyment of what is good and beautiful in music, rather than to yield to a desire for every-day, commonplace novelties, merely for the sake of attracting and amusing the audience. It may be well here to notice a statement which has been recently made in public, that the Concerts are of too high-class music for the frequenters, and that the programmes contain too much "Italian".

To these causes it is sought to attribute the falling away of the persons for whom they were originally designed. To the first allegation the only reply that can be given is, that the object of the Concerts is to afford rational amusement and to elevate and refine public taste and that under the system pursued, which embodied the class of music referred to, they have flourished for a period of upwards of eight years. To the second the answer is that an investigation of the schemes for the past two years shows but a very small proportion of "Italian" (which, however, has its admirers), and consequently it may be dismissed as an assertion unfounded and therefore worthless. But while the attendance of the threepenny class of frequenters fell off, the returns demonstrate that the sixpenny audience did not absent themselves in anything like the same proportion. It is, therefore, to be inferred that to other causes than the want of attraction in the music or the executants is to be traced the withdrawal of the "people" from their usual attendance at the Monday Evening Concerts. The following suggests itself as the real cause of the absence of a large proportion of the usual supporters. Immediately Bingley Hall was opened as a place of resort for equestrian and other amusements at a low charge for admission, a marked alteration was observed gradually to take place in the receipts at the Town Hall; and although that building is now closed for this specific purpose, yet during the past three years numerous houses have been licensed for performances and other diversions, in combination with music and refreshments, which have had the effect of raising a competition not previously in existence, and which assuredly has not failed to attract large numbers of the working classes from the Concerts. Without intending for one moment to reflect on the establishments referred to (it is not here the question whether or not they are wholesome places of recreation for the community), there can be no doubt but that their opening has created a successful opposition to the Monday Evening Concerts, and it is inferred that to them in good measure is to be attributed the want of support observable during the past two years at these formerly popular entertainments'.

NOTES TO THE ABOVE:
A. Threepence (usually pronounced 'thruppence' or 'thrippence') was equal to about ¼p. or about 38p today. (Sixpence was 2½p, equivalent in value to about 75p today).
B. Bingley Hall, demolished in 1984 to make way for the International Convention Centre.

This is a refreshingly direct and honest analysis of the general situation which is still pertinent now; and they make no bones about their desire to 'raise public taste'. As to the Monday Evening Concerts, these had been wound up in March 1854 and then re-opened in December 1855. The foregoing discussion was published on this latter occasion. The writer goes on to suggest that the lowest ticket price should still be threepence, so as to remain faithful to the original intention of making the best music available to those who could not otherwise afford to hear it, and that no lowering of standards should be contemplated. It would be preferable, said the writer of the article, that they should cease rather 'than that they should be made the vehicle of contributing amusement by the introduction and performance of frivolous and trashy selections of music, which would not only degrade the art, but pervert the object aimed at, namely, the intellectual advancement and refinement of the people, at whose request and for whom the Concerts were instituted'.

The second phase of these Monday Evening Concerts lasted at least until 1866, and programmes from both phases, 1844-54 and 1855-66, have survived. The first of these, from Monday 1st October 1849 at the Town Hall, reveal that the concerts began at 8 o'clock and were designed to finish at 9.30 p.m. The items played on this occasion included a setting of 'God Save the Queen' by John Bull, and an organ *Fantasia* by Johann Rinck, a pupil of J. S. Bach's best pupil, Kittel. Rinck evidently inherited the Bach tradition in performance, but not especially in composition. Selections from two of Rossini's opera were played - on the organ - as was an arrangement of Beethoven's overture, *Prometheus*. Vocal duets by Mendelssohn and Mozart, in the latter case 'Lá ci darem la mano' from *Don Giovanni,* were sung, and the concert ended with a madrigal, Festa's *Down in a flow'ry vale* (1540) sung by the full choir! This was a vastly popular item with the British public for a long period. On 18th March 1850, a note at the top of the programme pleads for fewer encores following complaints to the Trustees of the Organ that they make the programme go on beyond 9.30 p.m. They ask that audiences should use the privilege of calling for an encore more sparingly in order to prevent a shortening of the programmes. We have already seen how useless this plea could be.

After 1855, however, the programmes varied more widely and Monday 14th January 1859 saw the appearance of 'the wonderful blind Sardinian minstrel SIGNOR PICCO'. He was to perform 'two favourite pieces on the PASTORAL TIBIA'. The 'tibia utricularius' means bagpiper, but the picco pipe is a small type of recorder, and it was this that 'Signor Picco' played. He appeared in London in 1856, his first port-of-call there being Covent Garden Theatre, on 21st February This Italian peasant was an exceptional player, and his visit to Birmingham is yet further proof, if needed, of the town's capacity to attract whatever music was going on in the capital, at least up until the period of the two World Wars.

A month after the preceding event, on 7th February 1859, there was 'A Nicht wi' Burns', with four singers, one in full Highland costume, together with the Prince of Wales' harpist, Ellis Roberts; the proceedings being as usual under the direction of James Stimpson as organist and conductor. Then, a fortnight later, there was a performance of Sterndale Bennett's cantata for chorus and orchestra, *The May Queen*, written for the 1858 Leeds Festival six months earlier. What is noticeable is that Bennett's music was never presented at the Birmingham Festivals during Costa's reign as conductor, since the two had had a disagreement when both were involved in the Philharmonic Society's affairs, in London. Spohr's oratorio *The Last Judgement* was also given in this series, but in general the programmes were of the miscellaneous type so popular all through the century.

A concert on 30th March 1865 is of particular interest to us now, for, along with the obligatory singer, a Miss Banks, whose name appears more than once in the series and who had sung for the Harrison Celebrity Concerts (chapter 11), there appeared also the violinist Joachim. His quartet, Joachim, Louis Ries, H. Webb and the great 'cellist Piatti on this occasion, were also joined by Charles Hallé at the piano. Hallé played Beethoven's Sonata in D op. 28, in his own edition, and Joachim and Hallé played Beethoven's *'Kreutzer' Sonata* (Violin and Piano Sonata in A op. 47). Joachim's quartet played Beethoven's third *'Razumovsky' Quartet* (in C, op. 59 no. 3) and Haydn's Quartet in G op. 64 no. 4. Miss Bank's contributed a song by Dussek and 'In my wild mountain valley' (The Lily of Killarney). Our forbears were nothing if not catholic in their tastes! In this particular programme there is a note to the effect that the *Kreutzer Sonata* was first performed at the Monday Popular Concerts on 21st March 1859 by Wieniavsky (1835-80), the Polish-born violinist, and Arabella Goddard, the English pianist, both outstanding artists.

Artisans concerts
Another enterprise aimed at bringing good music to the less well-off were the so-called Artizans (sic) Concerts, presented by the Midland Musical Society from about 1880 to 1940. In the same area of activity was the Birmingham Musical Association, also founded in 1880. These will be considered in more detail in chapter 15. In general, there was increasing musical activity once the difficulties of the Hungry Forties began to pass and the growth of industry and the increased speed of communication due to the railways began to bring benefits to citizens lower down the income ladder. It is impossible to know about everything that was done, but let us take one or two examples of new musical societies established in the 1850s. We already know of the new lease of life given to the Festival Choral Society by Stockley, in 1855. Two years earlier a most important and prestigious series had been started by the impresario, Percy Harrison, and a whole chapter will be devoted to them. Three smaller organisations will first be discussed.

The Amateur Harmonic Association 1855-89

One is the Amateur Harmonic Association, founded in 1855. This body not only contributed a number of choral singers to the festivals, certainly up to 1885, but it also fostered the development of instrumental and orchestral playing. The original idea was simply that the chorus should meet regularly to get to know the oratorio repertoire and, also, give open rehearsals. Its name and objects are described in a society report, the one for 1872, as follows:

'The Society is designated "The Birmingham Amateur Harmonic Association". The declared objects are an Union of the best Vocal Amateur Talent of Birmingham for the study and practice of the higher class of musical compositions, and the attainment of proficiency, precision, and effect in choral and part singing. The music at first to be such as can be suitably performed without accompaniment, or with that of the organ only, but ultimately orchestral works, aided by first-class instrumentalists and principal vocalists.

All funds, after payment of incidental expenses, to be devoted to the direct patronage and encouragement of the Art in its living representatives, viz., Composers and Professional performers. The only exception to this Rule, shall be the profits arising from Concerts given for the furtherance of any specific object'.

NOTE:
> 'The Festival Orchestral Committee having kindly placed their valuable Library at the disposal of the Association for the purposes of practice, the Members are particularly requested to be very careful in the use of it, and not to take away any parts from the Rehearsal Room'.

The 'Amateur Harmonic' rehearsed during a good part of its existence in the lecture theatre of the old Midland Institute, then more or less where the present Birmingham Conservatoire now is. The society acquired a considerable library in their thirty-four years of existence which was bequeathed, logically enough, to the then Midland Institute School of Music. This was in 1889, when the society was dissolved. Now of course, the library belongs to the Institute School of Music's offspring, the Birmingham School of Music, lately renamed the Conservatoire. It contained a number of major works including Bach's *St. Matthew Passion,* and 'an overture' (unspecified) by him; various Handel oratorios, of course; Mozart and Haydn Masses and the latter's *The Seasons;* Beethoven's *Choral Symphony, Mass in D* and *Mount of Olives;* Schubert's *Song of Miriam* and *Grand Mass* in E flat; Hummel's *Mass in D* and a number of new works being given at the festivals plus various part-songs and madrigals.

A further Midland Institute connection was through the society's conductor and accompanist, A. J. Sutton and C. J. Stevens respectively. Both men taught singing classes at the Midland Institute. They must have been very competent since the society not only contributed choral singers to our festival choir, but also, from 1867, to the huge Handel Festivals at the Crystal Palace, London. Sutton was joint Chorus Master with Stockley at the festivals, from 1861.

The organisers were certainly very serious about all they did and there is even a printed admonition in one report, to those attending at the Crystal Palace, to be assiduous and on time at the rehearsals. Poor attendance at the Birmingham rehearsals could also invoke a fine, which appears to have been a necessary sanction, for the choralists do not seem to have been as serious about things as the organisers. The choir was 181-strong (72 sopranos, 36 altos, 32 tenors and 41 basses) but the average attendance at the weekly rehearsals in 1871, was only 93. Perhaps the fact that only a selected group could attend festivals discouraged the rest? Who knows?

The Cecilian Society
This body is, presumably, not connected with the St. Cecilia Society active in the singing of glees earlier in the century since, in 1861, it is announcing only its *fifth* annual concert. This was held on 27th December in J. Hardman's large room in Newhall Hill. The society was devoted to communal singing in a different style from that of the glee, and Pergolesi, Mozart and Mendelssohn were performed, with harmonium and two-piano accompaniment. A Mr. H. Gould conducted and a competent standard seems to have been attained.

The Flute Society
Another society, dedicated to making music among small groups of the people, was the Flute Society. For gentlemen to play the flute in groups had been as much a social activity in the instrumental sphere as glee-clubs were in the vocal one. A widespread interest in the instrument was obviously enormously increased by the fact that Frederick the Great of Prussia, grandson of England's Hanoverian King George I, was a skilled player. Between 1734 and 1740, just before becoming emperor, Frederick had been able to devote a great deal of time to music and literature. From this period, then, it was just as much a social 'plus point' for a gentleman to play the flute, as it was for a lady to play the harp. A Manchester flute society called the Gentlemen's Concerts was founded in 1774, which was really a band of twenty-six flutes, and in general, whenever an instrumental group was formed it was overburdened with flautists. Sometimes, as in Dublin, they so overwhelmed the other instruments they had to be limited in number. The craze affected the whole of the British Isles and it really seems that, for once, Birmingham may have been late in the field. It may be that informal groups did exist here earlier, which kept no record of their activities, but the formal Flute Society mentioned above, was not founded until 1871.

This was a private club admitting a handful of amateur flautists, a pianist and a conductor. They played mainly for their own pleasure but gave occasional and apparently successful concerts for charity. The society had its genesis in 1856 when the Stourbridge-born James Mathews (1827-1900) whom we have already encountered, founded the Birmingham Flute Trio and Quartet Society.[2] It became the Birmingham Flute Society in 1871 and was finally disbanded in the 1950s. Its useful library was also passed to the Birmingham School of Music, now the Birmingham Conservatoire. Several members of the highly and variously gifted Mathews family had early and important connections with the Birmingham and Midland Institute; something in James Mathews' mind no doubt, when the ultimate destiny of the library, should the society cease to exist, was decided.

A fuller account of chamber music in general in nineteenth century Birmingham will be given in chapter 17.

---

1. Ernest Legouvé, quoted by Henry Pleasants op. cit.
2. Margaret Lowe: *James Mathews and his Marvellous Flute* (Article in the *Magazine of the Black Country*. Winter 1992 vol. 25 no. 1).

Chapter 11

The Harrison Concerts.
Another gallery of celebrities

The subject of this chapter is in reality a continuation of the last one as being evidence of the fact that Birmingham was enjoying more music than just that presented at the Musical Festivals so that Sullivan's boa constrictor gibe was amusing but wrong. The information available about Harrison's Concerts is copious, since the majority of the programmes have been kept, and it will easily take up the whole of a chapter, which in any case these concerts merit.

It must be said immediately that this series was perhaps the most significant one to be put on in nineteenth century Birmingham, since it brought a very large number of the greatest musical stars of the age to the town regularly every year. The extraordinary thing is that it has attracted virtually no attention from anyone writing about the town's musical history so far. Sutcliffe Smith [1] bestows very little attention on these concerts; yet it seems to the present writer that not only did they play a very important part in keeping the musical flag flying between the festivals, they were in themselves trail blazers.

Beginning in 1853 and continued with great success until 1916, they made a great deal of money for their promoter in the process. They exploited the same kind of audience as the festivals yet, for a good part of their existence, were called Harrison's Popular Concerts. Thomas Harrison came to live in Birmingham in 1844 and died there on 19th January 1908, aged 89. Initially, he was assisted in the management of the concerts by Oscar Pollack, a later Birmingham correspondent of the *Musical Times*. Thomas's son, Percy, who took over his father's project, died less that ten years after his father, in December 1917, at the age of 71.

The Harrisons certainly exploited the musical public's love of singing stars but, by 1866, they were bringing in people who would play Haydn and Beethoven chamber music, and involving pianists who played Schubert, Chopin and Liszt. By 1875, the Hallé Orchestra was making its first visit to the town. This was all before Richter's arrival as festival conductor in 1882 and must have helped to develop people's musical taste and to prepare music-lovers for the changes in the festival programmes that Richter was able to make; of which more anon.

The concerts were presented at the Town Hall, of course, and there were four each season, two in the Autumn and two in the Spring. The long list of great vocalists who appeared is given below, in chronological order of their appearance in this series; that is, apart from Patti, who is given pride of place at the top.

	Adelina Patti	
Sims Reeves	Christine Nilsson	Kirkby Lunn
Guilia Grisi	Ben Davies	John McCormack
Mario	Nellie Melba	Luisa Tetrazzini
Clara Novello	Emma Albani	Elena Gerhardt
Hermine Rudersdorff	Clara Butt	Walter Hyde[4]
Theresa Tietjens	Alice Gomez	John Coates
Miss Banks[2]	Ada Crossley	Edna Thornton
Helen Sherrington[3]	Carrie James	Carrie Tubb
Edith Wynne	Kennerley Rumford	Maggie Teyte
Edward Lloyd	Robert Radford	Princess Iwa
Charles Santley	Louise Dale	Agnes Nicholls

The singers in Harrison's series

Some of the singers in the above list were in fact heard live by people still living today, as for example Elena Gerhardt. In a few cases also, recordings are extant. From these two sources we are able to learn of the high standard of the singers at these concerts and, by implication, at the Birmingham Musical Festivals. Running like a golden thread through the Harrison series, from 1874 to 1907, however, were the regular appearances of the incomparable Queen of Song, Adelina Patti. She came to sing for Harrison approximately every other year, on a total of fifteen occasions. Add to these fifteen appearances in the Harrison Celebrity Concerts her two festival appearances in 1861 and 1864, at the ages of 18 and 21 respectively, and we can appreciate how much the Birmingham public adored her. Some idea of her quality comes to us from contemporary comment, but we can now form an impression of it ourselves, on a compact disc, in a remastered version of a small part of a recording she made in 1906, just before she retired. She was 63 years of age at that time, but we can still hear the purity and richness of a voice that, quite obviously, must always have been incapable of emitting an ugly or harsh sound.

Many people in the later years of Patti's career were growing resistant to the Italian school of florid operatic singing, in an age when Schubert and Wagner had created a demand for a totally different vocal style. One of these objectors was a New York critic, Henry T. Finck, who later apologised for his merciless denunciation of Patti earlier, in the following terms:

'No doubt everything I said about Patti's shortcomings was true. She was infinitely more interested in showing off her lovely voice than in the music she sang. The composer was for her a mere peg to hang on her trills and frills... But as a singer

Chapter 11 - The Harrison Concerts. Another gallery of celebrities

she was glorious, so incomparable, that while under the spell of her vocal art the listeners forgot everything else and simply luxuriated in ecstatic bliss. I wrote... describing the charm of her voice and the ingratiating spontaneity of her singing. I consider myself fortunate in having been able to listen twice a week to the sweetest and most mellow voice the world has ever heard...

Patti was a nightingale; why ask more of her? In her way she was absolutely perfect, and perfection of any kind should be honored (sic) and extolled, without any of the buts and ifs on which I dwelt too much'.[5]

The same writer also thought, however, that Patti would have given one of her beautiful black eyes to have sung and acted in a Wagner opera.

Adelina Patti 1843-1919.

Bernard Shaw, also, writes of,

'Patti of the beautiful eloquent voice, so perfectly produced and controlled that its most delicate *pianissimo* reaches the remotest listener in the Albert Hall: Patti of the unerring ear, with her magical *roulade* soaring to heavenly altitudes: Patti of the pure strong tone that made 'God Save the Queen' sound fresh and noble at Covent Garden: Patti of the hushed, tender notes that reconcile rows of club-loving cynics to 'Home, Sweet Home'. This was the famous artist who last night sang 'Bel raggio' (from *Semiramide*) and 'Comin' thro' the Rye' incomparably'.

These extracts give us the flavour of the great Patti phenomenon, enjoyed by the audiences in Birmingham's own Town Hall, just as much as by those who saw and heard her at the Albert Hall or Covent Garden - or in New York. Harrison would have to pay her a large fee for this privilege, £600 equivalent to £18,000 now, but he also knew that every time she came he was sure of a packed house, with hundreds more in a jostling crowd outside, hoping against hope for the chance of a place in the hall. He also organised her English-Irish tour, between 26th October and 27th November 1891. This started in Birmingham and took her to Hanley, Manchester (Free Trade Hall), Huddersfield, Sheffield, London (Albert Hall), Brighton, Wolverhampton (The Drill Hall), Liverpool (old Philharmonic Hall), Dublin, Belfast and Cork. Patti, like Liszt and other soloists before her, toured with a concert party. This included a quartet of vocal soloists of good standard, and a solo pianist and solo violinist, both female.

The instrumentalists

But a procession of brilliant solo instrumentalists also troops its way through the Harrison list of performers, right from the beginning, when Madame Pleyel came in 1853, playing the ever-popular Fantasias on operatic airs by Prudent and Liszt. Charles Hallé, Joachim and the latter's quartet appeared in this series and in 1866, on 20th February at 8 p.m., we know that the quartet gave Haydn's Quartet op. 76 no. 2, Hallé a Beethoven Piano Sonata (op. 26 in A flat), and Joachim a *Romance in G* by the same composer. The Mendelssohn Piano Trio in C minor completed the programme. On this occasion the personnel of the quartet was slightly different from that the year before, at the Monday Popular Concerts. This time Joachim, Louis Ries, William Hann and Alfredo Piatti played, Hann having replaced Webb as violist. Later Ludwig Straus replaced Hann as we see from the following photograph.

This concert was graced by the presence of Sims Reeves and Miss Banks, the latter contributing lighter items. Reeves sang Beethoven's *Adelaïde,* accompanied by C. J. Stevens who was accompanist for the Amateur Harmonic society. Hallé, Joachim and Piatti were regular visitors to the Harrison series and, notably, the two last (sharing a programme with singers Lemmens-Sherrington and Vernon Rigby) were to combine their talents with those of Clara Schumann. On 17th February 1870, Madame Schumann, as she was called in the programme, played her husband's four *Nachtstücke* op. 23, also Mendelssohn's Scherzo in E minor. (Should this be B minor?).

The Joachim Quartet, 1888 (Joachim, Louis Ries, Ludwig Straus and Piatti).

Chapter 11 - The Harrison Concerts. Another gallery of celebrities

Left - Clara Schumann, 1819-1896. Right - Wilma Norman-Neruda, Lady Hallé, 1839-1911, leading a quartet 'At the Monday Pops'.

She was also pianist with Joachim and Piatti in Beethoven's Piano Trio in G major op. 1 no. 2 and with Joachim in Mozart's Violin and Piano Sonata in A (no. 17 of Hallé's edition, according to the programme). She had already visited the town in 1867, apparently, during a tour organised by John Chappell.

Both Harrisons must surely be given credit for enabling Birmingham to hear some of the finest artists available, in masterpieces from the chamber music repertoire. This was the case from the mid-1860s onward and indeed, from 1871, they seem to have run some Classical Chamber Concerts, as they were called, in the Masonic Hall, New Street. A string quartet led by Madame Norman-Neruda (later Lady Hallé) with Hallé at the piano played there – with the indispensable vocal solos from Madame Tellefsen – on Tuesday 19th December 1871. The series ticket cost one guinea (£1.1s or £1.05p) and tickets for the individual concerts were six, four and two shillings, or 30p, 20p, and 10p. It is hard to tell if this particular series lasted. One suspects not, since some of Stephen Stratton's Concerts at the same venue ran as Popular Chamber Concerts between 1879 and 1884.

The Hallé-Neruda connection with Harrison most certainly continued, however, and at the Town Hall on 19th November 1873 'The Celebrated Band of Mr. Charles Hallé', augmented to seventy performers gave what was probably the first of their many Birmingham concerts. The programme included Beethoven's *Leonora Overture* no. 3, Mendelssohn's *Italian* Symphony and small Schubert and Hérold items. The orchestra also accompanied Edith Wynne and Charles Santley in the duet 'Crudel, perché' from Mozart's *Figaro* with their conductor, Charles Hallé himself, in Weber's *Concert Piece* for piano and orchestra, op. 79.

Chamber music was not abandoned, and in March 1874 we find a Haydn Piano Trio in G being performed by Joachim and Piatti with the excellent Agnes Zimmerman at the piano. It may be noted in passing that Agnes Zimmerman also composed small-scale works, in the classical style, and edited the piano sonatas of Mozart and Beethoven.

The Hallé orchestra paid another visit to our Town Hall in January 1875 with Frederick Cowen as solo pianist. Cowen also appeared in this series as conductor of the orchestra Harrison employed for the majority of his concerts. Where the players came from for this orchestra it is not possible to be certain, but one guesses that its composition would be much as it was at the festivals, with most from London or the Hallé Orchestra and a small contingent from the home town. Again a list may be the simplest and clearest way of showing the distinguished instrumental soloists employed by Harrison, all of them of the highest calibre, with the years of their visits.

Instrumentalists at Harrisons Concerts, 1853-1916

Charles Hallé	piano and conductor	Regular visits
Joseph Joachim	violin	"
Alfredo Piatti	cello	"
Wilma Neruda, Lady Hallé	violin	"
August Wilhelmj	violin, 1875	
Arabella Goddard	piano, 1877	
James Stimpson	organ, 1878, 1879, 1880	
Hans von Bülow	1878★, 1880★	
C. W. Perkins	organ, 1898, 1905	
Walter Bache	piano, 1880	
Fanny Davies	piano, 1888, 1914, 1915	
Pablo Sarasate	violin, 1890, 1896, 1906	
Adelina de Lara	piano, 1894	
Arthur de Greef	piano, 1895, 1898, 1900	
Mark Hambourg	piano, 1897, 1914	
Nettie Carpenter	violin, 1897	
Adela Verne	piano, 1898	
Paderewski	piano, 1898, 1901, 1902, 1907, 1912	
Eugène Ysaÿe	violin, 1902, 1913	
Ferruccio Busoni	piano, 1902, 1906	
Jan Kubelik	violin, 1902, 1903, 1908	
Percy Grainger	piano, 1902	
Pablo Casals	'cello, 1912	
Wilhelm Backhaus	piano, 1913	
Fritz Kreisler	violin, 1913	
Marie Hall	violin, 1904	

Instrumentalists at Harrisons Concerts, 1853-1916 (Cont.)
Egon Petri   piano, 1904
Irene Scharrer   piano, 1909
Vladimir de Pachmann   piano, 1910
Albert Sammons   violin 1916
★ These recitals, as with several solo recitals, were held in the Masonic Hall.

Accompanists
C. J. Stevens   Date uncertain
F. T. Watkis   1902
G. H. Manton   1902, 1903
E. A. Sewell   1903, 1905, 1906
Frank Mummery   1904
Hamilton Harty   1904, 1908, 1909, 1916
Stanley Hawley   1906
R. J. Forbes   1907, 1910, 1912, 1913, 1914, 1915
Harold Craxton   1915

NOTE TO THE ABOVE:
A. This list is not exhaustive.

Programme notes were provided quite early on in the series. Those by Edgar F. Jacques (1901) were both informal in style and informative in substance, with musical quotations. Alfred Kalisch and Percy Pitt's were used on 3rd March 1906, for example, and were very short and factual, though themes were given. We are not surprised to see Ernest Newman's name at the foot of some notes in 1908. These quoted themes and gave some explanation, but were more succinct than those of Edgar Jacques, which were quite lengthy.

The widening of the repertoire has been mentioned as a feature of this series so perhaps we may pick out some examples. Joachim included some Bach in a programme on 11th March 1875. He played the *Andante* and *Allegro* from Bach's Third Sonata for violin in A minor, (presumably the third of Six Sonatas BWV 1014 to 1019). Von Bülow included Schubert's Impromptu op. 90 no. 3 in 1880 and the Birmingham-born Walter Bache championed his beloved Liszt at a concert in the same year. Another visiting pianist with a very long concert life, lasting well on into the twentieth century and who eventually gave radio recitals, was Adelina de Lara, a Clara Schumann *protégée*. She played a Wagner-Liszt transcription and a *Romance* by Tchaikovsky on 29th January, 1894. This last item was pencilled into the programme and was substituted for something else, obviously to commemorate the composer's death two months earlier. De Lara demonstrated that classical style which treated the piano as a friend with a beautiful voice, which had only to be conjured out of it by the most sensitive of touches. It was not an enemy to be conquered as sometimes seems to be the case today!

Mark Hambourg, in 1897, brought a Chopin and Liszt programme, while Arthur de Greef (1898) played Beethoven (the Piano Variations in C minor), Chopin, Brahms, Grieg, Saint-Saëns, Liszt, and a *Tarantella* of his own composing. Paderewski, on an Erard piano in the Town Hall on 28th March 1898, gave the *Brahms-Handel Variations*, Beethoven's Piano Sonata op. 57, a Schubert Impromptu in B flat, some Schubert-Liszt transcriptions with other items, and concluded with Liszt's Sixth *Rhapsodie* for piano. In 1901, he gave Beethoven's Sonata op. 111, Schumann's *Carnaval*, Chopin's *Ballade* in A flat and some Liszt. Ysaÿe and Busoni managed to include a Bach item in their contribution to a programme in 1902, as did Percy Grainger, later in the same year. For on 6th October he was to be found sharing a programme with Patti herself, together with Charles Santley, baritone, and Gregory Hast, tenor. The accompanist was F. T. Watkis. Patti sang 'Casta Diva' (Bellini: *Norma*), 'The Last Rose of Summer' and 'Quand tu chantes' by Gounod. Santley contributed 'O ruddier than the cherry' (Handel: *Acis and Galatea*) and Hast 'Un aura amorosa' from Mozart's *Così fan tutte*. Grainger played the contemporary Cyril Scott's *An English Waltz* and Tausig's piano arrangement of Bach's Toccata and Fugue in D minor for organ. We are not nowadays very happy with the Tausig arrangements but they then had the merit of drawing attention to Bach himself, perhaps kindling a desire to hear the music in its original form.

Thus it will be seen that Harrison still employed a judicious mixture of the frankly popular with items that were musically more demanding, but never did he deviate from his well-tried policy of finding the very best performers.

Picking up the threads again, in 1902 Grainger also played as accompanist for Alice Liebmann, in Grieg's Violin Sonata in C minor, composed 1886-7, fifteen years earlier. Then on 3rd December 1906 Busoni played Chopin and Liszt and Sarasate gave some unidentified Bach - either a violin sonata or two movements from an unaccompanied Partita.

In 1906 Willy Hess, leader of the Hallé Orchestra brought a string quartet which played Dvorak's Quartet in F op. 96 (The American) and the first movement of Beethoven's op. 18 no. 5. Casals, in 1912, played Boccherini, Lalo and Fauré and in 1914, Fanny Davies the pianist, who received her early training in Birmingham, performed Beethoven's Sonata op. 27 no. 1 and a Moskowski Concert Study.

There are here small straws in the wind of change in musical taste that do indicate the move away from the old Italian domination. Ironically, it was a singer, Elena Gerhardt, who presented the most boldly chosen programmes, in 1909 and 1911. An incomparable *lieder* singer, with taste and artistry of a high order, as well as the possessor of a beautiful voice, she gave the Birmingham audience groups of Schubert, Brahms, Wolf and Strauss songs. What a privilege! Did the audience appreciate just how lucky they were? Her accompanist in 1909 was Hamilton Harty.

Chapter 11 - The Harrison Concerts. Another gallery of celebrities

The Orchestras at Harrison's Concerts
The Hallé Orchestra, conducted by Charles Hallé came six times between 1873 and 1899, the Richter Concerts Orchestra gave one concert under Richter himself, the New Symphony Orchestra directed by Landon Ronald visited in 1908 and the London Symphony Orchestra conducted by Elgar, Henry Wood and Nikisch gave four concerts between 1905 and 1915. The Queen's Hall orchestra added a further four visits to this list, between 1905 and 1913. The programmes they all brought covered the then orchestral repertoire pretty extensively and one cannot help but think that these visits from nationally-known orchestras must have played a large part in the drive within the city to establish a permanent orchestra of its own.

As a postscript, an interesting feature of a number of Harrison Concerts were small groups of accomplished singers and instrumentalists contributing some lighter items. Such were the Meister Glee Singers; a quartet of four men, alto, tenor, baritone and bass, who visited in 1892 and 1901. They were William Sexton, Gregory Hast, W. G. Forington and Webster Norcross. At least one of these, Gregory Hast, went on to make a career as a solo singer, often appearing with Clara Butt. Then, in 1892, the 'Meister Singers' were assisted by the Fraser Quintette, five sisters whose capabilities can be listed as follows: Violet was a singer, Ida played violin and piano, Ethel the viola and piano, and Mabel and Stella both played the violin. Two other vocal quartets were the Dilettante Vocal Quartette (which consisted of four gentlemen!), and the Alexandra Ladies Quartet, which explains itself. They sang for Harrison in 1895 and 1906, respectively, the Alexandra Ladies appearing on this latter occasion in the same programme with Patti, Robert Radford, Ben Davies, solo pianist Elsie Horne and the accompanist Stanley Hawley.

Again on the lighter side, Harrison managed to capture the Gilbert and Sullivan singer George Grossmith for one of his 'Humorous and Musical Recitals'. Some of the sketches are listed with titles such as 'Affectations', 'Somebodies and Nobodies' (he was co-author with his brother of *Diary of a Nobody*) and 'Hey Diddle Diddle' 'as sung by an amateur glee party'. The programme announced that Mr. Grossmith would accompany himself on a Brinsmead Grand Pianoforte. The show was put on at the Temperance Hall in Temple Street on Monday and Tuesday 13th and 14th of October, 1902, at 8 p.m. Ticket prices were 3/- reserved and 2/- unreserved (three shillings and two shillings, or 15p and 10p) and admission was one shilling (1/- or 5p).

On 28th March 1916 the great 60-year-long Harrison series came to an end, because of Percy Harrison's retirement, followed by his death in 1917, his father having died in 1908. Clara Butt and five other soloists, with Harold Craxton as accompanist, performed at the final concert. Butt sang her usual repertoire of songs by Graham Peel, Stanford, Herbert Hughes and Frederick Cowen, adding what seems an uncharacteristic item for her, Debussy's *Air de Lia*. According to a piece in a local paper about Harrison's retirement, there were photographs of 'his' artists in his office, the one of Clara Butt being signed 'To Daddy, from Baby'. Harrison - presumably Percy - had introduced her to the musical world in her young days and to him she owed a great deal for the success of her career, which was mainly on the concert platform. This was true too of her husband, the baritone Kennerley Rumford, whom she married in 1900. To begin with, Harrison paid Clara Butt less than ten guineas (£10.10s or £10.50p) and, with a 'take' of over £1,000, it is no wonder that Harrison made money, even if there were other soloists to pay.

Another photograph in the Harrison office was of the pianist Paderewski, signed in this case 'To my dear Bishop'. Our younger concert organiser evidently looked like a robust parson, but this dedication, and that on Clara Butt's photograph, do show clearly the easy and perhaps affectionate relationship Harrison had with his artists. It is certain that Percy Harrison had always superintended his concerts personally, being an enthusiastic believer in his performers and in their music.

Clara Butt, contralto, 1873-1936.

Who attended these concerts? The series must have been sustained mainly by local people with the money, time and interest to spare, rather than drawing on an audience from far and wide, as the festivals did. With tickets costing two shillings and five shillings (10p and 25p) and programmes 1/- or 5p, a skilled craftsman, especially if he was not married, could save up and attend occasionally. The professional and business people, relatively much better off than today, could attend every concert. In any case a 'take' of over a £1,000 implies a full house of two thousand people. That the Harrisons had rendered a great service to Birmingham is indisputable. The fact that they made money out of it is something which should make us pause for thought and ask why this was. A discussion of this point will be taken up in the chapter about the end of the Musical Festivals.

---

1. J. Sutcliffe Smith: *The Story of Music in Birmingham*. Birmingham. 1945.
2. Miss Banks also appeared at the Monday Popular Concerts.
3. Helen Sherrington was known as Mme. Lemmens - Sherrington after her marriage to the Belgian composer, Lemmens.
4. Walter Hyde was born in Birmingham and received his initial training at the Midland Institute School of Music.
5. Quoted in Henry Pleasants. op. cit.

Chapter 12

Some Birmingham musical personalities

Edward, Walter and Constance Bache

The huge popularity of vocal music, both to be listened to and taken part in, brought many benefits, not the least of which was that it took thousands of people into the gloriously satisfying realm of fine and beautiful music. Wherever people gathered together, in churches or in houses, a choir or vocal group was sure to be formed, either officially or unofficially. The new, cheap editions of oratorios published by Novello were bought in vast quantities. In homes, young and old with a good ear and a modicum of voice, sang duets and quartets from the oratorios and operas they had heard and seen, and wanted to 'have a go at' themselves. A world of music was opened to many people which they might not otherwise have entered.

All this was very fine and desirable, but there was an undoubted imbalance which weighed against instrumental music, rather the reverse of the situation pertaining for most of the twentieth century. There were, however, a number of people who were anxious to make playing an instrument as much a matter of course for ordinary people as singing in a choir then was. If a sound foundation of generally available instrumental training were to be instituted, talents would emerge and from these, in turn, orchestras could be formed as readily as choirs had been. Stockley's effort to form a regular orchestra to accompany Festival Choral Society concerts have been detailed and his further success in the orchestral field will be described later.

Someone else who had been concerned about this problem was Edward Bache. His father, the Rev. Samuel Bache, was a Unitarian minister and noted teacher who also ran a Proprietory School, opened on the 12th October 1767 according to Aris's Birmingham Gazette. Among the pupils entrusted to his care were W. C. Gully, a later Speaker in the House of Commons, David Martineau, member of a prominent local family, and Charles Flower of Shakespeare Memorial Theatre fame. The school also took boarders. Three of Bache's own family of five sons and two daughters were outstandingly musical. These were Edward, Walter and Constance. Constance's account of the lives of these two brothers was published by Methuen in London in 1901, under the title of *Brother Musicians*.

Edward

If Edward's outstanding musical abilities showed themselves early it was not entirely surprising, since Mrs. Bache, the mother, was a gifted pianist. It was clear to his parents that Edward's should be a musical career. He was the eldest son, nine years older than pianist brother Walter who, in the end, made more of a mark in the musical world, since he enjoyed a longer life. By 1846, at the age of 13, Edward was talented enough to play under Mendelssohn's baton at the first performance of *Elijah*. He was a violin pupil of Alfred Mellon, at that time leader of the orchestra at the town's Theatre Royal. Even as a very small child, when he wanted to have the Hallelujah chorus played to him, Edward would seek out the family's volume of *Messiah*. By the age of three he wanted to look at a score of Beethoven's *Pastoral Symphony,* one supplied by a Birmingham music-seller no doubt. While having violin lessons from Mellon, he also had tuition in composition from the Town Hall organist, James Stimpson. In 1849, he moved to London and was taught by Sterndale Bennett. After that he went to Leipzig to study (as who did not in those days?) and heard and commented on the music of all kinds which he heard there. It was then that he appreciated how sound, back in Birmingham, James Stimpson's training had been.

After his return home in 1855, Edward Bache wrote a number of critical pieces about the Birmingham Musical Festival and also contributed to the still-existing *Birmingham Music Journal*. Then he prepared a series of chamber concerts to be given with a Mr. Deichmann. The first took place, but Bache was not well enough to undertake the second, and by the winter of 1857 he was mortally ill in Torquay where he had been sent in the vain of hope of some improvement. He died of tuberculosis on 24th August, 1858. A memorial window was dedicated to him in the new Church of the Messiah, in Broad Street, opened in 1862, where a concert was given in his memory in 1863.

Bache's own compositions are, of course, small in number and bear strong evidence of his devotion to Mendelssohn, and to his own teacher, Sterndale Bennett. We can only speculate about what he might have achieved had he lived to a mature age.

Walter

In a letter dated 12th February 1856, Edward is to be found advising his younger brother Walter not to take up the profession of music because, in England, he says, it is badly paid and poorly esteemed. Nevertheless, Walter Bache (1842-88) did become a musician, and was a good pianist and teacher. He became a professor of piano at the Royal Academy of Music and the arch-promoter of Liszt's music in England. Walter had been a pupil of Liszt and a Liszt-Bache Scholarship was later established at the Academy of Music in his memory.

Walter seems to have been a noble and selfless person, as well as a good musician. Liszt had taught him 'enthusiasm and the power of sustained hard work', and Walter was eternally grateful for that. Walter's charming and likeable nature was all his own, however.

Constance
The gifts bestowed on his sister Constance (1846-1903), were as much literary as musical. Treated by big brother as the little sister who tagged on behind, Constance was 'allowed' to sing in the chorus at some of Walter's concerts, but earned her own fame through her translations into English of *The Early Correspondence of Hans von Bülow* (1846) and the libretto of Humperdinck's opera *Hansel and Gretel*. This family, with its connections into the wider musical world, well beyond the confines of this town, seems to be typical of many of Birmingham's musical citizens - in all ages one suspects.

Edward Bache's plea
Even more relevant to the topic of nineteenth century developments in our musical life, however, is Edward Bache's passionate plea, in letters written in 1856, for more training to be organised for instrumentalists in Birmingham, capable of being used in, or even constituting, the festival orchestra.

Although Birmingham has the very best vocalists at its concerts and festivals, he writes, it often fails on the instrumental side. 'If an orchestra', he says 'could once be organised and kept up in Birmingham, there would be nothing to prevent our singers from availing themselves of its assistance; whereas at present the vocal music itself suffers from the want of proper accompaniments. To those who may urge that they care only for vocal music, and do not care for *fiddling* (a generic term often applied to orchestral performances by those who have never heard very good ones), the answer is that if there were an orchestra they would be able to hear their favourite vocal pieces rendered still more effectively than before'.

It is significant that Bache has to explain that most of such pieces were not written with a piano or organ accompaniment, which is what they usually got, but that the composers had expected an orchestra to be available. He goes on to point out that 'scandalously exorbitant terms are paid in England, and in England only, to a few foreign singers'. In this respect, he affirms, England is the laughing-stock of all continental nations, and it is well known that from Mozart's time onwards the 'English public were first gulled by the pretence of giving charitable concerts, and then plundered to the utmost extent' by these 'generous' performers. This was the 'musical entrance to John Bull's treasure-chambers'. Meanwhile, the bitter (and true) comment is added that the generality of indigenous musicians earn scarcely enough for their immediate wants.

Finally, Edward Bache calls for positive thinking and makes a wise comment which we would do well to heed today. He says that in England 'we are in too great

Left - F. Edward Bache.
Right - The Three B's - B sharp, B flat and B natural (Bülow, Buonamici and Walter Bache).

a habit of legislating for only an abnormal or negative state of society; whereas, by giving some attention to fostering the good which is, we should be spared much time wasted on correcting the evil'. He suggests that those who have derived a fortune from their commerce in Birmingham should aid those who, by their skills, have given pleasure to those more fortunate, while being unable to earn a proper living themselves. In any case, constant listening to good performances would raise everyone's standard, not least that majority of young ladies in England for whom music was a part of their education!

Thomas Anderton
Another Birmingham composer who did not make a big mark in the wider world was Thomas Anderton, born in 1836. He wrote a number of works for specific Birmingham occasions which were well-received locally, and he played an active part as a lecturer on musical topics at the Birmingham and Midland Institute. Some of his scores are available for inspection at the Birmingham Central Library.

What is more significant to us now is that Anderton was also running a series of Subscription Orchestral Concerts on Saturday afternoons at the Masonic Hall. Well-known soloists were employed and the concerts were certainly in existence by 1869, before William Stockley established his orchestral concerts in 1873.

Charles Lunn 1838-1906. A prophet without honour in his own country

One who obviously thought that the Midland Institute was not conducting its music operation to the best advantage was the Birmingham-born Charles Lunn. A tenor who trained in Italy, Lunn had a national reputation as a singer and writer on singing. His book *Philosophy of Voice,* in which he set out in clear terms the old teachings of Porpora and Manuel Garcia, ran into nine editions. In his ideas about the relationship of art to society he owed a great deal to his friend John Ruskin, art critic and thinker, to whose circle Lunn belonged. In this elevated sphere Lunn was valued, for he was evidently entertaining and well-informed. He was also a fearless advocate of his ideas, but this cut no ice in Birmingham and the colder his reception in the town, the more heated Lunn became. He wrote open letters, and had them printed at his own expense, 'for gratuitous circulation' and these were addressed to subsequent Mayors of Birmingham – still 'mayors' as Birmingham was not then a city. He pleaded for their support in the establishment of an Academy of Music in Birmingham.

Lunn did much to destroy his own case by letting his feelings muddle his thoughts, which made his letters long-winded, to say the least. After a cold and dusty answer from Joseph Chamberlain to his first letter, Lunn felt hurt and became defensive, which made things worse. His letters abound in *non-sequiturs* and he writes just as he thinks, moved by strong indignation against various entrenched groups and individuals. These people he sees as constituting a Birmingham musical establishment which is taking everything in the wrong direction. It is worth examining what he said in a little more detail for the light it sheds on music in general in the Birmingham of a century ago.

The continuing dominance of London

In a speech given in 1876, Joseph Chamberlain lamented the 'absorption of National Institutions in London'. Lunn pounced on this, believing that those with civic power would welcome ideas from local professional musicians. This would be especially so, Lunn thought, if they had experience, drawn from the wider world – as his was of course! – as to how musical education might best be put on a permanent institutional basis. In this belief he was mistaken. The civic powers preferred either to go about things in their own sweet way, or to do nothing at all. To make things worse, the Midland Institute was offended by the implication that the things it was already doing did not seriously count as a musical establishment. The slurs implied in Lunn's letters were all the more irritating in that they were essentially true. Lunn also attacked the Tonic Sol-fa-ists and on this issue came into direct conflict with Stockley, the 'Honorary Principal' of the vocal operation at the Institute.

Lunn was not alone among private music teachers in being thoroughly alarmed by developments at the Midland Institute. Hundreds of interested amateurs could go to the Institute and receive musical training at minimal cost, simply because they wanted to. The private teacher could not compete with this, and the Institute's own standards were being dragged down. This 'music education for all who want it' philosophy was not entirely abandoned until after 1970. As we shall see, it delayed the establishment of a fully professional conservatoire and perpetuated a certain discomfort in the face of excellence - if it was produced locally that is. This was another facet of the many points Lunn made in his open letters. Birmingham needed to see itself not just as a city, which it was by the time of his last letter (1893), but to be more like the capitals of the world. It should aim to lead in music as confidently as it did in manufacturing. It often produced good musicians, he wrote, but could not train them up to the highest excellence. He was also alarmed at the cost of importing expensive soloists, especially singers, from outside to the Festivals. Many in Birmingham, including Edward Bache, would have agreed with him about this, for it was one factor among others helping to bring about the demise of the Festivals in 1912.

Lunn points to the success, both artistic and financial, of his own pupils' concerts at the Town Hall. He also quotes in his defence glowing reviews of his book, *Philosophy of Voice,* culled from journals published in Milan, Leipzig, San Francisco and London. Much of his adverse criticism of his home town was clearly justified, however tactlessly expressed. With the final words of his last open letter, however, we can surely all agree when he writes that Birmingham should 'divest itself of all narrow-mindedness and pride, and the profession of all jealousy and conceit, and so by mutual union make Birmingham able to compete successfully in Art as it has hitherto competed successfully with the world in manufacture'.

Lunn moved to London in 1895, ostracized by his native city.

Chapter 13

Musical Education.
The establishment of the Midland Institute School of Music

It may help to consider first what happened to music education after the chantry schools were converted into grammar schools. The all-round education of Renaissance man, which most certainly included skill in music, had been swept aside in many places by the utilitarian ideas of the late Tudor period. This is interesting in the light of arguments still raging today about the proper place of music in schools - that is if it has any place at all of course! Outside the choir schools, boys were to be educated for the practicalities of mercantile or professional life, an aspect of pedagogic theory which increasingly separated the way boys and girls were educated. Any possibility of including music in the syllabus of the new independent and grammar schools seems to have related mainly to the ideas of the individual headmaster, or pedagogue as he was called in Birmingham. In his treatise of 1570, called *The Scholemaster,* Roger Ascham, tutor and secretary to Queen Elizabeth I, had expressed the thought that music was a reasonable study to help fit a man for life, provided not too much time was spent on it! On the other hand, William Kempe's *The Education of Children in Learning* (1588), does not mention music at all, while Richard Mulcaster, headmaster of Merchant Taylor's and St. Paul's Schools, in 1581 advocated the teaching of singing as a basic necessity. By contrast again, a specific statute of 1600, imposed on Blackburn Grammar School, founded in Elizabeth I's reign, decreed that 'writing, ciphering, singing and such-like' should be outside the normal curriculum, which embraced only the classics, arithmetic, geometry and cosmography. The governors had the fitting of the children for the world of work and trade firmly in the front of their minds. The 'such-like' mentioned in the above list were extras to be paid for, and among these was music.

General education in the eighteenth century was still scarce and sporadic in its provision, the churches having been the main providers of schooling for those of small means. Affluent parents, or ones in comfortable circumstances, employed private tutors or sent their children to some small private school. Education in music for the majority would mainly be a matter of having private teachers or simply singing hymns in the church schools. These could vary widely, with some surprisingly accomplished people cropping up in surprising places. Musico-genetic material does not look at a map or at the size of a person's house or income before deciding where to bestow itself. The family of a blacksmith in Middlesbrough, in about 1900, to take an example, were all outstandingly gifted musically.[1] Local teachers, perhaps the church organist or sometimes the incumbent himself, may have provided tuition in such a case, the gift of an excellent musical ear supplying the rest.

To focus more particularly on Birmingham, the attentive reader will already realise that there had always been some gifted musician or musicians living in the town, from the Gild's organist, Sir William Bothe and his predecessors, to the minstrels who entertained the Shuttleworths in 1609 and on, over the next hundred years and more, to Gunn, Broome, Barker, Kempson. Hobbs, Clarke, Simms and Alfred Mellon, to mention only some of those we know by name. We know quite certainly, too, that a number of these men offered *private* music teaching for those who could pay for it.

The huge population explosion in the country as a whole and the general migration to the towns, at the end of the eighteenth century, made a properly organised education system begin to seem an absolute necessity. By 1840, a number of churches in Birmingham and some benevolent individuals, were providing free schooling for the poorest children, the so-called Ragged Schools, while the longer established National or British schools made a charge for tuition. In 1850. however, two-thirds of children in school still left at the age of 10 to go to work, and it was to be a further fifty years before we achieved compulsory full-time education in this country, continuing into the teenage years. In spite of this, a lot of good work was done and some good foundations for further development laid.

As far as organised music teaching was concerned, we do know that 'music and singing' were introduced into the syllabus of the King Edward Foundation Elementary Schools from 1851, and their introduction in the Board Schools set up in 1870, together with the growth of large, well-attended Sunday Schools, were among developments which had their results in an ever-increasing interest in choral singing, in schools as well as in the adult world. Some specific societies for young people grew out of this movement between 1855 and 1880. One was the Sunday Schools Choral Union under the conductorship of different church organists. Between 1865 and 1878, and possibly for longer, a thousand children were involved in the Union's annual choral festivals, given at the Town Hall in aid of the Children's Hospital. Something of the order of sixteen schools took part in these.[2] Another society of this type, from 1855, was the Amateur Choral Union, whose members were drawn from the Board Schools in Bristol Street: and a third was the Tonic Sol-fa Society. The last requires a little more explanation.

Tonic sol-fa
The origins of the tonic sol-fa syllables, *doh, ray, me, fah, soh, lah, te, doh,* is to be found in the 'modes,' or 'moods', of the medieval period. The system as developed by John

Chapter 13 - Musical Education. The establishment of the Midland Institute School of Music

Curwen (1816-80), however, owes a great deal to a method used by a Miss Sarah Ann Glover for teaching her pupils in Norwich in the 1830s and 1840s. Both Curwen, a clergyman, and Miss Glover had religious and social as well as didactic aims, and believed that to teach children to read music was to confer an enormous benefit on them. They would learn to make music to the glory of God, and open their souls and minds to the peacable and heart-warming influence of great music. It would enable them either to sing or play it for themselves, or join with others for the same purpose.

The system attached a simple syllable to each note of the scale, from *doh* to *doh* as listed above. This was like a template which would fit any major key. It could be modified to fit the minor key, and also accommodate chromatic notes, notes raised or lowered a semitone in pitch by a sharp or flat placed before them. When flattened, syllables were given the vowel 'a' pronounced 'aw' (eg. *ray* became *ra*) and when sharpened the vowel given was 'e', pronounced 'ee' (e.g. *soh* became *se*). Curwen emphasised the importance of associating any note of the scale with its mental effect, especially as that effect related the note heard to the tonic, or *doh*. Thus *soh* (the dominant or fifth note of the scale) was bright, since it suggested the fanfare quality of the perfect fifth, and similar 'affects' were associated with every sol-fa syllable. This system was also very useful for teaching harmony to the average pupil. Once he or she had mastered the relationships of two triads, or chords, to each other in sol-fa terms (say the tonic to the dominant) this perception could then be applied to every other major or minor key. The arrival of atonal music cast a blight on the tonic sol-fa system and it has been abandoned completely as a teaching aid. Whatever its limitations, its merits or demerits, it was instrumental in establishing the idea that pretty well *every* child could be taught to read music. Miss Glover's Norwich Sol-fa Ladder, as she called her sol-fa chart (modulator), was a leg-up in musical terms for millions of children, during a period of about a hundred years.

Sarah Ann Glover, 1785-1867.

A perfect example of a rags-to-riches story brought about through tonic sol-fa is that of Henry Coward (1849-1944) of Sheffield. His own *Reminiscences* provide us with the details of his life.[3] Coward's father was a Sheffield grinder who was a banjo player and later a publican in Liverpool. His mother was a good singer. The father died when Henry was still young and the family moved back to Sheffield. At nine years of age, the boy was having to work as a trainee cutler and, in the absence of schooling, was teaching himself to read and write. He attended tonic sol-fa classes and then started a class of his own. This was good enough to give concerts, and Henry's success in this venture encouraged him to abandon his trade and become a school pupil-teacher. He was soon the headmaster of a primary school, working as a choral conductor at the same time. He formed an official Tonic Sol-fa Association in Sheffield and from this emerged the famed choral society, the Sheffield Musical Union. Coward conducted 60,000 children on the occasion of Queen Victoria's visit to Sheffield in 1887, and in 1895 he was appointed chorus-master to the newly-founded Sheffield Festival. After 1887, Coward decided to make music his career, and became a Doctor of Music (Oxford) and an FRCO (Fellow of the Royal College of Organists). He was also music critic of the *Sheffield Independent* for twelve years. He was knighted for his services to music.

John Curwen, 1816-1880.

Coward was loved and widely respected. The city of Sheffield bought the appropriate academic robes for him to wear on official occasions for example. In 1900 Elgar invited him to Birmingham to deliver an opinion on the problems the chorus was having at the rehearsals for the premiere of *The Dream of Gerontius*. Coward himself, however, never wavered from his advocacy of the tonic sol-fa method. He was the living proof that it could work as a gateway to an altogether different kind of life, being at the same time a temporary but satisfying release from the ugliness of the city around them for thousands of others.

In 1853 John Curwen established the Tonic Sol-fa Association, in 1863 the Curwen publishing house and in 1879 the Tonic Sol-fa College. From 1874, annual Tonic Sol-fa festivals were held at the Crystal Palace, with 3,000 young singers, plus tenors and basses, and nearly 30,000 people in the audience, There seems to have been an earlier huge gathering of this kind in Birmingham Town Hall in 1859, when six hundred singers are said to have come from within the town and from Coventry and Burton-on-Trent. This is an unconfirmed statement by J. Sutcliffe Smith (op. cit.) but it has to be said that it is supported by the *Musical Times* which reveals that the Tonic Sol-fa Association held a concert at the Music Hall, Birmingham, on 5th July 1858, under the direction of a Mr. F. Barnby, organist. The hall was well-filled and the music well-performed, according to the reviewer.

Adult Education in Music. The Midland Institute School of Music
Among local sol-fa enthusiasts was Weaver Stephens, who taught singing for the Midland Institute School of Music. The Birmingham and Midland Institute was

Chapter 13 - Musical Education. The establishment of the Midland Institute School of Music

formally established, by Act of Parliament, in 1854. The Act charged it with the task of encouraging 'knowledge of arts and sciences among all classes of people in Birmingham and the Midland counties'. This was a serious and important establishment in a way that may not be fully realised today, when education to the age of 18 is free for all and heavily subsidised after that. At that time, a chance to study mathematics, commerce and languages could open a door to a career otherwise debarred to people with limited schooling. The arts were regarded as having a different, but no less vital role as a civilising influence; for through them mental horizons were widened, fruitful co-operation with others was practised and above all the soul and the spirit were lifted above the purely material. Through its varied and numerous classes, the Birmingham and Midland Institute was a gateway to achievements and to personal development otherwise unattainable.

In 1859, Singing classes were organised by the Institute's Industrial Department under the Amateur Harmonic Association's conductor, A. J. Sutton. These did not prosper and were closed in 1861. Two years later, however, Penny Classes in Elementary Singing were started and were taken, very successfully, by Richard Rickard until 1865. Rickard was a Mathematics teacher at King Edward's School and an amateur flautist, and taught both Arithmetic and Singing at the Institute. After 1865, C. J. Stevens took over the Penny Classes and the numbers increased still more, 543 being the average number at each class! Anyone organising any kind of music course today must surely turn green with envy at the very thought of numbering their students in hundreds. The problem would have been how to organise such a large number, not how to attract more students.

An Advanced Singing class, on the other hand, did not thrive. It is noticeable, too, that Elementary Singing classes taken at venues in what are now inner city areas, and in certain suburbs, such as Harborne, did not always do very well either. Very much depended on the personality and dynamism of the teacher or conductor. In any case, if a class did not pay, the Institute could simply not afford to continue it. Classes which were well-attended, however, were the elementary and advanced violin classes, started in 1882. These were the Institute's response to the pressure from various quarters - Bache and Stockley for example - for more encouragement for instrumental playing. The Theory of Music classes given by the composer A. R. Gaul, from 1877, were also part of this movement. In 1885, classes in piano, solo singing for ladies, clarionet (sic), flute, 'cello and part-singing were added, and a year later, 1886, the whole endeavour was brought under an official umbrella, and called a School of Music. William Stockley was Honorary Principal, assisted by fourteen teachers.[4] A start had been made, and an attempt was in train to emulate the Royal Academy of Music, founded 1822-23, and the two newly-established bodies in London, the Royal College of Music and Trinity College of Music, both just opened in 1883, in London.

The music section of the Institute had 157 subscribers which, between 1882 and 1885, promoted some orchestral concerts. In Stockley's words,

'...the Midland Institute gave valuable help to instrumentalists by introducing orchestral concerts to their subscribers on Monday evenings as a relief to the usual lectures, and this not only proved an agreeable and instructive variety to the audience, by whom it was much appreciated, but also gave to the band the opportunity for the extra practice which they needed.

This was not the only occasion when the Midland Institute greatly helped the cause of music, for a similar instance must be recorded in their establishing a Madrigal Society under my conductorship, which not only afforded many accomplished amateurs the opportunity of practising unaccompanied singing but also - as in the case of orchestral concerts - gave pleasure to the members of the Institute by concerts given in alternation with the Monday lectures. Several composers of eminence honoured the Society by conducting their compositions at the concerts, and expressed themselves much pleased with the performances of the choir. Sir John Stainer assured me that he did not remember any singing of madrigals so good, except that of Mr. Henry Leslie's celebrated choir. My task as a teacher was a very easy one, as many of the members were excellent soloists, and all were good singers'.

The orchestral concerts had to be abandoned in 1885 because the number of subscribers was not large enough to fund them any more, but the Madrigal Society continued under Stockley's leadership. Entrants to this society were auditioned and they paid an annual subscription of five shillings (5/- or 25p). The choir gave a concert twice a year.

The question of funds, ever a vexed one, was exercising the minds of the Institute's officers very acutely at this particular period, and various methods were tried in order to raise money. A letter to the *Birmingham Post* from 'J.J.' of Bordesley Park Road, dated 25th March 1889, refers to a recital given earlier that month by the eminent pianist, Fanny Davies, in order to add to the funds. Miss Davies was trained in Birmingham by Charles Flavell and A. R. Gaul, and subsequently in Leipzig where she studied for two years with Clara Schumann. The letter from 'J.J.' makes it clear that he ranks himself among the working men who 'take a deep interest in the welfare of our local university - the Midland Institute'. He calls for someone with the eager, impassioned spirit of Charles Dickens, to whom the Institute owed so much for its inception, to cast in his lot with this important educational body. He adds however, that they might be able to manage without the support of a famous man like Dickens if –

'they always had the help which they might have anticipated from those around them. But whilst some were giving time they could ill spare in labour for the Institute, their fellow-citizens permitted them to stagger under a load of debt which cramped every energy and made despondent every thought'.

Plus ça change..!

Chapter 13 - Musical Education. The establishment of the Midland Institute School of Music

Here again we are seeing further signs of that same decline we have already noticed in connection with the profits from the festival. In spite of the town's population reaching unprecedented numbers, and higher ticket prices, the financial product from these prestigious events did not grow. Not only that, after 1876, they actually began to decrease. It is hardly surprising, therefore, that a relative infant like the Midland Institute, only thirty years old as compared to the festivals' one hundred, should be in difficulties.

Fundamental changes were ushered in by the founding of the official School of Music, in 1886. It was now regarded as a serious musical establishment, and most people welcomed this as a progressive step. Edward Bache would have done, no doubt, as might Charles Lunn even. Men like C. J. Stevens and William Stockley put their whole weight behind it, but everyone was spurred into further action when, in 1894, the respected music scholar, Ebenezer Prout, commented unfavourably on some of the Institute's pupils. He criticised, in particular, the custom of teaching in classes those subjects which ought to be taught on an individual basis. Vigorous efforts were made as a consequence of these strictures and, among other things, more teachers were recruited.

Collective teaching, of instruments and solo singing in particular, was ended. Among those who arrived as gifted tutors were Birmingham's own Dr. Charles Swinnerton Heap, also Max Mossel, the violinist.

By 1896, the external examiner, Frederick Corder, known to us now mainly for his translations into English of opera *libretti,* reported much more favourably on the general standard of achievement. By 1897, a pupil of the School, the young tenor Walter Hyde, won a scholarship to the Royal College of Music. He went on to become a renowned singer, particularly in the Wagnerian roles of Siegmund and Parsifal. He was also a noted oratorio singer - a visitor to the Festival (1909) and to the Harrison concerts (1910).

Meanwhile, the Institute continued what it saw as one of its main tasks, namely to present lectures. Distinguished musicians spoke on various topics. Among these were John Stainer, composer of the once popular oratorio *The Crucifixion,* A. G. Mackenzie, Principal of the Royal Academy of Music, and Arnold Dolmetsch, speaking respectively on 'Psalms and Carols, 'The Early Orchestra' and 'The Lute, the Viols, the Virginals and the Harp'.

In 1900 the Institute's school began both a new century and a new chapter in its history with the appointment of Granville Bantock as its Director. Not everyone was happy with the way things were going, however. In 1892, Weaver Stephens, the sol-fa specialist, had pointed out that the conservatoires taught the teachers but that the Midland Institute taught the people. For some years, even after Bantock's arrival, the Institute tried to do both. Had it separated the two functions - teaching the professionals and teaching the amateurs - more clearly in its corporate mind, things might have progressed faster and further. As things turned out, the schools gradually took over the business of teaching the amateurs from 1900, onwards, and the Institute failed to see what had happened. It did not concentrate properly on teaching the professionals. This delayed the establishment of a college of music able to compete with those in London and Manchester. More will be said on this topic in chapter 28.

The original Birmingham and Midland Institute, Paradise Street.

1. Lady Bell: *At the Works.* A study of a manufacturing town. London 1985.
2. Sunday Schools contributing singers to the Sunday Schools Choral Union festivals belonged to the churches of St. Andrew (Girls), St. Asaph,. St. Bartholomew, St. Clement, St. David (Edgbaston), St. George, St. John (Deritend), St. Luke, St. Lawrence, St. Mary, St. Mary (Moseley), St. Matthias, St. Mark, St. Thomas, Saltley and a school set up by Messrs. Chance, Oldbury.
3. Henry Coward: *Reminiscences* as quoted in (a) E. D. Mackerness: *Somewhere Further North.* A History of music in Sheffield. Sheffield, 1974 and (b) Herbert Antcliffe: *Henry Coward* (Article in *Grove's Dictionary of Music and Musicians*, Fifth edition.).
4. Midland Institute School of Music teachers in 1886: A. R. Gaul, class singing, theory, advanced harmony and counterpoint; W. Astley Langston, piano, organ, flute; Weaver Stephens, class singing, tonic sol-fa; Rowland Winn, choral singing; John Pierce, solo singing; R. Rickard, elementary violin; W. Cover, intermediate and advanced violin; Thomas Abbott, violin and 'cello; Frederic Ward, viola and orchestra; W. H. Johnson, double bass; G. W. Roberts, oboe; T. E. Pountney, clarionet (sic); Alfred Roberts, bassoon; H. Bell, brass instruments. Messrs. Abbott, Ward, Johnson, Roberts (both), Pountney, and Bell all played in the early twentieth century Birmingham orchestras to be described in later chapters.

Chapter 14

Nineteenth century church music in Birmingham

It must be admitted straight away that a good deal more research needs to be done into the music of the growing number of churches of all denominations in nineteenth century Birmingham. It is really a subject in itself. In spite of some decline in church-going and the growth of scepticism which had already begun, particularly among the men-folk, the church and its music nevertheless continued to be a source of inspiration to many. It also launched not a few musicians into wider participation in music of all kinds, besides sacred music. The break with village life for many around 1800, which had been centred round a parish church, sometimes put an end to an individual's church attendance which was never resumed. Very many folk, equally, made a bee-line for the nearest appropriate place of worship when they arrived in town, in order to maintain an important and familiar aspect of their lives. Some churches were built to serve the growing nineteenth century population, only to find that they were soon having to try very hard to keep their parishioners, as other pursuits lured then away, or the pace of church-building ran ahead of the numbers of church-attenders.

John Thackeray Bunce in his *Birmingham Sixty Years Ago* reports that in 1830 there had been no surpliced choirs in the town, but still the mixed choirs of men and women, usually in a gallery at the West end of the church. The psalms and responses were said, not sung, and the choir sang the hymns and, sometimes, the 'Gloria' at the end of the psalms. The whole effect, he confesses, was somewhat dull. The competition between the sacred and the secular, and to some extent between one church and another, led to a brightening of church services in Birmingham as the century wore on, however. The high church clergy, in the older more 'catholic' tradition, encouraged more ritualistic and colourful services. These either had music sung by a trained choir or no music at all, depending on the occasion. The evangelistic party, on the other hand, emphasised the preaching of the gospel and communal, congregational hymn singing. In this category were the non-conformist churches and in some of these there could be a good choir and a high standard of music. Carrs Lane Church, built in 1819, was an example.

It was perhaps in fact in the Roman Catholic tradition that some of the best music was to be found earlier in the nineteenth century. Following the Catholic Emancipation Act of 1829, the Roman Catholic Cathedral of St. Chad's, designed by Augustus Pugin, was built and finally consecrated in 1841. The organisation of the music was entrusted, as at Cardinal Newman's Birmingham Oratory, to the priesthood but the role of choirmaster was assigned in 1854 to John Hardman, one of the family associated with the design and making of stained glass. The sanctuary area was altered to accommodate the choir stalls and an organ. This lay-out continued until 1967 when the cathedral was refurbished. In 1879 the choir's excellent tradition was recognised by Bishop Ullathorn in his encyclical for their twenty-fifth anniversary. The Bishop, who was very musical, was a guiding spirit behind the music at St. Chad's. The idea he enunciated was that in music for the church the secular must not invade the sacred. Surely an example to be followed!

Somewhere between the musical extremes were the majority of the forty-six Church of England churches built in Birmingham by 1870. Increasingly these had a surpliced, trained choir, some of which were capable of singing anthems, while affording the congregation the opportunity of singing a decent range of hymns and psalms. Most town churches and chapels were provided with an organ, unlike country churches which often still had a little band of instrumentalists to play for the services. This meant that the standard of a church's music came increasingly to depend on the talents, or otherwise, of one man or woman, the organist and choirmaster. Birmingham was thus very fortunate in this respect for there was a good pool of very capable musicians to draw on. Once more, a short list will demonstrate the situation most clearly and concisely.

Some Birmingham Church Organists 1830-1900

Henry Simms	St. Philip's	1829 - 1871
C. J. B. Meacham	St. Philip's	1871 - 1888
Yates Mander	St. Philip's	1888 - 1898
A. G. Thomson	St. Philip's	1898 - 1901
W. C. Stockley	St. Stephen's	1850 - 1858
	St. Mary's	1858 - 1870
	St. Luke's	1870 - 1889
	Carrs Lane	1889 - 1902
George Halford	St. Mary's	1875 - 1877
	St. George's	1877 -
	St. Michael's Handsworth	Dates not known
A. R. Gaul	St. John's, Ladywood	1859
	St. Augustine's, Edgbaston	1868 - 1913
Samuel Simms (II)	St. Cyprian's, Hay Mills	1880 - 1885

Some Birmingham Church Organists 1830-1900 (Cont.)

Samuel Simms (III)	St. Cyprian's, Hay Mills	1885 - ?
Charles Stevens	St. Michael's Handsworth	Dates not known
A. J. Sutton	St. Thomas's Bath Row	Dates not known
Dr. Rowland Winn	Harborne Parish Church	Dates not known
Walter Brooks	St. Martin's, Birmingham	Dates not known
John Hardman	St. Chad's Cathedral	Dates not known

By 1846, choral services with a surpliced choir were also held at *St. Peter and St. Paul, Aston* and at *Holy Trinity, Bordesley*.

There are some familiar names in the above list, men active as choral conductors, as teachers or composers, whose high level of musicianship we already know of. That was also the age of the famous preacher. According to Stockley, for example, when he went to St. Mary's (now demolished) in 1858, Dr. Barrett was then at the height of his popularity, and the services were attended by very large congregations. A large congregation usually meant a large choir and plenty of scope for enthusiastic music-making. Sometimes there was more enthusiasm than discretion, however, and such seems to have been the case at St. Martin's at one point. Our evidence for this comes from G.A Osborne who compiled a *Birmingham Religious Scrapbook* which contains a section called *Church Music in Birmingham 1865 - 1900*. Of St. Martin's in 1871, it says:

'It possesses a tolerably good organ of twenty-four stops built by Elliott and Hill; enjoys the services of an excellent organist, Mr. Walter Brooks, and a somewhat powerful choir; but, with these advantages, the result is, musically, very unsatisfactory. The services are little more elaborate than those of the most sober conventicle. The Psalms for the day are read, not chanted, and the responses are treated in a similar manner. Last Sunday evening, the *Magnificat* was drawled to Henley in E flat. *The Nunc Dimittis* was sung service-wise to Ebdon in C. Both in these and in the metrical hymns, the congregation joined lustily. The organ played loudly to keep the whole together notwithstanding which, the large body of singers still lagged behind time... in one of the hymns, the last line of each verse was repeated three times and as a *coda* coupled with the last line but one was repeated a fourth time, the result of these repetitions was, in some verses, absurdity'.

In the above paragraph we are told that 'the organ played loudly'. How is it that the organ is the only instrument that can - apparently - play by itself!

The writer goes on to say that the congregation was allowed in seven minutes before the service began, but even so the first words he managed to hear after finally getting inside were those of the beginning of the Absolution. In other words he entirely missed the entrance of the choir and the first hymn. Those who managed to get in first must have been deafened by the opening and shutting of pew doors and the bustle of people settling into their seats.

Things were obviously much better, musically speaking, at St. Philip's in 1871, where cathedral use and a choral service had recently been established. There were eighteen boys in the choir and six paid adults. The organ was still in a West end gallery and was then about fifty years old. It had had a rebuilding in the 1820s by J. P. England, and was again altered and improved by Hill's in 1874.

A happy blend of noted preacher, good congregations and choir – and a fine organist to boot – was to be found at Carrs Lane. William Stockley speaks with great affection of the minister, Dr. Dale. He describes his time at Carrs Lane as the most pleasant of his organist's engagements. The committee and congregation treated him with 'great liberality and kindness' and his association with Dr. Dale was remembered by Stockley with 'pleasure and gratitude'. Dr. Dale attended the weekly rehearsals of the choir for a period of two years and when Stockley retired, thanked him for the help his music had given to Dale in his own work.

Finally, the very specific part the Roman Catholic Oratory, built in 1851, was to play in Birmingham's musical history will be recounted in the chapter on Elgar and Birmingham.

Chapter 15

By the people, for the people

It would be impossible to give a fully-detailed and exhaustive account of every organisation devoted to presenting choral music in Birmingham in the last part of the nineteenth century, particularly as everyone who could sing wanted to join a choir and sing all the works they heard – or heard about – at the Festivals. If enough like-minded people got together, then at the drop of a hat, another choral society was formed. We shall pursue the subject of the 'choral craze' in early twentieth century Birmingham in chapter 24. Here, we can only pick out two or three enterprises for closer scrutiny.

The Midland Musical Society
One of these was the Midland Musical Society. Eschewing all false modesty, it boldly dedicated itself to 'raising public taste' and gave three 'artizans concerts' a year at the Town Hall. No-one will be surprised to learn that it presented the best known works from the oratorio repertoire; Handel's *Judas Maccabaeus* and *Messiah* and Mendelssohn's *Elijah* for example. In addition, Gounod's *Redemption* was the great favourite for their Good Friday Concerts. Rehearsals were on Thursday evenings in the Priory Rooms, Upper Priory. Some concerts were for charity, yet the tickets, available through a dozen outlets in the city centre, were only priced at threepence, sixpence and a shilling (just over 1p, 2½p and 5p) equivalent to 30p, 75p and £1.50p now. Presumably it succeeded because performers who needed to *be* paid accepted modest fees. As was frequently the case at that time, there were often two thousand in the audience and two or three hundred on the platform. The band had about fifty players – 'good, but wanting refinement' – according to a pencilled comment in an old programme.

The guiding hand in the Midland Musical Society at the beginning was H. M. Stevenson. He was inspired by the idea of enabling even the poorest to have the pleasure and joy of listening to, or participating in, great music, just as their better-off fellow citizens had. After 1900, the Society responded to the change of atmosphere, widened its own musical horizons and presented works like Bantocks's *Atalanta in Calydon* for unaccompanied choir, for example. Instrumental works were also introduced into their programmes as time went on. More of this in due course.

Birmingham Musical Association
Another organisation which aimed to put on Saturday evening concerts of high class music, with low ticket prices, was the Birmingham Musical Association, founded in 1879 at the instigation of the local M.P. Jesse Collings. This was the society whose variable standard of performance so incensed Charles Lunn. Unlike the Midland Musical Society, above, it only had a short life.

A thread running through so many of the musical initiatives taken in nineteenth century Birmingham was the excellent and unashamed intention of improving, educating, uplifting, teaching, and then, of extending the benefits of all this to every level of society. At least if some turned their faces against what was generally agreed to be fine music, it would certainly not be because of lack of money.

Birmingham Choral and Orchestral Association and the Birmingham Choral Union
Finally, somewhat similar to the Midland Musical Society, in its later stages, was the Birmingham Choral and Orchestral Association, founded in 1882. Placing rather more emphasis on instrumental music, it too presented mixed orchestral and choral concerts; and in 1886, the Birmingham Choral Union embarked on its first century of active and honourable existence. In the years running up to 1900, a (monthly) Saturday evening series at the Town Hall seems to have been shared between the Choral Union, the Choral and Orchestral Association and the City Choral Society. Again, more will be said about these choirs in chapter 24, in the second part of this book.

Chapter 16

Stockley's Orchestra
1873-1897

Stockley looms large in several chapters of this book, but now we must turn the spotlight directly on him yet again, and pursue the story of his establishment of an orchestra.

First let us summarise Stockley's achievements so far. The music-selling business of Sabin and Stockley, became Stockley's alone when Sabin retired in 1889. From 1856, Stockley was conductor of the Festival Choral Society, which he himself had made nationally famous. He was chorus-master or joint chorus master at the Festivals from 1861 to 1894, entrusted by Michael Costa with first performances of new choral works, and he was first Honorary Principal of the Midland Institute School of Music. During all this time he was serving one church or another as organist and choirmaster. He must have had that special combination of both dynamism and the common touch to achieve all this, but it is probably his establishment of an orchestra, simply to give orchestral concerts, which was to have the most far reaching consequences for Birmingham's music. The launching of an orchestra in 1856 to play for the Festival Choral Society concerts was described in Chapter 8. This was done with a faith and hope which was soon justified. The launching of an orchestra *per se* eventually followed, and a series of 'Subscription Orchestral Concerts' was announced in 1873 in these words:

'Each concert will comprise a SYMPHONY and other Compositions of GREAT MASTERS and will be interspersed with VOCAL MUSIC, for which at least one Artiste of eminence will be engaged. The accompaniments will, as far as practicable, be ORCHESTRAL or with OBBLIGATI for solo Instruments'

The first piano accompanist was C.J. Stevens, but Rowland Winn was employed from the late 1870s onwards.

This first series 'gave much satisfaction to a limited audience' in Stockley's own words - and lost him a hundred pounds (£100)! This would be the equivalent of about £3,000 today. A number of public-spirited gentlemen [1] came forward to aid Stockley's brave project, however, and an orchestra gradually more able to compare favourably with Birmingham's choralists, instead of lagging far behind them, was built up over the next twenty-four years.

Three concerts a year were presented, always on Thursday evenings, and from 14th November 1880 onwards, programme-notes were provided by Andrew Deakin. A study of the programmes themselves reveals that a tally of 35 symphonies, 27 concertos, 55 operatic overtures and between 50 and 60 suites was marked up. Haydn is still grossly under-represented, by only one item. This was the last movement of his 'Symphony no. 7' which we came across in the 1820 festival programme.(chapter 5). Here it is nicknamed 'the Departure'. Why symphony no. 7 when in fact it was number 97 in C major? The answer is that a separate collection of the 'Salomon' or 'London' Symphonies was made, and number seven was the one in C major. The full list is given at the end of the chapter. [2] The name 'Departure' most probably refers to the fact that it was the last one of the first set to be performed in London, before Haydn's return to Vienna in 1792, and is not a name now used. It should not be confused with the Symphony no. 45 in F sharp minor, the so-called 'Farewell Symphony'. The London concert concerned was given at the beginning of May and Haydn went home in June. Notice also that these symphonies were made available in piano versions by publishers like Augener, also Breitkopf and Härtel, and were eagerly snapped up. These piano versions were, after all, the nineteenth century equivalent of the recording, the only way the ordinary music-lover could enjoy this music on a regular basis, in the comfort of his own home.

Four Mozart symphonies were played, in Stockley's programmes. All of Beethoven's are there except the *Choral Symphony*. Schubert was represented by Symphonies no. 8 and no. 9, namely the *'Unfinished'* and the *'Great C major'* symphonies. Schumann and Dvorak symphonies also appear, including the latter's ninth, 'From the New World'. Perhaps the best way of conveying the flavour of this series is to list the works in which Edward Elgar played when he was among Stockley's first violins, sharing third desk with Charles Hayward, son of the brilliant violinist Henry Hayward. This was between 1882 and 1889. Not the least of Stockley's contributions to music was the opportunity he gave to Elgar to play in a number of great masterpieces. This was of great importance because England's greatest indigenous composer since Purcell was largely self-taught. Everything he heard and played in was imprinted on this exceptional musical mind. He learnt from it, and it added new vocabulary to the 25-year-old composer's own musical language. All the pieces in the following list must therefore have contributed in one way or another to Elgar's musical development.

Works presented at William Stockley's orchestral concerts during the period in which Edward Elgar played as a first violin. 1882-1889

Wagner: *Die Meistersinger* (The Prize Song, sung by Edward Lloyd)
Sterndale Bennett: Overture to *Paradise and the Peri*
Caprice in E for piano and orchestra.
(solo piano: Rowland M. Winn)

Chapter 16 - Stockley's Orchestra 1873-1897

Works presented at William Stockley's orchestral concerts during the period in which Edward Elgar played as a first violin. 1882-1889 (Cont.)

F. H. Cowen:	Suite in D for strings
	Symphony no. 4.
Elgar:	*Intermezzo Mauresque.*
Mendelssohn:	Symphony no. 3. '*Scottish*'
	Symphony no. 4, '*Italian*'.
A.C. Mackenzie:	*Rhapsodie Ecossaise* op. 21
Dvorak:	*Slav Dances* op. 46 no. 6 and no. 8
Gade:	Symphony in B flat op. 20
Handel:	Organ Concerto no. 4 (soloist, James Stimpson)
Raff:	Italian Suite, *In the South*
Beethoven:	Symphony no. 8
	Piano Concerto no. 5
★Elgar:	*Sevillana* (orchestral sketch)
Meyerbeer:	*Grand Coronation March* from *Le Prophète*
Macfarren:	Violin Concerto in G min (soloist, J.T. Carrodus)
Sterndale Bennett:	Overture to *The May Queen*
Prout:	Symphony in F
Gade:	Symphony in C minor op. 5
Berlioz:	*Hungarian March* from *Faust*
Schumann:	Piano concerto in A minor (soloist, Fanny Davies)
Dvorak:	Symphony in D op. 60 (conducted by the composer)
Spohr:	Symphony no. 4, *The Power of Sound*.
Schubert:	Symphony no. 8, *The Unfinished*. The *andante* only.
Beethoven:	Symphony no. 5, in C min. op. 67
Wagner:	*Lohengrin*. Introduction to Act 3
Cherubini:	Overture to *Anacreon*
Stanford:	Symphony in F minor op. 28 '*Irish*'
Mendelssohn:	Overture to *Ruy Blas*
Cowen:	Symphony no. 5 in F
Flotow:	Overture to *Stradella*
Mendelssohn:	Piano Concerto in D min. op. 40 (soloist, Fanny Davies)
★Elgar:	Suite in D min. for orchestra
Beethoven:	Symphony no. 2 in D op. 36
Grieg:	*Two Elegiac Melodies* for string orchestra op. 34
Verdi:	Requiem (with Festival Choral Society 24th Feb. 1887)
Rheinberger:	Concerto for organ, string band and three horns, op. 137 (Soloist, C.W. Perkins)
Beethoven:	Symphony no. 1 in C op. 21

Works presented at William Stockley's orchestral concerts during the period in which Edward Elgar played as a first violin. 1882-1889 (Cont.)

Mackenzie: *Benedictus* for small orchestra op. 37
Meyerbeer: Grand March from *Schiller*
Schubert: Symphony no. 8, *'The Unfinished'* (complete)
Max Bruch: Violin Concerto in G min op. 26 (soloist, Nettie Carpenter)
Frederic Cliffe: Symphony no. 1 in C minor
Beethoven: Overture to *Egmont*.
Also a number of well-known Italian operatic arias.

We know from Elgar himself that the concert in which Dvorak conducted his own *Symphony* in D (no. 6) had a great influence on him, as did the first performance of Verdi's *Requiem* in Birmingham, in 1887. Elgar himself described the latter as 'a work I have always worshipped'. Further, the performance of Elgar's own pieces in Birmingham's Town Hall was of vital encouragement to him, going a little way towards giving him some of the confidence and reassurance which he so badly needed. The first piece, *Intermezzo mauresque,* was given on 13th December 1883 in fact. Stockley in his reminiscences gives the date as 1880 but this is a lapse of memory on his part, for Elgar is not listed among Stockley's players until 1882. In any case the event certainly attracted the attention of the national press, with all the attendant pleasures - and pains - of that, but at least people now knew of Mr. E. W. Elgar of Worcester. Stockley described Elgar's modesty on the occasion of this first performance and reports:

'I could not persuade him to conduct his "Intermezzo", or even to listen to its performance from the auditorium, but he insisted on playing in his place in the orchestra, from whence he came to the front in response to a most cordial demand from the audience'.

We can imagine the slim 26-year-old Elgar, already sporting his dark moustache, standing by the rostrum on the Town Hall platform, acknowledging the applause with his violin in his hand. In the appreciative audience were his mother and Helen Weaver, a sweetheart whom he was to lose.

Stockley gave many opportunities to other contemporary British musicians and included in the number were the Bache brothers, Edward and Walter. Edward Bache's *Romance* for flute and piano was played on 12th February 1874, and Walter Bache was piano soloist in Beethoven's *Fifth Piano Concerto* in E flat and in a Liszt *Hungarian Rhapsody,* in October 1878. No further works by Elgar were given in Stockley's series after the composer left the orchestra in 1889, and by the time his first masterpiece, the *Enigma Variations* came out, Stockley had retired. It fell to George Halford, Percy Harrison and the Musical Festival organisers to provide Elgar with Birmingham's handsomest tributes to his genius.

Chapter 16 - Stockley's Orchestra 1873-1897

Excluding the festival conductor, who was always a distinguished visitor, we can fairly claim Stockley as Birmingham's first established orchestral conductor, in spite of Anderton's earlier efforts. The appearance of a hand-over of his baton to George Halford in fact occurred in less than happy circumstances, for Halford did not so much succeed Stockley as push him aside. Halford's first orchestral concert was on 2nd November 1897, Stockley's farewell concert having taken place on 11th March of the same year. This might look like amicable co-operation, but according to Stockley it was not. It seems best to let him tell us what happened in his own words:

'My retirement from public work earlier that I had intended was caused by the formation of a syndicate to give concerts similar to mine, and my friends, the late Mr. Beale and Mr. George Johnstone, strongly advised me to retire rather than risk loss, at the same time informing me that the Festival Committee contemplated giving me a testimonial, and that this could be made of a more general character should I act on their advice'.

Stockley agreed to this suggestion and received an astoundingly generous sum of £500, at least £15,000 in today's values. Stockley continues:

'Dr. Rowland Winn, my loyal and efficient helper from his youth, at the Festival Choral Society, the Festival, and my own concerts, ventured to continue the orchestral concerts, but his efforts, unfortunately, resulted in considerable loss, and were discontinued at the end of the second year. The 'syndicate' was also unsuccessful financially and lost seriously on their ten years trial. I feel that I may be excused some pride in having succeeded in continuing the movement single-handed for twenty-four years with gradually increasing success, while the efforts of a powerful syndicate lasted only a short time'.

Here he is of course referring to the syndicate supporting George Halford and the much shorter life-span of Halford's series. This is not quite fair as we shall see in the chapter about Halford's orchestra (chapter 22) which was in reality an early and prestigious part of a strong new current in Birmingham's musical life.

On the lighter side and in a different sphere, typical also of Stockley's wide-ranging sympathies, is the special choral and orchestral concert he organised for cabmen, bus drivers and bus conductors, whose working hours precluded them from attendance at week day concerts. The band and chorus of the Festival Choral Society readily took part, and the Mayor, Alderman Richard Cadbury Barrow, authorised the free use of the Town Hall. A selection from *Messiah* was presented to a full and appreciative house one Sunday afternoon during Alderman Barrow's mayoralty (1888-9).

Stockleys' contribution to Birmingham's own musical life was incalculable. Not only did he develop a first-rate Festival Chorus and play a major part in starting to establish a proper School of Music, but he also helped to build up a pool of professional orchestral players in the city, and many of these are to be found playing in the later twentieth century orchestras - two of them in the City of Birmingham

Orchestra in 1920, namely the 'cellist, F. A. Ward, and the trombonist, F. Goddard.

There is no doubt that when he eventually retired, Stockley was already beginning to seem outdated and his limitations increasingly conspicuous, but there is no doubt either that without him the town's own music-making would have been immeasurably poorer. Without Stockley - and the Harrisons it should be added - Sullivan's 'boa constrictor' description of Birmingham might well have come true. Stockley obviously had the gift of enthusing people so that what had only been talked about before could actually come into being, and grow and thrive. When he arrived in Birmingham he proved himself to be 'the man of the moment', as Kempson and Moore had been before him, and he too must surely join them in Birmingham's musical pantheon. Where the Harrisons brought international musicians to Birmingham, Stockley played a huge part in building up the musical life within the city itself. Both made Sullivan's gibe seem more and more like an outsider's misconception.

William Stockley, 1830-1919.

---

1. President: J. B. Gausby. Also present: Dr. Harvey, Messrs. G. H. M. Muntz, W. N. Fisher, O. Suffield, T. Anderton, F. Cotton, J. Bagnall, W. J. Dale, J. Boraston, W. Fisher, W. H. Ball, W. Scott, W. Cottam and W. Aston. Pledges of support from non-attenders came from Messrs. T. Bragg, R. Peyton, G Zair, W. Hudson, Glydon and Rowlands.
2. The publisher Augener has no. 1 in E flat (now 103), no. 2 in D (104), no. 3 in E flat (99), no. 4 in D (101) no. 5 in D (93), no. 6 in G (94), no. 7 in C (97), no. 8 in B flat (96), no. 9 in C minor (95), no. 10 in D (86, a Paris Symphony), no. 11 in G (100), no. 12 in B flat (102). The publisher Breitkopf adds: no. 13 in G (?92), no. 14 in D (96).

Chapter 17

Chamber Music

Chamber music continued to play a surprisingly large part in Birmingham's musical life. Some of the Monday Evening Concerts had included music we would now consider as belonging to this category, as did some of Percy Harrison's. Some series, however, were entirely dedicated to the small-scale music repertoire. Such a one was started by a group of people devoted to instrumental chamber music who formed the Birmingham Musical Union in the late 1850s. Their series of concerts was given at Dee's Hotel, the venue for Boulton and Moore's earlier private concerts. First class musicians, some of them associated with the Midland Institute School of Music, gave concerts of chamber music 'taken from the best classical composers'. The Birmingham correspondent of the *Musical Times* is our source here, and he obviously thought them worth noticing. It seems to have been a monthly series. Louis Ries, violin, James Mathews, flute, also C. J. Ducheman and C. E. Flavell, pianists, were among the performers.

A further series was started by Stephen Stratton in 1862. Initially these were simply piano recitals, given by Stratton himself, or his pupils. One that he gave himself took place on 8th August, 1862 'on Kirkman's concert grand' and 'under the Eastern dome of the International Exhibition'. The programme was frankly popular and included a *Tarantelle* (which is not known) and a Fantasia on Themes from *Il Trovatore* by one B. Richards. A programme for one of Stratton's pupils' concerts has survived which is dated Friday evening 20th January 1871. This shows that the concert was held at the Plough and Harrow Hotel and was 'played on a new iron boudoir grand'. Then, in between 14th October 1879 and 18th March 1884, Stratton presented a regular series of what he called Popular Chamber Concerts at the Masonic Hall, New Street, later to become the Forum cinema. In five seasons he promoted twenty-eight concerts which usually took place in October and November, February and March, totalling four or five a year. There was a total of 136 works performed, covering 70 composers in all, including J. S. Bach, Bruch, Chopin, Mendelssohn, Mozart, Verdi and Wagner, together with chamber and piano music by the local composers Thomas Anderton, Edward Bache and Swinnerton Heap.

There had been a further series, called the Birmingham Chamber Concerts, as early as 1858, using leading players from the orchestral and chamber music world, such as Henry Hayward, Louis Ries and Daubert the 'cellist; also the Birmingham pianist, Charles Flavel. Later, Charles Swinnerton Heap too presented an annual series of chamber concerts at the Birmingham and Midland Institute which, unhappily, did not outlive him. These seem to have begun in the mid-1870s but perhaps, like Halford's orchestral concerts later, they were too demanding musically for their day; they did not use singers for example - or perhaps their trouble was that they were organised by an Englishman and, what was worse, a native of Birmingham! On the 24th January 1885, for example, a string quartet consisting of excellent players (Carrodus, Speelman, Bemhardt and Vieuxtemps) with Heap himself at the Piano, presented an interesting programme. This included Dvorak's Violin and Piano Sonata in F op. 57, a rarely heard Duo in G for violin and viola by Mozart and a Bach Chaconne in D minor played by Carrodus. The last item, according to the Musical Times 'took the audience by storm'. What it does not reveal, however, is the size of that same audience.

Also, in the 1880s, two enterprises are mentioned in current issues of the *Musical Times*. One was the Birmingham Musical Guild, which included among its performers the Birmingham clarinettist T. E. Pountney, and other competent local players, including solo pianists. They presented miscellaneous programmes of first-class music, and a concert on 2nd February 1888 included the Mozart Trio in E flat, K 498, for clarinet, viola and piano, Prout's Quartet in F, op. 18, for piano and strings, a Rubinstein Sonata in G for violin and piano (the *Andante* omitted) and Chopin's *Ballade* in A flat, op. 47, played by a Mrs. Richardson. A Weber item for clarinet, played by Pountney, was 'much applauded'.

This strand of Birmingham's musical life continued at a very competent level well on into the twentieth century and this will be described in chapter 25.

Chapter 18

Hans Richter. The Twilight of the Gods, The Musical Festivals 1885-1912

Hans Richter was born at Györ in Hungary on 4th April 1843, his father being Kapellmeister of the town. His mother, a noted singer, sang the part of Venus in Wagner's *Tannhäuser* when it was first performed in Vienna in 1857. Richter himself studied at the Vienna Conservatoire, taking horn and violin for his practical studies, and after working as an orchestral horn player he was recommended to Wagner as a conductor. He then worked with Wagner in Lucerne, between 1866 and 1867, and made the first fair copy of the score of *Die Meistersinger*. His career progressed from height to height and in 1876, after conducting the rehearsals of Wagner's *Der Ring des Niebelungen* cycle at Bayreuth, he was entrusted with the direction of the first performances. He also shared with Wagner the conducting of the Wagner concerts given at the Albert Hall, London, in 1877. In 1882, Richter introduced Wagner's *Ring* cycle, *Die Meistersinger* and *Tristan and Isolde* to London, his 'Richter Concerts' there (first called the Orchestral Festival Concerts) having been established in 1879. It was in this series that he demonstrated his grasp of the Beethoven symphonies, all of which he conducted from memory, and it was at this point in his career, in 1884, that he was invited to become the regular conductor of the Birmingham Musical Festivals.

Richter's London concerts were naturally much reduced in number from 1897, when he went to Manchester to take over the conductorship of the Hallé Orchestra, but he was able to introduce the *Ring* cycle in English to London audiences in 1909. That was the year of Richter's last Birmingham Festival, and in 1911 he retired from the Hallé Orchestra also, and spent his remaining five years in Bayreuth.

Richter in Birmingham

Richter's conductorship of nine Birmingham Musical Festivals covered the years 1885 to 1909. In a sense it was Birmingham's ultimate nineteenth century accolade, that a conductor of his great stature should agree to work here. His orchestral conducting was universally seen at that time as superb but he, in turn, only came to work in England because he found our orchestral musicians so good. By insisting on uniform bowing everywhere he went, he enabled the strings to reach their full potential and created one of those conductor-orchestra partnerships which can be so fruitful and influential. His knowledge and experience of playing orchestral instruments was probably unrivalled among conductors of that day, which naturally added to the respect in which he was held and, as a consequence, to the results he could achieve. He worked for, and got, a broad rich sound from his orchestras. Before going on to consider the effect of Richter's arrival on the Birmingham Musical Festival scene and the music played in his era, readers might like to have a comment on the great man himself from the harpist, Charles Collier. Collier played in all the early twentieth century orchestras in Birmingham but had been heard by Richter in 1897, who thereupon suggested that Collier should move to the Hallé - which he did in 1907. This is probably the only example of a Birmingham orchestral export to Manchester *at that time*, although things have changed since, with a recent CBSO co-leader, Lyn Fletcher, now leading the Hallé Orchestra in brilliant style. Collier writes in his reminiscences in the Hallé Centenary booklet in 1957 that he remembers vividly Richter's 'terrible piercing gaze'. Collier continues: 'kind enough at heart, he was a musical martinet if ever there was one'. Again we are told that if Richter caught players not looking at him he would stop the rehearsal instantly. "I know I am not good-looking", he would cry, "but you must still *look* at me". On one occasion, according to Collier, Richter stopped the fiddlers in the way he had that could almost paralyse a player. There was a breathless silence, then he said quietly: "I would remind you, gentlemen, that there are no prizes for those that get there first".

Hans Richter, 1843-1916.

To land this 'big fish' was to establish Birmingham even more firmly in the front row of the musical scene, and to have a new work presented at a Birmingham Festival was to 'arrive', as Elgar himself was well aware. What Birmingham played today would be heard and, if liked, played elsewhere tomorrow.

Chapter 18 - Hans Richter. The Twilight of the Gods, The Musical Festivals 1885-1912

The programmes
So what was played in Birmingham during Richter's reign?

As one would expect the emphasis in the programming shifted away from 'the Italian', although that did not entirely disappear, and towards the German repertoire. Generally speaking, items in any one concert were fewer and more substantial, and a wider range of composers was represented. One single change sums up the situation quite neatly. In 1891, *The Passion of our Lord according to St. Matthew* by J. S. Bach was sung, in full, on the Wednesday morning (7th October) This was a sign of change indeed, but the revolution was completed in 1900 when Bach's *St. Matthew Passion* actually displaced Handel's *Messiah* from its hallowed niche on Thursday morning (4th October 1900). In one way this was just as well. Our old friend William Pountney gives it as a general opinion that 'Mr. Richter's conception of Handel's *Messiah* will never be accepted by musicians imbued with the tradition - it was too slow and mechanical'. In other words, it was no longer in the more Italianate style. In any case, Richter was not at his best as a choral conductor. *Messiah* was back in its Thursday slot in 1903 and 1906, however, (also in 1912 after Richter had left) but in 1909 it was replaced by another Handel work, *Judas Maccabaeus*.

Otherwise, we find the following works being performed, which give some idea of the increasing scope of the festival. The date or dates given following each title refer of course to the dates of the Festivals at which they were performed. We may perhaps highlight Palestrina's *Stabat Mater* (1894), a Byrd Mass (1900), Purcell's *King Arthur*, complete, (1897), Bach's *Mass in B minor* (1903) and his Orchestral Suite no. 2 in B minor (1909), Berlioz' *Faust Legend* (1891, 1897 and 1909) and the same composer's *Messe des Morts* (1888) and *Te Deum* (1894). Glazounov's Sixth Symphony was played in 1900 and Bruckner's *Te Deum* was given its first performance in Britain on the evening of Friday 16th October 1903. Beethoven and Wagner were of course well-represented, the former by Symphonies nos. 3, 5, 7 and 9, the Violin Concerto and the Mass in D. It is very clear also that Richter was intent on making Brahms accepted in Birmingham, with an innings which included the Third and Second Symphonies (1888 and 1894) the *Alto Rhapsody* (1894 and 1903), the *Song of Destiny* for choir (1897 and 1909), the First Symphony (1897 and 1906) together with his *Variations on an Air by Haydn* (sic) (1897). Brahms' *German Requiem* can be added to this list, placed in the same programme as a Mass by Byrd, the Prelude to Wagner's *Parsifal* and Beethoven's Seventh Symphony. All these on Friday 5th October 1900. Dvorak's music was also given an honoured place by Richter. As well as the commissions, *The Spectre's Bride* in 1885 and the *Requiem* in 1891, his *Stabat Mater* (1888), overture *Husitska* (1894) and *Symphonic Variations* on an original theme op. 78 (1903) were performed.

It is noticeable that the symphonies of Haydn, Mozart and Schubert do not appear very often as compared to the 'bigger' more Romantic works by Schumann,

177

Berlioz, Bruckner and Brahms. Only one Haydn item was given in the nine Birmingham Festivals in which Richter was involved, namely his Symphony no. 101 in D, *The Clock*. Only two of Mozart's symphonies were played - numbers 39 and 40, although the latter was given three times. Schubert was represented by only one work, namely his Symphony no. 8 *'The Unfinished'* - given twice! What about the new works which were played?

Contemporary British Music at the Richter Festivals
Some forty-four contemporary British works were given at the last six Festivals, twenty of them first performances. Among the composers whose music was performed and which is still heard, were Stanford, Parry, Elgar and Delius. Their most substantial works were given at the last Festival in 1912, however, after Richter's departure. The other composers involved are known today by the very occasional appearances of their music in a programme, or sometimes just by name. These included Sterndale Bennett, Frederick Bridge, F .H. Corder, Edward German, A. C. Mackenzie, Percy Pitt, Ebenezer Prout and Arthur Somervell.

Richter himself only conducted those items that he was especially asked to conduct such as, for example, Samuel Coleridge Taylor's *Song of Hiawatha* and Elgar's *Dream of Gerontius*. Usually the composers conducted their works themselves. Unfortunately this seems to have carried with it a subtle suggestion of first and second-class music, one class being worth the great man's attention, the other not. It could also lead to a far from perfect performance.

Feelings ran high in Manchester on this point, where German domination of the music scene was being strongly resisted. In its first days, all the leading players of the Hallé Orchestra were foreign, usually German; although we see that by 1875, of the seventy-one players in the Hallé Orchestra performing at a Percy Harrison concert at Birmingham Town Hall, the English contingent had climbed to thirty-five, the 'natives' being most weakly represented in the first violins and at the Principals' desks. The situation by the end of the century was very different, but Mancunians still felt that British music itself would get nowhere if only German conductors, who naturally wanted to play German music, were employed. Richter replied that he was very willing to conduct British music but that failing eyesight made it increasingly difficult for him to study totally unfamiliar scores, especially in manuscript. This was a trifle specious since he tackled Elgar's *Dream of Gerontius* in Birmingham in 1900, was always willing to cope with a new Strauss work - and what could have been more complex than some Strauss scores?

Richter is also known to have set his face against Delius and his music, and we notice that that composer's *Sea Drift*, composed in 1906, was not played in Birmingham until 1912, after Richter had retired. Granville Bantock and his *Omar Khayyam*, given at the Birmingham Festivals in 1906 and 1909, also received

Chapter 18 - Hans Richter. The Twilight of the Gods, The Musical Festivals 1885-1912

something of a snub. When the work was first put on at the Hallé concerts Richter was invited to conduct, but in the end Bantock had to conduct it himself since Richter was 'tired', and 'forced to take the air' at Blackpool.[1]

Everyone who heard Richter conduct was always carried away by what he actually did, especially in his beloved German repertoire. It was what he did not do that concerned a growing number of English musicians, including Elgar, whose thoughts on the state of British music at that period will be considered in later chapters. In spite of these tensions, however, it is interesting and heartening to note the more enduring reputations of some of the later nineteenth century British composers such as Parry, Stanford and, of course, Elgar.

Performers and programme notes

The soloists at Richter's festivals were usually very fine, as they had always been, and the fact that a majority were English was an encouraging sign.[2] Some concern was already being expressed, however, at a certain decline from the old idea of total commitment to the 'mystery' or craft of singing. One who put this thought into words was, again, Elgar. More of this in due course.

Meanwhile, the chorus totalling about 350, was perhaps not now at its very best. In any case, such a very large number was not conducive to the most sensitive choral singing. Stockley was becoming an old man and retired in 1897. Swinnerton Heap's very brief reign as chorus-master did not have a chance to bring about the expected improvement before his untimely death in 1900. The orchestra was usually about 120-strong and could obviously not be a Birmingham-only band. The Hallé provided the backbone of it, but at least there were occasions when Stockley's orchestra was invited to accompany choral items, as for example at the 1885 festival. Among those providing programme notes by the way was Ernest Newman, considered as much a giant in his own sphere as Richter in his.

Practical arrangements

The practical arrangements for ballots for tickets continued, the venues for these changing over the years, from the Blue Coat School, used until 1882; to King Edward's School, New Street in 1885; to the Masonic Hall, New Street, 1891-97; and finally to a ticket office at 123, Colmore Row, which was Stockley's shop.

The benches in the Town Hall were changed to upholstered arm-chairs in 1891 but the organisers still managed to pack in over 2,000 people. How hot it must have been! At a more elevated level, it should be mentioned that C.W. Perkins re-opened the rebuilt Town Hall organ in 1890.

Before going on to consider the final Birmingham Musical Festival of 1912, we should perhaps pause a moment to take a last look at Richter's effect on festival programmes. As we have seen, Haydn, Mozart and Schubert were still scarcely represented and the big romantic orchestra, and its Germanic repertoire, took precedence over the smaller classical one. It has to be said, though, that Richter certainly delivered the festival from a tendency to both the grandiose and the sweetly-pretty elements of Costa's era, above all from the dominance of the operatic star and his or her party pieces. Brilliant as these could be, they were limiting, and it needed a large personality like Richter's to deal with the tyranny of the *prima donna*. There was on one occasion a head-on conflict between the conductor and a 'star' singer who wanted to pause on a note which happened to be her best one, when no pause was marked. W. H. Reed, in his book *Elgar as I knew him,* recounts Richter's implacable response to this: 'If Beethove' had wish to pause, he would have mark. He have not mark, so we do not make'. For Richter the music came first and this was an extremely important point to be made to everyone concerned at that time.

Music with a charitable purpose
After all, they were still putting on music to raise funds for a charity and not just for its own sake. All that was about to change, but before it did, there was one more festival and, on the other side of the argument, one can point out that without this charitable purpose some wonderful music would never have received the exposure and the appreciation it did.

The Last Birmingham Musical Festival in 1912
Conducted by Henry J. Wood, the array of music on offer and the talented musicians on hand to perform it really make one ask the question: why was it the

Henry J. Wood, 1869-1944.

Chapter 18 - Hans Richter. The Twilight of the Gods, The Musical Festivals 1885-1912

Birmingham Town Hall ca. 1905.

last? It seems best just to give the details of this festival swan-song and let them speak for themselves.

Among the soloists on this occasion were the singers Carrie Tubb, Aino Ackté, Clara Butt, Muriel Foster, John McCormack, Gervase Elwes and Clarence Whitehill. Solo instrumentalists were the pianists Moriz (Maurycy) Rosenthal, 'cellist Pablo Casals and the city's own organist, C. W. Perkins. The Chorus Master of the Hallé Chorus, R. H. Wilson, took charge of the choir and the conductor was Henry Wood. Analytical notes were provided by A. J. Jaeger, 'Nimrod' of the *Enigma Variations* of course.

Major works involved were, in date and time order, Elgar's *We are the Music Makers*, Sibelius's Fourth Symphony - 'first time of performance' - Liszt's Piano Concerto no. 1 in E flat, Bach's Third *Brandenburg Concerto* and his *St Matthew Passion*, Haydn's 'Cello Concerto in D, Richard Strauss's tone poem, *Don Quixote*, Verdi's *Manzoni Requiem*, Delius's *Sea Drift*, Brahms' *German Requiem*, Scriabine's *Prometheus*

(The Poem of Fire) and parts one and two of Elgar's *The Apostles* as a grand finale on the Friday evening. This final item was the very last to be given at the Festivals.

As a footnote, Sibelius' Fourth Symphony had already been played in Helsinki. Perhaps the phrase 'tried out' in Helsinki would be more accurate, since the Birmingham Festival had incomparably the greater status at that time.

---

1. Recounted by Havergal Brian in *On Music* op. cit.
2. Charles Santley, Edward Lloyd, Andrew Black, Ben Davies, John Coates, Plunket Greene Frangcon Davies, Robert Radford, Anna Williams, Muriel Foster, Kirkby Lunn and Agnes Nicholls all sang for Richtrer.

PART TWO
THE TWENTIETH CENTURY

Chapter 19

Introducing the twentieth century

Writing an account of music in Birmingham in the twentieth century presents the writer with a tremendous challenge. The first problem is the sheer quantity of evidence available. Every worthwhile musical event was recorded in some form or other. This record includes two major elements. On the one hand there are reviews and reports, both in the well-established local press and, particularly after 1980, nationally. On the other hand there are original programmes deposited locally. Here, both the Birmingham Central Library and the City of Birmingham Symphony Orchestra look after valuable archives as do the University of Birmingham and now the Birmingham Conservatoire. Compensating a little for this bewildering array of records is the fact that there are now several separate books on, for example, the City of Birmingham Symphony Orchestra, the Birmingham Philharmonic Orchestra, the Chamber Music Society, the Midland Musicians Concerts Society, the concert and opera programmes at Birmingham University's Barber Institute (a booklet entitled *The First Fifty Years*) and various personal reminiscences. All these are listed in the bibliography at the end of this volume. To some extent therefore the account in *Sounds Unlikely* can be viewed as a source of information for further enquiry as well as an account in itself.

The rich Pan-European Tradition; from the Urals to the Atlantic
Once again, however, the writer must enter a caveat. The account given in all the publications mentioned, including this present one, cannot deal with all that is now on offer in the city of Birmingham in the shape of jazz, pop, ethnic and world musics. These recent developments, are now making up a very busy 'scene' and a glance at a *What's On* magazine for the city for a fortnight in the Autumn of 2005 reveals that the coverage of music divides as between classical on the one hand and rock, pop, folk, roots, jazz and blues music on the other in a ratio of roughly 14 events to approximately 60 events - a ratio of about 1 to 4. It is very much to be hoped that someone who is knowledgeable about these comparatively new arrivals in the world of music in Birmingham will take on the task of describing the musical developments associated with the coming of jazz and swing music in the

Chapter 19 - Introducing the twentieth century

early part of the century, and with 'pop' music and the music brought by immigrants from the Caribbean Islands and the Indian sub-continent, from about 1960 onwards.

This present volume can only be a pointer towards what was on offer in the field of what is inaptly called 'classical music'. From the evidence of the *What's On* magazine it may be argued at this point that, at the beginning of the twenty-first century, the classical repertoire is only a part, perhaps a very small part, of what people now think of when they hear the word 'music'. This present account, however, only claims to trace the course of music in what might be termed the classical pan-European tradition as it has been performed and, with great pleasure, listened to in the city of Birmingham over the last millennium. Its long life so far argues a deep and abiding value for the human spirit and should, if the city follows its distinguished citizens of the past, guarantee its continuance in the Birmingham of the future.

When does the past become history?
The second problem is to answer the question: when do events become history? A useful rule is that they should be at least 30 years old before they can be seen in an objective perspective. To deal with events more recent than that may well be to pass a signal at red, doing so at one's peril. In this case, some risk must be taken, however. This is made a little less hazardous by the fact that the last twenty years of the century were clearly defined, musically speaking, by the presence of one charismatic personality, that of Simon Rattle. As musical Birmingham in 1980, when he arrived in the city, and that in 1998 when he left are almost two different places, this revolution can and must be described and celebrated in a separate, final section. Further, Simon Rattle has now moved to pastures new, and a description of what can only be called 'his' era may now be clearly defined and evaluated reasonably dispassionately.

The twentieth century pattern
To make the task of describing Birmingham's twentieth century classical music a little easier, an overall pattern in it was looked for. In fact of course, as always, there is a considerable amount of correlation between the country's general history and local musical fortunes. At first sight, the idea of an inverted sine curve for Birmingham's music seemed appropriate, with a gradual decline from a high point to a low point, followed by a slow and gradual recovery upwards. This does not quite fit the facts, however. There were distinct jolts down, and then up again, in 1914 and 1980 respectively. A better image, perhaps, and one more suited to the motor-manufacturing city Birmingham pre-eminently was in the twentieth century, is to imagine an expensive, well-built car running along impressively and smoothly in top gear, until in 1914 a disaster occurred. Parts were damaged which could not be replaced at such a time of national peril, and the car had to run in third gear as best it could. Being a well-

built car it did - for over 60 years! Everyone felt that it ought to be doing, and could do, better. The potential was there, but the resources and the funds were not. In difficult times, including two world wars and a massive economic slump between them, other things had priority. The car struggled gamely on, nevertheless, and someone arrived in 1980 who knew how to get it into top gear again. Not only that, he was able to persuade people to spend the money to add on all the new technology now available in the form of electric ignition, more valves, overhead camshaft and fuel injection, speaking figuratively!

To translate this image into musical terms, it is clear that in 1900, Birmingham could still attract international musicians of the highest calibre to its festivals. As has been described in previous chapters, to appear at a Birmingham Musical Festival had long been an important and highly valued part of an international musician's career, and this included composers as well as performers. To appear in Birmingham was an essential part of 'arriving' as a musician. Comments from the American, Lowell Mason in 1852 (see page 108) are worth repeating: 'The Birmingham Festival seems to move the whole musical kingdom. It brings together the very best talent that can be found and the works of the greatest masters are performed under circumstances more advantageous than elsewhere to be found in the world'.

Such was not the case between 1920 and 1980. Music in the city in this period was usually worthy, often very good and occasionally outstanding, but the likes of Stravinsky, Heifetz or Maria Callas, for example, did not eagerly seek to appear in Birmingham as a matter of course as Saint-Saëns, Paganini and Adelina Patti had done in the previous century, just to take some examples. It was no longer automatically one of the musical Meccas for the international megastar, although it was still true that very fine musicians, mostly resident in this country, continued to play as soloists with the city's official orchestra.

After 1980, the 'Rattle era' re-established that former international dimension, together with all the additional advantages of the recording and broadcasting technology available to him, in ways not even in existence back in 1900. Above all, Simon Rattle's own status, as well as his achievements with the city orchestra, played an important part in helping to secure a top-class concert hall for the city, in the shape of Symphony Hall, so long pleaded for in vain. Apart from its musical effects, the fine new purpose-built concert hall has literally changed the 'image' people have of music in Birmingham.

Three phases of the twentieth century in summary
Twentieth century music in Birmingham will, therefore, be considered in three main phases: 1900 to 1920 approximately, then 1920 to 1980 and finally 1980 to 2000.

The **first phase** will include the nineteenth century legacy together with the potential for one crucial new future development, namely an orchestra or orchestras

Chapter 19 - Introducing the twentieth century

actually based in the city. Apart from anything else, coming as it did before the electrical recording of sound, the plethora of new local orchestral and choral initiatives seem to have been spurred on by a sort of enterprising and exuberant 'do-it-yourself' spirit.

Just as an aside, perhaps an important one, it is relevant to remember here that Queen Victoria died in 1901 to be followed by her raffish but much more outward-looking son. At that time, too, all could now benefit from free education and better prospects in life. The so-called redbrick universities - Manchester, Birmingham, Liverpool, Leeds, Sheffield and Bristol - were all established at this period. In 1901 Marconi succeeded in sending a wireless signal across the Atlantic. Man had just learned to fly and the new motor car was increasingly seen in the streets - even if mostly owned by the better-off citizenry. Herbert Austin left Wolseley in 1905 to set up his motor works at Longbridge in Birmingham, and all manner of attendant industries, with prospects of better employment opportunities and more money to spend, followed on. London was still the capital city of an Empire which had put substantial pink areas all over the global map. The sky did indeed seem to be the limit and the clouds of war were as yet discerned by relatively few people but, in any case, wars happened hundreds or even thousands of miles away did they not? Even when, at the end of the first decade of the new century, the threat was more widely perceived, the prevailing very confident and positive spirit in the land gave rise to the idea that the country would be perfectly able to deal with it. When war did come in 1914, it was only after two years that the compulsory call-up for men was brought in. Above all, self-help was still the requirement for making progress, with as yet no social security system. Only in 1908 had an old age pension been introduced, followed in 1911 by a sickness and unemployment benefit scheme and only in 1942 did a full National Insurance scheme materialise. The motto was that if something needed doing it was a question of thinking what steps the individual, or a small group of active individuals, might take to do it - themselves!

The **second phase** will describe the middle years of war, slump and more war and of coasting along, musically speaking, as a respectable provincial industrial city. This might be characterised as 'reputable but regional' with a very strong dash of growing dependence on the state to provide everything for all, from cradle to grave. Organisations rather than individuals were more often than not the expected 'providers' for group music-making, with the individual artist only occasionally lucky enough to find influential patrons. Public funding for the arts in the shape of the Arts Council began at the period of the Second World War, but its funding was not generous by later European standards and grants to a few lucky organisations could lead to feelings of discouragement, even despair, among the unlucky. The BBC was rightly only a forum for the already accomplished and successful. A tightening of belts followed by a very slow process of letting them out was the order of the day all through this middle period of the century from about 1930 to 1960 – with an inevitable impact on the city's music. And recovery thereafter was impeded by the huge industrial unrest of the 1970s.

The **third phase**. This was, coincidentally, a time of growing personal and national prosperity, and a corresponding return of greater confidence and optimism. It was also a time when Birmingham's musical fortunes happened to take a most significant turn for the better. An attempt will be made to assess the huge impact of the great rekindling which occurred after 1980, in the 'Rattle era'. This had an impact which regained for the city's cultural life as a whole, the former international dimension – and more. Aiming for Everest this time, rather than merely the Matterhorn, perhaps?

Footnote
Some of the nineteenth century enterprises surviving into the twentieth century have already been described. In chapters 11 and 18, the distinguished performers appearing in Birmingham in the Harrison celebrity series (1854 to 1916) and in the last phase of the Music Festivals (1885 to 1912) respectively, were described in detail, demonstrating the high level of music-making – and of the music-makers still prepared to visit. Other musical threads are also picked up in the chapters to follow, the most important one being an account of the various efforts to build up a capable professional orchestra in the city. On the other hand, all the chapters describing the first phase of the twentieth century also contain in them important pointers to those factors which would bear most significantly on what happened to music in the city during the second two phases of the century.

Chapter 20

Phase One: Birmingham Musical Festival – Cause of death

The main purpose of this chapter is to examine why the great Music Festivals, while surviving into the first part of the twentieth century, and lending their high status to the city at that period, did not long survive the developments the new century brought with it.

Festival finances
Let us look first at the receipts and profits from the festivals after the building of the Town Hall in 1834 and until their demise in 1912.

	General Receipts	Nett Produce (sic)
1834	13 527	5 489
1837	11 224	2 173
1840	9 516	2 362
1843	8 822	2 916
1846	11 638	5 508
1849	10 332	2 448
1852	11 660	4 704
1855	12 745	3 108
1858	11 041	2 731
1861	11 453	3 043
1864	13 777	5 256
1867	14 397	5 541
1870	14 635	6 084
1873	16 076	6 577
1876	15 374	6 071
1879	12 304	3 010
1882	15 217	4 703
1885	13 715	3 360
1888	11 829	2 500
1891	14 572	5 516

(Cont.)	General Receipts	Nett Produce (sic)
1894	13 580	4 517
1897	14 282	5 147
1900	15 282	6 009
1903	14 007	4 521
1906	13 600	4 415
1909	11 817	3 791
1912	10 831	1 549

NOTE:
Figures given to the nearest pound (£1)

It was pointed out earlier that the net profit at the final Musical Festival in 1912 dropped to a level which had already been achieved in the eighteenth century, in 1799, and had always been surpassed thereafter, until the final year. In 1799 the town had about 75,000 citizens and by 1912 half a million, about seven times as many. If that part of the population interested in music had grown proportionately, there should by 1912 already have been the need for an even bigger concert hall and a net profit of about £10,850 not a mere £1,549. As things actually were, it is doubtful if such a hall could have been filled, still less that 14,000 people would have been clamouring to attend any one festival event held in it. Was some of this due to the fact that Festival audience members from elsewhere were fewer in number? Was the annual family holiday at the seaside now the preferred option? What other factors were at work?

In aid of the General Hospital?
There is another aspect of the matter which might be pointed out here for we know, too, that in 1799, the general receipts were only £2,544, while the net profit was £1,470 (57% of takings). In 1912, the equivalent figures were respectively, £10,831 and £1,549 (only 14% of the total takings). In other words, the total profit from all these great organisational and musical efforts was falling and, in any case, the enterprise was costing a great deal more to put on. At the same time, the numbers attending, and the ticket prices, had not increased correspondingly, nor had the donations. It is also clear that by 1900 artists were charging, relatively, much more for their services than they had done a hundred years earlier; particularly striking when one reflects that many of the later singers in particular were simply front-rank soloists, rather than great stars. This was certainly a complaint at the time. In 1897, for example, payments were made as follows:

Chapter 20 - Phase One: Birmingham Musical Festival - Cause of death

	Fees			Approximate Present-day equivalent
	£.	s.	d.	£.
Principals Ten singers, organist, chorus-master and conductor (Richter)	2 129	8	0	60,000.00
Orchestra	2 249	4	6	60, 000.00
Choir	1 408	10	0	30,000.00
TOTAL	**5 787**	**2**	**6**	**150,000.00**

In other words, soloists were clearly absorbing far too high a proportion of the total costs, over a third in fact.

Some of the net profit was apparently, and rather crucially, being boosted by personal donations. In 1885 donations during and after the festival totalled £3,509. Without these donations the festival itself, which only made a profit of £3,360, would simply have broken even and no more. Thus the enterprise already, twenty years before its demise, depended heavily on straightforward sponsorship from generous individuals. Many must have asked why they did not simply donate the money direct to the hospital, if the festivals were no longer generating the *extra* money they once did?

Changing musical tastes

Thinking of those who particularly cared for music, however, one may ask why the festivals could not have continued as purely musical events, provided always that they were indeed able to break even. Some such thing might just have continued had it not been for the outbreak of the First World War in 1914. There was a certain amount of 'keeping the homes fires burning' during the war, and London theatres for example, put on some popular shows. In Birmingham, however, the Hippodrome was closed between 1914 and 1917, the Town Hall was commandeered on two occasions, in 1914 and in 1918, and the town as a whole much occupied with the production of munitions. It was not a propitious time for thinking about musical festivals in aid of charity.

In contrast to all this, several different new *orchestral* series were put on in this 1900 to 1920 period, as we shall see, and a growing number of people were enthusiastic about the idea of exploring the orchestral repertoire and of having a city-funded orchestra to play it. Here was a change in musical taste in fact. Was this change in taste connected to some extent with the increasing mechanisation of life? As the machine had replaced physical effort, the motor-car the horse-drawn vehicle and, in the front of everyone's mind in 1918, the tank had replaced the cavalry, so the instrument would oust the unaided human voice from its musical primacy at that time. A large symphony orchestra can certainly suggest great power, but it can also offer a huge range of tonal colour, a range to beat anything even a large choir can produce. It can also lead the listener into a world of musical ideas, not in any way limited by words. These must have been crucial points in its favour for those sated with choral music. The reader may care to think about these propositions and agree or disagree.

A decline in standards?
It has to be said that there was indeed some decline in the standards of performance at the later Festivals. In 1919, W. P. in *Birmingham and Music* comments on the very favourable remarks made about the Festivals back in 1852 by Lowell Mason of New York (page 108). W. P. suggests that 'this is placing Birmingham on a pinnacle surely'. Further, in his book *A Mingled Chime*, Thomas Beecham is also less than complimentary about the Festivals he attended in the Richter period. He writes that the level of performance 'was rarely higher than adequate, as the time and facilities for rehearsal were never anything like sufficient'. In addition, we have the testimony of the noted harpist, Charles Collier, writing in 1957 - whom we met in the chapter on 'Richter's' Festivals - that the orchestras in those days 'did not work as hard as they do today' It is clear, too, that as the nineteenth century progressed, larger-scale works were given at the Festivals and the specialist orchestras of the early nineteenth century were not employed. An almost ad hoc orchestral situation pertained. A very large number of singers and instrumentalists were almost thrown together at a relatively late stage in the proceedings and the thing gradually became more of a jamboree than a finished performance.

The end of a musical era
Whatever the reasons, it was the repertoire of the symphony orchestra which was increasingly enthusing the more enterprising spirits in the musical world, and it should be pointed out that Birmingham's Music Festivals, with their strong celebration of choral and vocal music, were not the only festivals based in an industrial city which did not survive far into the twentieth century. The Manchester and Sheffield Festivals also fell by the wayside, although Leeds managed to go on until after the Second World War. Further, as people became more aware of the potential of the symphony orchestra they were correspondingly more aware of the need for more disciplined playing in this sphere, and of the sustained effort and background organisation which would be needed to bring this about. Musical energies were gradually being redirected.

Social changes
Other changes were occurring which would also affect people's attitude profoundly. Increasingly, services like social welfare, education and health would be

Chapter 20 - Phase One: Birmingham Musical Festival - Cause of death

paid out of taxes and local rates from 1900 onwards. The days of the large subscription list of individual benefactors was coming to a close, as personal taxation grew to crushing levels. As so often, this bore most heavily on those in the middle income group. Since many Birmingham workers were well-paid, it also hit some skilled artisans. This was not just due to the 1914 war, but had started much earlier, when the financial burden of supporting the British Empire had begun seriously to be felt.

While some few individual investors did very well out of colonial enterprises, and were influential enough to insist that they were continued, the British as a whole certainly did not.[1] The dependent territories expected the mother country not only to defend them, but also to fund services like railways and communications systems in addition, leaving them, on the other hand, free to develop other projects for their own benefit. Income tax in Britain had first been levied in 1799, during the Napoleonic Wars, but by 1851 it was, because of our colonial commitments, both permanent and heavy. The British citizen was the most heavily-taxed in the world, with a level almost three and a half times that of other developed countries in 1860, and still two and a half times as great in 1912. Because of the way the tax system was devised and because it was the middle-class which carried most of the weight of this, it affected just those people whose energy and generosity had been most vital in maintaining the success of the Birmingham Musical Festivals. The situation was at its worst in 1906 when the middle-class contribution to the state coffers was far higher, pound for pound, than that of the upper class, since unearned income was not taxed and a super-tax on the very rich did not come in until 1910. The least well-paid were, naturally, exempt from tax.

It is not surprising therefore that festival takings ceased to rise after 1876, and that at the succeeding twelve festivals they only exceeded £5,000 at three of them, one of those being in 1900, the year of Elgar's *Gerontius*. By this time, many people had both less spare income and at the same time a growing inclination to think that the government, which took so much off them in tax, ought to take on some of the benevolent tasks formerly undertaken by benevolent individuals.

The effect of World War
The general disillusion following the First World War, with its five million Allied deaths, three million German and Austrian casualties and a total of twenty-one million wounded, meant that nothing would ever be the same again. The spirit of the festivals, leisurely, graciously-garbed, and including much music with an openly expressed religious component, had been extinguished, never to be rekindled in the same form. People were more inclined towards more frivolous distractions after the war. Easier travel, regular holidays and more organised sport for all competed, between the two World Wars, for what money was to spare.

Cause of death?

So, higher artists' fees, not matched by increased audiences and donations, a general reduction of disposable income, especially among the middle classes, the depression after the 1914 war, and, finally, the change in musical taste with the shift away from vocal towards instrumental music all seem to have played a part in ending the notable 144-year-long era of the Birmingham Musical Festival. Causes of death, plural, rather than cause of death, singular.

---

1. Lance. E. Davis and Robert A. Huttenback: *Mammon and the Pursuit of Empire.* The Economy of British Imperialism. 1860-1912. Cambridge. 1986.

Chapter 21

Elgar and Birmingham

Edward Elgar 1857-1934

Many people think of Birmingham as being the scene of some painful experiences for Elgar and this has tended to detract from the honourable part the city played in his development, and the services he rendered, in turn, to the city. This section is an attempt to put the picture back into focus.

Elgar as orchestral violinist and composer in Birmingham
As we saw in chapter 16, Edward Elgar was first associated with the city in the nineteenth century, as an orchestral violinist, his membership of Stockley's orchestra affording the budding composer valuable extra experience of the orchestral repertoire and, in 1885, the experience of playing in a Birmingham Musical Festival. In that same year, Stockley's band provided the accompanying orchestra for the performance of two British choral works by Bridge and Stanford, the latter a full oratorio. The fact that Stanford was less than five years older than Elgar spurred on the latter to think in terms of composing on a much larger scale than he had previously attempted.

The performance of Elgar's pieces *Intermezzo mauresque, Sevillana* and *Suite in D minor* in 1883, 1885 and 1888, has been described in the same chapter. These Birmingham performances brought Elgar to the attention of a wider audience, which put some further pressure on him to progress to something more ambitious. It also gave him a little public appreciation and encouragement, something he always badly needed.

Elgar as a major composer at the Birmingham Festivals
Birmingham came back into Elgar's life in 1900 in no uncertain fashion, making the twentieth century the most high-profile part of his association with the city. He was by now the composer of an acknowledged masterpiece, the *Enigma Variations* of 1899, heard in London by influential members of the Birmingham Festival scene. Elgar had also married a gifted wife and now had a source of sympathy, gentle pressure, encouragement and admiration permanently at his side.[1] He felt able to accept the Birmingham Festival Committee's commission for a full-scale oratorio, and the subject, Cardinal Newman's poem *The Dream of Gerontius,* was agreed. The chairman of the Festival Committee, G. H. Johnstone, assured the composer that no difficulty would arise because of the Roman Catholic theology of the poem, which included

the idea of Purgatory. Please note that this assurance was given to Elgar on 1st January 1900 about a large-scale work which was to be performed early in October the same year! On 12th January Elgar went to the Birmingham Oratory, Hagley Road, to ask Cardinal Newman's executor, Father Neville, for permission to adapt the words of the poem for the libretto. Ten days later, Novello agreed to publish the new work at G. H. Johnstone's request, and Johnstone undertook all the negotiations with the publisher on Elgar's behalf. By the end of February the music was well in hand and Elgar was able to play some of it to close and appreciative friends. By early May, however, everyone was beginning to be uneasy about the timing of the arrangements for publishing the score and, most of all, about how there was ever going to be enough time to rehearse the work.

It could be said that Murphy's Law was in operation with a vengeance; if that is not too vulgar an idea to associate with a work such as *The Dream of Gerontius*. On 11th June Charles Swinnerton Heap died. A highly enterprising and successful choral conductor (among many other things as we have seen), Heap had taken over the Festival Choral Society from Stockley in 1897 and great things had been hoped for. To make matters even worse, Richter himself would not be available until just before the festival, so there was no alternative but to entrust the rehearsal of the new work to Stockley. At last, on 20th August the first choral rehearsal was called, with Stockley singing in the solo parts, as he had always been able to do.[2] A week later progress was reported, but there was great anxiety among members of the chorus itself. Stockley was slow now, and physically quite feeble. Shortened rehearsals meant that some of the Wolverhampton contingent, for example, hardly sang at all, and wondered why they had bothered to make the journey to Birmingham.[3]

The next step was for Stockley to invite Elgar to take a choral rehearsal himself. Elgar worked on many important points and politely professed himself pleased (but of course). Alice Elgar, more concerned with the sound of the music itself, was transported. Henry Coward, the noted Sheffield musician, whom we have already met, was asked by Elgar to come and deliver an opinion. Coward made himself scarce after the rehearsal, however, and that was ominous. Then, to add still further to the difficulties, the publication of the orchestral parts was delayed and Richter himself first saw the score on 23rd September, with only ten days to go to the first performance. The first full rehearsal, with everyone there, soloists, chorus, orchestra - and Richter - was on Saturday afternoon, 29th September Guests, friends, *and* members of the press were also present in the hall. As anxiety increased, so tempers rose, none more so then Elgar's which finally erupted in a tirade against them all for getting 'everything wrong'. His desperation was wholly understandable but not at all wise. It alienated many, and when it came to the performance on the following Wednesday (taken too slowly by Richter, probably for safety), some of the audience suspected deliberate sabotage. E. A. Baughan, writing in the *Musical Standard* (13th Oct.) opined:

Chapter 21 - Elgar and Birmingham

'Doubtless Mr. Elgar's protest took the spirit out of the chorus, and it seems to have so seriously injured the pride of many that it is quite a question if they did their loyal best with the composition on Wednesday morning'.

What were the main faults of the performance? The soloists were far from ideal, Richter was not in full command being, as we have said, less than the finest of choral conductors, and the orchestral players were virtually sight-reading their parts. It was the chorus most of all, however, which showed itself unequal to its novel task. As a contemporary *Musical Times* commentator put it, it was not that the choral parts were exceptionally difficult but only that they were 'of a kind to which choralists are not yet accustomed'. The tenors in particular were defeated by the chromatic writing and, either by accident or partly by design, sang flat.[4]

A balanced account of the affair is given by Dora Powell née Penny, 'Dorabella' of the *Enigma Variations*. In her book about Elgar, she quotes her own diary entry after the first performance. It says: 'Too wonderful and clever to describe here, but performance not good'. She then goes on:

'I remember well wondering what to put. The performance lacked so much of what one knew was there. The chorus had not had enough time to learn their music: the Elgar idiom was like a foreign tongue that cannot be mastered in a few weeks. To crown all, a soloist began one of his 'pieces' a semitone flat - or was it sharp? - *and stuck to it* - (bless his heart!) He was so upset about it afterwards. It was all rather dreadful and I felt afterwards that I wanted to get home quickly and meet nobody. The poor Elgars had escaped back to their hotel and saw no one - how my heart ached for him and what he must have felt that day!'

Yet after what was a nightmare experience for Elgar and some of his closest friends, the audience in the Town Hall broke all the rules about 'no audible expression of applause' at the morning performance, and gave him a tremendous ovation. Like Alice Elgar, many listeners had heard the great new music shining through the chaotic performance and had been prepared to ignore - or did not fully appreciate - what was amiss up on the platform. German musicians in the Town Hall invited by A. J. Jaeger of the Novello publishing house - 'Nimrod' of the *Enigma Variations* - were bowled over. Within a year Professor Julius Buths, who was one of them, supervised a performance of the work in Düsseldorf. This was a great triumph and after it, Alice Elgar recorded in her diary that 'R. Strauss made a beautiful speech about Meister Elgar, no end of toasts'. In a letter to Alfred Littleton, Chairman of Novello, Elgar himself wrote: 'Richard Strauss, who never speechifies if he can help it, made a really noble oration over Gerontius - I wish you could have heard it - & it was worth some years of anguish - now I trust over - to hear him call me Meister'. (Quoted in Jerrold Northrop Moore op. cit.). Extracts from *Gerontius* were given at the Worcester Festival in 1901, and it was given complete at the Sheffield Festival in 1902, conducted by Henry Wood. The admirable Muriel Foster sang the Angel and John Coates was the excellent Gerontius on that occasion. The *Dream of Gerontius* went into the regular repertoire both here and in Germany, and eventually on the American continent. It was a great triumph for English music in the end, and a vindication of the discernment and faith of the Birmingham Festival Committee. This was rewarded when Elgar agreed to a further commission from them in December 1901, ready for the 1903 festival. They, in return, guaranteed the proper training of the chorus, now under the direction of R. H. Wilson who had been the Hallé chorus-master in Richter's time.

So, in the event, Elgar forgave Birmingham so far as to entrust its festival with three further first performances, and a chance to redeem itself with a repeat performance of the *Dream of Gerontius* in the Town Hall in 1909. The second Elgar oratorio for Birmingham, *The Apostles*, was given in 1903, conducted by the composer, but only parts 1 and 2 were ready in time. Nevertheless, it was a tremendous success and confirmed Elgar as a major, not to say, great composer. Richter even thought it the greatest work since Beethoven's *Mass in D* according to a letter from R. H. Wilson to Elgar.

Edward Elgar In 1900.

This time, Elgar had conducted the work himself and the soloists had been, as far as was practicable, singers of his own choosing. These were Emma Albani as the Virgin and Angel, Muriel Foster as Mary Magdalene, John Coates as St. John, Kennerley Rumford as St. Peter, Ffrangcon Davies as Jesus and Andrew Black as Judas. The chorus, trained by Wilson, sang with dedication and enthusiasm under Elgar, conscious no doubt that they must efface the memory of the *Gerontius* difficulties three years before. Everything was back on course as far as Elgar and Birmingham were concerned, and set fair for them to complete a most rewarding voyage together. Another performance of *The Apostles* was given at the 1906 Festival, along with the premiere of the second in what was intended to be a trilogy of oratorios, namely *The Kingdom*. This time Agnes Nicholls, William Higley and Charles Clarke replaced Albani, Kennerley Rumford and Andrew Black as Mary, Peter and Judas. Nicholls, Higley and John Coates joined Muriel Foster, ever Elgar's preferred mezzo-soprano, in *The Kingdom*. Again, Elgar conducted his own works.

It was clear even then that the inspiration in *The Apostles* was at a lower level than in *Gerontius*, and *The Kingdom* below that again. Ernest Newman deprecated the whole idea of the trilogy and said, in print, that Elgar should be concentrating on the orchestral repertoire; with which most people would now agree. Newman acknowledges however that 'Elgar is now so consummate a master of effect, particularly of orchestral and choral effect, that he can almost persuade us against our own judgement that the actual tissue of the music is better than it really is' *(Birmingham Daily Post,* 4th October 1906). This did not prevent audiences for the Elgar works from being huge, and his prominent position at the Birmingham Festivals did an enormous amount to make the whole country, and much of the rest of the world, aware of England's Edward Elgar. The international dimension of Birmingham's musical life was clearly still in existence.

The 1909 festival presented the best of Elgar's music and Birmingham was quite able to make up for the past. Richter conducted *Gerontius* and Elgar's Symphony no. 1 in A flat, first performed in Manchester the previous December. As this was Richter's last festival, it was particularly fortunate that everything went well.

Muriel Foster, mezzo - soprano, 1877-1937.

Finally, in 1912, Birmingham was vouchsafed another Elgar premiere. This was *The Music Makers,* with Muriel Foster as soloist, together with chorus and orchestra. Elgar himself conducted. Critics appeared to think – and one cannot but agree with them – that the inferior poem by Arthur O'Shaughnessy undermined the piece, and was unworthy of Elgar's genius. This was not helped by the fact that Elgar included in it quotations from some of his own finest works which pointed up the difference in the levels of inspiration of the words and the music, to the detriment of the former. This was all the more of a pity for Elgar's, and England's, musical reputation, since it was followed by a fine new work by a foreigner. This was the *Symphony no. 4 in A minor* by Sibelius, commissioned for the festival and conducted by the composer. Perhaps another performance of parts one and two of *The Apostles* on the Friday evening – the very last music ever to be performed at the Birmingham Musical Festivals – made up for this. We may perhaps reflect too, that the festivals had ended, as they began, with a choral work 'made in England'. This time, however, it was made by a born Englishman.

Elgar was given pride of place at the last five festivals and it obviously cannot be said for one moment that the relationship between Elgar and the Birmingham Musical Festival people was other than very cordial and friendly. Elgar knew what he owed to them. He even bore no grudge against Stockley for his part in the unfortunate 1900 *Gerontius* affair, remembering instead all the good Stockley had done for Birmingham – and for Elgar himself as well.

Elgar and the groves of academe

Evidence of the respect in which Elgar was held in Birmingham is the fact that he was both a visitor to the Midland Institute School of Music and, from 1905 to 1908, Birmingham University's first Professor of Music. The Chair of Music was established in 1905, through the generosity of Richard Peyton, a manufacturing chemist, Birmingham City Councillor, amateur painter and keen music-lover. We have met him already, in chapter 9, sorting out the 'hot rolls' incident at a rehearsal of Gade's *The Crusaders* in 1876. The chair was to carry a stipend of £400 (now worth £12,000), together with a stipulation that it would only be set up if Elgar agreed to accept it. He had no taste for teaching in any shape or form, quite the reverse, but felt that because of all the opportunities the city had afforded him he must accept, and so secure for its new university a Department of Music. Here, incidentally, we are seeing another specifically twentieth century development in that Birmingham, along with several other industrial cities, is becoming a university city for the first time.

An inaugural lecture was required from the new professor of course, and this was given in the large theatre of the Midland Institute, then in Paradise Street, on 16th March 1905.

Other lectures followed. The full title of the inaugural lecture was *A Future for English Music*. The remaining lectures were on *English Composers* (Nov. 1), *Brahms' Symphony no. 3* (Nov. 8), *English Executants* (Nov. 29), *Critics* (Dec. 6) and *Retrospect* (Dec. 13). Two further lectures were given by Elgar in November 1906, one on *Orchestration* and one on Mozart's *Symphony* no. 40 in G minor.

Elgar's Birmingham lectures have been edited from Elgar's own hand-written notes by Dr. Percy M. Young and readers are able to see for themselves what Elgar said. At the time, they created some consternation, some of his hearers being uncomfortably aware, especially at the inaugural lecture, that some of his general criticisms had specific people in mind. He seemed almost to be 'doing a Charles Lunn' all over again, inspired by a chip on the shoulder; flailing about verbally and making what seemed to be veiled attacks on well-known figures in the music world; failing to clarify the very important positive points he was trying to make; becoming incoherent and going on too long! Rosa Burley, a long-standing friend of the family and headmistress of The Mount School in Malvern, where Elgar had once taught violin and at which his daughter was a pupil, described it as 'one of the most embarrassing failures to which it has ever been my misfortune to listen'.[5] Nevertheless, musical opinion, as expressed in the press and music journals, seems to have welcomed the serious underlying points that Elgar was making - or seemed to be trying to make.

Anxious, like so many more, over the state of indigenous English - we would say British - music, Elgar pleaded for our musicians to be well-versed in music through practical music-making. He spoke against dry academicism, also against the insipid technical correctness of much British music. Elgar called it 'white'. Better to be exuberant and vulgar, and perhaps make some harmonic 'mistakes' than to have no good red blood and no real inspiration at all. The refinement would come later. Elgar stated quite boldly that he found most of the recently-composed music commonplace and that was why it never held an abiding place in the public's affections. He excepted Sir Hubert Parry from these criticisms, but by not mentioning Stanford, set the cat among the pigeons and gave great offence in a powerful quarter. Stanford was Professor of Composition at the Royal College of Music.

The remedy, Elgar suggested, was not to whine in a misconceived imitation of Mendelssohn, nor 'groan' like a follower of Brahms, nor 'shriek' as Richard Strauss in his most livid rages; it was not even to try to imitate the native English style of Purcell. He pleaded, instead, that 'the younger men' should draw their inspiration more from their own country, from their own literature, - and in spite of what many would say - from their own climate. Good Heavens! Was not Shakespeare a Warwickshire man, and were they not in his own country and county? The younger generation must cease from imitation.

One significant suggestion Elgar made which bore good fruit was about the importance of an excellent university music library and it must be said that he himself took practical and generous steps in the matter, setting things on the right road. Significantly, he also urged the establishment of a permanent orchestra in the city, while praising the famous choral society. He confessed to having learned a good deal about choral effect 'under our revered chief, Mr. Stockley'. (So certainly no hard feelings were harboured!) He speaks also of encouraging opera in the town, either English opera or opera in English.

Some of this was all very fine, but Elgar then returned to his attack on living composers of works produced between 1880 and 1900. The results of these were cold and left him unmoved, he said. Great dexterity was displayed in the technical finish of the works, but there was absolutely nothing new. The student of orchestration and choral writing would learn better from a French or German composer. What was needed was something growing out of our own soil and, to quote him, 'something broad, noble, chivalrous, healthy and above all, an out-of-door sort of spirit'. 'To arrive at this', he continued, 'it will be necessary to throw over all imitation. It will be necessary to begin to look at things in a different spirit'. He also commented that it was time to put an end to the sad situation where composers hailed as budding geniuses at thirty had dwindled to nonentities by the time they were fifty or sixty.

With a final salute to Granville Bantock and the Midland Institute School of Music, with whom he looked forward to co-operating, Elgar ended with a quotation from David Hume: 'We place our lever in Heaven and by it we can move the world'.

Of course this was not a tactful lecture for a new Professor of Music to give, but it was all-too-truthful and caused an enormous stir. At least two reports, one in the *Birmingham Post* on 17th March 1905 and the other in the April issue of *Musical Opinion* admitted that there was justice in what he had said and that, on balance, he was right to say it.

In the subsequent lectures, Elgar expressed great satisfaction at the excellence being attained by English orchestral musicians - as opposed to continental ones is the idea implied here. He was much less happy about our string soloists, our conductors and singers. There was only one conductor who did nothing but conduct, as opposed to conducting and composing, or conducting and training choirs, and that was Henry J. Wood - a 'giant' in Elgar's estimation - and he added that some system for training conductors ought to be devised. As to singers, both solo and choral, he pleaded for more general education, more study and real understanding of the text. There were still too many 'brainless singers' about. Choruses should cease being efficient machines, and soloists should cease to indulge in foolish and inappropriate emphasis on one particular word, merely for its sound and effect. In other words, Elgar wanted more intelligence in singers and, from solo singers in particular, a much greater sense of drama. He cited with approval the following singers: Charles Santley, Ffrangcon Davies, Andrew Black, John Coates, Muriel Foster, Kirkby Lunn.

As to organists, Elgar felt more than satisfied with the situation in England, which had some of the best organists anywhere. Indeed they did not have to go out of Birmingham for a shining example. He was speaking, of course, of C. W. Perkins, the City Organist from 1888 to 1923.

In the lecture on critics, Elgar spoke scathingly of reports which merely described the appearance of the audience, and how many of them had attended the musical event concerned. He asked for the men who wrote about performances of music to be well-read in literature and knowledgeable about art as well as about music. He praised the new breed of critic represented by Ernest Newman, E. A. Baughan and Alfred Kalisch.

Apart from the controversy which the lectures had caused, Elgar found their preparation extremely worrisome and wanted to concentrate on his own composition. The series of lectures for October and November 1907 were therefore given instead by an American academic, Thomas Whitney Surette, and by H. Walford Davies and Ernest Newman. Surette spoke on the music dramas of Wagner, on Russian music and on Beethoven's Fifth Symphony, Davies on church music and modern harmony and Newman on new forms in music. These were held in the large lecture hall of the university, then in Edmund Street, approximately where the present Central Library now is.

Much of what Elgar rightly asked for in his lectures, muddled and badly expressed as it was, has since come about. His own music, and that of Holst, Vaughan Williams,

Walton, Britten and Tippett for example, has a firm place in the repertoire. Foreign musicians admire it and perform it. Our music critics are expected as a matter of course to be musically knowledgeable and television and radio music presenters are frequently, though not always, practising musicians themselves. During the twentieth century, the country produced some internationally acclaimed conductors and singers, and our organists could - and can - still vie with the best. There have also been more university and conservatoire places available for music students. Yet there is, at the beginning of the twenty-first century, increasing concern about the future for classical music in this country, and its marginalisation in schools and in the public media. There is particular concern about the absence of Singing from the schools curriculum. We need another figure of the calibre of an Elgar to lead a revival against the over-utilitarian and profit-led contemporary culture.

Mason College, Edmund Street, before 1886 (Later the University of Birmingham) This is where the present Central Library now stands.

When the time came to plan the 1908 lectures, Elgar was immersed in the preparation of his first symphony and wrote to resign from the Chair of Music. This was a relief to everyone, even Richard Peyton, who considered that three years had been wasted. This was not quite fair, it should be said, as the Music Department still benefits from its library, the University Music Society and the Great Hall organ, which Elgar had encouraged. Granville Bantock was appointed as new Professor of Music at Birmingham University in succession to Elgar on 4th November 1908. This was very far from being the end of Elgar's association with Birmingham however, but in future he would appear in his more natural roles; as composer and conductor.

Elgar as conductor
Elgar came to Birmingham as a conductor on several occasions, including three times with the London Symphony Orchestra in Harrison's series. These visits were in 1905, 1915, and 1916. (Please see chapter 11 for details). He also conducted one

of Halford's concerts on 21st January 1902. (see chapter 22). Perhaps the fitting climax to it all was when, in October 1920, Elgar came to conduct an opening concert of the newly formed, city-subsidised symphony orchestra, the City of Birmingham Orchestra. He later confessed to his biographer, Robert Buckley, that he was on that occasion powerfully conscious of that place at the third desk of the first violins where he himself used to sit, when playing in Stockley's orchestra, nearly forty years earlier.

Whatever the ups and downs of Elgar's relationship with Birmingham, it must be said that it was both long (from 1882) and fruitful, for both parties. Elgar, a rather taut and nervous figure, must have made the trip from Snow Hill station, along Colmore Row, to the Town Hall, on dozens of occasions, with occasional excursions either next door to the Midland Institute, then still in Paradise Street, or across the road to the University, in Edmund Street, Those central areas, now so changed but remembered by older citizens of Birmingham, must have been extremely familiar to the man who was the first great English composer for two centuries. Alas, he did not much like the place apparently. Writing to Lady Alice Wortley after the 1912 festival, he hopes that she is 'rested and quiet after that hideous Birmingham'. Perhaps he was thinking principally of the stresses and strains of the festival itself, but in any case the epithet is in marked contrast to the words used by William Hutton in 1741 when he admired the bright cleanliness of the uncrowded town. (chapter 4).

Nevertheless, it is good to think that Elgar conducted the City of Birmingham Orchestra, then in its infancy. One cannot help but think he would be absolutely delighted with to-day's grown-up orchestra, though what he would have to say about other aspects of contemporary music and music-making one trembles to think.

Postscript

Elgar provided the incidental music for a play about Beau Brummel, at the Theatre Royal, New Street, in November 1928. He himself conducted at the first night, but neither play nor music attracted attention. Elgar's music was, in any case, suffering a temporary eclipse in the 1920s.

Finally, it was the noted Birmingham physician, Arthur Thomson, then attached to the General Hospital and later Dean of the Medical School, who was consulted by Elgar, in Birmingham, after the death of Alice Elgar and who attended Elgar in his final illness. Inevitably perhaps, a sad end to a long association with the city.

So we see Elgar associated, among other things, with two absolutely vital strands of twentieth century music in Birmingham, namely the development of higher music education institutions, and the moves towards the establishment of a regular, securely-based first-class orchestra in the city. The next chapter will focus on one important enterprise which moved things along quite significantly towards this latter goal.

Chapter 21 - Elgar and Birmingham

1. Letter from Mrs. G. Sutcliffe to Roger Fiske published in *The Gramophone* July 1957 p. 4. Quoted from J. N. Moore: *Edward Elgar: A Creative Life.*
2. For some amusing descriptions of how he 'filled in' at performances, for horns, bassoons, singers and anyone else who missed a few notes, please refer to his book, W. Stockley op. cit.
3. Mrs. Richard Powell: *Edward Elgar: memories of a variation.*
4. For the chronology of events connected with the first performance of the *Dream of Gerontius* the writer has drawn heavily on Jerrold Northrop Moore's *Elgar: A Creative Life.*
5. Rosa Burley: *Edward Elgar: the record of a friendship.*

Chapter 22

Halford's concerts

It is time to examine in more detail how the growing importance of the symphony orchestra *per se* showed itself in Birmingham. And since the fortunes of orchestral music came to dominate the shape of music in Birmingham in the twentieth century, as the Festivals did in the nineteenth, then this is a crucial chapter. It describes a most important further development along the road to establishing a permanent resident orchestra in the city, following Stockley's initial nineteenth century enterprise in this field. (see chapter 16).

As we have seen, Stockley felt that, in effect, he had been ousted by George Halford's orchestra and the syndicate that supported it. A slightly different view of the situation, however, comes from a Wolverhampton newspaper of January 1928, although which one is not at present known. A friend of the writer of the piece recalls the circumstances in which the Halford concerts started as follows:

'At that time the only professional orchestral body in the district was Stockley's Orchestra. This was utilised for four orchestral concerts - at Mr. Stockley's risk and expense - and for the Festival Choral Society concerts. It was drawn largely from theatre bands in the district and from Gilmer's Military Band. Cornets alone were used, and when a trumpet was required for the *Messiah* or *Samson* the player was engaged from London. As an illustration of the lack of players of reputation, in the orchestra of 130 players for the Triennial Festivals only 12 or 14 local players were engaged, all the rest being from the London or the Hallé Band. Mr. Halford went to the Continent to study conducting, and on his return the Halford Concerts were started. The cornet was cast out and the players told they must learn the trumpet or men would be engaged in London. Of course they "switched over". Mr. Freeman, father of Mr. Harry Freeman, became the principal trumpeter, and never again was a solo trumpeter called from London. High class programmes were given at eight orchestral concerts each season'.

(There is an inaccuracy in the above account as Stockley's concerts were only a cost to himself in the first season, after which he acquired backers. See chapter 16).

The reasons for the eventual failure of George Halford's venture will emerge; but more immediately, who were the people who formed the syndicate to back him? The president was the Lord Mayor of Birmingham, vice-presidents being the

Duchess of Hamilton, Earl Howe and Viscount Cobham. Among the other 54 members of it were Harrison Barrow, Charles Bassano of Old Hill, Miss Helen Cadbury, C. W. Dixon, A. R. Gaul, G. H. Kenrick, A. F. Martineau, H. F. Osler, C. W. Perkins, E. W. Priestley, Rowland M. Winn, W. H. Ryland and most crucially of all for the future, Neville Chamberlain. Local people will recognise some influential names in this list. In addition, Chamberlain's involvement in the enterprise was no doubt an important factor in his subsequent support for the founding of a city-funded orchestra.

Let us turn to the orchestra itself and survey the music it played. It had a string section of 12.10.8.8.8, triple woodwind, and the usual brass and percussion of an early twentieth century orchestra. The joint leaders of the orchestra were Ernest Schiever, leader of Richter's orchestra but based in Liverpool, and Fred Ward. Ward had actually played as a first violin in Stockley's orchestra and was a tutor at the Midland Institute School of Music during the 1890s. These two were joint leaders, also, of the Festival orchestra at that time. It was to Ward that Elgar dedicated a piece for violin and piano, *La Capricieuse,* composed in 1891. The principal flautist, too, was 'imported' but the principal viola was J. A. Beard, a local resident, later a member of the city's official orchestra and father of that orchestra's leader from 1920 to 1932, namely Paul Beard. Indeed, an increasing number of orchestral players were Birmingham-based as time went on, as will be seen in the next chapter. (chapter 23). It may perhaps interest concert-goers to see the lay-out of the orchestra on the Town Hall platform, as given in an article by Havergal Brian in 1905; a factor which Brian believed contributed to the fine ensemble in *tutti* passages.

BRASS		PERCUSSION		BASSES
VIOLINS	HORNS		BASSOONS	CELLOS
VIOLINS	OBOES		CLARINETS	VIOLAS
		FLUTES		
		(Conductor)		

This unusual arrangement has all the strings at the sides and all the wind instruments in the middle.

In general the programmes have a modern look. The 'vocal spots' occurred more rarely and when they did, were more 'meaty'. Notice that the concerts were held on Tuesday evenings, fortnightly between October and March, with about ten in a season. There was no interval in these concerts.

Halford conformed to the custom of the time and did not neglect contemporary British composers. On 21st January 1902, Elgar himself came to conduct his own overture, *Cockaigne,* and two new Military Marches, no. 1 and no. 2 *(Pomp and*

Circumstance). The *Cockaigne* overture had had its premiere at the Queen's Hall, London, six months before and the marches had first appeared, to a warm welcome, in Liverpool under Rodewald the previous October (1901). Halford conducted the other orchestral works in that programme, which also included some Granville Bantock songs. Elgar's *Enigma Variations* were performed on 8th December 1903 in company with Tchaikovsky's Fifth Symphony and the Mozart Piano Concerto no. 20 in D minor K. 466. Elgar's *Sea Pictures* were sung by Ada Crossley in March 1907, with *Variations on an African Air* by Coleridge-Taylor given at the same concert. The programme on 25th November 1902 included a symphonic poem, *A Summer Night*, by Rutland Boughton. Many will only know Boughton as the composer of the opera *The Immortal Hour*, given at the original Birmingham Repertory Theatre, in Station Street, in 1922, and then taken to the Regent Theatre in London - brief moments of glory not to be repeated. Boughton was a teacher at the Midland Institute School of Music from 1904.

A weighty programme on 29th March 1904 is worth mentioning since the Strauss tone-poems *Also sprach Zarathustra* and *Ein Heldenleben* framed Wotan's Farewell and the Fire Music from Wagner's *Die Walküre*, with Wotan sung by Andrew Black. The composer Havergal Brian wrote in glowing terms of Halford's interpretation of the Strauss works. He spoke of the 'climaxes... so huge, so immense, and yet achieved with a calm that is almost terrible in its intensity'.

Another impressive Halford achievement was to secure a visit from Richard Strauss himself to conduct a concert in his series. This was on 20th December 1904. A review in the *Musical Times* reveals that the programme consisted of three Strauss tone poems: *Don Juan, Tod und Verklärung* and *Ein Heldenleben*. The reviewer tells us that 'the performance of each, *directed by the composer*, brought out all their special points, and our local orchestra achieved triumph after triumph. Strauss's Violin Concerto (op. 8), with Mr. Max Mossel as soloist, made a great impression. Dr. Strauss had a reception of the most enthusiastic description, and the performance of every number evoked the heartiest applause'.

Halford was something of a purist in his programme-planning and set out to explore the symphonic repertoire for its own sake. All Beethoven's Symphonies were given, including the ninth; Borodin's Second Symphony (8th Nov. 1898) and Bruckner's Fourth Symphony (27th Oct. 1903) are also to be found. The Bruckner and Borodin would be an innovation in Birmingham where symphonies still had to be carefully chosen and taken in very small doses. Halford was daring to extend a little further what Richter had begun at the Festivals. Festival audiences had for long accepted Beethoven and Mendelssohn symphonies, but Richter added Schumann, Dvorák and Brahms, so Halford's excursions into Bruckner and Borodin continued that exploration of the symphonic repertoire. To play seven of the Beethoven symphonies in the one year, as Halford did in 1904-5, would certainly be a challenge to those who still felt more at home with the vocal-and-orchestral repertoire, spiced with a small admixture of lighter, more romantic orchestral pieces.

The best laid plans - the question of the first British performance of Rachmaninov's Second Piano Concerto

It is clear that Halford's orchestra was taken very seriously by many outstanding musicians elsewhere, some of whom came to conduct it, as we have seen, and some of whom were prepared to write for it, as was Rachmaninov evidently. Havergal Brian asserts that Rachmaninov wrote his Piano Concerto no. 2 in C minor for George Halford in Birmingham. The facts of the matter are these. Rachmaninov was invited to come to London in 1900 to play his own first *Piano Concerto,* written between 1890 and 1891, and revised in 1917. He was obviously not very happy with this work, however, and promised to write a better one 'for England' according to some authorities, 'for London' according to others. According to Brian, it was 'for Birmingham'. In any case the promise was apparently made to the Secretary of the Royal Philharmonic Society in London and, indeed, on 29th May 1902 the concerto was played for the Philharmonic by the pianist Sapellnikov, with Frederic Cowen conducting. This is claimed as the first English performance, but it was probably only so by default. The first English performance of Rachmaninov's Piano Concerto no. 2 was programmed for a Halford concert at Birmingham Town Hall on 4th March 1902, with George Halford conducting and Alexandre Siloti as soloist. This would have taken place nearly three months before the London performance, and a review in the *Musical Times* of 1st April 1902 suggests that it should have been earlier still. Perhaps we should leave the *Musical Times* to explain.

'Rachmaninoff's Pianoforte Concerto was down *for the second time*, with M. Siloti as soloist, but *again* Mr. Halford was disappointed through the illness of the pianist. Mr. Leonard Borwick, at short notice, stepped into the breach, and his splendid playing in Beethoven's *Third Concerto* (in C minor) and in the Caprice, *Africa* of Saint-Saëns, more than made up for any disappointment the audience might have felt'. *(Musical Times* 1st April 1902).

NOTE:
The Caprice *Africa* was in fact a Fantasy for piano and orchestra.

Exactly a year later, the April issue of the same journal reveals that, on 24th February 1903, the 'long promised Piano Concerto no. 2 by Rachmaninoff', with M. Siloti as soloist, at last received its Birmingham premiere; thus beating Manchester by two days! The third English performance was given by the Hallé Orchestra on 26th February, 'the first time at these concerts', and again Siloti was at the piano, with Richter conducting.

Halford and Halford's Orchestra with Kreisler as soloist. Kreisler's last concert with them was on 7th November 1905 in the Town Hall.

Commenting on the Birmingham performance, the *Musical Times* reviewer wrote that 'the performance was superb, but the work requires more than one hearing. It is very complex, fully scored and, in places, noisy'. Meanwhile, in May 1902, the London performance of the work had taken place, and thus was Birmingham cheated of a British premiere. The fact remains, however, that Halford's orchestra had been thought worthy of the honour, even if fate snatched it away.

If the Halford concerts failed after ten years it certainly cannot have been because of the soloists employed, who were all outstanding. For after all, Birmingham was still in touch with the international music circuit in this first phase of the twentieth century and most soloists would be known already to Birmingham audiences, through Harrison's concerts and the Music Festivals. Here are some of them.

Joachim	Beethoven: Violin Concerto	28.02.1899
Fanny Davies	Brahms: Piano Concerto no. 1 in D minor	31.10.1899
Max Mossel	Sinding: Violin Concerto in A op. 45	19.03.1901
Rowland Winn	Beethoven: Fantaisie op. 80 for piano, chorus and orchestra	02.04.1901
Busoni	Beethoven: Piano Concerto no. 5	12.11.1901
Ÿsaye	Vieuxtemps: Violin concerto in E (Andante & Rondo)	26.11.1901
Ernst von Dohnányi	Variations on a Nursery Tune (his own) Beethoven: Piano Concerto no. 5	28.10.1902
Rosina Buckman	Wagner: *Tannhäuser* (Elisabeth's Greeting)	18.03.1902
Alexandre Siloti	Rachmaninov: Piano concerto no. 2 in C minor Originally planned for: Given on:	04.03.1902 24.02.1903

Fritz Kreisler	Beethoven: Violin Concerto	10.02.1903
	Tartini: *Il Trillo di Diavolo*	
Mrs. Henry J. Wood	Strauss: Group of songs	22.11.1904
Egon Petri	Saint-Saëns: Piano Concerto no. 5 in F	14.03.1905
Percy Grainger	Tchaikovsky: Piano Concerto no. 1	21.11.1905
Lady Hallé (Wilma Norman–Neruda)	Max Bruch: Violin Concerto in G minor	30.10.1906
Marie Hall	Max Bruch: Violin Concerto in G minor	12.02.1907

Bantock's Symphonic Poem *Lalla Rookh* should be added to the above list. It was given on 24th February 1903 but according to the *Musical Times was* 'not good enough in performance for criticism'.

Other appearances worth mentioning are Leonard Borwick in Beethoven's Piano Concerto no. 4 in G, Carl Fuchs in a Haydn 'Cello concerto, Kathleen Arnold in Mozart's Piano Concerto no. 20 in D minor K 466 and Frederick Dawson in the Franck Variations for Piano and Orchestra. Note also that Rosina Buckman, mentioned in the above list, came from New Zealand and trained at the Midland Institute School of Music, subsequently making a noted career in the Melba Opera Company and as a leading soprano in Beecham's companies.

Other aspects of Halford's work encompassed choir training and lecturing. It was the Halford Choir, assisted by the chorus of the Stourbridge Concerts Society, which performed in Beethoven's *Choral Symphony,* also in the same composer's *Fantaisie* op. 80, on 2nd April 1901. As to the lectures, these seem to have been given only occasionally, but what did happen on a regular basis was the sale of analytical notes, written by Andrew Deakin, ten days before each concert. They were made available through Priestley's music shop, Colmore Row. Open rehearsals were organised and an extract from a programme in November, 1897 contains the following, given verbatim:

NOTICE:
'As the symphony by Brahms (no. 2) is comparatively new to Birmingham audiences, and the Poéme Lyrique by Glazounov quite new, Mr. Halford will be glad if any of his Subscribers care to attend the final rehearsal for this Concert, to be held in the Town Hall on Tuesday November 30th at 2 p.m. Subscribers will be admitted at Door A, on production of their Serial Tickets, which on this occasion are not transferable'.

NOTE TO THE ABOVE:
A. The author takes no responsibility for the wrong accent on the word 'poème' in the above notice!

Among the lectures, one was given by Halford early in the series, in connection with the third performance in England of Richard Strauss' *Ein Heldenleben*. The announcement explains:

'Because of the complexity and magnitude of this, Mr. Halford (assisted by Miss K. Thomas at the piano) will give an explanatory lecture in the Small Theatre of the Birmingham and Midland Institute kindly placed at his disposal by the Institute Council. On Saturday March 21st at 8 p.m. prompt'.

It adds that 'Mr. Halford will feel honoured by the attendance of anyone who feels interested'.

That was in the early days when people were still feeling 'interested'. By 1906. however, the interest had declined to such an extent that Joseph Bennett, Music Critic of the *Daily Telegraph* wrote a bleak review on 2nd March 1906, deploring the lack of support for such excellent concerts. This was occasioned by a depressingly small audience at the previous concert, and the writer reflected that the series was only kept alive by guarantors, being otherwise unable to make both ends meet. This, of course, is the same situation that applied to the Festivals. Bennett further commented that George Halford was deaf to suggestions that he should make the programmes more popular, and wondered how much longer he could hold on. The answer was: not very long. Why was this?

Havergal Brian in the book *Havergal Brian On Music* comments as follows. 'Constant playing under its own and distinguished conductors, has made the Halford band a most pliable instrument. The attack, the manner - almost effortless - in which a *forte* rises from the faintest *pianissimo*, the perfect phrasing, are several features of this fine orchestra. Cross-bowing among the strings is practically unknown. Judging by the youthful appearance of the majority of the members of the orchestra, young blood obtains full sympathy'.

Elgar's interest
Elgar is known to have been very supportive of the Halford enterprise because he thought it just the kind of thing to help forward what he took to be the right vision of a future for English music. He particularly congratulated Halford on arranging the visits of Richard Strauss to Birmingham, and told Halford that he and Lady Elgar had been much pleased with a Halford Orchestra performance of two of Elgar's own pieces. Halford's letter of thanks to Elgar for his visit to the concerts includes the words: 'I think it was awfully kind of you to come when you didn't know me or anything about me but now I hope we may always be friends. We are both working for one object, the advancement of our art...'[1]

A very different view of Halford's orchestra is to be found in Ernest Newman's review in the *Birmingham Daily Post* of a Halford Orchestra performance towards the end of its life. (27th March 1907). The critic writes of accompaniments badly played, and elsewhere a 'rhythmless scurry'. The Brahms First Symphony had 'many serious blemishes some of them technical, some intellectual. The whole reading lacked unity; there was no conception of the symphony as one great harmoniously wrought totality......There was a good deal of fuzzy tone and muddled playing in the three last movements; and the dynamics were often disregarded'.

What is one to make of these very different opinions? Had Halford simply lost heart at this stage, or was it simply a basic inadequacy in himself as a conductor, as opposed to his obvious enterprise in setting up an orchestra which he hoped might eventually be supported out of public funding? Without any recordings we cannot judge for ourselves.

Finally, why did Halford's orchestra only give full seasons of concerts under the Halford name between 2nd November 1897 and 9th April 1907? Was the programme content of some of these concerts too demanding? Some commentators suggest that the failure of this enterprise, and others which followed, was because Birmingham was not yet ready for 'orchestra-only' programmes, and was still too addicted to choral music. If that was the reason, why did interest in the Festivals with their feast of vocal music also fall off? Did the standard of orchestral playing fall off? Or was a non-musical reason at work? Apparently Halford concert nights were all too often played to the accompaniment of every type of foul weather imaginable! In any case, the answer is not a simple one, as we saw in chapter 20.

What is certain is that Halford continued the build-up of a pool of Birmingham-based orchestral players. As early as 1901, Halford himself recalled that when the orchestra started, four years earlier, about half of the eighty musicians involved were from London or from Midland towns such as Cheltenham, Worcester and Wolverhampton. By 1901, however, only five 'foreigners' were needed, the rest being residents of Birmingham (*Daily Argus*, 20th February 1901). This being so, and whatever his shortcomings and those of his new players, Halford must be credited with helping to build up a most important basis for the foundation, twenty years later, of a city-funded orchestra.

---

1. Elgar, edited Percy M. Young: *A Future for English Music and other lectures.* London. 1968.

Chapter 23

An Orchestral Medley

Stockley's series of orchestral concerts from 1879 to 1897 followed by the Halford series spanning the years 1897 to 1907, both seemed to be set fair to make regular orchestral concerts in Birmingham an expected feature of the city's musical life and in this they can both be said to have succeeded.

The survival of Stockley's Orchestra may have depended to some extent on the maintenance of that variety of musical genre so beloved of the Victorians in their programme planning. Well-known symphonic music was interspersed by the always expected vocal items, some of them accompanied on the piano. Halford on the other hand was not so ready to pander to popular taste. His purpose was to present full-scale and quite demanding symphonic concerts, regularly introducing something entirely new, and his project in that form lasted only ten years. Nevertheless, when Halford's series faltered no-one was going to leave it at that. Both his enterprise and Stockley's had made regular orchestral concerts in Birmingham an expected feature of the city's musical life. In any case, given the successful establishment of the Hallé Orchestra in Manchester in 1857 and Dan Godfrey's Bournemouth Symphony Orchestra in 1893, it was now even more widely thought to be high time for a similar establishment for Birmingham. Not only had Birmingham had the premier Music Festival of the nineteenth century, and the finest chorus, but its population of some 900,000 was now exceeding that of any other city except London. Not to have a permanent orchestra would be something of a disgrace!

Of other smaller orchestral enterprises besides those of Stockley and Halford, active at this period, two were actually functioning in the nineteenth century, namely the City of Birmingham Police Band, giving annual charity concerts at the Town Hall from the 1880s, and the Edgbaston Philharmonic Orchestra. More will be said about the Police Band in chapter 27. A programme for the Edgbaston orchestra dated 31st January 1891 reveals a small band of 29 players listed as having six first and six second violins, three violas and three 'cellos, two double basses with double wind and horns, plus cornet, tuba and timpani. They seem to have played fairly 'slight' orchestral items, laced with the occasional Beethoven symphony. The conductor was S. S. Stratton and the 'accompanyist' Dr. W. T. Belcher. In the list of players we see some familiar Birmingham names, there being two Rylands (first violin and timpani), a

Feeney (second violin) and H. W. Stratton (oboe). The third enterprise, under the auspices of Granville Bantock, was a band entitled the Amateur Orchestral Society, and a programme dated the 12th December 1904 shows them giving a Berlioz concert at the Birmingham and Midland Institute.

Orchestral 'musical chairs'
The diminishing audiences for the Halford Concerts were both a setback and an opportunity, and opportunism on the part of several noted conductors and local promoters of orchestral music was certainly a hallmark of the period between 1907 and 1920. Attempts to fill the gap left by the reduction of the Halford series were numerous and intertwined and some were relatively short-lived. A bewildering number of orchestral enterprises tried their luck in the city, in what can only be described as a kind of musical chairs, until the City of Birmingham Orchestra sat securely in the last seat. The struggle was characterised as 'internecine' by Beecham but at least it was productive in the end!

The Birmingham Symphony Orchestra
At some time before the autumn of 1907 the guarantors of Halford's concerts had apparently decided to reduce the concert season from ten concerts to four. A comment in the *Musical Times* at that time states that the annual series of ten concerts of the Halford Concerts Society is discontinued because of 'a large reduction in the guarantee fund and inadequate support for these excellent concerts by the general public'. A series of four was proposed instead of the usual ten. It seems to be of some relevance here that an 'Inaugural Concert of the Birmingham Symphony Orchestra' had already been given on 4th April 1906, before the demise of the Halford series as such, which was conducted by Henry Wood. Havergal Brian (op. cit.) writes that 'Mr. Halford, after spending thousands of pounds to establish orchestral music in Birmingham, had to give in owing to lack of public support. The members of his orchestra have formed themselves into the Birmingham Symphony Orchestra'. It seems fair to conclude from all of this that the sponsors or other persons – perhaps they were the 'Birmingham Concerts Society' – had decided that their efforts would benefit from fewer concerts and the presence from time to time of more prestigious and widely known musical personalities.

Orchestral players in Birmingham
The present writer makes no apology for a most significant digression at this point. The list of players for this concert in April 1906, under the title 'Birmingham Symphony Orchestra', is extremely interesting and very well worth examining. Two significant statistics emerge. The first is that there are 66 of them, 49 of whom will be found in other orchestras in the city over the next ten or fifteen years, which suggests

that they were all locally based. Cornelius Meachem, for example, is to be found in the Birmingham Philharmonic Orchestra in 1910-11, Richard Wassell's Orchestra, 1916-19, Beecham's Birmingham Orchestra 1917-18 and the City of Birmingham Orchestra in 1920. The flautist George Bromley, related to the pianist Tom Bromley and a tutor in flute-playing at the Midland Institute School of Music, is likewise to be found in the same four orchestras. George Bromley was born in Newcastle-upon-Tyne and came to live in Aston. Aged 30 in the 1901 census, he was thus 50 years of age when he became second flute in the City of Birmingham Orchestra in 1920. F. Goddard, a Midland Institute School of Music tutor in trombone, even goes right through, playing in all the professional orchestras from the Stockley Orchestra in 1897 to the City Orchestra in 1920, always occupying the Principal's chair.

This brings us to a second statistic which is that 15 of these Birmingham Symphony Orchestra players in 1906 eventually played in the City of Birmingham Orchestra in 1920. These are C. Meachem and M. Reidy, first violins, F. E. Goddard first and then second violin, H. Timperley, second violin, J. A. Beard and W. H. Ward, violas, F. A. Ward, 'cello, Arthur and Edmund Cockerill, double basses, W. Heard and G. Bromley, flutes, J. W. Ward and J. Thomas, clarinets, A. Clarke, bassoon and F. Goddard, trombone. Further, 32 of the 75 players in the 1920 City of Birmingham Orchestra had already played in one or other of the orchestras mentioned in this chapter. No doubt some of these players were in Halford's original orchestra, back in 1897.

This clearly reveals the growing pool of good local orchestral players, capable of forming the bedrock of personnel required for a permanent city symphony orchestra.

The Birmingham Symphony Orchestra continued
It is clear too that, in spite of setbacks, Halford continued to play an active part as an orchestral conductor in the city, as will be seen from the fact that in January 1907 it was recorded that the 'newly-formed' Birmingham Symphony Orchestra, so called, were giving symphony concerts and being conducted by Henry Wood, Landon Ronald, Richter, and Halford himself. Richter's visit was seen as further strengthening the orchestra's reputation and, according to Oscar Pollack, the *Musical Times* critic, a 'splendid concert' conducted by Halford was given in that same season, in March 1907. Havergal Brian's statement that 'The members of his (Halford's) orchestra have formed themselves into the Birmingham Symphony Orchestra, run on co-operative lines' cannot as yet be verified. Whatever had actually gone on behind the scenes, what transpired was that for the 1907-08 season a different name, the Birmingham Concerts Society, was adopted for the more 'serious' Tuesday evening concerts and four of these were indeed given under that title during the 1907-08 season with Halford, Allen Gill and Frederick Cowen the conductors. This body, the Birmingham Concerts Society, should not by the way be confused with the Birmingham Orchestral Concerts Society. (see below).

Chapter 23 - An Orchestral Medley

The new formula, using visiting conductors, seems to have been effective, since for the next season, in 1908-09, eight Tuesday evening concerts were announced instead of four, to be conducted by Henri Verbrugghen, Charles Stanford, Allen Gill and Frederic Cowen, Halford himself conducting the other four. It is noticeable that this series was also given on Tuesday evenings as Halford's had been; a fact of some significance perhaps.

Soloists such as Nellie Melba – in a concert conducted by Landon Ronald – and Charles Santley continued to play an important part in bringing in audiences and the pianist, 'our own' Arthur Cooke, 'created a sensation' under Halford's baton in January 1907. Cooke was a piano tutor at the Midland Institute School of Music.

Meanwhile, again under the title Birmingham Symphony Orchestra, what one can only surmise was virtually the same band of players, but perhaps slightly fewer in number, gave Popular Saturday Night concerts at the Town Hall and these continued until 1918. Again many of them were conducted by Halford, with visiting conductors adding extra audience pulling-power for one reason or another. For example, our 'clever pianist' Arthur Cooke conducted on New Year's Day in 1910 so that local supporters and pupils would probably swell the audience here. On the other hand the celebrity factor must have operated when Richter gave his services at a Benevolent Fund Concert on 31st March 1909. Other visitors who came to conduct were Frederic Cowen, Edward German, Arthur W. Payne of the Llandudno Pavilion Concerts (in May 1907) and Julian Clifford conductor of the Harrogate Kursaal (in April 1912). The orchestra also featured in connection with other events, giving nightly concerts during the Arts and Crafts Exhibition at the Town Hall between 20th and 24th September 1910 for example. We see here, therefore, the germ of the idea that there might be a local orchestra which would automatically be thought of when any orchestral music was required for other major events in the city.

Finally, we may note that Oscar Pollack in the *Musical Times* in September 1910 informs his readers that the Birmingham Symphony Orchestra is, significantly, contributing most of the players to the new Birmingham Philharmonic Society. (See below).

Uninvited visitors! The Birmingham Orchestral Concerts Society

In the Autumn of 1907 the *Musical Times* in its Birmingham section informed readers that 'a new scheme that came as a great surprise to local musicians was made known on June 10th (1907), according to which it is proposed to give eight orchestral concerts on a grand scale at the Town Hall next season'. Three were to be by the Hallé Orchestra conducted by Richter, three by the Queen's Hall Orchestra conducted by Henry Wood, Max Fiedler of Hamburg and Landon Ronald. These concerts would use some local players and the orchestra totalled a hundred. Elgar, Holst and Max Fiedler are quoted by the *Musical Times* as supporters of a guarantee fund for this enterprise. There were also promises of support from the Lord Mayor, Henry Sayer, and the local leading citizens Messrs. Beale, Lodge, Peyton, Johnstone and Bragg. The series began with a concert conducted by Richter on 16th October 1907. This venture, which included visiting orchestras as has been said, and should not be confused with the Birmingham Concerts Society (see above), did not last beyond this first season in spite of the strong local support.

Promenade Concerts
Meanwhile Landon Ronald was presenting his annual Promenade Concerts at the Theatre Royal. These were organised by the noted violinist Max Mossel, were conducted by Ronald and ran for three weeks in May or June. The orchestra was 70-strong and the players described as mostly local. Again, the question of the rise in the number of resident orchestral players will be considered separately. This series was viewed by the local critic Oscar Pollack as a valuable 'educational force' and was according to him artistically as well as financially successful. In spite of setbacks, the Promenade Concerts lasted from 1905 to 1914.

Handsworth Orchestral Society
As with Edgbaston, it was possible for this well-established middle class suburb to think in terms of having an orchestra and this body is recorded as presenting a concert at the Town Hall in 1908.

The Birmingham Philharmonic Society
Yet another enterprise was announced in a prospectus issued in July 1910. It should not by the way be connected with the later Birmingham Philharmonic Society which was started in 1941 and is still active. This earlier Birmingham Philharmonic did in fact owe a very great deal to the Birmingham Symphony Orchestra and therefore to Halford. The avowed object of this new body was 'to place orchestral music in Birmingham on a permanent footing and develop local resources'. Given what had already been achieved by others in the field, this was perhaps a little insensitive.

An orchestra of eighty players was planned, 'selected from the best available players in the district and supplemented by principals from London and elsewhere' - but not it seems from the Hallé Orchestra any more. In fact, as we can see from their orchestral lists, a large proportion of these eighty players had already played in the Birmingham Symphony Orchestra. Eight concerts were to be given in the first season, with Landon Ronald, George Herschel, Wassilli Safonoff, Henry J. Wood, Thomas Beecham and Fritz Cassirer engaged as the conductors. A report on one of these concerts in the *Musical Times* for November of the same year comments that 'the weakest portion of the orchestra are the strings, lacking in body and tone-power to make up a first-class orchestra'. A portent of things to come, as we shall see.

Chapter 23 - An Orchestral Medley

A glimpse into one of the concerts in this series vouchsafed us by the *Musical Times* informs us that Thomas Beecham was 'much more in sympathy with Brahms than with Sir Edward Elgar's Second Symphony'. It adds that 'Ackté in the Dance of the Seven Veils (from Richard Strauss's *Salomé*) made her glorious voice soar above the tremendous orchestra'. On this occasion she must have known her music it has to be said. She was the lady who ruined the ensembles in a performance of Verdi's *Manzoni Requiem* at the last Musical Festival in 1912 and was snubbed in the artist's room afterwards by Elgar no less. Also in the programme was Havergal Brian's orchestral piece *For Valour*, a Mozart Minuet for four horns and orchestra (no K number given of course) and the Entracte from Delius' *A Village Romeo and Juliet*, the Good Friday Music from Wagner's *Parsifal* and the Ride of the Valkyries from his *Die Walküre*. It adds that the Dance of the Seven Veils was repeated at the close of the concert. Again, we see here that combination of the apparently insatiable appetite for long programmes, together with a willingness to listen to recently composed music. Whatever else, there was evidently a great desire to promote 'the new'.

As this last initiative owed a great deal to Granville Bantock, Bantock himself and all that he helped to promote will be considered separately and in more detail in due course.

The Great War
The Great War of 1914 to 1918 changed many things for ever of course. There was an initial halt to most musical activities all over the country, the eventual compulsory call-up of the young men from 1916 onwards having an effect on orchestral personnel everywhere. In Birmingham the requisitioning of the Town Hall for various periods was an added difficulty. Nevertheless, the launching of orchestral concert series soon continued almost unabated, in spite of it all! One small new feature in the way of band music offered to the citizens which might be added here was the playing of Regimental Bands in the city's public parks.

Midland Concert Promoters' Association
Indeed, the by now unstoppable movement towards the establishment of a permanent orchestra in the city was not killed off in spite of war. This is something that Thomas Beecham comments on in his book *A Mingled Chime*. He tells us that in the summer of 1916 he 'received an invitation to attend a meeting in Birmingham summoned to consider the best way of forming a municipal orchestra'. He continues, 'It was surprising that what had proved impossible in peace time should be regarded a feasible in the middle of a world war, but so many unexpected things had happened since 1914 that this perhaps was but one more to be added to the list'.

What was happening in Birmingham was that a number of leading local citizens, foremost among them being Neville Chamberlain, Lord Mayor in 1916-17 and

1917-18, were keen to see the establishment of an official, publicly-funded orchestra in the city. On 26th September 1916 the inauguration took place of a 'New Birmingham Society' to work towards that end.

We have a very full account of what happened from Thomas Beecham (op. cit.) following his invitation to the Birmingham meeting. No apology is made for quoting it rather fully.

'So there I went and duly attended several gatherings, at which all the trite sentiments ever uttered upon such a subject anywhere since life began were rolled out by one speaker after another. How necessary it was for Birmingham to have an orchestra, what a valuable contribution to the city's culture it would be, how the plan ought to be supported by everyone, and what a wonderful thing music was with its power to inspire and uplift! But of any idea how to put it into practical operation there was little evidence; certainly no one seemed ready to spend any of his own money on it, and the Lord Mayor, Mr. Neville Chamberlain, was very clear that the present was not the time to add one farthing to the rates in the interest of the fine arts'.

'This negative kind of zeal was as usual getting us nowhere, but I did discover among the representatives of about half a dozen leading societies a much greater willingness to co-operate than formerly, and I told Mr. Chamberlain that if the scheme under discussion did not materialise he might let me know, as I had the skeleton of another in my head which might result in something tangible. A little while after I did hear from him that he saw no immediate chance of any civic project being carried into effect, and that I was free to work out something on my own lines if I wished to do so. As soon therefore as I could go to Birmingham again I called into consultation two or three energetic spirits whom I had known in earlier days, obtained a list of the concerts given during the past season by all the societies operating within a radius of thirty miles, and finding it to be larger than I expected, invited their managers to come and see me'.

'They all attended and I told them that I was willing to engage an orchestra on a permanent basis for six or seven months in the year, if I could rely on their co-operation; which meant simply an understanding from them to use it for the whole of their concerts. The cost as far as they were concerned would be no more than in previous seasons; indeed, if they cared to lengthen their respective series it would be less, in view of the conditions under which the new body of players would be working. On satisfying themselves that there was no catch or snag in the proposal they unanimously consented, and my next step was to ask the principal supporters of the seasons I had conducted in 1911, 1912 and 1913 if they would join me in reviving them, as it would hardly do to have a resident orchestra in the town playing only for choral societies. This too was agreed, and I set about the task of founding yet another institution, which I maintained in this fashion for two years without incurring more than a reasonable loss. I was preparing to continue for a third when my representative in the town notified me that

Chapter 23 - An Orchestral Medley

the Government had taken possession of every building where music could be given and asked what was to be done about it. I replied that the proposition was transparently clear: no hall, no music; and that it was for Birmingham to decide if this was what it wanted. As none of the local authorities took enough interest in the matter to intervene and preserve the existence of the young organisation, I had no alternative but to abandon it, and once again the adverse fate which frowned upon every serious enterprise in Birmingham had got the better of us. But the effort was not entirely in vain. I had demonstrated that the thing could be done in a practical and fairly economical way, and a few years later the city council came forward with a grant which brought about the establishment of an actual municipal orchestra'.

The efforts towards achieving an orchestra funded by the city during war-time having, rather unsurprisingly, to be abandoned, nevertheless there were in fact two new orchestral initiatives in 1916 to help to fill that gap, both surviving to the crucial year of 1920. These were orchestras appearing under the names of Richard Wassell and Appleby Matthews. Before describing these, however, one other enterprise has to be mentioned.

The New Philharmonic Society

Earlier, in December 1915, a new 'amateur' orchestra had announced its presence on the ever-changing orchestral scene. This was to be conducted by H. M. Stevenson junior, in other words Matthew Stevenson, son of the guiding spirit behind the Midland Musical Society, formed to give low-priced concerts in the 1880s. (chapter 15). Priestley's, the music shop, presented this new orchestra which performed at the Grand Hotel. In spite of claiming to be an amateur orchestra there was some professional stiffening from some London players, one or two very experienced local orchestral musicians and some Midland Institute School of Music students. The programmes are, refreshingly, a little out of the ordinary with Arnold Dolmetsch performing at one with six violas and six vocalists and Russian orchestral music featuring in a Saturday night concert in December 1916. The latter was with the Appleby Matthews choir and the New Philharmonic Orchestra, in scenes from Mussorgsky's *Boris Godounov*. In October 1919 they gave a concert in aid of a fund to secure an organ for the Royal Institution for the Blind in Harborne. This orchestra does not seem to have survived the establishment of the City of Birmingham Orchestra.

Richard Wassell's Orchestra

From 1916 onwards, then, two new luminaries appear in the Birmingham orchestral firmament namely Richard Wassell and Appleby Matthews. Wassell's orchestra first. In March 1916, Wassell organised a concert in aid of Red Cross funds in which a 'well-balanced orchestra performed to a packed Town Hall'. (*Musical Times*). Then, in September 1916 it was announced that Wassell intended to present three concerts during the 1916-17 season. Notable pianists such as Mark Hambourg, Benno Moseiwitsch (the pianist's preferred spelling of his name), Arthur de Greef and Irene Scharrer played a prominent part in Wassell's concerts which, under the title Wassell Concert Society, survived as has been said until the 1919-20 season. Wassell also seems to have presented some popular concerts - one on 2nd March 1918, for example, with Irene Scharrer as pianist playing to a packed Town Hall. Dale Forty the music business in New Street provided all Wassell's concert management.

The *Musical Times'* reports of this series on different occasions spoke of 'well-schooled players performing to a packed Town Hall' and of Wassell conducting 'with conspicuous ability'. Again we should notice that 24 of the players who had played for Wassell between 1916 and 1920 appeared in due course in the City of Birmingham Orchestra in 1920.

Six Hallé Concerts in Birmingham
These concerts were organised in the 1916-17 season, Thomas Beecham and Landon Ronald conducting four of them, with another in conjunction with the Birmingham Festival Choral Society. The first concert was given in the presence of the Lord Mayor and Mrs. Chamberlain. The second of the series in December 1916 was given in conjunction with the Appleby Matthews Choir who sang Elgar's *To Women* and *For the Fallen*, the soloist Carrie Tubb's voice like a 'clear silver bell' (*Musical Times*).

The New Birmingham Symphony Orchestra 1917-18
This was the Beecham initiative described by the conductor in the paragraph above, entitled Midland Concert Promoters Association. Birmingham, along with other cities, must be eternally grateful to Thomas Beecham for his determination, and his personal generosity, in helping to keep alive the interest in achieving the highest standards in both orchestral music and in opera in this country. His operatic ventures in the city will be dealt with elsewhere, but it must have been encouraging that Beecham was able to use very many local players in this latest orchestral venture. It is true that he used six Hallé players - but only six! Of the total of 58 musicians, 37 of them were experienced local people and, with the six Hallé players it means that only the remaining 15 were from elsewhere. It must be marked as great progress if a conductor of Beecham's calibre was prepared to use so many Birmingham players. These concerts seem to have been held on Sunday evenings.

Beecham Orchestral Concerts 1918-19
It may perhaps be surmised that these concerts were in fact a sequel to those described in the previous paragraph. These were held on Tuesday evenings and given, to begin with at any rate, in the Central Hall in Corporation Street because of the requisitioning of the Town Hall by the government in September and October of 1918.

Chapter 23 - An Orchestral Medley

It is interesting to see from contemporary comment that audiences were greatly increased at this period by the large number of people brought to the city to do war work.

The Appleby Matthews Orchestra

Appleby Matthews was a versatile, energetic and persuasive personality who could attract and motivate singers, instrumentalists – and concert promoters! He was active as a church organist, a choral conductor and, most significantly in the present context, as an orchestral conductor, he himself being a capable violinist and violist. Beresford King-Smith gives an admirable and amusing portrayal of the confident Matthews in his book *Crescendo* (op. cit.), a history of the City of Birmingham Symphony Orchestra. Suffice it to say here that between 1916 and 1920, Appleby Matthews ran a succession of orchestral concert seasons with an orchestra presented under his own name. The earliest reference to this found by the author is to a concert on 16th July 1916 at the Town Hall in which forty players were involved, led by Alex Cohen. In the 1917-18 season, twelve Monday evening concerts were given at the Repertory Theatre, then still in Station Street. Then on 4th October 1916, Matthews conducted the first *complete* performance of Elgar's choral trilogy, *The Spirit of England,* with his chorus and orchestra and soprano soloist. Part of the work, *For the Fallen*, had already been given in Leeds two years before, under the composer's baton. In the following season, 1918-19, forty Sunday concerts were promoted at the Scala Theatre and then, in 1919-20, thirty-six concerts were announced also given on Sundays, these in the 'magnificent and up-to-date Futurist Cinema'. The first one of this last season, on 7th September 1919, was given to a packed house according to the *Musical Times*. To quote further from the same journal, 'Evidently these excellent concerts have come to stay and there is no doubt that there is a public for them so long as Mr. Appleby Matthews gives the music his patrons want and that appeals to them. The first programme was a mixture of the classical and modern, as also was the second, and the same rule will to a certain extent prevail throughout the season. The orchestra has been augmented and fine performances have been given of Mozart's E flat Symphony, Wagner's *Siegfried Idyll*, the Overture to *Rosamunde* and Dvorak's bright and spirited *Carnaval Overture*. Mr. Alex Cohen, an excellent violinist, is again the leader of the orchestra'.

One stage nearer regular arts funding – and a city orchestra?

In June 1919 the then Lord Mayor, W. A. Cadbury, welcomed delegates of the British Music Convention to Birmingham's Grand Hotel. Part of the aim of this convention was 'to foster British genius' but as far as Birmingham in particular was concerned to encourage musicians to stay in the city and not to try their fortune in London. This seems to have been the idea of the 'music industries'. The proposal was that one penny be paid on every pound of sale 'towards educating the nation to a larger appreciation of music, thereby promoting the expansion of the music industries'. In other words when you bought a piano or volumes of music, a percentage of the price would go to a music fund. Apart from anything else, it was an instance of enlightened self-interest, of course. It was also yet another glimmer of the idea that a future for the arts could only be assured if some form of regular, systematised funding was forthcoming, as was by then the case with publicly-funded free state education. This was a portent of the future – with an 'official' city orchestra and, who knows, a sort of national arts organisation for the funding of the arts?

Chapter 24

The Choral craze

There were even more choirs in Birmingham between 1900 and 1920 - almost thirty of them - than there were attempts to set up a permanent orchestra, with a regular established series of concerts. The task of describing these choirs is much more straightforward, however.

It can be assumed that the vast majority of the singers were residents of Birmingham, its suburbs and satellite towns. Some of them certainly belonged to more than one choir, but the choirs themselves were separate, local organisations with (on the whole) recognisably different titles and, one assumes, separate organising committees. The amazingly large number of these enterprises show us the huge enthusiasm for singing at that time. Everyone has a voice, of course, and music can (usually!) be made with it, without the expense of buying an instrument. There is also something extrovert about singing which suited the temper of that enterprising and confident - perhaps over-confident - age, something touched on in the previous chapter. One member of the Birmingham City Choral Society, Edwin Elliott,[1] to take an example, also belonged not only to the Victorian Concert Party and Victorian Quartette but also to the Birmingham City Choral Society's offspring, the Select Choir. Membership of the Co-operative Choir and various church choirs at different times were added to his list.

All this was encouraged by schools which now had a daily assembly with hymns and, increasingly, regular singing classes in school time. Many men, religious or not, belonged to church choirs and had learned their craft there. For those who acquired a real love of choral singing either from school or church there were some thirty choirs in Birmingham to choose from. It was possible to aim for one with a suitable standard for your own abilities and singing a repertoire you enjoyed. In addition there was the Competition Festival to be described in due course (chapter 26), which invited junior and senior school choirs to compete.

The Birmingham Festival Chorus
The leader in the choral field during the first score of years in the twentieth century was, inevitably, the famed Festival Choral Society. Still preparing for and singing in the Festivals until 1912, it kept itself in good shape with regular concerts in the non-festival years between. Not until 1916, the year after what

should have been the next Festival, did the collapse of its *raison d'être* begin to affect it. Further difficulties followed when George Sinclair, the choir's conductor from 1900, after Stockley's retirement and Swinnerton Heap's untimely death, died himself in 1917. Sinclair, one of Elgar's *Enigma Variations* - the owner of dog Dan - was an experienced choral conductor as well as being organist of Hereford Cathedral.

The choir's 'non-Festival' concerts offered a regular Boxing Night *Messiah*, with Elgar's *Dream of Gerontius* on 14th November 1904, for example, Muriel Foster, John Coates and Ffrangcon-Davies as the soloists. This was one of the regular Spring and Autumn concerts, some of these occasionally performed with the Hallé Orchestra in attendance - its usual Festival partner. A further performance of the *Dream of Gerontius* with 'Captain' John Coates as Gerontius came at the very end of Sinclair's time as conductor, in October 1916. Sinclair died the following February.

The only concert by the choir recorded by the *Musical Times* in 1917 is the usual Boxing Night *Messiah* - conducted by 'Lt.' Allen K. Blackall. The same journal reports in February 1918 that Granville Bantock's *Omar Khayyam* is to be conducted the following month by Thomas Beecham, who is duly elected as the new Festival Choral Society conductor in June of the same year. Further announcements revealed that music to be performed in the following months would include Berlioz' *The Damnation of Faust*, Handel's *Messiah* (as usual), a Wagner selection, Debussy's *Blessed Damozel* and Bach's B minor Mass. The great baritone, Robert Radford, one of the Beecham Opera Company's stars, would be among the soloists. Lt. Allen K. Blackall, so-styled, was the official chorus-master.

Again, a Beecham association with Birmingham came in a short burst (as it did with the City Choral Society earlier on) for later that year Henry Wood became the choir's conductor, staying with it for the next four years.

The Birmingham City Choral Society 1899-1908
According to Edwin Elliott, the City Choral Society was formed as a sort of junior rival to the Festival Chorus. In Elliott's own words, it consisted of younger people who 'could not get into the other society but wanted to be in one'. F.W. Beard, uncle of Paul Beard, was its chorus-master, although at concerts in 1902-4 he appears as conductor also. Auditions were held and there were some 250 singers. Rehearsals took place in the small theatre of the original Birmingham and Midland Institute which was on the site of the present Conservatoire. There were usually three concerts a year with soloists, organ and orchestra. Initially having no subscription, an entry fee of 5 shillings (25p) was asked for in the second season. Of course the choir had to finance itself using members' fees, fines for missed rehearsals(!) and season ticket revenue. Anyone wishing to resign was asked to make this fact known as soon as

possible as there was a waiting list. Numbers had built up from 250 to 335 in only the second year. Dorothy Silk, a student of the Midland Institute School of Music and later an admired solo soprano, was a member of this choir.

The choir performed recent works such as Stanford's *Phaudrig Crohoore* a ballad for chorus and orchestra composed in 1896 for the Norwich Festival. They gave this in 1902. Coleridge Taylor's *Hiawatha's Wedding Feast* composed in 1898 was offered both in 1899 and in 1904. The latter was favourably reviewed in the *Musical Times*.

Henry Coward conducted the choir in the 1906-7 season and in April 1907 it was announced that Rutland Boughton was to take over these duties since Fred Beard had 'gone to the Antipodes'. Beard had originally gone to Australia for a visit but liked it so much he stayed. At this point Thomas Beecham was invited to take charge of the 1907-8 season with his own 'new orchestra' but this did not prevent the demise of the choir in 1908 due to lack of funds. An all too familiar problem!

The Choral Union

Established in 1886, with Thomas Facer as its first choirmaster and conductor, this choir maintained a robust life on into the twentieth century and is still in existence, even if in a more modest way. In the early years of the twentieth century it was to be found described in the musical press as giving seasons of Saturday evening concerts at the Town Hall. The brilliant C. W. Perkins was their organist, accompanying performances of Handel's *Messiah* and Haydn's *Creation* for example. In 1902 they had performed a dramatised version of *Ben Hur* composed by their conductor. In May 1912 Facer retired after 25 years' service to be succeeded by Richard Wassell. In the Spring of 1914 the choir, all 356 of them, gave Edward German's *Merrie England* under Wassell's 'able conductorship' (*Musical Times*) and Wassell is again commended for a performance of Gounod's *Messe Solonelle*, this time with Wassell's orchestra. This on 11th November 1916. On 6th October 1919, however, the same choir, again under Wassell, was lambasted in the *Birmingham Post* by A. J. Sheldon for a poor performance of Handel's *Judas Maccabaeus*. Since similar severe criticisms were extended by the same (admittedly caustic) critic to Appleby Matthews' choir in this same month, one might be forgiven for thinking that the 1914 to 1918 war and the absence of young male singers away in the services might have had something to do with this. Indeed, this is confirmed by a comment in the *Musical Times* for October 1916 that choral music was being much affected by the Great War and the consequent call-up into the forces reducing the number of male singers.

Birmingham Choral and Orchestral Association

Founded in 1882 (see chapter 15) this was an organisation that did what its title implied and continued to present instrumental as well as choral music, with an emphasis on the choral. As well as presenting the standard oratorios they occasionally broke some new ground as for example with Benedict's *The Lily of Killarney* in 1908 (to a crowded Town Hall), Gaul's *Bard of Avon* in 1914, and with Edward German's *Tom Jones* and Elgar's *King Olaf* during the 1919 to 1920 season. These last-mentioned works have not worn well but at least this organisation was prepared to risk presenting recently composed music. On the instrumental front, they were bold enough to present Tchaikovsky's First Piano Concerto and we find the ever-popular local pianist Arthur Cooke playing piano solos at one of their concerts in 1918.

The Midland Musical Society
Another survival from the nineteenth century (chapter 15), this organisation remained true to its original brief of giving popular oratorio concerts with low ticket prices but did not hesitate to add an orchestral element to their programmes. In the Spring of 1907, for example, they combined with the Birmingham and Handsworth Orchestral Society to give their annual Good Friday concert. In 1908 they presented Gounod's *Redemption*, an 1882 Birmingham Festival commission, and in the same year, the same forces under Johann Hock again presented some 'praiseworthy orchestral items'. (*Musical Times*). On 16th April Max Bruch's Violin Concerto was given with the local violinist and teacher, Arthur Hytch, as the soloist. For their 100th concert, on 19th October 1908, honouring their popular oratorio tradition they presented Sullivan's *Golden Legend*.

The Good Friday of 1909 brought the established favourite Mendelssohn's *Elijah* to their large following and later in the same season a novelty in the shape of Frederick Cowen's *Sleeping Beauty*, composed for the Birmingham Festival in 1885. In September 1914, undaunted by the onset of war, this society was ahead in announcing its future season's programme which was to consist of Elgar's *Black Knight*, Dvorak's *The Spectre's Bride* and Bach's *St. John Passion*.

Other ventures
The indefatigable Appleby Matthews was also a choral conductor, and not just in Birmingham it should be added. In the *Musical Times* of January 1914 it was announced that a concert by the 'newly-formed Matthews Birmingham Choir' of 50 mixed voices will be given in the Grosvenor Room of the Grand Hotel. Subsequently it was described as 'admirable in every way' by Oscar Pollack. Slotted into this programme were violin solos played by Felix Salmond accompanied by Clarence Raybould. Later, in 1916, they presented a programme of Russian orchestral music, presumably using Matthews' own orchestra, with the choir in scenes from Moussorgsky's *Boris Godounov*. Later in the same season they performed Haydn's *Creation* when even the kindly Pollack commented that 'sometimes they were carried away by abundant temperament', but at least that 'imparted enthusiasm'.

Chapter 24 - The Choral craze

Perhaps two more choral ventures should be mentioned briefly before simply appending a list of the many other choirs active in this very singing-minded first phase of the century.

Music at the Cathedral

St. Philip's Church became the city's cathedral in 1905 when the diocese of Birmingham was created. The following year Edwin Stephenson was appointed organist and we find some beautiful and, for the time, adventurous music being sung during his tenure of the post. In 1909 in Holy Week, the week leading up to Easter, items by Palestrina and Allegri were sung together with a selection of numbers from Bach's *St. Matthew Passion*. Later, in October of the same year, music by Byrd and Tallis was added to yet more items by Palestrina. On 8th March 1912 the whole of the *St. Matthew Passion* was given with Stephenson conducting, Appleby Matthews at the organ and a Dr. Reynolds providing the continuo part reportedly on the clavichord. This was obviously not their first attempt at scaling the peak of this musical Everest, since the *Musical Times* comments that this performance was 'better than last year' and 'deeply impressive and appealing'.

From today's perspective, it may perhaps be surmised that, given the smaller scale of performance which would have to be the case in the Cathedral, Stephenson's efforts could well have been nearer to what would now be regarded as the 'authentic' Bach style - certainly nearer than the large choral society performance in a large hall. Their standard was sufficiently high for them to have been invited by the impresario, Oscar Pollack, to give a concert at the Botanical Gardens in June 1907.

The New Choral Society

This was initially described as Rutland Boughton's New Choral Society and was started in 1908. At first it seems to have given fairly regular concerts but from December 1911, after Boughton's departure from the city, was directed and trained by Miller Johnstone, he who established an early Conservatoire of Music in 1912 at the Queens' College Chambers, Paradise Street. (see chapter 26). Johnstone seems to have replaced this enterprise with his own Miller Johnstone Madrigal Choir which is to be found at a Dale Forty concert with the New Symphony Orchestra under Landon Ronald, and prestigious soloists (*Musical Times* July 1912). Thereafter this choir seems to disappear from the local musical scene.

Distinguished Visitors

Major choirs came from Glasgow, Sheffield and Wolverhampton (the Festival Choral Society) at this period, the Glasgow choir, 300 strong, singing with our 'local symphony band' under George Halford.

For the rest – a list
It is impossible to be certain about the standard achieved – or not achieved – by some of these choirs but at the very least they were providing an opportunity for many ordinary people to learn to read music, to experience it 'from the inside' and to join with others in the joy of singing. Can as much be claimed a century later?

>Birmingham Madrigal Society Choir (Halford)
>Birmingham Philharmonic Choir
>Choir of the Welsh Calvinistic Church
>Midland Gleemen (formerly Mr. Savill's Male Voice Choir)
>New Philharmonic Society
>Welsh Society – annual concert at Town Hall with for example the New Symphony Orchestra in 1908, conducted by Landon Ronald, with prestigious soloists.
>Birmingham Victoria Male Choir (great success at Town Hall 1909)
>Male Voice Choir (under Harrison of Celebrity Concerts)
>Tala Choral Society (announced in 1911, the Taylor and Law Works Choir directed by A.G.Cooper)
>Birmingham Madrigal Singers at Queens College
>Birmingham Ladies Choir trained by Johnson Peters
>Midland Adult School Union
>Barfield Choir
>Madame Gell's Ladies Choir
>Ladies Choir conducted by Richard Wassell

Choirs from suburbs and surrounding towns with their years of formation:

>West Bromwich 1907
>Moseley Choral Society 1908
>Shirley Institute Choral Society 1908
>Darlaston, Edgbaston, Erdington and Sutton Choral Societies 1910

As a footnote, it can be added that the Barfield Choir sang Bantock's *Vanity of Vanities* during this period, described in the local press as a 'disappointing work' but the choir making 'an excellent show' in it.

The programmes
In general, the stranglehold of the popular favourites from the Handel repertoire together with Mendelssohn's *Elijah* continued but as in the previous century some recent works were also programmed, with contemporary English composers being given a good innings. Some small strands of other things were also beginning to creep in now

Chapter 24 - The Choral craze

and then - such as items by Wagner and Moussorgsky - and as we have seen, the sacred repertoire of Palestrina, Byrd and J. S. Bach for example, at the Anglican Cathedral.

Once again a view from Beecham is pertinent. He tells us that he had been innocently impressed with the enthusiasm of the City Choral Society (see above) over his suggestions of performing old and little-known choral pieces. He goes on: 'There was no one I knew to warn me that this particular organisation was regarded as the very stronghold of reaction by the insurrectionists, and that I as its conductor would be attacked as the master criminal of the conspiracy to put the musical clock back a hundred years or more. It was bad enough to inflict on them works like *The Seasons* of Haydn or the *Dettingen Te Deum* of Handel, but when it came to a Mass of Cherubini and a selection or two from my minor French and Italian masters of the seventeenth and eighteenth centuries I was made to feel that I ought to be banished for ever from the society of all decent people'.

No surprise then that Beecham's association with the City Choral Society did not last. One wonders if the choir itself would have lasted much longer if it had embraced Beecham's ideas and made itself more interesting by singing fresh repertoire.

What of standards? We learn from Elgar, in one of his Inaugural Lectures as new Professor of Music at Birmingham University in 1905, that British choirs are our 'great insular wonder'. They are highly trained, he thinks, 'to a perfection of finish and attack never before attempted', and in some ways, he adds, this is over-training. Elgar thinks that they do not always sing with sufficient understanding of either the musical style or the import of the words, and sometimes make up for this by an affected and artificial emphasis on one particular word; as for example the word 'jarr'd' in the line: 'Till disproportioned sin, *Jarr'd* against nature's chime...'

It has to be admitted, even so, that to be dubbed a 'great insular wonder' is a worthwhile achievement! In any case, we can only envy their many opportunities to sing, along with other people, for the pure joy of singing.

---

1. Information drawn from a diary and reminiscences of Edwin Elliot, kindly supplied by his daughter Margery Elliot.

Chapter 25

A miscellany 1900-1920

Chamber Music

At that time, of course, the only way to hear first class performances of the solo and small ensemble repertoire, played by distinguished performers, was 'in the flesh'. As with orchestral and choral music, outlined in the two previous chapters, there were many local enterprises in this field, some achieving a high standard. In that respect it may be argued that the music-lover in early twentieth century Birmingham was quite as fortunate as Birmingham audiences today, when radio and recordings in various formats entertain the music lover rather than live music. This is especially so if we bear in mind that some of the performers involved were, as we know from their later recordings, very good indeed.

A series of chamber concerts which used a large number of prestigious foreign soloists, run by a foreigner and thriving accordingly, was the one organised between 1898 and 1925 by Max Mossel. Mossel, at one time leader of the Concertgebouw Orchestra in his native Holland, was brought to Birmingham in 1895, as we have seen, to teach at the now properly constituted Midland Institute School of Music. He had previously run first-class chamber concerts in Glasgow and elsewhere and was as much known for his concert promotion as for his other activities. In addition to his teaching, these included leading his own string quartet. So to some extent Mossel was doing what Harrison was doing in his Celebrity Concerts, but on a smaller and more intimate scale.

Some of the concerts were held in the Grosvenor Rooms of the Grand Hotel and these from 1910 onwards were referred to as Drawing Room Concerts. The names of many of the artists Mossel employed are already familiar to us because of their visits to other Birmingham musical events and, indeed, some of the names involved still resonate in the mind of the music lover today. The violinists Sarasate and Ÿsaye, as well as the pianists Busoni, Fanny Davies, the eccentric Vladimir Pachmann and a Clara Schumann pupil, Mathilde Verne, are among this number. At the same time, Mossel did not neglect really promising young artists. For example, the violinist Marie Hall appeared in this series at the age of 21. A Mossel pupil for a short while, having had lessons from Elgar and Wilhelmj before that, it was she who played the first performance of Vaughan Williams' *The Lark Ascending* and introduced sonatas by Rutland Boughton into her programmes. Mark Hambourg, the pianist, came in 1910 at the age of 31, and shared a programme with others including the tenor Gervase Elwes, educated at the Oratory School in Birmingham and a notable Gerontius. In the same year the 26-year-old Dorothy Silk, who trained at the Midland Institute School of Music in the early Bantock era, sang a group of Wolf songs, songs which require great subtlety of imagination and alertness in their performance. Mossel also did some very successful talent spotting among younger foreign artists. Busoni's pupil, Egon Petri, was invited in 1913 when he was 32. He played the Franck *Prelude, Chorale and Fugue*, the Liszt *Reminiscences of Don Juan* and the Chopin Piano Sonata in B minor. At the same recital the Dutch contralto, Julia Culp, then 30, sang Schubert, Lully and Loewe items together with some old English tunes. The 25-year-old Moiseiwitsch visited Birmingham in 1915, playing the Brahms-Handel Variations, two Debussy pieces (*Jardins sous la Pluie* and *Clair de Lune*), and Liszt's *Venezia e Napoli*. Moiseiwitsch also accompanied his wife, the Australian-born violinist Daisy Kennedy, herself only 22, in Schumann's Sonata for Violin and Piano in A minor, opus 105. People of the writer's generation remember performances by most of these younger artists who were promoted by Mossel, when they were in their maturer years, and can attest to their virtuoso quality - and the success of the careers that followed. So again Birmingham was able to hear music-making at its best if it so desired.

Mossel's concerts were more often than not on Thursday evenings and tickets for them could be booked at Messrs. Stockley of 123 Colmore Row. Stockley's, together with Priestley and Sons of Colmore Row and Paradise Street, also supplied the pianos for the concerts. The 'business enterprise' spirit of the age is clearly seen here, an inevitable element in the situation, given the lack of any public funding for the arts. The make of piano and its supplier were advertised on the programmes and we are told that Mark Hambourg played on a Brinsmead and Irene Scharrer on a Bechstein from Priestleys, Hamilton Harty accompanying Julia Culp and George Henschel in 1911 on a Blüthner. Chappell and Steinway pianos were also used, according to the preference of the pianist concerned presumably.

Mossel's series was a relatively successful one and spanned just over a quarter of a century being finally discontinued in 1925. They certainly did not lack competition but their success undoubtedly owed a considerable amount to Mossel's ability to spot winners and the consequent musical public's trust in him. If we look at a concert at the Temperance Hall in the Spring of 1903 given by Holden-White, piano, Percy Sharman, violin, and Bertie Withers, 'cello, for example, the *Musical Times* tells us that these musicians 'gave an excellent programme… to a mere handful of auditors' because 'the artists were not known'. The commentator here is, presumably the always supportive Oscar Pollack.

Other important venues used for chamber music besides the Grand Hotel Grosvenor Room and the Temperance Hall in Temple Street, already mentioned, were the Masonic Hall in New Street, the Botanical Gardens in Edgbaston, the Royal Birmingham Society of Artists Gallery (RBSA) in New Street, Queens College in Paradise Street and even, occasionally the Prince of Wales Theatre. Chamber concerts given by the Midland Institute School of Music will be considered separately.

The RBSA Gallery was the choice of the *Musical Times* correspondent for Birmingham at the time, Oscar Pollack. He promoted Musical Matineés there, held weekly on Saturday afternoons between April and June when the Spring art exhibitions were on. Incidentally, we may perhaps remind ourselves that Pollack himself, born in 1838, was at the age of only 16 entrusted by Thomas Harrison, the father of Percy, with the management of his celebrity concerts. He was also music critic for the *Birmingham Mail*. Pollack himself gives us an idea of his aims in the chamber music field. Involved with the great musical stars as he must have been, it appears that he was also very conscious of the difficulty young musicians had, and always will have, in climbing on to the performance ladder in the first place. His bulletin from Birmingham in the *Musical Times* for June 1906, referring to the current season, informs readers that 'as hitherto, a great number of new vocalists and instrumentalists were given a hearing who would otherwise have found it difficult to secure an appearance'. It seems therefore that Birmingham's musical public had plenty of opportunity to hone their critical skills by hearing the full range of talent, from the young hopeful through to the the established virtuoso.

Pollack's RBSA series ran from early in the century until the time when he seems to have begun to reduce his musical activities, in about 1916 - at the age of 78! As well as the Musical Matinées at the RBSA Gallery, Pollack had also promoted some vocal and instrumental concerts at the Botanical Gardens with what seems to have been a grand climax in 1918 when he arranged a concert of vocal and choral items plus violin and piano pieces, played by the highly talented Birmingham musicians, Paul Beard and Arthur Cooke.

Meanwhile, the ubiquitous Max Mossel was clearly not prepared to tie himself to one venue, let alone to one city, as we have seen. In 1908, at the Temperance Hall this time, he presented outstanding British talent in the shape of the pianist Fanny Davies, trained in Birmingham and Leipzig, and the tenor Gervase Elwes her frequent colleague. During his season the following year, Mossel invited the Schiever Quartet to play, but this time at the Masonic Hall. The German-born Ernst Schiever had studied under Joachim, was a member of the Joachim Quartet, but from 1878 onwards he made Liverpool his headquarters and always led the orchestra there when Richter conducted.

In 1910 another venue featured on the Birmingham chamber music scene, this time the Windsor Room at the Grand Hotel. It was used for concerts organised by a Miss Violet Banks, also aiming to introduce new artists. Further information is there none about this venture, so perhaps even the kindly Pollack decided that a discreet silence would be best?

Chapter 25 - A miscellany 1900-1920

In the 1909-10 season Dale Forty seem to have made their entrance on to this particular scene and for two or three seasons at least, presented six concerts per season. In 1910 they invited the pianists Wilhelm Backhaus (no less) and Mark Hambourg. Backhaus was in this country during that year as a visiting piano professor at what was then the Royal Manchester College of Music. Later, six concerts promoted by Dale Forty in the 1912-13 season featured the Catterall Quartet, the Miller Johnstone Madrigal Choir, together with prestigious visitors in the shape of the New Symphony Orchestra conducted by Landon Ronald.

The RBSA was also the venue for some of the Birmingham Chamber Concerts Society concerts, again organised by the indefatigable Max Mossel – who else? From this time onwards the Chamber Concerts Society seems to have featured just local professional musicians, with Catterall, Max Mossel and Appleby Matthews themselves providing the performances. Also in 1914, the newly-formed Birmingham Strings Club, its leading lights Christine Ratcliff, Clarence Raybould and Clifford Roberts, used the RBSA 'new rooms' as the scene of its activities. This organisation was formed 'to enable amateurs to practice all branches of chamber music', to work for high standards and to give occasional concerts.

Again from 1914 onwards, more Matinées Musicales were presented by a Madame Minadieu. Her series seems to have drawn performers from a wider field and with two of her matinées on the 10th and 12th November 1914 she crowded the Repertory Theatre in Station Street with large audiences to raise funds for the Birmingham Prince of Wales' War Fund. Subsequently she arranged further Matinées Musicales, four each season, this time at the Grand Hotel. These were like Max Mossel's series in terms of the excellence of the artists employed, some nationally known, others promising newcomers. The singer Plunkett Greene appeared, also Arthur Catterall, Beatrice Hewitt, the pianists Adela Verne and William Murdoch, violist Lionel Tertis together with Harold Craxton and G. H. Manton as the accompanists. Older readers will remember the excellence of these musicians. By 1920, however, Mme. Minadieu was ill and her concerts were discontinued. Beatrice Hewitt herself gave three Saturday concerts at the Repertory Theatre with Arthur Catterall, Paul Beard and Johann Hock among the players. This in 1919.

Yet another enterprise had appeared in the late Summer of 1916 when the first of four chamber concerts was organised by Appleby Matthews. On 12th July, Matthews himself with the violinist Arthur Catterall played violin sonatas by Grieg, Delius and Franck. Finally in this period Richard Wassell just gets in on the act with some Chamber Concerts at the RBSA.

On the bigger stage. Celebrities and Opera Stars
Perhaps the reader should be reminded here that the account of the most important series of Celebrity Concerts at this period, those promoted by the Harrisons and already

described in chapter 11, stretched forward into this first phase of the twentieth century, to 1916 in fact. Dale Forty moved into this sphere in 1916, presenting Clara Butt and Agnes Nicholls at the Town Hall but, in general, successors to Harrison's series will be described in the section on phase two of the twentieth century. In any case it can be seen that the best orchestras and the great soloists were still being heard by the Birmingham public, along with the local orchestral and choral music already described.

Celebrities in a generous mood - two charity concerts
Before moving on to what was on offer operatically speaking, two charity concerts might be mentioned which certainly exploited the celebrity factor. The first was in May 1910 in aid of the NSPCC and using the services of the admirable Muriel Foster, Elgar's preferred contralto. According to the *Musical Times* report her performance amply demonstrated ' her glorious voice and dramatic style'. Then at the end of 1915 a whole line-up of first class singers and instrumentalists gave their services at the Town Hall to raise money for the St. John Ambulance Brigade. They were singers Dorothy Silk, Birmingham-trained, also Muriel Foster 'a great attraction', the Walsall-born tenor Frank Mullings, the pianist Irene Scharrer, violinist Max Mossel, accompanists G. H. Manton and O'Connor Morris and last but not least our own great city organist, a 'shining example' according to Elgar, C. W. Perkins. All of these performers would draw large audiences, contributing substantially to the charities concerned.

Opera
As we have seen a good deal of chamber music was given by locally connected people who were mostly professional, some with a country-wide reputation. For fully professional operatic performances, however, Birmingham relied, as it still does, on visiting companies. The most distinguished of these were the Moody Manners, Carl Rosa and D'Oyly Carte companies and last but not least, the Beecham Opera Company.

The Moody Manners Company played a week in 1907 at the Prince of Wales Theatre in Broad Street with a 'magnificent version' of Verdi's *Aida*. This opera had not been seen in Birmingham since 1893. The following January they brought two 'novelties', Puccini's *Madam Butterfly* and *La Bohème*, three and seven years old respectively. The following June they gave Verdi's *La Traviata* and Halévy's *La Juive*, throwing in Wagner's *Tannhäuser*, Gounod's *Faust*, Wallace's *Maritana* and again *Butterfly*, for good measure. The Moody Manners Company had been set up in 1889 by the bass Charles Manners and his wife, the Cornish soprano Fanny Moody. It consisted of two travelling companies numbering 175 and 95. Among their singers was the tenor John Coates, noted for his technical artistry and for being the best British Tristan and Siegfried. The company was very popular for a number of years but sadly had to wind up its affairs in 1916 - there was considerable competition in this field of course. Its main visits to Birmingham were between 1907 and 1910.

Chapter 25 - A miscellany 1900-1920

Three other companies which appeared in Birmingham in 1910 were the Italian Opera Company, the Carl Rosa Opera Company – the doyen of touring companies – plus the D'Oyly Carte Company, all usually at the Prince of Wales Theatre. The first of these seems to have disappeared thereafter, no doubt absorbed into one of the other larger touring companies. The Carl Rosa was a different matter in spite of some ups and downs. After a bad patch between 1900 and 1907 when there had been some financial mismanagement, the Carl Rosa went on the road again certainly visiting Birmingham, most notably in 1910, 1912 and 1918 bringing with them an operatic feast. In 1912 their programme consisted of thirteen operas over a two-week period! This company had come into being in 1875 due to the efforts of the German-born violinist Karl Rose who was married to the singer Euphrosyne Parepa. He actually bought the Royal Alexandra Theatre in Liverpool and set about bringing the standard grand opera repertoire to his audiences, in English. He also encouraged the composition of new operas such as Goring Thomas's *Esmeralda* in 1883 and Stanford's *The Canterbury Pilgrims* in 1884. Most of these were as short-lived as many of the Birmingham Festival oratorios but were popular at the time. The three touring companies as a whole survived many vicissitudes, ringing down the last curtain in 1960. The most important point to be made, probably, is that subscription tickets for the provincial tours were available *at all prices*. You did not need to be wealthy to hear some of the greatest operas, and some of the finest singing - from the likes of Eva Turner for example.

Just after the war the Carl Rosa had taken over two other touring companies, one of them the Turner Company which itself had visited Birmingham independently, but was considered by the *Musical Times* commentator to be 'not top rank'. Presumably the Carl Rosa 'cherry-picked' the best of their talent, those who were selected subsequently doing better, presumably, with the bigger, more successful company. Certainly the Carl Rosa Company had an eye for talent and recruited three generations of the Goossens family as conductors, the third being Eugene Goossens of whom we will hear more now from Thomas Beecham. In his book *A Mingled Chime*, Beecham tells us how he had first used the young Goossens' services in 1915, throwing the 22-year-old Eugene in at the deep end, trusting him to cope with two new works, namely Stanford's *The Critic* and Ethel Smyth's *The Boatswain's Mate*. Beecham writes that 'from the start the resourceful youth had comported himself with the baton as if he had been a veteran... His coolness and facility were phenomenal'. This is an accolade indeed from such a source. This is also further evidence of the level of talent that the Carl Rosa Company looked for at that period. They gave the public good value for their money, in every sense, with a wide range of operas well performed.

The year 1910 was certainly a busy one, and the *Musical Times* correspondent's observation to this effect is rather intriguing. The opera scene was especially crowded for in addition to visits from the Carl Rosa and Moody Manners Companies, with generous repertoires of operas, another touring company, the D'Oyly Carte Company, was added to the strength. The London-born Rupert D'Oyly Carte had been manager for the likes of the great tenor Mario, for the diva Adelina Patti and for the composer Gounod, all of whom we have met in these pages. He it was, too, who commissioned Gilbert and Sullivan's *Trial by Jury* in 1875, subsequently building his own theatre, the Savoy Theatre in London, to produce more Gilbert and Sullivan operas. His venture into Grand Opera was not a particularly happy one, however, but as far as Birmingham was concerned his company provided them with a couple of seasons in 1910 and 1916, both times at the Prince of Wales Theatre.

Yet another visiting company was the O'Mara Company which came in 1914 and played the Bordesley Palace Theatre with Wallace's *Maritana*, Verdi's *Il Trovatore* and Balfe's *The Bohemian Girl*. O'Mara himself had appeared as a favourite tenor in the Moody Manners Company and also later in Beecham's Company - of whom more next.

There is no doubt that the most prestigious of all these visiting companies was the Beecham Opera Company. What happened was that yet another touring company, the Denhof Company, had been formed in 1910 by a German musician, specifically to give performances of Wagner's *Ring Cycle* in the English provinces. This had from the first toured major cities, adding Debussy's *Pelléas et Mélisande*, Richard Strauss's *Der Rosenkavalier* (both in English) and Mozart's *The Magic Flute* to the menu. After two weeks of a first visit to Birmingham and its third visit to Manchester in 1913, both very badly attended, the company was deep in debt. Thomas Beecham had been one of the company's conductors and he now took it over, along with some of its best singers, among them Marie Brema, Agnes Nicholls, Birmingham's own Walter Hyde, also Frederic Austin, a pupil of Birmingham's Charles Lunn, (see chapter 12) and the great bass, Robert Radford.

A graphic description, as ever, of what happened is given by Beecham in his book *A Mingled Chime*.

'I called in a brace of auditors, procured the seating plans of all the theatres due to be visited, worked the telephone line in a score of directions, and after twenty-four hours discovered that if we could sell out every seat for each remaining performance for the rest of the tour we had a sporting chance of getting through fairly well after all. How could this be done? Only with a hurricane of publicity that would reach and wake up even the most lethargic and indifferent creature who had ever heard the terms *music* and *opera*'.

In fact, of course, results could not all be fully achieved overnight and the second week, in Manchester, was abandoned. The Sheffield tour went ahead, however, 'with fair success', according to Beecham. The first performance in Birmingham of Wagner's *Ring Cycle* took place at the Prince of Wales Theatre in Birmingham in 1913. In the event, between 1913 and 1919 the Beecham Opera Company brought twenty-one operas to Birmingham, the Carl Rosa Company adding its contribution of thirteen. The year 1918 was certainly a 'bumper' year for opera as far as Birmingham was concerned. The June issue of the *Musical Times* reports that the Beecham Opera Company had just visited, packing the theatre for its season of performances and in the following Autumn both the Carl Rosa Company and the Beecham Companies came, each with the usual comprehensive selection of operas. Large numbers of government workers brought to the city at the end of the war were also particularly addicted to opera it seems.

Other companies appear fleetingly as for example the Quinlan Company and, in 1914, the Castillano Italian and English Company. Some smaller and local operatic ventures should also be mentioned. The Birmingham Amateur Operatic Company was used at some of the Birmingham and Midland Institute's annual Conversaziones and the Institute's own opera class gave public performances, again at the Institute.

All in all, it was possible for the Birmingham opera buff to hear most of the great operas, past and recent, and in most cases they were well performed. Nor was it all beyond the reach of the less well off citizen. We are given pause for thought, however, by Elgar's remarks in one of his Birmingham University Inaugural Lectures in 1905. He admits that England has some fine voice teachers but that we 'lack dramatic singers because we have no real dramatic art'. Further, 'dressed-up dolls and dummies fill the stage at most of our theatres... These people cannot act... they only dress up and pretend to be somebody else'. He asks that singers sing with understanding and intelligence. Among the operatic singers he excepts from his strictures are John Coates and Kirkby Lunn.

Birmingham's Musical Diet – a summary and an omission repaired

It is clear that the music-lover in the city had a remarkably wide range of music to choose from. The orchestral, choral, chamber music and operatic repertoires were very well covered, quite a number of the organisations concerned making a point of performing new music and ranging more widely into the European repertoire. A considerable number of great performing talents were also on offer, and that they were great we can often hear for ourselves in that a lot of them survived into the recorded music age. Alternatively, older people today knew others, now dead, whose judgement they trusted and who praised what they had heard.

One category of musician we have not so far considered is that of the organist. Of the city organist of that time we have read Elgar's golden opinion. The organists in general, however, played an even more crucial part then ever in providing the underpinning for much good teaching of music, training in singing and general musicianship. Organists were still very much community musicians, embedded in the musical fabric of society. The major city churches in Birmingham have ever prided themselves on possessing good organists and the reader is reminded of the more detailed accounts of all that its organists contributed to the city's music, to be found in chapters 14 and 28.

Chapter 26

Granville Bantock – larger than life

We turn at last to the man who more than anyone energised Birmingham's inner musical life in this first phase of the twentieth century. Bantock was 20 years of age when he began his musical training at the Royal Academy of Music, having originally been destined for the Indian Civil Service. At the Academy he studied composition, winning the Macfarren Scholarship, and had a one-act opera of his given at the Crystal Palace, conducted by no less a figure than August Manns. Between 1892 and 1896 Bantock edited the *New Quarterly Review* and obtained a good deal of conducting experience in touring opera and then at the Royalty Theatre in London. He also organised concerts of orchestral and chamber music by contemporary English composers.

He quitted the London musical ambit when he moved to New Brighton in Cheshire to take charge of a military band which played for Summer visitors. New Brighton is on the Mersey coast of the Wirral peninsula, almost opposite Liverpool. The military band played for dancing but Bantock, being Bantock, gradually slotted more musically substantial items between the dances, eventually building the band up into a symphony orchestra. He saw to it, too, that English music by the 'greats' of the day - Parry, Stanford and Elgar - was played. He also encouraged Sibelius whose music had not yet been heard outside his native Finland. The two men became friends and Sibelius subsequently came to conduct his own works in England, and that certainly included Birmingham as we have seen.

A momentous day for Birmingham followed in 1900 when Bantock accepted the new full-time post as Principal of the Midland Institute School of Music on Elgar's recommendation. Here was another of those key moments in Birmingham's musical history which opened up great new possibilities. We have already seen how Joseph Moore and William Stockley upgraded the Musical Festivals and the Festival Chorus respectively. Bantock was to do the same in several areas of the city's musical life.

Bantock was a protean character, able to adapt himself to various roles, as conductor, organiser, educator and composer. Being hugely enterprising, energetic and above all enthusiastic himself, he was able to motivate and energise almost every

Chapter 26 - Granville Bantock - larger than life

aspect of musical life in the city, not least in the area of music education. He could also inspire affection - and had a mischievous sense of humour as we shall see.

As far as the School of Music was concerned Bantock found what was still to some extent, in spite of some progress made, an amorphous collection of music classes. He immediately set about building up the instrumental teaching staff thereby enabling the school to produce capable orchestral musicians. By 1910 he could claim that about seventy per cent of the players then in local orchestras were products of the Institute School of Music. There was a very positive and cheerful sense of progress in the air. For Bantock was humorous, but above all very interested in his individual students whom he tried to get to know by name. They found however that the relationship was very much on the boss's terms and there was a clear mark in the sand between them which they could not cross!

The growing success of the School was then advertised more widely and after 1907, when this happened, students came from elsewhere to study music in Birmingham. In fact some new staff members had already been arriving, willing to come to Birmingham if it meant working for Bantock. One such was Ernest Newman who had early joined the staff to teach singing and the rudiments of music. Newman also worked as Music Critic for the *Birmingham Post* and became in due course a foremost authority on the operas of Wagner. Sadly Birmingham lost Newman in 1906 to go to the *Manchester Guardian*, then considered a more prestigious newspaper than the *Birmingham Post*. Other notable members of staff were Rutland Boughton and F.W. Beard, uncle of Paul Beard. In any case, all the members of staff were carefully chosen and their work and attendance as carefully monitored when they did arrive, more than one not having their appointment renewed if they did not give satisfaction.

Bantock saw to it that choral singing and orchestral playing were both part of the curriculum as well as the theory of music. He also started an opera class which he took himself and by 1903 the class was able to present costumed and staged scenes from Mozart's *The Magic Flute* with orchestral accompaniment. The orchestra was formed from the School's own students with members of staff in the section leaders' chairs.

Students who made a success of their future careers included the soprano of the silvery voice, Dorothy Silk, whom we have met and will meet again. There were also Julius Harrison and Clarence Raybould, who subsequently had successful conducting careers, W. Greenhouse Allt, later a Principal of Trinity College of Music – and a younger member of the Beard family, Paul Beard, who was to play as Principal Viola in the City of Birmingham Orchestra, then as Leader, finally moving to London to lead the BBC Symphony Orchestra with great distinction. As for Julius Harrison, in spite of his subsequent very distinguished conducting career, it was in fact a composition prize that he had won while under Bantock's tutelage, the adjudicators being Ernest Newman, Coleridge Taylor and Delius himself. Again, it was not as a potential conductor that Raybould gained his initial distinction but as an organist. He took the FRCO (Fellow of the Royal College of Organists) examination while at the School, this diploma being a generally agreed sign of the ability to reach a recital standard of performance. Raybould then went on to become one of Bantock's students in the Birmingham University Music Department.

For yes, indeed, not satisfied that he was already doing all he could to build up Birmingham's musical life, Bantock had accepted the Chair of Music at Birmingham University in 1908. This was in succession to Elgar and again on Elgar's own recommendation. Here Bantock went ahead and established a curriculum which is still the basis of what is expected - or at least hoped for - from students today. Students would be expected to study not only harmony and counterpoint and be able themselves to produce samples of music written in all the typical styles, but they would also be expected to study music from every period and of every genre. At that time these historical studies began no further back than the sixteenth century, rather than from much earlier, as now. Students would also be expected to study orchestration, that is the ability to adapt other genres of music, such as for example a piano piece, for orchestra. Further, a compulsory part of the course would be attending the Institute School of Music for instrumental or singing lessons. This last relationship is one that still exists, university students still attending the Conservatoire for their practical lessons. There was in the first half of the twentieth century a jibe going around that too many Doctors of Music could not play any instrument very well. Clearly, Bantock was having none of that!

Granville Bantock.

In passing, one wonders what Bantock's reaction was to Miller Johnstone's attempt to set up a Conservatoire in 1912, housed nearby in Queen's College Chambers? Whatever it was, this particular conservatoire did not survive.

An account of Bantock's work as Principal and Professor of the Midland Institute School of Music and University of Birmingham Department of Music, respectively, does not end our description of his educational work. He saw very clearly, as some members of today's educational establishment do not, that the foundation of a healthy musical life in the country is laid in the schools. By his time, schooling was both compulsory and free and what was more, singing and dancing were regularly taught in the Elementary Schools, the equivalent of today's Primary Schools. Part of giving people an incentive to do both these activities well, the Competition Festival movement had been initiated in the nineteenth century and very much encouraged by John Curwen in the 1860s. (chapter 13). Usually, festivals were set up through some local initiative, the local festival then being able to become part of the British Federation of Music Festivals. Birmingham's Competition Festival was started by Bantock in 1912, to be under the presidency of whoever was the current Lord Mayor. Choral classes and country dancing classes featured prominently as well as solo classes and by 1924 there there were two hundred competing children's choirs drawn from the city's Elementary Schools. This Festival was held every two years. In 1920, for example, Cecil Sharp, the folk-song collector and Sidney H. Nicholson, founder of the School of English Church Music to give it its original title, were among the adjudicators.

Many people, including the writer, are uneasy at the idea of introducing the element of competition into the business of making music, but it must be admitted that these events would be an exciting occasion for people, making participators and audiences alike more acute and discriminating listeners. For better or worse, Birmingham's Competition Festival in this form ended in 1932. Perhaps we should just leave the reader with the following report from the *Birmingham Mail* of 25th June 1919.

Children and Music, forming the taste of the next generation. Birmingham's progress

...'educational work among children will determine whether the next generation will redeem us from the old reproach, which is still levelled at us in some quarters, of being the most unmusical among the nations of Europe. Birmingham cannot claim to be more musically alive, collectively, than Manchester, Liverpool or Leeds, but we are blessed with some educationalists who are individually very much alive musically and they want to guarantee us a musical posterity.

Quietly, but effectively, much useful educational work is being done among the children of Birmingham which is engendering a widespread love of music for its own sake. Of recent years it has been accompanied by a notable improvement in the standard of music which children are able to appreciate, and also by a growing love of good instrumental music. In the elementary schools both teachers and scholars have been encouraged to aim at the highest and best in musical expression. The competitive musical festivals have given a great impetus in this direction. Any student of music who looks through the syllabuses of the festivals may see for himself how far the children have progressed. Audiences by no means uncritical, hearing Birmingham's elementary school children sing for the first time, have exhibited considerable surprise at their finished performance.

As for the methods in use, the younger children are taught action songs requiring of them not only understanding of the music and the capacity to render it, but also grace in action. It is remarkable to find the children from the poorer quarters excelling in such efforts. The little children from the area around St. Jude's, hard by New Street Station, have taken first prize on more that one occasion in competition from children all over the city. To hear these children sing - children often ill-clad, often needy – would give a greater impulse to your democratic sympathies than fifty speeches by conventional demagogues. As an indication of the quality of the music taught one need only mention that the works most in favour among the children themselves are 'Where the Bee Sucks' (Dr. Arne's melody from 'The Tempest'), 'Robin Hood and 'The Red, the Green and the Yellow', the two latter being the folk-songs of these titles.

The older children are set more ambitious tasks. Two-part songs there are which illustrate better than any other how older children are feeling their way to interpretation of mood and feeling. They are 'The Cloud' by Rubinstein and 'Drake's Drum' by Coleridge Taylor. No fewer that twenty-three choirs from boys', girls' and mixed day schools prepared these pieces for the last competitive festival and everyone who was privileged to hear their rendering of them was struck by the easily accomplished transition from the opposed moods of the two... many other instances might be furnished to show that the trite part-songs of twenty years ago, which had little, if any, musical worth, would not do for the children of this generation. Composers of high rank are being induced to write for school children pieces which would not have been dreamt of twenty years ago. Indeed it is not uncommon for a composer to come down to Birmingham specially to hear school children sing one of his compositions. It follows, of course, that the musical training of Birmingham school children goes considerably beyond the requirements of the Government curriculum. The time allowed in the ordinary Government curriculum could not produce these musical results'.

Plus ça change!

Finally, Bantock was a composer! Sadly this really has to be put last, as his own music has been the least enduring product of his hugely creative life. His energy was apparently limitless and in general he lived an amazingly productive life according to his own very bright lights. Unfortunately the music he himself composed also had little limit or control put on it and sometimes a rather grandiose structure clothed what were not very memorable musical ideas. There has however been some resurgence of interest in his more successful music and pieces like the *Pagan Symphony*, the slighter *Fifine at the Fair* and *Two Heroic Ballads,* as well as other works, have recently appeared on compact disc.

With such a generous and productive personality we must not end on a down beat. One of Bantock's successors as Principal of the Midland Institute School of Music was Christopher Edmunds. He has left us some amusing reminiscences of Bantock in a recorded BBC interview with Peter Spaull in 1972. Men in those days were much more prone to a certain kind of practical joking and Granville Bantock was clearly one of these. It was quite on the cards for a student or member of staff to be invited to Bantocks's room for an interview, only to enter the room and find the great man wearing a comic red nose! What *are* you supposed to do in such a

Chapter 26 - Granville Bantock - larger than life

situation? Outside visitors on the other hand might enter his room, be invited to take off their coats and hang them up on the hook behind the door, only to find it was made of rubber, the coat flopping unceremoniously to the floor!

Granville Bantock - a gargantuan character. He is most certainly another in the city's musical pantheon who made all the difference, for the better, to its musical life.

Chapter 27

Phase Two: A City Orchestra – The new musical flagship

Reputable but Regional – Courage in Adversity

At last, in 1920, the efforts of the Midland Concerts Promoters who had first met in 1916 (chapter 23) bore fruit. In the four intervening years, leading local citizens, many of whom were also significantly on the City Council, had continued to be active. Two previous Lord Mayors in particular, namely Neville Chamberlain and David Brooks, as well as Granville Bantock on the musical front, finally persuaded the Council to make £1,250 available annually for the running of a City of Birmingham Orchestra; this for an experimental period of five years from 1920 to 1925. In the event, of course, the city has quite crucially continued its support ever since. As the title of this chapter implies, this orchestra has borne the main responsibility for upholding Birmingham's musical reputation in the musical world for eighty-five years to date – this is over half as long as the great Musical Festivals performed the same task.

For the authoritative and comprehensive account of the city orchestra's history it is not possible to do better than read Beresford King-Smith's book *Crescendo!* (see Bibliography). This is a very enjoyable and balanced account by the orchestra's present Archivist, one who has been involved with the orchestra since 1964 in managerial and administrative capacities. It would be a work of supererogation to attempt any such full account in this present volume; but it would also be absolutely impossible to offer the reader a balanced picture of the city's musical history without leaving him or her with a clear idea of the importance of the role the city's orchestra has played and does play on the Birmingham musical scene in the twentieth century. This applies both to its more modest past as well as to the prestigious, high-profile present.

Appleby Matthews. Conductor 1920–24

The first conductor of the official city orchestra was, in the end, T. Appleby Matthews whom we have met already in previous chapters, as conductor of his own orchestra and of the City of Birmingham Police Band, and as choral conductor, violist, organist and chamber ensemble pianist. Given that in many ways he and Richard Wassell were very comparable as to musical experience, it is interesting that it was Matthews who was finally chosen to conduct this new and important body, with Wassell as his deputy. Apparently, it was the preference of two local music critics, A. J. Sheldon and Robert Buckley, for the more ebullient Matthews which probably tipped the balance in his favour Some local musicians still alive today do clearly retain a vivid memory of Matthews' presence and of the huge contribution he made to music in the area; certainly he had enormous drive and indeed 'nerve'. As King-Smith recounts (op. cit.), Matthews made an offer to the committee involved in launching the orchestra which is almost breath-taking in its self-belief. He suggested (in the name of economy of course) that the fee of £450 for 30 concerts in the inaugural season which he had been offered as conductor should be changed, and that he should receive £1,000 for his services both as conductor and as secretary-cum-manager. He clearly wanted to manage as well as conduct but was he qualified to succeed in both tasks or would he fall between the two stools?

In the event, things initially went ahead as Matthews suggested and on Sunday evening 5th September 1920, the new City of Birmingham Orchestra gave its first concert, conducted by Appleby Matthews in the Theatre Royal, New Street - a popular venue. The orchestra probably numbered about 45 on this occasion, with Alex Cohen as Leader. The *Musical Times* commented that it was an advantage that the public were long accustomed to Sunday evening concerts, clearly shown by the audiences for Matthews' concerts at the Futurist Cinema in the previous season, and that it was a shrewd move to choose a Sunday for this important occasion. The same journal also commented that a foundation had been laid on a sure base and that success was promised. For this particular occasion some modern English music featured and the programme included Granville Bantock's Overture *Saul*, Elgar's *Serenade for Strings* op. 20 ('beautifully played') and also Tchaikovsky's Fourth Symphony. Even at that date, however, there was the inevitable vocalist. This was the local baritone, Herbert Simmonds. In the event, even the demanding A. J. Sheldon of the *Birmingham Post* was full of praise.

The launch and the start of the voyage

The inaugural concert in the Symphony Concerts Series - as opposed to the popular Sunday Evening Concerts - was given on the 10th November 1920 with Elgar very appropriately conducting on this landmark occasion. Elgar's own music was naturally and fittingly offered, namely his symphonic study, *Falstaff*, the Second Symphony and the first performance in Birmingham of his 'Cello Concerto with Felix Salmond as soloist. Later in this first season, the *Musical Times* Birmingham correspondent records a visit to Birmingham on Thursday 15th December 1921 of the Hallé Orchestra's conductor, Hamilton Harty, to conduct the new orchestra, and comments on Harty's magnificent command over 'a fine band'. The programme included Berlioz' *Symphonie Fantastique*, Handel's *Water Music* and two contemporary British works, Bantock's *The*

Sea Reivers and a piece for solo piano by Arnold Bax from 1915 called *In a Vodka Shop,* this last piece having 'no special attraction' according to the *Musical Times* critic - nor a very appealing title it has to be said! The piece must have been bad if this usually encouraging commentator wrote thus! Rosina Buckman, who had received part of her training at the Midland Institute School of Music, sang 'Ritorna vincitor' from Verdi's *Aida* 'with dramatic force'. So even here, we see the taste for the 'vocal spot' in the programme still alive and kicking even in the supposedly more serious Thursday series. Nevertheless, and very importantly, major recent British works were indeed programmed, as for example when Vaughan Williams conducted his own Symphony no. 2, the *London,* in the Spring of 1921, and Holst's *Hymn of Jesus* and Arnold Bax's newly-composed First Symphony were performed in the 1923-24 season.

During this first season, the country's best woodwind Principals appeared in the orchestra, in the shape of Leon Goossens, oboe, Haydn Draper, clarinet, Wilfred James, bassoon and Alfred Brain, horn. As an aside, Alfred Brain, the elder brother of Aubrey Brain and uncle of Dennis, subsequently moved to the United States to play in the Damrosch Orchestra, eventually taking American citizenship. At this same period, in the Spring of 1921, Dan Godfrey, conductor of the Bournemouth orchestra, secured outstanding performances from the Birmingham band and Godfrey himself had thereby formed a favourable opinion of the new City of Birmingham Orchestra which had played inspiringly under his beat. Another favourable review appeared in the *Musical Times* in the same year when a concert at the Theatre Royal commemorating the 150th. anniversary of Beethoven's birth was described as 'spirited and quite admirable in tone and technique'. A very good start was being made.

Concerts in Birmingham satellite towns were also arranged but further, and very importantly, a successful series of concerts for children was inaugurated under Matthews' guidance in February 1921, to be held on certain Saturday afternoons in the Town Hall. To their very great credit, those who have decided orchestral policy have all along sought to bring the joy of great classical music, well played, to the city's younger generation. This has taken slightly different forms over the years, but the intention has usually, and rightly, been there.

So, the orchestra had been launched with success, and praise and encouragement had come from various respected quarters. There were also, inevitably, factors in the situation which would require some changes in the future. It does seem as if Appleby Matthews was still prone to programme the more old-fashioned type of miscellaneous concert, with items of very varied kinds, and not just in his more popular Sunday series. He had also fallen foul of the new Amalgamated Musicians Union by using members of the City Police Band in the orchestra. It was of course, as ever, a matter of working within a very prescribed budget, in a situation where there were still many 'unknowns'. The players' payment was very low and uncertain,

Chapter 27 - Phase Two: A City Orchestra - The new musical flagship

Appleby Matthews.

and when Matthews used 'amateurs' from the City Police band to swell the numbers this upset the Union. Unionism generally was now an established fact of British life and union involvement in the orchestra's affairs would eventually come to a painful crisis in the 1970s. At that early stage of the orchestra's existence, when the finances were simply not sufficient to play the players a professional rate, let alone a regular professional salary, Union protection for the poorly-paid employee, certainly those working on a casual basis, was a necessary factor in the situation and had to be taken into account.

Building up the orchestral finances

As to the financial situation itself, the initial grant of £1,250 from the city for the first year came, in effect, with no strings attached. This sum was expected to help to defray the expected shortfall of some £2,500 which represented the difference between the expected orchestral running costs of £8,500 and a hoped-for revenue, mainly from ticket sales, of £6,000. Guarantees from individual supporters were expected to be £1,250. In fact, at the end of the first season the shortfall was some £1,432 only too soon to rise to £2,000. Influential civic leaders behind this project must have thought it their responsibility not to let things get worse before doing anything about it. In 1922 a species of Development Plan was set up. In addition, a special Appeal was launched by Lady Brooks, wife of Sir David Brooks whom we have already met, together with Gerald Forty, a doughty and influential friend to the orchestra. This appeal urged music-lovers in the city suburbs to make a commitment to encouraging attendance at the orchestra's concerts. Matthews himself also tried various strategies including giving popular low-priced concerts in the suburbs which were very well attended. Finally the subsidised Sunday series was replaced by a series of 24 concerts to be held at the Futurist Theatre, a space with good acoustics. These were to be on Sundays still, but with the orchestra undertaking them on a co-operative basis.

In summary then, a city orchestra had been launched and received much praise, and at the same time the standard of the playing of the City Police Band had been raised. Interest among the citizens of Birmingham themselves in their new orchestra had been encouraged in various ways, by the Appeal and by suburban concerts which replaced some of the Sunday concerts, the latter not being sufficiently patronised by those able to buy the highest priced tickets apparently. The Children's Concerts were continued and visits to surrounding towns such as Cheltenham, Tamworth and Wolverhampton had been arranged. The orchestra was also formally established as an official society under the Friendly Societies Act and acquired a Chairman (its third in as many years) who fortunately stayed with them until 1931. This was A.G. Macdonald who was also, and importantly, a City Councillor.

And then discord...

Ominously for him, in 1922 Matthews found himself relieved of any involvement in the management of the finances of the orchestra and £350 was deducted from his annual salary of £1,000 in order to pay a General Secretary. Audiences were not increasing sufficiently, the orchestra itself was reduced to a mere 35 players and, what was worse, a message came from David Brooks himself, that the City Council might not continue the grant after the end of the 1924-25 season. In the end, after four years as conductor, Appleby Matthews' contract with the orchestra was not renewed. This was done incorrectly, in the legal sense, and as a consequence Matthews was advised to pursue an action against wrongful dismissal, which was successful. The orchestra had to make an out of court settlement in Matthews' favour of £600.

Plainly, Appleby Matthews was an initiator and not an 'organisation man'. He had made a huge contribution to Birmingham's musical life, often on his own initiative, not least by forming his own orchestra back in 1916. It must have been a miserable experience for him to have to go on working in the city where he had been so publicly demoted. Though later conductors of the city orchestra also had to relinquish their post in less than happy circumstances, none of them had to go on living in the area of his humiliation as Matthews did. Sometimes hasty-tempered it has to be said, Matthews had not been a skilful diplomatist. Used to running his own shows, working with and under the control of other people clearly did not come easily to him. Even so, Birmingham should not forget the very large contribution this physically diminutive man made to this most crucial element in the city's twentieth century musical life. At least the Civic Society had already awarded him with its Gold Medal which was seen as a real mark of distinction.

Adrian Boult. CBO Conductor 1924-30
Adrian Boult took over the conductorship of the orchestra at the age of 35, coming to Birmingham with some prestigious conducting achievements on the wider national scene already behind him. He had studied at the Leipzig Conservatoire and observed the great Nikisch at work. In 1914, at the age of 25, he joined the staff at Covent Garden and in 1918 he had conducted the first performance of Holst's *The Planets* at the composer's invitation. This was at a privately organised concert at the Queens Hall. A year later he was the chief conductor for the Autumn season of Diaghilev's Ballet Russe and joined the teaching staff of the Royal College of Music.

Apart from all this important experience, Adrian Boult's personality was totally different from that of Appleby Matthews. A public school and Oxford educated man, he was urbane and carried with him an impression of quiet confidence. According to one

Adrian Boult (photograph by Constantine).

recently retired CBSO player, he was able to go before an orchestra and say, as he metaphorically twirled his moustache, 'just a few points please, gentlemen'. After working on these, he would then take command of the proceedings and achieve a workmanlike and professional performance. Not a man with what today we would call great charisma, he was certainly a conductor with great musical integrity whom composers and listeners alike trusted and respected.

In 1923, Boult had accepted the conductorship of the Birmingham Festival Choral Society (see chapter 24) in succession to Henry Wood and some think he may have agreed to do this because he knew that an opportunity with the city orchestra was opening up. In any case, Boult had already conducted the orchestra himself in a performance of Rachmaninov's Second Symphony in the Spring of 1921, so he knew its potential.

Adrian Boult's relationship with the city

Was this appointment successful? The answer must be 'yes'. Boult's ability to command an orchestra was not in doubt but, at this juncture in the orchestra's history, it was important that there should be someone at the helm who had other qualities as well as great musicianship. These Adrian Boult certainly had. He immediately identified himself with the city by happily complying with the orchestra management's requirement that its conductor be resident in the city. He even paid the rent of an office in Birmingham out of his own pocket. Further, he was at ease with the influential Lord Mayors, ex-Lord Mayors, Aldermen, City Councillors and other leading citizens, some of them wealthy business-men, who had so crucially used their considerable influence in establishing - and maintaining - an official orchestra for the city. This was important in any case, but important, too, at this particular juncture in that their support would be more likely to be forthcoming for some new initiatives being proposed by Boult.

For example, Boult was keen to reduce the orchestra's Summer break, when players would perforce migrate to the seaside there to earn much-needed money - and to learn slovenly playing habits in pier orchestras which had to be unlearned in the Autumn. He therefore introduced the idea of adding to the orchestra's regular schedule by giving more concerts in Midland towns such as Cheltenham (for a few weeks), also in Midland public schools such as Rugby, Oundle, Shrewsbury and Repton. He further made a point of introducing 'great foreigners', to use his own words, to CBO concerts, not least the conductors Bruno Walter and Ernest Ansermet. Dohnányi was also invited, in the triple roles of pianist, composer and conductor - at one and the same concert incidentally. On the other hand, some of the orchestra's players were given the opportunity to play at Covent Garden and in the new permanent Wireless Symphony Orchestra, an experience which would no doubt widen their horizons and raise their expectations of themselves in a valuable way. Boult hoped that all these kinds of development would in the end lead to the Management being able to offer the players

Chapter 27 - Phase Two: A City Orchestra - The new musical flagship

contracts for nine or ten months of the year. That did not come until later, but it is clear evidence of the wider vision that this conductor brought to the orchestra's affairs.

Did Boult himself enjoy his Birmingham experience? The answer seems to have been: yes. In his autobiography, *My Own Trumpet*, he tells us:

'I found Birmingham in every way a happy place to work in. A cheerful bracing climate - how I noticed this on returning at 9 p.m. after my weekly day at the R.C.M (in London) - and a wonderful group of city fathers, who all belonged to the Union Club where I often lunched. Someone said that Edgbaston was responsible for the good government of Birmingham. Edgbaston was the closest dormitory: it actually began about a mile from the Town Hall; but only another half mile from there, one came to the edge of a valley which included ten or twelve houses with thirty-acre gardens each, one with 200 acres, and a great allotment field of 100 acres, all joining each other. Big business men when they retired, had no wish to move away (as was the general rule in Liverpool for instance). They stayed where they were, and interested themselves in public work, and so the public work was well done'. (Boult's time in Birmingham also indirectly furnished him with a beloved wife and four ready-made children, all of whom gave him a warm family life from 1933 onwards).

Joseph Chamberlain and the great tradition of civic responsibility

One has to say that this tradition of municipal responsibility for the civic, social and cultural welfare of the city owed a great deal to Joseph Chamberlain initially, one which later members of his family and other leading local citizens were also to follow. This concept owed much in turn to the influence of Birmingham's great non-denominational preacher, George Dawson, and his emphasis on practical Christianity.

The programmes 1924-30

What of the programmes? In 1925 it is clear that the *Musical Times* correspondent for Birmingham was pleased and impressed by the obvious intention of providing a platform for contemporary British composers. British works included Bax's *Symphonic Variations* (1917) with Harriet Cohen as the piano soloist, Bliss's *Colour Symphony* (1922) and John Ireland's *Symphonic Rhapsody, Mai Dun* (1921). In the same season, on 13th October 1925, Gustav Holst was the visiting conductor who guided performances of Haydn's Symphony no. 99 in E flat and his own Suite, *Beni Mora*. The *Fancy* section of Holst's new Choral Symphony was also included in a programme conducted by Boult, Wagner's Overture to *Die Meistersinger* and Ravel's *Pavane for a Dead Infanta* completing the programme.

In October 1926, the *Musical Times* gives a brief run-down of the music to be played in the forthcoming season, 1926 to 1927, the concerts to be held on Thursdays rather than on Tuesdays as formerly. The list is wide-ranging and included Bach's 'Triple Concerto', Harty's *With the Wild Geese*, Honegger's *Pastorale d'Eté*, Richard

Strauss' Tone Poem, *Don Quixote* and Brahms' Second Piano Concerto. The list of symphonies includes all nine by Beethoven, Borodin's second, Mahler's fourth, Schubert's seventh, eighth and ninth (sic) and Schumann's third and fourth. Another major Mahler work offered by Boult was given during his final season in Birmingham, 1929 to 1930. This was *Das Lied von der Erde* in which Astra Desmond and Steuart Wilson were the vocal soloists. Was Schubert's Seventh Symphony, listed above, what we would now call the Sixth Symphony in C one wonders?

It should be pointed out that for very many people in the audiences of those days, before the prevalence of radio and the recording media, the opportunity to hear such a rich variety of works was really relished. There was no other way to hear them at that point after all and this new orchestra was making the most valuable contribution to the health and wealth of the city's cultural life, and providing many people with huge and satisfying enjoyment they would not otherwise have had. The following is just a sample of what was on offer in the final phase with Adrian Boult as conductor. Further modern English works were heard in January 1929 at the West End Cinema when Boult conducted Schubert's Sixth Symphony along with two works for small orchestra, namely Butterworth's *Two English Idylls* (1911) and Bantock's *Old English Suite* (1909). Towards the end of the same month Dohnányi came to the city to conduct Beethoven's Symphony no. 3, the *Eroica*, his own *Ruralia Hungarica* and to play the piano in his own *Variations on a Nursery Tune* under Boult's baton. Bringing foreign composers to the city was something that Boult wanted to encourage. On 10th October 1929 the audience was given Schumann's Third Symphony, Arnold Bax's Symphonic Poem, *November Woods* (1917) and Dvorak's Violin Concerto with Isolde Menges as soloist. Later that month Boult conducted the orchestra in Arensky's Piano Concerto, an interesting item, and on 16th February 1930, Medtner's Piano Concerto was heard, with Birmingham pianist Edna Iles as soloist. In May 1930, Adrian Boult conducted his Farewell Concert and his successor Leslie Heward was announced. Boult had conducted this season in order not to let Birmingham down. He had already accepted an invitation to become Director of Music of the BBC and in fact, according to his own testimony (op. cit.), he regretted the departure from Birmingham for various reasons, but he must have known that in the end to go to London was a step up the career ladder that he must take.

The Town Hall showing its age
Coming down to practicalities for a moment, in this same season part of the Town Hall ceiling collapsed, thus delaying yet again any possibility of finding the money for a purpose-built concert hall. The subsequent repairs and alterations involved putting two new galleries at the back of the hall, creating the very idiosyncratic acoustics endured by audiences until 1991 and the move to Symphony Hall.

As a postscript to this section on Boult's tenure of the orchestra's conductorship, it was hardly surprising that after all his expenditure of energy and enterprise, Boult was

Chapter 27 - Phase Two: A City Orchestra - The new musical flagship

taken ill in 1927, the deputy conductor Joseph Lewis taking over his duties during his absence on a cruise which happily restored him to health. Like many men who 'don't look very robust' Adrian Boult lived to the age of 94, happily for the world of music!

The Union again

The Union's now regular involvement in the orchestra's affairs again surfaced when players from elsewhere were used to augment the orchestra, not yet as large as a true symphony orchestra should be. Visiting players were paid for rehearsals whereas regular players were not. The Union demanded that this practice should cease. A Players' Committee was set up at this point to deal with such matters in the future and is still in existence at the time of writing.

Leslie Heward CBO Conductor 1930-1943

Heward, the third conductor of the CBO was a Yorkshireman. The son of an organist, he was educated at the Manchester Cathedral Choir School, something which came about due to the influence of Sydney H. Nicholson, founder of the School of English Church Music. In 1914 at the age of 17, Heward became Organist and Choirmaster of St. Andrew's Church in Ancoats, Manchester, also an assistant organist at Manchester Cathedral, going on at the age of 20 to the Royal College of Music in London as the possessor of a scholarship in Composition. After his training, he was appointed as an assistant Music Master at Eton College. He subsequently conducted for the British National Opera Company, doing some compositions for the Gaiety Theatre at the same period. Most relevant to his future work in Birmingham was his appointment as Musical Director of the South African Broadcasting Corporation and Conductor of the Cape Town Orchestra, this between 1924 and 1927. He immediately raised the standard of this orchestra's playing to such an extent that they were invited to come to England and play in London at the Empire Exhibition at Wembley in 1925.

Still only 33 years of age when he came to Birmingham, Heward soon gained the respect of players and audiences alike by his formidable musicianship. Together with his sense of humour, this was an excellent recipe for further progress. Nevertheless his personality never intruded on the music and according to the testimony of the distinguished critic Eric Blom, at the time on the staff of the *Birmingham Post*, 'he was catholic in his tastes and so much more intent on letting the music speak for itself than on exhibiting his own interpretative personality that he was able to do justice to the work of any composer'. Heward would do his best even with a piece by a composer whose music he probably did not much like and would always 'give a conscientious and excellent performance'. Eric Blom also writes that the orchestra was at this point in its history 'as good as may be found in a continental town of similar importance'. So, progress being made indeed, but the orchestra not yet as good as the best! Respectable but still regional.

It is certain that the orchestra respected Heward for his total grasp of the scores, and some personal reactions from musically knowledgeable audience members at the time, related to the writer, indicate that they too shared this respect for him, admiring him as 'a great man'. On one occasion, according to these witnesses, the soloist in a concerto had a complete memory lapse whereupon Heward handed them his own full score and conducted the rest of the piece from memory.

On the financial front at this point the situation was not quite as rosy and the 1939 to 1940 season ended with a deficit of £1,000. In November 1940, however, the *Musical Times* reported that a Trust Fund created at this point by Miss Margaret Frances Pugh brought some relief.

War - a spur to progress?

In September 1939, the initial cessation of orchestral activity brought about by the BBC's decision to lay off its musicians, affected the BBC Midland Orchestra and thereby the city orchestra. In addition, the Town Hall was immediately requisitioned and surrounded by sand bags, an ominous sign. A month later, however, the Orchestra Committee, concerned about the effect on players' livelihoods, came to a decision to soldier on and a series of concerts was announced. Heward's contract had been suspended but in any case his health was necessitating a stay in a sanatorium and it was Victor Hely-Hutchinson, then Professor of Music at Birmingham University, who stepped into the breach. He conducted the concerts for that season, given by the City of Birmingham (Emergency) Orchestra, so-called, in the Large Theatre of the Midland Institute. This was until a further temporary contract for Leslie Heward could be negotiated. After their return to the Town Hall in 1940, the area around the Town Hall was bombed and the hall suffered some damage. Hundreds of people in the city were killed. Concerts continued, however, and there is no doubt that the generous and variously gifted Hely-Hutchinson had played an important role in ensuring their survival.

Just as an aside, the wry comments made by Beecham back in 1916 about doing in wartime what had been deemed impossible when at peace, seemed to apply again here. In fact, from the beginning of the Second World War, after the initial uncertainty, the Arts were seen as a way of doing that essential thing in wartime, keeping up public morale. This was something of a fight-for-life gesture against the very real menace of invasion by a fascist political regime. People attended cinemas and concerts in large numbers, in spite of the ever present possibility of an air-raid, for the camaraderie it brought and the distraction from the awful news. The author remembers the seats behind the orchestra at the lovely new Liverpool Philharmonic Hall filled at concerts by members of H. M. Forces admitted for sixpence (2½p). This in the earlier part of the war.

Chapter 27 - Phase Two: A City Orchestra - The new musical flagship

The programmes

As to the programmes, these continued to be an eclectic and interesting exploration for all concerned at that date. What might be called the main-stream, 'standard' repertoire of Haydn, Mozart, Beethoven and Schubert symphonies, with some by Schumann and Brahms, continued to feature, with the occasional foray into Bach and Handel, the latter usually 'arranged' it has to be said, and in the 'romantic' rather than the baroque style we would expect today. More recent works continued to be introduced, such as Edward German's Second Symphony on 20th December 1931, Sibelius' Second Symphony on 3rd January 1932, Vaughan Williams's *Job* in October 1932, with the new orchestra leader, Alfred Cave, as soloist. Heward was certainly also a great advocate of Sibelius' music. In the same month John Foulds' *Dynamic Triptych* was also played. The music of John Foulds has interestingly been espoused by the present conductor, Sakari Oramo, and an impressive recording of several pieces on CD was released in 2004. William Walton's First Symphony, composed between 1932 and 1935, was given 'for the first time outside London' in one of the Tuesday evening concerts late in 1935. At that time, this was a challenging work. John Ireland's Piano Concerto (1932) was played in the same season.

Leslie Heward.

It is also noteworthy that it was under Leslie Heward that the orchestra made its first commercial gramophone recordings. By December 1940, after his first stay in a sanatorium, Heward had been well enough to conduct these, and music for strings by Mozart and Tchaikovsky, and songs with the soprano Gwen Catley, were performed.

An unhappy ending

Birmingham lost this brilliant man at the point where many were only just beginning to realise his stature. The invitation to Heward from the Hallé Orchestra's management to take over the conductorship of that orchestra was a clear sign of the respect in which Heward was now held in the wider musical world. He accepted the invitation at the end of 1942 and the CBSO management faced the task of finding another conductor for the 1943 to 1944 season onwards. Very sadly fate had other ideas for Heward himself. A victim of tuberculosis, he did nothing to safeguard his health, continuing to smoke and drink heavily - and work too hard - even after a second period in a sanatorium. There were as yet no generally available antibiotics and Heward must have suspected the likely outcome of his condition, whatever he did. He died on 3rd May 1943.

George Weldon CBO Conductor 1944-51

Born in Chichester in 1908, George Weldon went to Sherborne School and, in spite of what he claimed was an undistinguished career there, managed to gain a Music Prize to go to the Royal College of Music when he was 17. There he studied conducting under Malcolm Sargent and Aylmer Buesst. From 1937 to 1939 he assisted Julius Harrison, conductor of the Hastings Municipal Orchestra, and worked also with the London Symphony Orchestra and the International Ballet. In 1943, Weldon was appointed as Conductor of the City of Birmingham Choir, following the death of his predecessor, G. D. Cunningham, one of Birmingham's great City Organists. More will be said about Cunningham in due course.

Weldon's personality

According to concert-goers of the time who have spoken to the author, Weldon was 'a flamboyant fellow' particularly adored by the young ladies not least, one suspects, because of his having one leg shorter than the other, so walking with a limp. Romantic female protectiveness perhaps kicked in here! In addition, Weldon was devoted to a succession of fast - some very fast - cars, even taking part in an official motor race, something which in its turn would be very good for his image among the young men.

Raising standards

All this appealing veneer in fact covered a thoroughly professional and committed dedication to the orchestra's fortunes and a capacity for hard work. Initially contracted to the orchestra for one season, 1943 to 1944, and then for a further three, Weldon was particularly concerned - and rightly it has to be said - about the unreliable quality of the string tone, especially that of the first violins. Part of this was due to the small size of the orchestra, only 60 in number, implying a string section of some 40 players. What was more, as things were at that time, these would vary at almost every concert as to personnel. The true 'symphony orchestra' sound required a total of at least 20 *more* players in the orchestra than this, implying a total of 80 and a string section of about 60. If in turn they were always the *same* players, because they had a permanent contract, this would enable the building up of a larger, much more cohesive body of string players with a consistent standard, to the great benefit of the orchestra as a whole. The wind players in an orchestra often have to play as soloists, and recordings that Weldon made with the orchestra reveal some very good wind soloists, both wood and brass, with competent but hardly rich or exciting string tone. In fact, rank and file string players, especially the violinists, were too often content to hide behind the section leaders, and individual auditions when occasionally carried out often revealed unacceptable standards.

Permanent contracts for the players

Weldon spent much time in auditioning new players and in doing all he could to raise the standard of playing. He also urged the establishment of a permanent orchestra, so increasing the players' own commitment. Of course, all this would cost money but Weldon had the support of Ulric Brunner, the orchestra's Secretary and Librarian at that time, who presented a scheme for a permanent orchestra to the Chairman of the Executive Sub-Committee. In the event, the very helpful link with the BBC, which had offered extra employment, ended when permanent contracts for the CBO players were established in 1944. Weldon's official appointment was now as Musical Director and Conductor of the orchestra at a salary of £2,000 a year. This seems high for those days - twice what a bank manager earned for example at that time - but we are talking about someone who had to absorb and physically conduct the music played in a significant proportion of nearly 200 two-hour concerts every year, with rehearsals and recordings added in, some of all this involving travelling to other towns and cities.

Problems with programme-planning in wartime

It is clear from reports from the time that by 1943 the concert-going public in Birmingham either attended in droves or, just as unpredictably, stayed away. The usual soul-searching over programme-planning went on - to go for the popular, or for the new and challenging? Piano concertos were a sure-fire draw, also - usually - the music of Tchaikovsky, though less predictably in this latter case apparently. So, do we recognise that for some young people the oldest of old chestnuts is for them an entirely new and exciting experience, or do we make a very earnest attempt to extend the boundaries of the public's musical repertoire? In the event Weldon was accused of veering too much towards the former with light-weight shorter pieces - though some of these were new, and British, it has to be said. Major works by Saint-Saëns, Brahms, Dvořák, Sibelius, Elgar and major new symphonies by Vaughan Williams (fifth), Rubbra (third) and Walton (first), for example, appeared more frequently *after* the war.

In October 1943 the first three Sunday programmes at the Town Hall included Dvořák's Fourth Symphony (now known as no. 8 in G), Tchaikovsky's Piano Concerto no. 1 with Mark Hambourg as soloist, the Schumann Piano Concerto with Louis Kentner, Tchaikovsky's Fifth Symphony, Brahms Second Symphony, Beethoven's Third Piano Concerto with Kathleen Long, and Walton's new *Spitfire* Prelude and Fugue. All these pieces were audience-pullers at the time.

The experiment of a week of Promenade Concerts was tried in August 1945 which was highly successful. This was perhaps not so surprising given the 'holidays at home' culture which war had imposed on the nation. In the event, this innovation was continued and extended to three weeks instead of one and the Summer Proms continued on into the Rattle era. In any case, in September 1944 the *Musical Times* speaks of the orchestra packing the Town Hall and Eric Blom in the *Birmingham Post* asks 'will the orchestra please oblige by giving a bad performance for a change?' Clearly Weldon's policies were having some success.

A challenge
Not everyone was to agree with Blom's comment, however, and a correspondence in the *Musical Times* between May and September 1945 refers back to something that had happened the previous November, in 1944. John Stone, a critic for the *Birmingham Weekly Post* had got into very hot water because of his challenge to what he saw as the complacent view of the orchestra's playing held by some, and endorsed by most of the other critics, in opposition to a very different view held by a considerable body of listeners in the city. One would imagine in the light of all this, he said, that 'the strings consisted of an amalgam of Menuhins, Tertises, Piattis and Bottesinis; that our woodwind outshone any combination of Amadios, Leon Goossenses, Drapers and Camdens; that the Brains had nothing on our horns; and that the percussion were likewise peerless'. The imperfections cropped up time and again, Stone wrote, only to be ignored by the other critics, to the detriment of the orchestra's real progress.

The shock of seeing these views expressed in print was too much for the city orchestra authorities, we are told, and a letter went from the office of the orchestra, signed by the secretary, asking Stone to return the press tickets that admitted him to the orchestra's concerts. Who was really behind this action one wonders? In any case, Stone then received another letter, this time from the editor of the *Birmingham*

Weekly Post, saying that 'acting on Lord Iliffe's instructions' (Lord Iliffe was the proprietor of the journal), 'I shall no longer require your weekly articles on music'. An article in the *Musical Times*, in May 1945, follows this with the comment that 'there are many evidences among us of an inclination towards methods that, if used by foreign oppressors, we should not hesitate to describe, however free from conscious evil intent, as tending towards the setting up of Fascist ways'. Stone was accused by the 'orchestral establishment' of harming the orchestra's reputation. He replied in turn that low standards on the part of the players would give the Philistines on the Council every excuse to argue for the ending of the city's grant to it. Further comment from the *Musical Times* (June 1945) added that whether the orchestra agrees or disagrees with Stone's strictures 'when they (the orchestra) invite criticism by sending tickets they should make it clear beforehand that unfavourable criticism is not within the scope of the invitation. We know what would happen to those notices in British newspaper offices; with one exception, the *Birmingham Weekly Post*'.

Finally, Lord Iliffe having been publicly dragged into this, wrote to the *Musical Times* himself, having to come down heavily, as he knew he must, on the side of press freedom. Even so, John Stone's services as a local music critic were never again required.

One cannot help but think that Weldon himself would have been in agreement with what John Stone had written. In a letter to the orchestra manager in January 1944 he had expressed the hope that the critic Eric Blom would 'go for' the players, especially the violins, and that he, George Weldon, was determined to raise standards. (Quoted by King-Smith op. cit.)

Programme planning again

By 1945, however, there seem to be some complaints about the prevalence of standard programmes and well-known soloists, although one totally unfamiliar work had appeared at the end of 1944, namely Liapounov's *Ukrainian Fantasy* for piano and orchestra with the local pianist Wilfred Ridgway as the soloist. Some of the pieces played in the 1944 to 1945 season do seem very slight. These included Guy Graham's *Landsman's Hornpipe*, Rowley's *Burlesque Quadrille* and Gordon Jacob's *Passacaglia, Russian Interlude* and *Galop Joyeux*. They may have been attractive but they have not survived in the orchestral repertoire. Many piano concertos were in the programmes – using successively, it was noted, four women and two men as soloists, hardly surprising in the middle of a world war with all able-bodied younger men called up into the forces!

Weldon as conductor

The inclusion of so many shorter works in the programmes did not mean that Weldon was not good at shaping a really big piece. In fact he seems to have been particularly good at doing just that. Two comments from John Waterhouse, who was *Birmingham Post* Music Critic at the time, can be quoted from the contributions Waterhouse also made to the *Penguin Music Guides* of the mid-1940s. The first is from the December 1946 number.

'Mr. Weldon repeatedly shows himself a master in the building up of large structures, and in the holding together of those which, like the Elgar A flat Symphony, are apt to creak and come apart if left to themselves. But he has also fashioned many small things exquisitely'.

Further evidence of Weldon's Elgarian sympathies is given by the *Musical Times* in a report in August 1951: 'It is scarcely surprising, then, that when the orchestra gave two concerts in the Royal Festival Hall, (during the Festival of Britain) on 20 and 21 June, Elgar's *Falstaff* brought forth the most authoritative playing. The music flowed along, with its numerous incidents of drama, humour, pageantry and sentiment all faithfully and lovingly realised'.

Weldon could be flamboyant we have been told. What of his conducting? That verged on the flamboyant too at times. This from the *Penguin Music Guide* (May 1947) and the pen of John Waterhouse again:

'Our high opinion of Mr. Weldon steadily grows. There was a time not long ago when some of us feared that he might be tempted to turn down the ruinous road, so congested with conductors these days, of superfluous and histrionic gesticulation.

George Weldon.

One recalls an alarming occasion when he waved the horns through their swaying seconds in the love-theme of Tchaikovsky's *Romeo and Juliet* so that the total effect was suggestive of seagulls, an image unlikely to have been part of the composer's programmatic intentions. To overcome the temptation towards this sort of thing must, for a sensitive conductor with the inevitable goggling and pestering battalion of "fans", be an iron test of integrity. But there is every evidence that Mr. Weldon has overcome it'.

Post war doldrums and the attempts to weather them
A year later in the *Penguin Music Guide* for October 1948, however, John Waterhouse now describes a rather gloomy situation.

'The decline is due, I think, to two causes: to the nation-wide passing of the big orchestral boom; and to the fact that, in the long run, two orchestral concerts a week proved too much for the city's musical digestion. Only those at grips with the orchestra's economic complexities can say whether there is a way round this latter problem; but I am quite sure that, if two concerts there must be, a discreet but continual seasoning of novelty is more likely to stimulate the digestion than is a still further narrowing of the diet'.

Some items in the orchestra's programmes between 1948 and 1949 must have been new to audiences at that time, it must be said, these including Bach's Concerto for two violins and strings BWV 1043, Shostakovich's Ninth Symphony, Bliss's Piano Concerto with Shulamith Shafir as soloist, Medtner's First Piano Concerto again with Edna Iles as pianist, Vaughan Williams' challenging new Sixth Symphony, Samuel Barber's First Symphony, Gordon Jacob's Rhapsody for cor anglais and orchestra and Alan Rawsthorne's Piano Concerto. At the same period, 1949, an official CBSO Journal was announced to be edited by Ruth Gipps, chorus master of the City of Birmingham Choir. Visits by the orchestra to other towns and cities continued.

George Weldon's efforts to improve the standard of playing, the string playing in particular, had certainly already had some effect. The orchestral lists in 1946 might include some 64 players. Five years later, in 1951, Weldon had 73 players, 40 of whom were new members of the team, with only 33 survivors from the previous era. All this was indeed radical surgery - painful for some who were never engaged again, but very beneficial to the reputation of the immediate post-war orchestra. All very necessary if the orchestra was to survive post-war 'austerity' and the parlous state of the country's finances at that time. In February 1948, Weldon had also insisted that the orchestra should in future be known as the City of Birmingham *Symphony* Orchestra; from now on therefore CBSO and not CBO.

Later, on 3rd September 1951 John Waterhouse, writing in the *Birmingham Post* about the current CBSO prospectus comments that the CBSO programmes 'compare not unfavourably with those of most other British orchestras' and that in the first year or two of Mr. Weldon's direction they were positively enterprising but afterwards veered this way and that, new pieces being very brief and slight with a limited selection of major composers - as we have already seen.

By 1950, sadly, the orchestra's financial deficit amounted to at least £5,000 probably considerably more. To add to the woe, three highly-respected, long-serving and active members of the orchestra's management hierarchy retired or resigned at this point, namely Gerald Forty, Byng Kenrick and Hamilton Baines. All of these men had been, as we would say, heavy-hitters in the city's affairs. Two of the crucial new incumbents, as Chairman and Executive Chairman, were Stephen Lloyd and Bill Russell, both of whom also proved to be formidable guardians of the orchestra's affairs, but also much more 'hands-on' in their involvement, which alarmed some people but was to be extremely beneficial in fact. One of their first initiatives was to set up a City of Birmingham Orchestral Endowment Fund in 1950 which, within two years, was holding a very useful capital sum of money, some £8,000 - a significant amount of money at that time. Other initiatives were to follow.

To help with ticket sales, an imaginative new idea was then launched and blocks of tickets were sent out to offices and factories to be offered for resale to employees. This was followed up by the invitation to the employers to commit themselves to purchasing vouchers which could then be offered on to their workers - an early species of sponsorship perhaps? Weldon himself, feeling that the orchestra's rather conventional publicity in an era of paper shortage was too muted, had a personal letter from himself to the Promenaders put inside the programmes at these very well-attended events, urging them to attend the forthcoming regular Winter season concerts.

Weldon's dismissal
None of this was enough to save George Weldon however. There was, in addition to the anxiety over the finances, some anti-Weldon feeling among certain influential local musicians. Faced with all of this, Lloyd and Russell seem to have decided to take drastic action. They initiated moves to appoint Rudolf Schwarz as CBSO conductor and this was more or less a done deal before George Weldon knew anything about it. It was then suggested to Weldon himself that he should not (*could* not in fact) renew his contract and his appointment as Conductor of the CBSO came to a bitter end. He himself seems to have been dignified in defeat. John Barbirolli on the other hand was furious, and offered Weldon the post of Associate Conductor of the Hallé Orchestra, which he accepted. Weldon never held a principal permanent conducting post again and died in Cape Town while out there to conduct. According to his companion, Gerard Prideaux-Lightfoot, he died of an overdose of painkillers being taken for depression and the pain from his leg. One cannot but feel that he did not deserve such an end to all his efforts.

Did it simply come down to a matter of the management deciding that finding a more prestigious conductor to replace Weldon, as Boult had replaced Matthews in

1924, was again needed, or were other factors at work? We will probably never know, but one cannot help but feel that Weldon was to some extent unfairly held responsible for factors which had been in reality the product of the very difficult circumstances of total war – and its difficult aftermath.

Rudolf Schwarz CBSO Conductor 1951-1957

Schwarz's first concert with the CBSO was given a warm ovation. It was something that promised 'immensely well for the future' according to John Waterhouse, who also writes that the coming programmes are the 'best, liveliest and wisest offered by any major British orchestra since the war'.

Born in Vienna, Rudolf Schwarz, 46 years old when he came to Birmingham, had been conducting the Düsseldorf Opera back in 1924 at the age of 19. His subsequent post as conductor of the Jewish Cultural Organisation in Berlin inevitably drew attention from the Nazis, leading to internment in a labour camp from 1943 to 1945. This involved torture and physical injury. After that Schwarz had gone to Sweden to attempt to recover his health and was then invited to Bournemouth to conduct its Symphony Orchestra in 1947, taking British citizenship in 1952, after his arrival in Birmingham.

Did Schwarz provide the kind of leadership and training the orchestra still so much needed and did he provide the sort of fare likely to attract larger audiences? On the whole he appears to have done. Schwarz was a fine musician, of course, and he was meticulous in the preparation of the music to be performed, although the players did not find the whole process so much fun as it had been with George Weldon, according to the diary of the 'cellist Gwen Berry (quoted in King-Smith op. cit). As to programmes, Schwarz was certainly generous to the music of his British hosts, now his compatriots. Early in his time in Birmingham, Bax's Third Symphony, Moeran's *Sinfonietta,* Richard Arnell's Piano Concerto, Rubbra's Fifth Symphony, Vaughan Williams Symphony no. 2, *A London Symphony* and, in lighter vein, Josef Holbrooke's Variations on the Theme of *Three Blind Mice* appear in the programmes. Alongside these went works such as Roussel's Third Symphony, Schubert's Ninth and Beethoven's Fifth symphonies together with Debussy's *Nocturnes*, Reger's Variations on a Theme of Mozart and Hindemith's *Metamorphoses*.

The Feeney Trust

Importantly, the first two Feeney Trust commissions were performed in December 1955 and December 1956, respectively Bliss's *Meditations on a Theme of John Blow* and Tippett's Piano Concerto. This last was broadcast, but the *Musical Times*' critic's rather disillusioned comment at the time was 'What with a good deal of shaky playing, poor reception and a tendency to somnolence – the radio critic's occupational sickness – I should have welcomed a second broadcast'. What was at fault? – the work, the

Rudolf Schwarz.

performance or the critic? All three probably, would be the answer. The general reaction to 'new music' will be discussed later in this chapter.

Schwarz's final season as conductor of the CBSO in 1956-1957, concluded with a concert at the Royal Festival Hall in London. Schubert's Ninth Symphony was 'the crown of the concert' according to Noel Goodwin in the *Musical Times* of May 1957. Goodwin wrote of the problems of the great C major Symphony's dynamics which were solved on this occasion 'by maintaining an ideal balance of tone between sections at all levels'. How Beecham would have approved of that! Goodwin goes on, 'The music emerged with an unusual freshness and sparkle, if not with the full weight of its grandeur' and then also comments on something noticed by orchestra and soloists alike, that Schwarz's beat was not always easy to follow. He continues: 'Since the vagaries of Mr. Schwarz's beat usually mean that his points are made with the heel instead of the tip of his baton, it may be that he would achieve better results without it'. In spite of this, however, Schwarz was generally acknowledged as a most perceptive interpreter and his departure for London in 1957, where he took over the BBC Symphony Orchestra, as Adrian Boult had done in 1930, is testimony to the wider recognition of his gifts. On this occasion, Schwarz was replacing Malcolm Sargent.

A firmer financial footing

Meanwhile, the orchestra's financial situation had been put on a firmer foundation. It should be pointed out that the establishment of an Arts Council for Great Britain in 1946 meant, among many other things, an extra tranche of funding for the CBSO, in addition to the funding received from the city. By 1952, the sums involved were £19,000 from the city and £11,000 from the Arts Council. The post-war Labour government was keen to encourage the Arts, and to make them available to the whole population. Jennie Lee, the wife of Aneurin Bevan, founder of the National Health Service, was to be an enthusiastic Arts Minister and very supportive of the idea of public funding for the Arts. This general policy was reflected more specifically in Birmingham when Alderman Albert Bradbeer, a previous Birmingham Lord Mayor, a member of the Labour party and now leader of the Labour group on the city council, followed this general government policy and secured the granting of an interest-free loan of £20,000 to the orchestra to be paid back at the rate of £2,000 annually. This all contrasts favourably with the situation in Manchester as regards funding for the Hallé Orchestra incidentally. Historically, the Hallé had been the product of nineteenth century private enterprise alone, with no Neville Chamberlain, with his local political connections, taking an active part in the matter. Many members of the Manchester City Council could not see why they should now be involved at all, let alone make public money available This, of course, was also true in Birmingham but with the difference that in Birmingham the orchestra did have some very influential 'friends at court' so to speak, to fight their case, and in the long run fight it very effectively. Birmingham still did not have a decent concert hall, however, something that Albert Bradbeer, mentioned above, called for - yet again in vain.

The players

What of the orchestra itself at this point? They were now a permanent orchestra, with much more security and Weldon had managed to bring in some new blood, but there was still some very unsatisfactory playing among the string players. Certainly some of the comments Schwarz made on players he auditioned make very depressing reading. One can understand why he could appear rather glum and surly at times, at rehearsals, again according to Gwen Berry's diary, already mentioned (page 265). (King-Smith op. cit.) He does not seem, however, to have had the sort of involved determination that Weldon had in the business of improving the standard of the players and perhaps his eye was in the long run on a more prestigious conducting appointment elsewhere, most probably in London. In any case, an appeal for new players would no doubt occasion some sinking of the heart in those who had to manage the orchestra's finances. Maintaining the *status quo* would be hard enough, but a windfall in the shape of a generous donation of £11,000 from Harry Payne to help in paying for new players appeared at this point, and orchestral numbers rose to 71. Sadly, this money ran out after three seasons.

In spite of all this, there is no doubt that Schwarz could inspire the orchestra at concerts, so that it gave the best it could and, in spite of deficiencies, could come up with a 'high standard of performance' something appreciated by its next conductor. And how hard they worked, with 167 concerts in the season, arranged in Tuesday, Thursday, Saturday and Sunday series. Over a hundred concerts were in Birmingham, the rest in other towns which as always of course implied travelling as well. This was a heavy commitment for a relatively small symphony orchestra, with inadequate rehearsal time. Schwarz's appointment as conductor of the BBC Symphony Orchestra came in 1957 and so Birmingham lost another conductor to the London scene.

Andrzej Panufnik CBSO Conductor 1957-1959

The son of a violin maker father and a violinist mother, Panufnik entered the Warsaw Conservatory in 1932 where he took classes in percussion before concentrating on composition. Graduating in 1936 he then studied conducting with Felix Weingartner in Vienna, moved to Paris where he had more conducting lessons, and returned to Warsaw just before Hitler's invasion of Poland. He continued to compose in spite of all the difficulties associated first with the war and, after it, with living behind the Iron Curtain under the Stalinist communist regime in Poland.

Panufnik continued his conducting career, working successively with the Krakov and Warsaw Philharmonic Orchestras, also abroad in Western Europe. One of these visits gave him the chance to defect, and he escaped to England in 1954. Conducting provided him with his only means of support in his new country, where he was little known, and his appointment as Conductor of the CBSO in 1957, in succession to Schwarz, was certainly a way of making his name more widely known and giving him financial security, even if not a really lasting satisfaction. It is easy to see why he left his post in Birmingham after only two years and returned to his real love - composition. His reputation as a composer was growing and, in spite of the BBC's then current rejection of music rooted in anything traditional, his recognition was sufficient for him to risk abandoning a regular paid post.

Some interesting pieces were presented in Birmingham under Panufnik's baton, however, not least the Feeney Trusts's third commission, Rubbra's Seventh Symphony given on 1st October 1957. Harold Rutland in the *Musical Times* for November 1957 commented as follows: 'Andrzej Panufnik and the CBSO had clearly taken immense pains to secure a faithful presentation of the work'. He went on: 'In the first part of the programme the strings of the Orchestra gave us some clear and vital playing in Avison's Concerto no. 13 in D (evidence of Mr. Panufnik's keen interest in eighteenth century English music), and Hans Henkemans was the soloist in an admirable performance of Mozart's Piano Concerto in D minor. The concert was an important musical event. Where, however, were Birmingham's music-lovers? It was disappointing to see so many empty seats'.

Not a totally encouraging beginning for someone making his way in a new country, all the more depressing given the upheaval caused when the management of the orchestra warned 16 violinists about their standards of playing, and an ensuing strike was only narrowly averted. One can only wonder if the inclusion of some more very unfamiliar works in the programme in the New Year 1958 - Farkas's Harp Concertino, Malipiero's Two-Piano Concerto and Bloch's Symphony for trombone and orchestra - made things better or worse.

The Associate conductors

There had been another new conducting appointment made by the orchestra management in 1957 when Meredith Davies was brought in as a second Associate Conductor, Harold Gray continuing as Associate. Gray himself was originally appointed in 1924 as secretary and musical amanuensis to Adrian Boult, his first conducting appearance with the orchestra following in 1930. More will be said about him and his long association with the orchestra in due course. Davies on the other hand had been chosen from a list of 150 applicants, reduced to a short list of four, and in August 1958 won critical approval in the *Musical Times* from Hugh Ottaway writing about broadcast music. He comments that there was 'a good performance, sensitive yet masculine, of Delius's *Song of the High Hills*. Meredith Davies conducted the City of Birmingham Symphony orchestra, which has raised its standards considerably in the last six months or so'.

A policy of exploration was continued as far as repertoire was concerned in the 1958 to 1959 season and the list of recently-composed works included Lennox Berkeley's Second Symphony, commissioned by the orchestra through the Feeney Trust, Panufnik's own *Sinfonia Elegiaca* and *Tragic Overture*, Anthony Lewis's *Canzona, Homage to Purcell*, Peter Wishart's *Concerto for Orchestra* and, going abroad, Nielsen's Fifth Symphony. Lewis and Wishart incidentally were, respectively, Professor and staff member of the University of Birmingham Music Department at the time.

The standard of string-playing yet again

The battle for better players still needed to continue, Panufnik probably not being the ideal person to undertake it. In 1958, the question of the old-fashioned violin playing in particular, still used by some in the orchestra, not least the leader, Norris Stanley, really came to a head. The old style involved the constant use of *portamenti* - slithers and slides between notes - a practice that Malcolm Sargent had been able to weed out of the Liverpool orchestra back in the 1940s as a very active and decisive 'new broom' able to make a new start, in a fine new hall. Panufnik was not so fortunate in the cultural climate which prevailed while he was in Birmingham and not surprisingly he resigned from the conductor's post in 1959. This was then offered to Meredith Davies who wisely refused, rightly considering that he was not yet ready for such a responsibility. In fact he was engaged in the 1960s by Benjamin Britten to conduct several of his operas at Aldeburgh and elsewhere, afterwards also holding a number of posts as choral director of several well-known choirs, confirming his mastery of the British choral tradition.

In the interim 1959-60

The orchestra was fortunate in being able to obtain the services of Adrian Boult, now Sir Adrian Boult, for some concerts in the coming season. He, along with the two Associate Conductors, Meredith Davies and Harold Gray, kept an enterprising series going in the 1959 to 1960 season, and until a new permanent appointment could be made. In the Tuesday Series of concerts Meredith Davies conducted Rawsthorne's Symphony no. 2 on 29th September, this being another Feeney Trust commission.

Harold Gray (photograph by Constantine).

That was given a London performance three days later at the Royal Festival Hall. Further 'Tuesday Series' items included Holst's *Egdon Heath* and *The Planets* and Stravinsky's *Dumbarton Oaks* Concerto - all these conducted by Davies - with Boult conducting Walton's Cello Concerto, Amaryllis Fleming the soloist. The Thursday series featured Robert Simpson's Violin Concerto, the orchestra's own Ernest Element as soloist, and a number of major British works by Elgar, Vaughan Williams and Delius. In addition, Mahler's Fourth Symphony was added to the mix and Benjamin Britten came to conduct his own *Spring Symphony*. The Sunday series continued as before.

Contemporary music - an aside

We have seen that all through the nineteenth century and up to this point in the twentieth, recently composed music, not least British music, was played and enjoyed. In the twentieth century, music by Prokofiev, Shostakovich, Sibelius, Delius, Vaughan Williams, Holst and Walton was appreciated when it was new and is still enjoyed today. From about 1960 onwards there was to be a change. Atonal systems using no key at all, the twelve-tone experiments of Schoenberg which were germinating in his mind at the beginning of the First World War and developed after it, and aleatoric procedures using the element of chance were all experimented with by some of the mid-century composers. Many audience members found this very difficult to comprehend let alone enjoy. This posed a dilemma for programme planners. Were they to encourage new music, as the Arts Council urged, even if it drove away audiences, or were they to risk becoming stuck in a repetitive round of the familiar and popular? This is a question which has to be borne in mind from this point onwards.

Hugo Rignold CBSO Conductor 1960-1967

Born in Kingston-upon-Thames in 1905 of musical parents, Hugo Rignold spent his childhood in Canada. He won a scholarship to the Royal Academy of Music in London, where he had violin, viola, oboe and trumpet lessons with the leading players of the day, gaining all the major prizes. As with many musicians at that period of slump, poverty and huge unemployment, first the light-music scene and then His Majesty's Forces furnished Hugo Rignold with his early career opportunities and the ability to earn a living. He became the lead violinist with Jack Hylton's Orchestra, an orchestra whose light music style and relatively small numbers in fact called for a considerable degree of precision from each performer. The RAF furnished what was for Rignold a more suitable opportunity and he was able to lead and eventually guest-conduct the Cairo Symphony Orchestra. In this capacity, he received favourable notices from Richard Capell, *Daily Telegraph* Music Critic at the time, abroad as a war correspondent for the paper. These led to Rignold's work with the Palestine Symphony Orchestra.

Hugo Rignold and the CBSO rehearsing in Nottingham.

After the war, Hugo Rignold worked as Principal Viola with the Royal Opera House Orchestra and after that as conductor of the Liverpool Philharmonic Orchestra, as it then was. One principal player in the Liverpool Orchestra at that time expressed to the author her great respect for 'Riggy', particularly because of his success as an orchestral trainer. He was thoroughly professional and workmanlike, always expecting the same attitude from his players and only harsh, she said, with those who did not bother to give of their best. He was just what Birmingham's orchestra needed at that point in its history.

By 1955 even more new names were appearing in the orchestral lists - young blood from a new post-war generation, with some long-serving players no longer listed - but the total number of players still only 73. It is probably true to say that neither Schwarz nor Panufnik, fine musicians though they were, were quite as committed to the future of Birmingham and its orchestra as would have been desirable, although Schwarz had recruited some new younger blood to the strength. Hugo Rignold's conscientiousness and his engagement with the orchestral players, as players, was exactly the right prescription at this point. As early as April 1961, the *Musical Times* is commenting that Hugo Rignold had begun well and is 'obtaining a more disciplined and vigorous response from the players'.

Chapter 27 - Phase Two: A City Orchestra - The new musical flagship

The programming question again

What of the programmes at this period? Perhaps they could be summed up as a good solid representation of the core symphonic repertoire, surrounded by less substantial pieces with perhaps more audience-pulling power - just a bit 'easier on the ear' so to speak. Occasionally there was a really special occasion, a land-mark. One such was the memorable first performance by the orchestra of Britten's *War Requiem* in the new Coventry Cathedral, the composer and Meredith Davies co-conducting, along with the Coventry Festival Choir and soloists Heather Harper (standing in for Galina Vishnevskaya), Peter Pears and Dietrich Fischer-Dieskau. This memorable performance was broadcast. (30th May 1962).

From time to time there was a programme devoted to one composer as for example an all-Beethoven programme at a Sunday concert in October 1964 and an all-Sibelius one a year later, the latter composer especially dear to Hugo Rignold's heart. This whole conception could perhaps be derided as conventional but at that date, with classical music swept away to the Third Programme (predecessor of Radio 3), far fewer recordings of classical music, and pop music increasingly dominating the scene, concerts such as these were the main opportunity of getting to know the great orchestral repertoire. In spite of some adverse criticism, such programmes were a rich feast of some of the finest examples of our great and inspiring musical inheritance. Something to be treasured indeed.

The recent work was not, however, always very popular with many audience members if the truth were told, and such items were usually tucked into the middle of the programme with the more 'palatable', or should one say familiar, items to begin and end! This policy could, of course, occasionally backfire and end by completely pleasing no-one.

A further Feeney Trust Commission given on 31st October 1963 with Harold Gray conducting was Bliss's *Mary of Magdala* with the City of Birmingham Choir. Elizabeth Maconchy's *Serenata Concertante*, also a Feeney Trust commission. Adrian Cruft's *Prospero's Island*, Roberto Gerhard's *Alegrias*, John Joubert's First Symphony and symphonies by Egon Wellesz, William Matthias and Richard Rodney Bennett were later added to the mix. Guest orchestras also appeared - the Polish Radio Orchestra in 1969, the BBC Symphony Orchestra in 1963, the Bournemouth Orchestra the following year for example. In turn, the CBSO performed elsewhere - at the Three Choirs Festival, in opera in North Wales, in seasons with the Welsh National Opera and, a hopeful sign for the future, abroad in Czechoslovakia.

Some negatives…

In other less desirable ways, too, this period was quite eventful. There was a sort of abortive strike in 1965, really just a walk-out on the part of the players, due to the demotion of a violinist, a contretemps in which nobody, including Rignold himself, acted very diplomatically but which passed off without doing too much damage. This was nevertheless a portent of what was to come during the next conductor's period of office and which continued to simmer under the surface from time to time. Meanwhile there was a threat of a reduction in the orchestra's grant from the city. In fact this ended in an increase in the city's grant, funds from the Arts Council and from other surrounding local authorities in the area continuing in addition.

There had for some years been much talk about Birmingham being the country's Second City. It was certainly so as regards its population and its industry at that time, also in the current 1960s reshaping of the city, with its radical city centre redevelopment and ring road. It gradually dawned on even the most die-hard Philistine that a major city in the civilised world must not only have busy shopping and commercial centres but also fine theatres, a first-class art gallery, library, museum and - even - a first-rate symphony orchestra, performing in a decent, modern concert hall. It was also dawning on those involved in any way with Arts funding that where Germany and France respectively were spending the equivalent of about £7.50 and £5.00 per head of the population on the arts, we in the United Kingdom spent 50p. We had not in fact much to be proud about in this respect at that point.

...and some positives. An International Wind Competition and a recording
Meanwhile and much more positively, an International Wind Competition was held over the period of a week in May 1966. This was most instructive and fascinating to see and hear, for players and audience alike - even if audience attendance was disappointingly and rather disgracefully small. From this contest, with dark hair, cut short back and sides, a bespectacled young Ulster flautist named James Galway emerged, joint winner in a very competitive field with the French oboist, Maurice Bourgue. This had been an excellent show-case for Birmingham and its orchestra with a visiting jury of leading musicians, chaired by Adrian Boult, and had helped to launch important careers. Another very positive event was a visit to London to make a record of the Bliss *Music for Strings* and his *Meditations on a Theme by John Blow*, the latter a Feeney Trust Commission first performed by the CBSO under Schwarz in 1955. This was the orchestra's first recording since 1947. It was felt at the time as encouraging evidence of progress. An interesting and exciting event, particularly for the professional musicians in the audience, was the visit in 1967 of the eminent French musician and teacher, Nadia Boulanger, who conducted an authoritative performance of Fauré's *Requiem*. It was a memorable experience to see this almost legendary woman, who had taught so many eminent composers and performers, 'in the flesh', taking easy and masterly control of the large forces involved. These included members of the University of Birmingham Chorus, since a previous Professor of Music, Anthony Lewis, had been a favourite pupil of Boulanger.

On a practical note the orchestra also acquired its own, very large and useful instruments van.

The long-serving Harold Gray should be mentioned here, conducting a concert in 1967, forty years on into his 55-year association with the orchestra. In May of that year the *Musical Times* critic wrote as follows: 'On February 23rd the Associate Conductor, Harold Gray, played Nielsen's Sixth for the first time in Birmingham. Gray is usually worth hearing in Scandinavian music for which he seems to have an affinity - he gave a spectacular account of Nielsen's Third some time ago. The Sixth however has the reputation of being an uneven work, but Gray made these problematical central movements sound much more logical than I recall ever having heard them'.

In 1967, instead of renewing Rignold's three-year contract the orchestral management offered him one year only. He was understandably upset by this and riposted by handing in his resignation. Rignold completed the forthcoming season, ending up with a concert at which audience and orchestra alike gave him a standing ovation. This at a Prom in July 1968. What lay behind this management decision? It may have been a re-run of the Weldon-Schwarz changeover when the man who had slaved at raising the standard of every player in the orchestra was replaced by a more glamourous - and in each case foreign - personality. What was the grass-roots feeling? Many discerning local musicians known to the author had admired the growing sense amongst the players, particularly the wind and brass players, that it mattered very much how each one of them, individually, played. And this even extended to the back desk strings - for most of the time! One might still occasionally overhear an 'announcement' during the interval, from a string player, most often a violinist, that for the rest of the evening they would go 'on automatic pilot', very annoying for a paying audience member! - and no good for playing standards. Many much-admired performances were secured, nevertheless, which was inspiring and heartening for those concerned for the state of classical music in the city. At the same period, however, the *Birmingham Post* was fielding a Music Critic, Kenneth Dommett, who was adopting a particularly negative attitude. Many musically informed folk who attended a concert and then read the review of it in the paper next morning wondered if they had been to the same concert! This certainly did not help. This was interesting in that Dommett had written in the *Musical Times* shortly before this, in May 1966, as follows: 'The other concerts were conducted by Hugo Rignold who has done wonders for this orchestra'.

Clearly there was a strand of opinion which was dissatisfied with the current situation. There had in fact been sustained criticism from local musical scholars that the programmes were not imaginative enough. Again in the *Musical Times*, this time in December 1962, Nigel Fortune had commented: 'The orchestra and their chief conductor, Hugo Rignold, deserve support not only for what they do but for how they do it – their *Eroica* was splendidly vital, and they supported equally convincingly Ralph Holmes's superb account of the Berg (Violin Concerto). We hear almost no very recent music here; it is to be hoped that names like Boulez and Maxwell Davies will appear in programmes soon. In general the two concert series are well balanced – though not entirely so: three Brahms concertos and four early works by Sibelius on the one hand, *one* Haydn symphony on the other'. In the following October (1963) the same commentator writes: '...the enterprising concerts of 1962-3 seemed to be not well supported, so I suppose it is not surprising that the CBSO have virtually ceased to form, lead or coax public taste but have started to follow it. We are to have not a note of Bruckner, Schoenberg, Berg, Webern, Stravinsky, Bartók or Nielsen. Mahler, Britten and Hindemith are represented by a single work each...' Added to all of this, when a new piece was played the music itself was frequently less than enthusiastically reviewed. So what was to be done?

There is no doubt that any promoter of classical music at that time faced the same problems. The influence of television and pop music continued to grow apace, attention spans were reducing in any case, while new classical music was, as has been pointed out, very often very unpalatable for the ordinary concert-goer at that time. In Birmingham's case, the Town Hall was one of the most miserable concert halls in the country and there was always, as everywhere, anxiety over funding. It is possible, too, that Rignold himself was suffering from declining energies.

Whatever the reasons, a new conductor for the city orchestras was sought and the appointment of Louis Frémaux was made, following a season conducted by various conductors including Frémaux, most of whom were viewed as possible successors to Rignold.

Louis Frémaux CBSO Conductor 1969-1978
Born in the Pas-de-Calais in 1921, Louis Frémaux' first musical studies were at the Conservatoire in Valenciennes. Service in the French Résistance and with the Foreign Legion resulted in his been decorated, twice, with the Croix de Guerre. After the war he resumed his musical training at the Paris Conservatoire, winning a First Prize for conducting in 1952. As conductor of the Monte Carlo Opera Orchestra he made several award-winning recordings with that and other orchestras. In 1968 Frémaux became conductor of the Rhône-Alpes Philharmonic Orchestra in Lyon and in the same year conducted concerts abroad, some in this country. In 1969 he was made a Chevalier de La Légion d'Honneur.

Louis Frémaux conducted his first regular Thursday concert with the CBSO on 25th September 1969. The season's programmes were by and large in the usual symphony orchestra concert format very loosely described as 'overture plus concerto plus symphony' or the equivalent, with seasonings of commissions, and vocal or choral items. The deputies Maurice Handford, Staff Conductor, and Harold Gray, Associate Conductor, continued to play an important part in maintaining an interesting programme. Handford, who came to Birmingham in 1970, had been Principal Horn and Assistant Conductor with the Hallé Orchestra.

Growing enthusiasm
From the beginning, Frémaux seems to have generated a feeling of excitement and enthusiasm. The *Sunday Times* wrote of the orchestra having acquired 'a wrist second to none' and that it 'took no more than its scarcely perceptive direction of a handful of strings and continuo in the Vivaldi accompaniment to prove the musical feeling that controls it. There could be great days ahead for the CBSO with Frémaux'. This was a review of his first concert on 25th October, which was what might be called something of a 'fun' concert using that much-abused term in the proper way. It consisted of Britten's *Young Person's Guide to the Orchestra*, a Vivaldi Guitar Concerto in D major, the first British performance of *Cinq Métaboles* by Dutilleux, Castelnuovo-Tedesco's Guitar Concerto and the second suite taken from Ravel's

Louis Frémaux at the Town Hall in rehearsal with the CBSO (photograph by Alan Wood).

Daphnis and Chloë. Frémaux also conducted the concert a week later when the eminent soprano, Elizabeth Schwarzkopf, sang some of Desdemona's music from Verdi's opera *Otello*. A new Feeney Commission was featured the following March, namely Kenneth Leighton's Piano Concerto no. 3, clearly an item that Frémaux himself would certainly want to be in charge of.

In December 1969 the *Musical Times* wrote as follows: 'Initial impressions of a virtuoso conductor, flamboyant and aiming chiefly for purely physical excitement, were soon dispelled by Frémaux' versatility and depth of musical insight. The orchestra has played Mozart with an unaccustomed elegance, Brahms with a rich, even sonority and Bartók's *The Miraculous Mandarin* received a performance of assured virtuosity capturing all its drama and variety of emotion'.

Frémaux gained further critical approval with a performance of another recent work, Richard Rodney Bennett's Symphony no. 2 on 12th February 1970. *The Times* critic comments that 'no modern work could have been better chosen to reveal these players' present state of health. Wind and brass chording was particularly impressive in this excellently rehearsed performance, so, too, was the delicacy of the frequently exposed strings. Everyone seemed imaginatively involved'. The present writer's comment would be that a significant portion of what Frémaux could now achieve owed a great deal to what Hugo Rignold had already taught the orchestra. What was Louis Frémaux adding to that? He brought a livelier sense of excitement than it had been in Hugo Rignold's nature to do, thorough professional though he was. What Louis Frémaux seemed to have par excellence, however, was the gift of conveying to an orchestra what he expected of them almost telepathically, with the minimum of movement. In turn, this exercised the orchestral players' gift of 'seeing through the backs of their heads!' It is the sort of subtle body language seen elsewhere only perhaps in the reputable auction room, where the flicker of an eyelid secures a wanted item! Commentators described Frémaux' performances as having 'an airy brilliance' (Noel Goodwin). His panache and vivacity were infectious and all of this certainly pleased audience members, who attended in increasing numbers.

The following season, 1970 to 1971, was the orchestra's 50th anniversary and it opened with Mozart's Symphony no. 33 in B flat, Bach's Double Concerto in D minor for two violins with the two joint-leaders, Felix Kok and John Bradbury, as soloists. The concert concluded with Holst's *The Planets* with the City of Birmingham Choir ladies in the final movement. This programme was conducted by Frémaux who also took charge of concerts on 11th and 18th February when the Birmingham University Musical Society Chorus (11th Feb.) and the Birmingham School of Music Choir (18th Feb.) were added to the strength. The works in question were, respectively, the Symphony, *Roméo et Juliette* by Berlioz, Messiaen's *Trois Petites Liturgies de la Présence Divine*, with Shostakovitch's Tenth Symphony at the second concert. English soloists were used; singers Barbara Robotham, John Mitchinson and Michael Rippon in the Berlioz and, in the Messiaen, John McCabe, piano, and John Morton, Ondes Martenot.

Welcome visitors
Two somewhat 'different' concerts in the season occurred when the English Chamber orchestra under Raymond Leppard played four of Bach's *Brandenburg* Concertos and when a Saturday Gala Pop featured an Opera Night with Harold Gray conducting and Josephine Barstow and David Hughes as soloists, the latter a Birmingham man, popular and well-known from television appearances.

More about the repertoire
Several programmes again used the device of concentrating on the music of one composer. An all-Walton programme celebrated that composer's 70th birthday in March 1972, with Maurice Handford conducting, together with Yehudi Menuhin in the Viola Concerto, conducted by the composer. In January 1975 three concerts of this kind were featured, the composers concerned being Tippett, Beethoven and Ravel. Maurice Handford conducted the Beethoven concert, Frémaux himself the Tippett and, of course, the Ravel. The dedication to the music of one composer came to a notable climax when a Beethoven Festival was mounted in April 1975. Six of the symphonies (not 2, 4 or 9), all the piano concertos, the *Missa Solemnis* and *Choral Fantasia* were given, together with the *Diabelli* Variations in a recital played by Hans Richter-Haaser. The *Musical Times* comments at this point on the maintenance of high standards under Frémaux. It should be noted here that this sustained progress had been made at this point, during most of 1974, against a background of IRA fire bomb attacks on the city, culminating in the infamous pub bombs of 22nd November 1974. Then, and thereafter for some time, audiences had to queue to get into the Town Hall, while their cases and handbags were searched for possible bombs.

More major French music was added to the orchestra's repertoire when Berlioz' *Grande Messe des Morts* was given, (6th February 1975), the newly established CBSO Chorus showing off its paces in this. This was then successfully recorded by the same forces. They appeared the following week in Mahler's Symphony no. 3. More French music, Ravel's *Rhapsodie Espagnole* and Berlioz' *Symphonie Fantastique* framed John McCabe's new song-cycle *Notturni ed Alba* with Jill Gomez as soloist in a concert in October 1975. This last item was also recorded. Two more performances involving the CBSO Chorus were given in the early part of 1976 when they sang in Poulenc's *Gloria* (15th January) and subsequently in Bach's Magnificat in D and Beethoven's Ninth Symphony (8th April). Visiting ensembles included Les Percussions de Strasbourg (January 1975) who played contemporary music including a new work by Harrison Birtwistle and, in February 1976, the English Chamber Orchestra.

All in all, Birmingham was getting a very wide-ranging musical diet, with music from many periods and many countries on offer. Audience numbers had gone up by a third to over the 80%-full mark and tours and, importantly, recordings were being added to the orchestra's activities - and to its reputation. Among the recordings was a memorable and perhaps definitive performance of Saint-Saëns *Organ Symphony*, whose incisive sparkle no other recording has ever quite captured. There was also a Prom appearance at the Albert Hall in London in September in 1975 - a significant token of national recognition. The CBSO Chorus had been established in 1973, an initiative from Frémaux himself, with the baritone, Gordon Clinton, at that time Principal of the Birmingham School of Music, appointed as its first chorus-master. The chorus very quickly gained an admirable reputation.

The orchestra was also now established as a Limited Company and the number of corporate sponsors was being built up. Other ancillary activities were encouraged, such as the Birmingham Marketing Project funded by the Arts Council and some really serious sums of money were forthcoming from the newly-recruited industrial sponsors such as Imperial Metal Industries and H. Samuel the jewellers. All this helped to establish the orchestra more firmly in the public mind. There was even, yet again, talk of a new concert hall and indeed Louis Frémaux expressed himself prepared to think of going elsewhere if a new hall, or at least the hope of one, did not materialise.

Orchestral unrest
The talk of going elsewhere was in fact a warning signal. Union trouble was again brewing up in no uncertain terms. This was in any case the period of huge union militancy all over the country, with frequent strikes, inflation in double figures, power-cuts and a three-day working week all part of the general woe and culminating in the 1978 to 1979 'Winter of discontent'. The 'them and us' pattern of thought as between management and men was rife, with glaring faults on both sides - not least the former. Birmingham in particular was the scene of many mass meetings and strikes, most notoriously those called by a Shop Steward at the Longbridge car works, one Derek Robinson, known generally as 'Red Robbo'. The general atmosphere undoubtedly affected the orchestra, who were hard-worked and not very well-paid and its conductor could not have been unaware of this. Some players expressed the idea that they were seen as no more than a species of shop-floor worker or factory hand, others took the opposite view, that it was rather childish to make a fuss. It may perhaps be added in passing that the writer's own purely personal view would be that belonging to a Union, rather than to a professional association, may have tended to suggest thinking along the lines of wages for the players, rather than a professional salary with all that that implied.

All this general agitation came to a head in February 1978 at a rehearsal for a concert and recording. The viola section had lost its principal and another player to

London and, what was worse, a second leading player happened to be ill, so that a depleted section would have to be led by a sub-principal. Frémaux felt that this would not secure the performance he wanted so that when a former sub-principal violist was available to come back from London to lead the section for this occasion, Louis Frémaux expected him to occupy the front desk of the section. The union-minded players in the orchestra would have none of this - their own, present CBSO player would lead, and no-one else. The 'visitor' would sit at the back, or there would be a strike. As was usually the case at that time, everyone who should have taken a stand caved in. Frémaux felt let down but had to pocket his pride. Another crisis loomed, however, which did bring things to a head. Preparations were in hand for a further performance of Britten's *War Requiem* to be given at the Royal Festival Hall in London and recorded. Because of the loss of players to London and the generally negative atmosphere, Louis Frémaux felt that the orchestra was not in a fit state to do itself justice. Meanwhile, the orchestra's Union Representative had discovered that the Manager, the long-serving and efficient Arthur Baker, who had in fact done much to build the orchestra up, had been acting as agent for Frémaux personally, 'on the side' so to speak. What was more, he was turning down some prestigious dates for the orchestra itself.

It is revealing, and one has to say typical of the time, that the Management Committee were not really fully aware of all this. When the full seriousness of the situation did come to their notice a meeting was held and subsequently both Conductor and General Manager were suddenly gone, both resolutely keeping their counsel, which was very frustrating for all those left behind, not least the press! Sadly, Louis Frémaux has never been allowed to work for the CBSO since then, although he has subsequently conducted a concert given by the National Youth Orchestra of Great Britain at Symphony Hall, at which he received a tumultuous ovation.

An ill wind...
The general consternation was immediately followed by the need to act quickly to cover the rest of the 1977 to 1978 season and to carry out the plans for 1978 to 1979. Obviously this would also function as the necessary opportunity of hearing a series of different conductors, with a view to finding a successor to Frémaux. Some very positive consequences in fact emerged from this very unhappy episode. The immediate need for a suitable conductor to take charge of a second Beethoven Festival, already planned for May 1978, resulted in a Music Agent putting forward the name of the experienced Swiss conductor, Erich Schmid, who was able to make himself available. Schmid's friendly dignity, and his complete understanding of the Classical period of European music, using the term in its correct sense and referring to the age of Haydn, Mozart and Beethoven, won him great respect from audience and players alike. He was subsequently appointed Principal Guest Conductor for the period 1979 to 1982. Another positive consequence was the decision to have players' representatives on a

slimmed-down Committee of Management. There had been some discomfiture at the realisation that so much unrest had gone undetected by the 'top brass' as it might be expressed, and a determination that it should not happen again.

Harold Gray
It was in 1979, also, that after fifty-five years the orchestra's long-standing and dependable Associate Conductor, Harold Gray, retired. The occasion was suitably marked by presentations to him from various bodies and - typically - from him to the orchestra. It had always been possible to rely on Harold Gray to step in and conduct a concert at very short notice, some of these performances being among his very best. Nevertheless many of his scheduled appearances on the podium also won him high praise as we have seen.

Omens of a bright future
Finally, in addition to these other positive consequences it so happened that a rising star in the conducting heavens was at the right point in his career to take on the full responsibility of holding a permanent conductor's post. Among the fine conductors who visited Birmingham between 1978 and 1980 was a young man called Simon Rattle. He came with a growing reputation among the *cognoscenti* in the musical world which suggested that this was a very serious talent indeed and no mere 'infant prodigy' with no staying power. The concert he conducted in Birmingham Town Hall on 14th December 1978, which concluded with Nielsen's Fourth Symphony perhaps prophetically called the 'Inextinguishable', confirmed the idea in many minds, including the writer's, that here was someone on his way up who would take the orchestra up with him. Both conductor and orchestra would then learn and widen the repertoire together and would have a very personal stake in how they played it. Such proved to be the case. The revolutionary effect of this young 24-year -old's appointment will form the concluding chapter of this book.

The orchestra's proud role
This brief account of the city orchestra's first sixty years ends, then, on a note of great hope, the culmination of a huge amount of effort and dedication on the part of all concerned over a period of 60 years. The ups and downs have been briefly described but, as has already been indicated, anyone who wishes to get the full and intriguing story, from the inside, is again referred to King Smith's book (op. cit.) This writer simply says that the city should be very proud that it has gone on supporting, through thick and sometimes very thin, an organisation - an orchestra - which perhaps more that any other is a pinnacle of the achievements of civilised man. The product of the soul and mind of a Beethoven, for example, is recreated for many people, by another

group of people, prepared to train for years and practice and prepare for hours to make that happen. Man at his co-operative best perhaps?

In spite of difficulties and deficiencies over the years, the City of Birmingham Symphony Orchestra had already brought pleasure to thousands of appreciative listeners since its inception, enriching the city's cultural and communal life in the process. The faith and perseverance of all those involved, behind the scenes or on the platform, modest or prestigious, unpaid or paid is something the city should be grateful for. This faith and perseverance was about to be amply rewarded.

Chapter 28

Again, what else?

More orchestras...

Increasing prosperity and the consequent ability to afford to buy a musical instrument meant that instrumental classes offered by the Midland Institute School of Music, especially from 1900 when Granville Bantock became its Principal, were increasingly well-attended. As we have seen, staff and star pupils were then to be found playing in one or other of the various orchestras appearing in the city. This before the establishment of the City of Birmingham Orchestra in 1920. Many others again played in smaller ensembles, but in either case, it meant that there was a core of very capable instrumentalists and a growing awareness and appreciation of the orchestral repertoire. After 1920, the establishment of an 'official' orchestra did not preclude the establishment of other orchestras, however. Nor did visits from orchestras from elsewhere cease of course. Here, only an outline of all the various 'other' orchestral concerts on offer in the city between 1920 and 1980 can be attempted.

Another Birmingham enterprise appeared in 1921, the first of several which contributed to the local orchestral scene during these middle years of the twentieth century. This was the Moseley Musical Club String Orchestra under T. Henry Smith which attempted the Tchaikovsky First Piano Concerto with Irene Scharrer as the pianist. Smith had been leader of three bands; Richard Wassell's Orchestra, the Birmingham Orchestra organised by Beecham in 1916 to 1917, and the Midland Music Society Orchestra. Other visitors at this point were, rather intriguingly, the Southern Syncopated Orchestra of Negro Players and Singers making a special visit to Birmingham and giving six evening concerts and five matinées at the Town Hall. The *Musical Times* comments 'The entertainment proved as novel as it was interesting'. Yet another new enterprise was the New Concerts Society which lived up to the 'new' in its title by presenting music by the contemporary composers Kodály, Delius and Ravel. By 1923 they were announcing a season of six concerts.

In November 1926, perhaps most significantly, there was a report of a 'feast of lovely music' provided by the Birmingham Wireless Station Orchestra who gave Handel's opera, *Semele,* in a concert version. This is the first small sign of the revolution in musical life about to affect everyone, musicians and audiences, in one way or another, for better or for worse, from now on. The role of the wireless – or

Chapter 28 - Again, what else?

the radio - will be looked at again. The BBC Midland Orchestra was eventually established in 1934 with Leslie Heward as its conductor. At that point a number of its players were also used by the city orchestra which had to pay the BBC for their individual appearances, thus not employing them on a regular basis. This meant that the city orchestra had to fit in with the BBC over the use of players for particular concerts, but at least it relieved the CBO's financial situation at that time, by giving the players concerned much needed extra employment which the city orchestra could not afford.

In 1927, the City of Birmingham Police Band were still giving their charity concerts - and playing them very well apparently. A concert that year included an 'excellent performance of Mendelssohn's Scotch Symphony (sic)', this according to the *Musical Times*. This particular concert was the first of its regular series of six given at the West End Picture House under Walter O'Donnell, who conducted his own *Gaelic Fantasy* on that occasion. The Midland Institute School of Music Orchestra continued to give the occasional public concert and Johann Hock's concerts at Queens College Chambers, which were partly solo and partly chamber concerts, also featured his Philharmonic String Orchestra. Again, interestingly for us today, given the interest of the CBSO's present conductor, Sakari Oramo, in John Foulds, Foulds' *Hellas*, a suite of six pieces in Grecian modes (musical modes that is) was performed by Hock's orchestra in 1933.

Yet another orchestra came on the scene in 1934, when the 'newly-formed' Birmingham Chamber Orchestra announced future programmes of the music of Elgar, Delius, Sibelius and Bantock. It may be asked if this orchestra was connected with, or grew out of, the Moseley Music Club since it too was conducted by T. Henry Smith. Still another orchestra announcing itself was the Birmingham String Orchestra, proposing to give concerts in the 1934 to 1935 season. This was to be conducted by Wilfred Ridgway - he of the Ridgdowne Duo formed with Herbert Downes, the latter a member of a notable local family of musicians. We shall meet them again when we look at the chamber music of this period.

The music of local composers, on the other hand, was also being given the chance to be heard. Johann Hock's Birmingham Philharmonic Orchestra, for example, played Julius Harrison's *Cornish Holiday Sketches*, Variations on *'Down Among the Dead Men'* by Cyril Christopher and a Symphony for Strings by Christopher Edmunds in the 1936 to 1937 season. More of these composers later in this chapter. Unusual repertoire of a different kind was explored by Hock and the same orchestra in February 1939, when a Sammartini symphony was included in a programme. Little known by the general musical public today, Giovanni Sammartini was perhaps the most prominent of those composers writing in the newly developing symphonic form just prior to the time of Haydn and Mozart. He wrote some seventy symphonies in fact, simpler than later music in the genre, but symphonies nevertheless. His music was known to both Haydn and Mozart.

Distinguished orchestral visitors continued to come to Birmingham in the shape of, for example, the Royal Albert Hall Orchestra in February 1921, the London Symphony Orchestra, under Beecham, in 1923, the Berlin Philharmonic Orchestra in 1935 and the Prague Philharmonic in 1938. During the Second World War such visits continued, at least as far as English orchestras were concerned of course, as part of the effort to cheer everyone up a little. The London Philharmonic Orchestra played twice daily at the Hippodrome Theatre during the first week of October in 1940 and the Western Command Orchestra under Harold Gray appeared in December 1942. The Liverpool Philharmonic Orchestra directed by Malcolm Sargent, brought two concerts in 1943. This did not add up to many concerts but at least it was giving Birmingham a chance to keep in touch with what orchestras besides its own were doing

In March 1940, a New Midland Orchestra, under Harold Gray played one of the Priestley concerts at the old Repertory Theatre in Station Street and gave another concert the following month at the Town Hall. By 1942, however, Hock's Philharmonic String Orchestra and the String Orchestral Society seem to have ceased their operations and a new generation of Birmingham orchestras, other than the city orchestra itself, would be appearing from now on. Different visiting orchestras, other than symphony orchestras, would also be introduced. In November 1942, under the auspices of the Council for the Encouragement of Music and the Arts (CEMA), the Jacques String Orchestra, directed by Reginald Jacques, played at the Town Hall on 30th September 1943. Corelli's *Christmas Concerto* and three of Bach's *Brandenburg Concertos* were offered in their programmes. They were followed by the Boyd Neel Orchestra, an orchestra known to many at the time through its many broadcasts and recordings. Boyd Neel trained as a doctor but gave up medicine for music, eventually leaving this country for Canada because of the United Kingdom's poor support for the Arts. More will be said on this point later.

Further visits followed from the London Philharmonic Orchestra which did quite a lot of provincial visits during the war. A band simply called the National Symphony Orchestra also came to Birmingham at this stage. Then, in September 1944, the Hallé Orchestra came to play in the Big Top - a circus tent - in New Street. This involved a short series of concerts, the tent was crammed and hundreds of people were turned away. The following month Harold Gray conducted massed amateurs in a concert which included Haydn's Trumpet Concerto with W. J. Overton as soloist.

Perhaps the first of a number of local enterprises immediately after the war - fairly short-lived - was the Midland Symphony Orchestra, stepping on to the stage in December 1945. It is difficult to tell if this orchestra bore any relationship to the New Midland Orchestra which had played concerts under Harold Gray in

Chapter 28 - *Again, what else?*

1940, but in any case one of its main functions seems to have been to accompany the Midland Opera Company, under Victor Fleming. The war itself had not in fact put an end to all new Birmingham orchestral enterprises for in 1941, the Birmingham Philharmonic Orchestra was established and is still offering concerts today (2006). This was, and is, an amateur orchestra, set up originally by Ernest Powell. They first appeared as the South Birmingham Orchestra and accompanied a performance of Handel's *Messiah* in November 1941. Having twenty-four players initially, this band soon grew into a full-sized symphony orchestra. It has always attained a highly competent standard - obviously - or it would not have survived so long. Occasionally students and some senior school pupils have played in the orchestra, gaining very useful experience. The comprehensive history of the Birmingham Philharmonic Orchestra is covered in a book by Margaret Worsley written in 1999 (see bibliography). Her account lists the many concert venues, in this country and abroad, where the orchestra has played, together with a very impressive repertoire list. This enterprise clearly hit the right balance between being at a very good amateur level and not having to pay fees, on the one hand, and achieving a high enough standard to build up a following, on the other. One can only congratulate them.

From 1946, certain visiting orchestras would be appearing at the Barber Evening concerts at the University of Birmingham. These will be covered later in this chapter. After the war, too, the BBC Midland Orchestra and the BBC Midland Light Orchestra would be broadcasting regular concerts. These were in fact virtually one and the same orchestra, working under two different conductors, according to the repertoire involved. Then, in 1957, what one can only call a very significant new, smaller orchestra played its first concert in the city. This was Orchestra da Camera, often referred to as OdaC. It was soon seen as an important additional element on Birmingham's orchestral scene, playing in a widely varied repertoire. In 1962, for example, at one of its own regular Saturday evening concerts, the programme contained works by Skalkottas and Peter Wishart, the latter a member of the University of Birmingham Music Department staff. It played equally successfully with the Bach Choir at that choir's concerts and, in contrast, for the Midland Music Makers Grand Opera Company. In 1969, Orchestra da Camera was appointed as the official Aston University orchestra. Their last concert to be noted by the Birmingham correspondent of the *Musical Times* was in May 1972 when the orchestra played under Graham Treacher in Peter Dickinson's Concerto for strings, percussion and electronic organ. John Joubert, at that time Reader in Music at the University of Birmingham, was also invited to write for them. Based mainly in the county areas of Warwickshire, this enterprise has a strong educational element as well as giving concerts, some of which are in Birmingham.

Meanwhile, in 1956, Blyth Major, the CBSO's Orchestra Manager from 1952 to 1959, had launched the Midland Youth Orchestra which he himself conducted. He was followed by James Langley whom we find conducting a charity concert in November 1974 for example. The *Musical Times* comments on 'the excellent standards' these young people achieved - in such 'big' works as Brahms' First Symphony and Tchaikovsky's First Piano Concerto it should be noted. This orchestra was also to provide the CBSO with some players. It gave its final concert on 11 July 2004, and was succeeded by the CBSO Youth Orchestra.

Finally, mention should be made, first, of the short-lived Birmingham Sinfonietta, under the CBSO's principal horn player, Timothy Reynish, which sadly only lasted from 1974 to 1977, when Reynish moved to Manchester; and second, of two youth orchestras, namely the Academy of St Philip's Orchestra and the Birmingham Schools Symphony Orchestra. The Academy of St. Philip's Orchestra was set up by Anthony Fleming, assisted by his wife, the 'cellist Naomi Butterworth. As Birmingham Cathedral became the venue for their concerts, the Provost gave permission for the St. Philip's name to be used for their title. Again, a remarkably high standard was reached by these young players, but as with Timothy Reynish's Birmingham Sinfonietta, this orchestra did not survive the departure of its original organiser to work elsewhere. The Birmingham Schools Symphony Orchestra on the other hand survives. Now under what is today called the Birmingham Schools Music Service, it gives its concerts at the Adrian Boult Hall, in the Birmingham Conservatoire, and is one of the twenty-one central ensembles and twenty seven area ensembles supported by the Service.

It seems that the orchestras which now manage to survive are more usually large and prestigious in themselves or attached to a larger organisation, such as an opera or ballet company, or under the umbrella of a major symphony orchestra. Only that way can they achieve the status, and the subsequent funding and publicity to succeed in a very competitive world, today dominated in any case by a very different type of music, mainly pop music in its various guises.

In choirs and places where they sing...1920-1980

Before the second world war, there were still plenty of opportunities for keen singers to join a choir and a goodly diet of enjoyable choral concerts to listen to. This can be no more than a very condensed description of these.

Taking the doyen of Birmingham choirs first, the Birmingham Festival Choral Society continued to put on a regular season of concerts until the outbreak of war in 1939. Sadly some of these were not very well-attended, but this was to be a frequent complaint during these middle years of the twentieth century. Conducted successively by the extremely distinguished conductors, Henry Wood, Adrian Boult, Leslie Heward and the City Organist, G. D. Cunningham, it offered the usual oratorio

Chapter 28 - Again, what else?

repertoire but with fairly frequent forays into something new. Two examples would be Debussy's *Blessed Damozel* in April 1921 under Henry Wood and later, Walton's *Belshazzar's Feast* sung in 1933 with the city orchestra. Going in the opposite direction, time-wise, they offered Bach's *Christmas Oratorio* instead of *Messiah* in 1932. In the same year there was some Palestrina in one of their programmes and two years later, William Byrd's *Great Service*. This was unfamiliar repertoire for many concert-goers at that time. The *Great Service* was given in May 1934 in the University of Birmingham's Great Hall, conducted by the Associate Conductor of the city orchestra, Harold Gray, with Cyril Christopher providing organ items. At what appears to have been their last concert before the war Dvořák's *Stabat Mater* was performed, conducted by Gray.

The war certainly hit choirs very hard as may be imagined. With the universal call-up of younger men, and young women also expected to do some kind of war-work, numbers were much depleted and a great deal of choral activity ceased, and not always just 'for the duration'. In the case of the Festival Choral Society, it struggled to continue with about thirty singers and this remnant was rescued in 1962 by Madame Aird-Briscoe, who combined it with two of her own small choirs, probably her Oriana and Rubery Choirs. Energetic and ambitious, she improved the standard to such an extent that the newly-constituted Festival Chorus was able to perform Bach's *St. Matthew Passion* in the Town Hall, with the CBSO, only two years later. The author can vouch for it that Madame Aird-Briscoe was very proud of the fact that, at that point in its history, she was the only woman ever to have conducted the city orchestra. Jeremy Patterson took over from Madame, who wanted to retire, in 1969 and guided the choir for thirty-five years. He recruited new young singers, instituted entry by audition with regular three-yearly auditions thereafter and developed the choir's ability to sing contemporary music, the choir commissioning nine of these itself. Since 2005 Patrick Larley has been the Music Director.

It has to be said that the City of Birmingham Choir, established in 1921, really gained on the Festival Choral Society. Certainly it has survived until the present day but, not suffering as much of a decline as the older choir, it was well-placed to be the choir of choice to perform with the city orchestra, before the formation of the CBSO Chorus. Never afraid of exploring the choral repertoire in both directions as regards dates, they are to be found singing Vaughan Williams' recently composed Mass in November 1922 and, two years later, Purcell's *Dido and Aeneas*. In the years 1929 and 1930, they gave Bantock's *Golden Journey to Samarkand* under Malcolm Sargent and the same composer's *Omar Khayyam* directed by their conductor, G. D. Cunningham, or G. D. as he was affectionately called.

In 1935, Delius' *Sea Drift* conducted by Harold Gray was added to the list and in 1938 Bloch's *Sacred Service* was given, 'heard in Europe but new to this country', again under their own conductor's baton.

G. D. Cunningham, Birmingham City Organist and Festival Choral Society Conductor.

This choir's post-war life continued to be vigorous, in spite of the dearth of choral concerts during the war. In 1948 George Cunningham died and was succeeded by David Willcocks. The choir successfully continued its regular concerts, usually appearing with the CBSO. A year after the premiere of Britten's *War Requiem*, the City Choir also presented this work, in Birmingham. This in April 1963. Some imperfections were commented on in the *Musical Times* which was not happy about the lack of strength 'both tonally and numerically particularly among the men'. The choir was not alone in this defect at that time. Rueful memories of some of the whole-hearted singing of former northern choirs tended to come to mind in contrast. This situation may not have been unconnected to the pop revolution just getting going. A very different kind of vocalisation was on offer, all of it microphone-assisted, and young people were beginning to turn away from classical music in all its manifestations, not least its vocal ones. We begin to see here also the erosion of singing in schools, especially among teenagers.

Nevertheless in 1982 the City Choir tackled with great credit and sincerity Messiaen's difficult *La Transfiguration*, with local professional soloists drawn from the city orchestra, together with the pianist Peter Donohoe. This had been very carefully prepared, and was extremely well-controlled in performance by Christopher

Chapter 28 - Again, what else?

Robinson. Given in the Town Hall, it was very warmly received by the audience, and 'even the London critics were impressed', according to the choir's own account of its history. This booklet is entitled *The Robinson Years,* for Robinson conducted the choir for 36 years, from 1964 to 2002. This choir still thrives, singing at Symphony Hall, with the CBSO, and independently, and providing its amateur members with the great pleasure of singing great music. On their website there is a complaint about the fact that the BBC used to broadcast their concerts in the 1950s and 1960s, less often in the 1970s and now not at all. The effect of BBC policy, for good or ill, on classical music nationally and locally will be discussed in due course.

The origins of the Birmingham Bach Choir are quite difficult to disentangle. The choir's own website states that it was originally founded in 1919 and re-formed in 1947. This is probably an understandable simplification, because the facts in certain records suggest a more complicated picture. In May 1921, a Birmingham Bach 'Society', directed by Bernard Jackson, gave a Bach, Schütz, Handel programme. In 1924 we meet them again in the pages of the *Musical Times* singing music by Purcell and Buxtehude. In 1926 they are called the Bach 'Choir' but again directed by Bernard Jackson. This can only be surmised, but it seems that this organisation did not continue - or at least not in the same form - for in 1930 a Bach 'Cantata Club' was formed, affiliated to the London Bach Society and conducted by Allan Blackall, then Organist and Choirmaster of Warwick Parish Church, and in due course Principal of the Midland Institute School of Music from 1934 to 1945. In 1930, the Bach 'Club' gave a concert in Birmingham Cathedral directed by Blackall with the cathedral organist Fred Dunhill assisting. Given different names at different times, what is clearly the same organisation, but now called the Bach 'Choir', is giving its seventh season in 1937 (so certainly this is the club established in 1930) and opening with a tribute to the late Fred Dunnill, its previous conductor. After 1937 the conductor was T.W. North. This society did not confine itself to the music of Bach, nor simply to concerts. Earlier music by Palestrina, Vittoria, Byrd and Tallis, for example, was occasionally given, and lectures were also included, one in 1936 for example by Victor Hely-Hutchinson on Bach's keyboard music.

The war also put an end to this last choir's activities but in 1947 the Birmingham Bach Choir, under the aegis of the Bach Society, (now sure of its title!) was re-established. It was again the cathedral organist, Willis Grant this time, who played a major part in setting up this type of specialist choir, dedicated to the music of Bach and some of Bach's predecessors. Subsequent conductors were Roy Massey, another Birmingham Cathedral organist, and Richard Butt, who was also a BBC Producer in the Midland Region. Butt's conductorship lasted 26 years, between 1966 and 1992, and encompassed the highlight of a visit to Leipzig to sing in the church, St. Thomas's, where Bach himself held his last appointment. The present conductor is

Paul Spicer, also conductor of the acclaimed Finzi Singers, and he has succeeded in enabling the Birmingham Bach Choir to be invited to give the annual Symphony Hall performance of Bach's *St. Matthew Passion,* on Good Friday, in succession to the London Bach Choir now that David Willcocks has retired.

One of the longest-established choirs in the city we have already met, in chapter 15, namely the Birmingham Choral Union, established in 1886 and having some 350 members by 1914. This choir was still apparently prepared to admit anyone who simply wanted to join in 'a good sing' and as we saw in chapter 24 (The Choral Craze) they sometimes received some unflattering reviews from the critics. In 1920 signs of a more serious purpose began to show and in that year a performance by them of Elgar's *King Olaf* was noticed in the *Musical Times*, which commented on Richard Wassell's 'tactful and watchful' conducting. Appleby Matthews then took over from Wassell and in 1949 achieved a performance by the choir of Elgar's *Dream of Gerontius.* This was given with the City of Birmingham Symphony Orchestra, thus realising Matthews' ambition for the choir. In that same year Matthews died and the Choral Union acquired the young Denis Crosby as their conductor, he who also became organist at St. Chad's Cathedral. In 1951, the *Musical Times* again provides a review which comments that Denis Crosby showed great ability when he conducted the choir in Julius Harrison's Mass in C. Sadly, Crosby died in 1954 at the age of only 32, for under him membership had again grown and programmes had become more adventurous. More happily, he was followed by Harold Gray, Associate Conductor of the city orchestra, who continued the regular concerts, with the orchestra, and maintained a very good level of performance until he left them in 1975. Richard Silk and David Sadler succeeded Gray as conductors. The Choral Union is still active today, after 120 years, though on a somewhat more modest scale. Their present conductor is Colin Baines, and they continue to raise money for charities.

Inevitably, given the perennial desire of many Birmingham citizens to sing, if they did not want to join a big choir, there was over the years a choice of smaller choirs on offer. If you were a school teacher there were from 1938 the Birmingham Singers. The Clarion Singers, a workers' choir, founded in 1940 is still active After the war, in 1952, the Russell Green Singers gave their first concert. Born in 1909, Green himself was an organist and composer, having trained at the Birmingham School of Music and later studying with Herbert Howells. In 1959, however, he decided to emigrate to Canada and we read no more of his choir, at least in the pages of the *Musical Times*. Schoolchildren were also of course encouraged to sing in choirs and in 1949, with the old Competition Festivals no longer on offer, the city's Music Education Adviser, Desmond MacMahon, set up a Birmingham Children's Choir.

A further small specialist choir in the 1960s was the Hamish Preston Choir, giving a debut concert at St. Augustine's Church, Edgbaston, on 12th November

Chapter 28 - Again, what else?

1962. The *Musical Times* comments that this is an important event for the Midlands... 'we need regular performances by a hand-picked choir of this calibre'. There were in fact eighteen singers, comprising five sopranos and five basses four altos and four tenors. The report goes on to comment that several members were experienced soloists 'but Mr. Preston blended some highly-distinctive voices into a satisfying whole'. On 30th November 1964 the choir combined with Orchestra da Camera in unfamiliar music by two members of the Bach family. The role of the University singers will be described in a later section.

In the 1970s, two new choral enterprises were launched which were to have a significant role in the future, able to hold their own with distinction in the period after 1980, when the international dimension to Birmingham's music returned along with the arrival of the young Simon Rattle. The CBSO Chorus owed its existence to the initiative of the orchestra's conductor at the time, Louis Frémaux. In 1973, as we have seen, the recently retired Head of the Birmingham School of Music, Gordon Clinton, himself a singer, was invited to accept the responsibility for training the newly-formed chorus. A year later, in 1974, Anthony Cross writing in the *Musical Times* commented as follows. 'Many doubted both its (the CBSO Chorus's) necessity and feasibility in such a choral stronghold. Nevertheless, with plenty of work in the coming season its future now seems assured and artistically it has amply justified itself'. Cross further reports that the predominantly youthful choir (all were then under the age of 45) 'proved to be a responsive, well-blended body of singers with a wide range of tone colour and dynamics. Its existence has already stimulated a healthy competitive spirit shown by the splendid singing of the City Choir in Beethoven's Ninth'. This on 4th April 1974. The CBSO chorus's further progress is described in the next chapter (chapter 29).

At the other end of the scale but only as to size was Ex Cathedra founded by Jeffrey Skidmore with some forty singers. This was a body of singers chosen for having voices with a special purity of tone, and a high degree of musicianship. Eminently successful ever since, it has built itself a formidable reputation as a crack ensemble in demand in Birmingham and abroad, and making some very fine recordings. It undertakes a surprisingly wide range of music suitable for a small specialist choir. It has become, in its own right, a further strand in the international nature of music within Birmingham itself.

Finally, in different genres, are the many Gospel Choirs and Folk Clubs in and around the city. Brought by the arrival of West Indians in Birmingham in the 1960s, some of the Gospel Choirs reach a very accomplished standard indeed and are a further manifestation of the universal human desire to sing. Long may it continue.

The same could be said about our own indigenous folk song. What was described in a previous chapter, (chapter 4) as happening to folk melody in the later part of the eighteenth century in fact continued, and by the end of the nineteenth century people like Cecil Sharp were touring the countryside, noting down as many old tunes as they could, the 'respectable' ones then being included in school song books and sung in many schools up to about the 1960s. It was to be 'incomers' to England, however, who best retained the ability to sing songs in the true folk tradition. One particular example might be cited, namely Cecilia Costello, born in Ireland in 1883, but living for most of her life in Birmingham. In spite of having acquired a fine Birmingham accent, she sang her Irish folk songs as she had heard them in childhood, and of these she remembered a considerable number. The head of the BBC Recorded Programmes Library arranged to have these recorded in the early 1950s. An LP of this was issued in 1975 but is now, unfortunately, deleted from the catalogue.

After 1945, when American recordings became more readily available in Britain, the influence of transatlantic folk-singers spread and became a well-established aspect of our musical scene. Since some American folk-songs have British roots, then to some extent our own musical heritage was brought back to us, and rekindled some interest in the folk song tradition, including our own. Some people argue that there is a psychological difference if a folk tune is broadcast, so that thousands of people are hearing it at the same time. This carries with it a sense of social pressure and the idea that this is 'how it should be done'. This can remove the sense of spontaneity and those essential ingredients of folk song, the personal input from the performer and the element of improvisation.

This is a huge subject and one in which the writer is not an expert. Perhaps the last word should go to A. L. Lloyd. In his book *Folk Song in England* (see bibliography) he writes: 'The revival was strengthened by the enquiring minds of many young people who, searching for the roots of jazz found themselves led to American folk-song and thence back to their own shores, to an interest in their native stuff and a desire to perform it. True, they incline to treat their traditional music in a variety of non-traditional ways, with voice-production, instrumentation, rhythmical treatment, etc, borrowed from the worlds of commercial light music. Whether the material is thereby enriched or impoverished is arguable; it is less arguable that, through new treatments, many fine folk tunes and texts are made valid for thousands of performers and listeners whose musical interests would otherwise be limited to the banalities of Denmark Street'. What is certain is that, as with other forms of music, this genre is well represented in Birmingham.

....opera in the city 1920-1980

The city was certainly not richly provided with opera between 1920 and what turned out to be the beginning of the Welsh National Opera Company's regular seasons in Birmingham in 1969 when the Alexandra Theatre was the venue. Back in

Chapter 28 - Again, what else?

1921 and 1922 it was Barry Jackson, at the old Birmingham Repertory Theatre in Station Street, who catered for Birmingham's opera lovers, with Mozart's *Così fan tutte* and Rutland Boughton's *The Immortal Hour* for example. There were also premieres of Messager's *Monsieur Beaucaire*, Ethel Smyth's *Fête galante* and Bantock's *The Seal-Woman* between 1919 and 1924. A concert version of Handel's *Semele* was the Birmingham Wireless Station's contribution in this genre in 1926.

The Covent Garden Opera visited in 1929, 1930 and 1941, playing the Prince of Wales Theatre in Broad Street and in 1930 offering Puccini's *Turandot*, the latter with the incomparable Eva Turner no less. The city was doubly fortunate in 1941 since Sadlers Wells Opera also came, performing Arne's *Thomas and Sally* and Purcell's *Dido and Aeneas*, this time at the Theatre Royal in New Street. After the war, in 1949, a local society, the Midland Music Makers Grand Opera Society, moved to fill the operatic gap. Directed by Arthur Street, they were not shy of tackling pieces such as Berlioz' *The Trojans*, Rossini's *William Tell* and *The Thieving Magpie* or Borodin's *Prince Igor* for example. In 1969 they took the bold step of mounting a performance of Wagner's early opera *Die Feen*, not performed for many years, and given in the company's own translation. In 1974 Sadlers Wells brought a memorable week-long *Ring Cycle* to an enlarged Hippodrome Theatre. There were also occasional visits from Scottish National Opera, Opera North and Glyndebourne Touring Opera.

Since 1969, Welsh National Opera has continued to be the city's main source of professionally-produced grand opera. Its chorus has itself been fully professional since 1973 and its orchestra also has an independent role, playing concerts all over the world in its own right. Initially the company had used local orchestras when it toured, being fortunate in Birmingham to have the services of CBSO players. This was much better than in some places, but it has to be said that playing for an opera is a different business from playing on the concert platform.

From 1959, an operatic venture of a different kind was launched, this time at the Barber Institute of Fine Arts in the University of Birmingham. Baroque operas were presented, most often Handel's, to be given in the correct, 'authentic' musical style, with a small instrumental ensemble, and singers using the decorations of the vocal line in the way which was expected at the time of the operas' composition. Here the reader must be referred to a history of the first fifty years of the Barber Evening Concerts and Operas, 1946 to 1996, written and compiled by Fiona M. Palmer (See bibliography). It must be said, however, that this style of opera does not always appeal to the lover of grand opera nor to every musician. The frequent use of women in masculine roles, and of the counter tenor voice, is not to everyone's taste. The so-called *da capo* arias, where the first section of an aria is repeated in a decorated form after the middle section, can also be a stumbling block. On the positive side, however, ventures such as the Barber Operas have undoubtedly brought this type of music to a much wider audience.

The performance which those who attended most remember, probably, is that of Handel's *Admeto* in May 1968. This had Maureen Lehane, Sheila Armstrong and the young Janet Baker in the cast. Of the last-named, Winton Dean in the *Musical Times* wrote that it was difficult to speak of Janet Baker's singing in the role of Admeto in measured terms. He goes on: 'It was a superlative performance by any standard, brilliant, secure and profoundly expressive and supported by acting of touching eloquence. There is something about the timbre of the voice that goes to the heart of Handel's style'. Lehane and Armstrong also received very high praise. Dennis Maunder was the producer on this occasion, with the current Professor of Music, Anthony Lewis, who had instigated the project, in charge of the music of course.

In 1976, Felicity Lott was a radiant Cleopatra in Handel's *Giulio Cesare* and indeed the university's Music Department was very proud of the part it had played in helping to further the careers, in their early stages, of outstanding singers such as Janet Baker and Felicity Lott.

The Birmingham University Guild gave some admirable fully-staged and orchestra-accompanied performances of major operas. In April 1964, for example, the Guild gave a performance of Gay's *Beggars Opera* when Damian Cranmer, as Assistant Music Director, conducted an excellent orchestra. In 1967, Andrew Tillett conducted Gluck's *Iphigénie en Aulide* and a year later Clive Timms directed Verdi's *Un Ballo in Maschera*. The Midland Institute School of Music, under its various succeeding titles gave annual operatic performances, but the crises in the School of Music's fortunes after the second world war and up to 1970 militated against the development of a real approach to professional standards. Both singers and orchestra could vary from year to year with some unhappy results – but also some surprisingly good ones. After 1970, opera rehearsals were no longer in the evenings but only in the daytime and thus only available to full time students. From 1976 the operatic training was constituted as a graduate school and increasingly effective productions were mounted, the orchestral accompaniment steadily improving over the years.

The Midlands Arts Centre (mac) at Cannon Hill Park has put on operas for children since 1973 and in 1976 inaugurated major productions. Another important home-based operatic enterprise was the City of Birmingham Touring Opera started at the end of the period we are considering. Funded by the city and the Arts Council and known since 2001 as the Birmingham Opera Company, its aim is to involve members of the community by taking opera to what might be termed 'non-operatic' venues. The operas are performed in English and involve people from every part of Birmingham's population, giving them the opportunity to perform alongside internationally-known musicians. The choice of operas is uncompromising and in 2002 Beethoven's *Fidelio* was produced in a huge tent in the grounds of Aston Hall, and broadcast. This enterprise does not entirely belong to the middle part of the twentieth century although it was initiated within it, but it seemed important to take notice of this innovative venture.

As a small postscript to this section on opera, the tenor Webster Booth might be mentioned. Born in Birmingham in 1902, Booth was educated at the Lincoln Cathedral Choir School and at Aston Commercial College, Birmingham. He was a versatile artist, appearing initially with the D'Oyly Carte Company in London, and subsequently in films and on television. This did not prevent him from being an effective oratorio singer as well, but he is perhaps best remembered now for his partnership in light music, in the theatre and on radio, with the soprano Anne Ziegler.

As to some of the many musicals and pantomimes on offer in Birmingham the reader can best be referred to Victor J. Price's book, *Birmingham, Theatres, Concert and Music Halls* (see bibliography).

.... and church choirs and organists 1920-1980

During this period very many of Birmingham's parish churches could boast a good choir directed by a capable, even brilliant, organist. This was, and is, particularly true of the city and inner city churches, particularly the Anglican and Roman Catholic Cathedrals, although churches such as St. Martins (the parish church of Birmingham) St. Paul's in the Jewellery Quarter, St. Alban's, St George's Edgbaston, Edgbaston and Harborne Parish Churches, St. Augustine's Edgbaston and last but not least the Birmingham Oratory, should be added to the list. The Cathedrals of St. Philips and St Chad's still have boy choristers even today (2006), although at St Chad's, the Roman Catholic Cathedral, the boys are not used at High Mass, when a chamber choir sings instead. A high standard of music has been maintained there by Roger Hill and, since 1979, by David Saint who, like Marcus Huxley at Birmingham Cathedral, is also an organ recitalist - as was of course one of Huxley's predecessors at St. Philip's, Roy Massey. A former organist at St. Chad's, previously at the Oratory, was Denis Crosby whom we have met, ably conducting the Choral Union between 1949 and his early death in 1954. He had begun his organist's career as assistant to Edward Bairstow, the organist at York Minster, and there is a warming ecumenicism here. It often seems that if a church has a fine organ and a good choir, and the music aids the worship, an organist may well be less concerned about which religious denomination is involved.

Birmingham is very well provided for in terms of organs with, for example, the William Hill organ at the Town Hall, rebuilt by Mander in 1983 to 1984, the Norman and Beard instrument in the Great Hall at the University of Birmingham and the Harrison organ at St. Martin's, Birmingham's parish church. Since 1980, the city has acquired the Klais organ at Symphony Hall, inaugurated in 2001. Large and forceful it is particularly good when required to play with an orchestra, but perhaps the finest of all is the Walker organ at St. Chad's Cathedral, opened in 1994.

In the case of the churches, a fine organ will usually raise the expectations of church congregations. Some very good organists are therefore appointed and the organists themselves then contribute much to the community in many ways, not just by training the choir in church, but much more widely than that; for example by training secular choirs, teaching privately or in schools or colleges, and usually being particularly strong in musicianship.

It is impossible to do more here than sketch in a general picture as there are so many churches and they do not issue music programmes to be deposited in some convenient archive, reasonably easy to consult. A little difficult for the historian! However, here are a few references to musical activity in the organ world gleaned mainly from various issues of the *Musical Times*. For example, in 1921 Richard Wassell was appointed Organist and Choirmaster at St. Martin's Parish Church and in that same year the organ at the Royal Institute for the Blind in Harborne was opened with a recital given by the city organist of the time, C.W. Perkins. The money to buy this organ had been provided by various fund-raising efforts. In April 1933, G. D. Cunningham gave a recital on the rebuilt Town Hall organ and this was broadcast. The critic's comment was that they had rarely enjoyed a broadcast organ recital so much, a reminder that it was very difficult in those days to achieve a satisfactory reproduction of the sound from so large an instrument. In 1936, Willis Grant, who had been Assistant Organist at Lincoln Cathedral, took over at St. Philips. His contribution to the musical life of the city in another capacity, in connection with the Bach Choir, we have already seen. After the war, in 1951, the annual Organists' Congress was held in Birmingham, the programme of events including a recital by a brilliant young King Edward's School pupil, T. F. H. Oxley, who was already a Fellow of the Royal College of Organists (FRCO). A recital by T.W. North, Walsall's Borough Organist on the organ of the Birmingham University Great Hall was also included, as was a BBC Midland Orchestra concert under Gilbert Vinter which was broadcast.

In 1957, a new organ was opened at Edgbaston Parish Church built by Hill, Norman and Beard and in that same year the *Musical Times* reports that regular concerts, not connected with the church festivals, were being given at St. Martin's, directed by the organist, Geoffrey Fletcher. St Martin's had also had its organ rebuilt two years previously, and recitals by Thalben-Ball, O. H. Peasgood and Francis Jackson were arranged to celebrate this. In 1957 the same journal reports that the recitals given in the Town Hall by the current city organist, George Thalben Ball, were well-attended. Twenty years later, that was sadly not the case. There was some resurgence of interest when the young Thomas Trotter was appointed to the City Organist post in 1983, but it is mainly to the organ recitals at Symphony Hall that we now look, to provide us with some renewed interest in organ music.

Chapter 28 - Again, what else?

George Thalben-Ball.

Music in miniature - chamber music 1920-1980
Max Mossel's celebrity concerts just survive into this middle phase of the twentieth century and some of his final ones seem to be particularly 'starry'. The list in the 1925 to 1926 season includes the singers Elizabeth Schumann and Dorothy Silk, the 'cellist Pablo Casals, Rubinstein the pianist and also Maurice Ravel. The last is interesting. Ravel certainly toured in this country from time to time, but in the absence of any surviving programmes for this particular season, it has been impossible to know in what capacity he came or what he might have played. Mossel presented celebrity concerts, but most of the chamber music concerts in Birmingham were then, as now, the product of initiatives from local players, especially the orchestral players. It was more difficult to attract audiences for local players than for celebrities of course, and if quite a number of musicians were trying to do the same sort of thing it divided the relatively small musical public for this kind of music. As time went on, there was increasing competition from radio and recordings. It is not surprising that some of these local initiatives, worthwhile as they were, were relatively short-lived.

Alfred Cave, Leader of the City Orchestra after Alex Cohen, promoted chamber concerts between 1923 and 1925, as did Arthur Catterall, with his Quartet. A Birmingham Ladies Quartet was active at this period, two of whose members were the violist Lena Wood and the 'cellist Gwen Berry. Gwen Berry was accepted into the city orchestra in 1929 and we read far less of the Ladies Quartet after that date. Dale Forty, the music sellers, also promoted this type of concert, in which orchestral musicians often performed. On 10th January 1933, the Unity Quartet, led by Henry Holst, formerly leader of the Berlin Philharmonic Orchestra and later leader of the Liverpool Philharmonic Orchestra, played at a Dale Forty concert. At this same period, Paul Beard, another orchestral luminary of course, gave a concert with local pianist and composer Dorothy Howell, at which they played one of her compositions. And another Birmingham composer was featured when Christopher Edmunds' Piano Quintet was performed at one off Hock's mid-day concerts in the Spring of 1933. Beatrice Hewitt, a pianist who taught for Bantock at the School of Music, promoted some afternoon concerts at the Royal Birmingham Society of Artists, then in New Street, in which she herself played, joining other local musicians J. S. Bridge, Paul Beard and Johann Hock in one of Fauré's Piano Quartets for example. Hock himself organised what was probably the most successful series, though even this only seemed to cover the years 1923 to 1930. Hock's Birmingham Philharmonic String Orchestra on the other hand, which he also ran, seems to have survived until the beginning of World War Two. Various other societies in the chamber music field appear at this point, as for example the Midland Arts Fellowship, the Birmingham Music Guild and a Chamber Music Club, but these do not feature in the record after the war. There was even a Max Mossel Club which promoted concerts for a while. This was started in 1929, ten years after the death of Mossel himself, but again it did not long survive.

During the war years it seems to have been the Ridgdowne Series which kept the home-based chamber music fire alight. This was formed by the violinist Herbert Downes and the pianist Wilfred Ridgeway, already mentioned. Immediately after the war, the chamber music scene was apparently completely deserted. At this juncture, another Dutch violinist arrived in the city who acted to fill this gap. This was Harry van der Lyn who reached this country as a refugee from German-occupied Holland, possessing only what he stood up in - and his violin. He was accepted into the CBSO as a first violinist and presented his own long-lived series of concerts under the title of The Midland Chamber Players. From 1952, however, it was to be the Birmingham Chamber Music Society which came to dominate this genre of music in the city. To go back a little, the Barber Institute was already promoting from 1940 onwards some fine chamber concerts and recitals using the best of local talent, and there was certainly a University Music Society in existence. In addition, the Barber Evening Concerts were presenting very distinguished nationally-known performers from 1946 onwards. Given this background at the university, it was not surprising that Wilfred Mellers, then Staff Tutor at the University's Extramural Department, should conceive the idea of taking great chamber music to 'town' rather than just to 'gown'. From 1952 therefore, the city has had a society dedicated solely to presenting the finest, internationally famous chamber ensembles, most often string quartets, in Birmingham. This is still in existence after nearly fifty-four years, with relatively few changes in the personnel running the society in that time. The key to success was clearly the possibility opened to local people of seeing and hearing world-class musicians in the flesh, close up so to speak. Again, a booklet was produced in 1992 which gave some account of the first forty years of the society and a very impressive list of those who came to play for it.

Standards just very occasionally varied a little but in general the society was enabling people to hear performers of the very highest calibre. It was possible to go to the packed room in the City Art Gallery (now its restaurant) in anticipation of a musical treat. This room held about four hundred people, and when full, as it always was, and in warmer weather, it could feel like the Black Hole of Calcutta. But still people came and queued at the hall doors, waiting to take those seats not occupied that Saturday night by subscribers. This had not been the case when the society first started in the 1950s but within ten years, certainly, this series of concerts was over-subscribed and for musicians and a certain section of the musical public it was the city's musical 'jewel in the crown' at that time, not least because of its international dimension. Memorable performances were given over the years by, for example, the Smetana Quartet playing from memory, the Beaux Arts Trio, the Nash Ensemble, the Alban Berg Quartet. The season's chamber ensemble format was usually broken by one concert which perhaps featured a solo singer. Two of these occasions may be mentioned, first a truly memorable recital by the young Janet Baker with Geoffrey Parsons at the piano, and second a definitive performance of Messiaen's *Harawi* by the soprano Noelle Barker with pianist and Messiaen specialist, Robert Sherlaw Johnson.

By the 1960s the Arts Council was bringing pressure to bear on musical societies to include new works in their programmes, which did not necessarily make life easy for a society presenting a repertoire whose core and heart lies in music composed between, say, 1750 and 1950. Nevertheless, the need to attract some public funding was, and is, essential for any arts organisation, and John Joubert and John Casken, both with University of Birmingham connections, were among those commissioned to write for the society. Sadly the refurbishment of the City Art Gallery meant that the society had to move and, initially, it took up residence at Birmingham Cathedral where four hundred people seemed rather lost. Cold rather than heat was the problem here and, with the resonant acoustic, the sense of intimacy was also lost. A second move was made in 1987, this time to the comfortable but still too large Adrian Boult Hall, in the new Birmingham Conservatoire building. This improved the situation but today (2006) even this prestigious society is facing some of the problems endemic in our pop-dominated world.

Funding for the arts in this country in the 1970s

To turn aside from the Birmingham Chamber Music Society, another society presenting soloists and small ensembles was one started by the author in 1968. Apart from the

University of Birmingham Musical Society's lunch-time concerts, at which students and younger performers could appear, mainly at lunch-time and to a mainly university audience, there was very little in the city centre at that time which provided a platform for Birmingham's and the Midlands' own resident musical talent. Once more there is a booklet giving a brief history of the RBSA/Midland Musicians Society concerts from 1968 to 1978 (see bibliography). This society gave six or seven concerts a season and over its ten years presented 164 performers with a Midlands connection, several of them young prize-winners who went on to make very successful professional careers. Among these were Francis Greer, pianist, organist and composer, the flautist, Philippa Davies, the 'cellist Michal Kaznovsky, and singers Lynda Russell and David Wilson-Johnson. Twelve members of the CBSO during that period also appeared in the series. The critics took the enterprise seriously from the start and attended regularly. In October 1970 a *Birmingham Post* critic, Christopher Morley, wrote as follows: 'The atmosphere of serious music-making in such civilised surroundings (a drawing-room hung with paintings) reminds one of the 18th century subscription concerts. I strongly urge the Birmingham concert-going circuit to put in an appearance at the society's next concert'.

The first venue for these concerts was the RBSA Gallery then in New Street, which also gave the series its first name. Unfortunately this society also had a change of venue forced on it by circumstances beyond its control and in 1972 moved first to Carrs Lane Church and then to the Birmingham and Midland Institute's small theatre in Margaret Street. The moves and the consequent change of name were not helpful and at the beginning of what had to be the final season the critic Lyndon Jenkins wrote 'The Midlands Musicians Series is now entering its tenth season, with plans which have an undimmed look about them despite setbacks. What it now needs is a solid show of public recognition in support of the praiseworthy aims it pursues: a decent audience saw the season launched but surely there is enough interest in this city and region to take every one of the 120 seats in the small theatre at the BMI'.

More serious in the long run was the lack of funding from the regional arts council. Better financial support would have helped with both fees and publicity, thus helping to attract bigger audiences. As this society was dedicated quite specifically to presenting high-quality Midlands performers and composers, it might have been expected to have been a prime candidate for funding from West Midlands Arts, as the regional arts council was then called. Other than a life-saving proportion of the fee bill paid by the National Federation of Music Societies, then an independent body, no public funding was forthcoming. Forms were filled in, Music Officers appealed to, but all to no avail. Why was this? The implication seemed to be that the choice of programme was too 'traditional', not experimental or 'politically correct', - and that in spite of the young performers and a number of new works which were performed. The background to all this, and an important reason for mentioning it, is the sheer niggardliness of arts funding there has been in this country.

Chapter 28 - Again, what else?

It has already been pointed out that the United Kingdom's contribution to the arts was running at 50p per head of population at that time as compared to £5 and £7.50 in France and Germany. In his book (op. cit.), King-Smith reveals that in 1970, the CBSO received in grant-plus-guarantee from the city and the Arts Council a total of £137,000, whereas the comparable figure for the Rotterdam Philharmonic Orchestra was £390,000. In the 1980s, Munich was spending £4.9 million on its single orchestra where Britain spent £4.7 million on all its symphony and chamber orchestras put together. Today in 2006, the National Lottery has added two billion pounds to arts funding, but again this raises some contentious issues since not everyone who plays the lottery is interested in classical music, which in turn affects the way the money is allocated. In any case, what is the definition of 'the arts'.

Meanwhile back in the 1970s a number of orchestral musicians took things into their own hands and formed small chamber groups. The Amati Ensemble, formed from leading members of the city orchestra, was perhaps the most prominent of them. This ensemble consisted of the usual string quartet plus double bass, flute, oboe, clarinet, bassoon and horn under the direction of the orchestra's Principal Horn, Timothy Reynish. The Amati Ensemble clearly achieved a standard high enough to be asked to appear in a Birmingham Chamber Music concert in November 1972. Sadly and typically, this ensemble did not survive the departure of its director and other of the players for richer pastures in Manchester and London. A subsequent co-leader of the city orchestra, John Bradbury, also set up two ensembles, a string quartet and a piano trio, the last with his wife Eira West as pianist. The trio commissioned a work from Gunilla Lowenstein a Swedish composer resident for many years in Birmingham, which was played at a Midland Musicians Society concert in March 1976. Again, this quartet and trio did not survive the Bradburys' departure for London. Two other enterprises should be mentioned, one the Halcyon Consort consisting of baroque recorder, viola da gamba and harpsichord and, in contrast, the basing of the Contemporary Music Network at Aston University.

The Grosvenor Concerts, held during the 1980s, was another admirable venture in this field. Held in the Grosvenor Rooms of the Grand Hotel, they presented soloists of the calibre of the pianist John Lill and violinist Nigel Kennedy. Like many enterprises of this kind, they had a relatively short life.

The important role of the new CBSO Centre in providing a home for chamber music, mainly but not exclusively performed by members of the orchestra, will be touched on in the final chapter. An important new ingredient is the fact that the status of the CBSO players is now far more secure than their counterparts in London, so the flight to London is now often reversed, and players often stay longer than was usual thirty years ago. In any case the Centre itself provides its own continuity.

Music in Miniature on the large stage

Between the wars, the Harold Holt series of celebrity concerts continued, bringing to Birmingham singers such as Galli-Curci, Jeritza, Conchita Supervia, Frieda Leider, Liza Lehmann, Elisabeth Schumann and the instrumentalists Pachmann, Cortot, Rachmaninov and Kreisler. Wilfrid van Wyck brought the pianists Maurycy Rosenthal, Artur Rubinstein and Alexander Borovsky who gave their recitals in the Large Theatre of the Midland Institute. Josef Riley, with a music business in Birmingham, seems to have continued in the Max Mossel tradition of dedicating a series to the best of talent resident in this country. The singer Margaret Balfour and the pianists Iso Elinson and Irene Scharrer, for example, appeared in his concerts.

After 1945, little was attempted in the Harrison and Harold Holt tradition at first but in 1966 an admirable attempt at reinstating this aspect of the city's musical life was made by Reginald Vincent, 'an enlightened local record dealer' as the *Musical Times* described him at the time. Rubinstein, and the singers de los Angeles and Schwarzkopf, for example, attracted full houses the first time they came but not so successfully the second time. Others, equally talented but less fêted and publicised, such as the oboist Leon Goossens, drew an audience to the Town Hall numbered in mere hundreds. The series shockingly foundered for lack of support and due to financial loss. Unfortunately Vincent had not taken on board Beecham's skill's as a publicist but it must be said that the difficult cultural climate, already discussed, again had an effect in this case. A similar series subsequently launched by Elizabeth Laverack had, equally, to be abandoned, in spite of her greater consciousness of the need for good publicity and presentation.

Higher Education. University and Conservatoire

The University Music Department has continued to be faithful to the essence of Bantock's prescription for a thorough and balanced music course, both theoretical and practical, preparing students for the world of music who have a thorough grounding in how to write music in different styles, a thorough understanding of how pieces of music are constructed, and of the styles of music in every period over the last millennium, together with keyboard harmony, ear training and writing down music from dictation. Not least they must be able to play two instruments, or offer an instrument and singing, be able to conduct, and belong to the university choir or orchestra. The link established with the School of Music in Bantock's time is maintained as far as instrumental or singing lessons are concerned, and students have gone and still go to the Conservatoire for these. Some students play in Friday lunch-time concerts at the Barber Institute, and attending the fully-professional Barber Evening concerts is available to them without of course moving off the university campus.

The Barber Evening Concerts are always supervised by the current Peyton and Barber Professor of Music and these have usually reflected their special tastes and

Chapter 28 - Again, what else?

interests. Anthony Lewis's interest in baroque opera was reflected in the establishment of the Barber Operas, given between 1959 and 1991. His successor Ivor Keys was anxious to promote contemporary music as well as that of the classical period. The Early Music Festival will be mentioned later.

The progress made by the Conservatoire was far less smooth. As a species of 'everyman's university' at a time without free and compulsory education, the Birmingham and Midland Institute, established in 1854, with its penny classes in music among its courses was seized on by anyone wanting to learn. A fairly chaotic situation as regards the music was regularised in 1886 when Stockley and others established it formally as a School, with students working for nationally recognised examinations, which Bantock took charge of in 1900. Bantock did all the right things to turn the enterprise into a respected college of music but once his strong character no longer influenced the situation, the old Midland Institute ethos tended to re-emerge more strongly. There was still the obligation to remain open to the reasonably gifted amateur, as well as to cater for those who wished to pursue a professional career. This was made more difficult by the fact that the 'amateurs' far outnumbered the 'professionals'. Bantock's successor, Allan K. Blackall, to his credit managed to maintain and improve standards in spite of the fact that the war was making everything more difficult. The building was damaged by the bombing, and macks and umbrellas were necessary in some rooms! Edmunds took over as Principal in 1945 and during his tenure, student numbers increased and the orchestra was re-established.

The purpose of the School's training programme was now focussed increasingly on providing teachers for schools, since under the 1944 Education Act, Music was to be a compulsory subject in the curriculum. This meant a larger student body. How was it to be accommodated in the original Midland Institute building? Even more crucially, how were the students to be selected for entrance to the School? Edmunds mourned the waste of time, energy and precious space on that forty per cent of the student population which was not capable of taking full advantage of the training on offer. There was at the same time increasing pressure from the schools' inspectorate to raise standards and Edmunds had to cope with that on the one hand, together with an unsympathetic attitude from the Institute Council on the other. This tension led to his resignation in 1956. His place was taken by the singer, Steuart Wilson, who in spite of the continuance of the acrimonious atmosphere, managed to see to it that the school's results improved. Nevertheless, part-time students still outnumbered full-timers in a ratio of ten to one.

The crux of the unhappy atmosphere at the school, was the very uncomfortable relationship between the Council of the Midland Institute and its subordinate offspring, the Committee of the School of Music. A letter to the *Birmingham Post* in February 1960 from the Rev. F. Lunt, Chief Master of King Edward's School, himself a member of the Institute Council, sums up the problem.

'It has been for a long time now that I have kept these troubles under my hat; I have been terribly shocked at the government, or rather misgovernment, of the School of Music... I have been driven to the conclusion that the leadership of the Institute just tolerates the School of Music, and does so only for the sake of the money it brings in. And that is a tidy sum, £13,000 for the management of the School. Here is I think, a unique cultural and educational feature of this great city... it is in a sorry state, moribund, riddled by intrigue and run by internal manipulation, preferring hole-in-the-corner methods to the light...'

This got into the national press and Steuart Wilson himself concluded the correspondence with a letter of his own to the *Birmingham Post* in which he said that he did not like municipal enterprises but that after three years' experience of the government of the Institute and their mismanagement, 'I now would prefer any municipality to be in charge'.

Eventually of course that is what happened and the Birmingham Education Department took the school over, though not before the recommendation to the Institute Council to appoint Gordon Clinton, in succession to Steuart Wilson who had resigned, had been accepted. Clinton initially faced the same situation as his predecessors, with only 40 full-time students now, and an orchestra that was, in his words, 'absolutely diabolical'. Clinton also faced the move from the Institute to temporary quarters in the old Midlands Electricity Board building in Dale End. The building of the ring road in the 1960s forced the Institute itself to move to smaller premises in Margaret Street. So at last the child was able to separate from its parent and from 1970 approximately, the School of Music could really set out on the path of becoming a conservatoire and aiming to bear some comparison with its London and Manchester counterparts. An important step along this road was becoming a constituent college of the Birmingham Polytechnic, as it then was.

The School was still, however, hampered by the obligation to produce teachers, for private and school music teaching. Students worked for the Associate and Graduate Diploma of the School, the Associate Diploma in particular still being related to teaching. Performance standards were being worked on, however, and Harold Gray took charge of the orchestra, members of the city orchestra visiting to teach. The teaching of part-time students was phased out and. the opera classes were held in the day from 1970 onwards so that they too were only available to full-time students. A formal graduate opera school was established, achieving some very good results and some highly successful productions followed. In 1970, too, Frank Downes was appointed as full-time head of Instrumental Studies, a move which led to all the instrumental teaching being effectively co-ordinated. Another step forward was taken when the School with its 200 full-time students, moved to its new purpose-built premises in Paradise Circus in February 1973. At this point the violinist Louis Carus became the School's Principal in succession to Gordon Clinton, and the importance of the instrumental teaching was naturally emphasised even more. There was, however, some difference of opinion between Carus and his Head of the Instrumental Department, the horn player, Frank Downes. Carus wanted more emphasis on individual practice, Downes on actually playing in the orchestra. They managed to resolve their differences and the standard of instrumental playing continued to improve. This still did not do anything to further the careers of pianists and singers, however, and a Gulbenkian Report in 1975 suggested that pianists (and organists too, surely) should learn transposition (putting a piece of music into a different key), continuo playing and accompaniment. True - but again what about singers? Not all wish to join an opera company, nor may their voices be suitable for opera. What was to prepare them for making a living?

Louis Carus also initiated what is now the Birmingham Conservatoire Association, a society of supporters who are ex-students, members of staff, other musicians and music-lovers. Members receive *Fanfare*, an attractively produced journal. It was Carus too who had to cope with explaining the practical and financial requirements of a college of music to the Polytechnic authorities who were used to the requirements of a totally different kind of student training. The accommodation was successfully made, however. Since 1989, the former School has been a Conservatoire, with expectations raised and gradually being achieved. It continues to offer concerts which are open to the public, and a professionally-presented printed programme is issued each term.

The task of teaching the music teachers is now undertaken by the Education Department of the University of Central England and the Conservatoire can concentrate on training performers, and preparing them to carve out a career based on a high level of performance which must, however, inevitably involve the ability to undertake the other musical activities needed to earn a livelihood.

In the schools, music was still an expected part of the curriculum until the end of this period in every kind of school, be it independent, grammar, technical, secondary modern or junior. Most had a daily assembly of some kind which still often included singing a hymn. The City Music Adviser's Department organised the peripatetic instrumental teachers and supervised and conducted the orchestras and bands, whose players were drawn from all over the city. After 1960 it gradually became more difficult to engage some pupils in classical music, especially boys and especially after the age of 12 or 13. Some schools today (2006) have very little music provision at all on their own premises, - or where they did have a good music room, it became more common to find guitars and keyboards in it, as well as the piano or a violin for example. With so many different 'musics' at large in the city, the schools have to try to reflect this, but there is a real danger that many children will never be introduced to European classical music at all, while others do have the chance to become extraordinarily adept at performing it. Meanwhile many trained private music teachers continue to exercise the craft of developing the musical skills of private individuals, children and adults alike. A considerable proportion of their number are represented by the Birmingham Centre of the Incorporated Society of Musicians. Promising pupils have been able to take part in the Birmingham and Northfield competitive music festivals, begun in 1941 and 1950 respectively and still active in 2006.

Scholars and composers

It is to the University of Birmingham and the Conservatoire that one naturally first looks to find those who delve deeply into the study of music, or seek to compose it themselves, and there are indeed a number of Birmingham-based people who have made a valuable contribution in these ways.

Perhaps we should take the less well-known Sydney Grew (1879-1949) first. Born in Birmingham, Grew studied at the Midland Institute School of Music and from 1926, with the encouragement of his friend Adrian Boult, he founded and edited *The British Musician*. This was a monthly magazine commenting on musical works, on books about music, on local concerts and on recently-issued gramophone records. Grew's books include *The Art of the Player-Piano* (1921) and two volumes of *Our Favourite Musicians* (1922-1923). A volume on Bach in the *Master Musicians* series was written in collaboration with his wife, Eva Mary Grew.

Two nationally-known names which more readily spring to mind in connection with music scholarship, are those of Ernest Newman and Eric Blom. Ernest Newman we have already met (chapter 26) since he was in Birmingham in the early part of the twentieth century, but Eric Blom was active in Birmingham during the middle phase we are considering here. Critic for the *Birmingham Post* between 1931 and 1946, some of his comments are reported in the chapter on the first sixty years of the city orchestra (chapter 27). Blom was an excellent linguist and translated biographies of Mozart and Schubert into English. He also loved the English language for its own sake and cared very much about how it was used. This gift was exercised when he edited the *Everyman Dictionary of Music* and the fifth edition of the *Grove Dictionary of Music and Musicians*. The *Birmingham Post* is to be congratulated on being able to attract someone of this calibre to work for it for some fifteen years.

All the university music staff, in fact, were writing books on music or contributing to music journals or in some cases on their editorial staff, the aim being to further a better understanding of music, past and present, so that it could be more intelligently performed. Much work has gone into the music of the seventeenth century and here Nigel Fortune may perhaps be singled out. He made some important contributions to our knowledge, editing among many other things, articles, with Anthony Lewis, on opera and church music from 1630 to 1750 for the *New Oxford History of Music*. These have been a part of the important exploration of music of this earlier time, with the result that it has been brought to life for us, more nearly in the way in which it may have originally been heard. Before this was Jack Westrup, holder of the Chair of Music from 1944 to 1947, who had a formidable list of scholarly works to his credit and was a leading musicologist of his day. The University Singers, directed by John Whenham have been mentioned along with other choirs as singing, in particular, in the Birmingham Early Music Festival. This began in the mid-1980s as a week-long festival at St. Alban's church in the days when the late Ian Ledsham, then the university's Music Librarian, was organist. When Ledsham left St Alban's, senior members of the Music Department staff including Colin Timms and John Whenham, took charge and this is now a major project in the Autumn term, taking music of the seventeenth and eighteenth centuries to venues in and around Birmingham, and presenting a wide range of specialist instrumental and vocal ensembles. Timms and Whenham have since been joined by Mary O'Neill as the university members of the Board of Management. Pat Ryan is the Festival Administrator.

In this connection David Munrow must be included. Born in Birmingham in 1942, Munrow initially read English at Cambridge, where he founded a group to perform early music. He then returned to Birmingham to spend a year studying seventeenth century music in the University Music Department. A visit to South America had kindled his interest in folk instruments and the techniques needed to play them. Soon in demand as a recorder player, he taught the instrument at the Royal College of Music and in 1967 formed the Early Music Consort of London with James Bowman, Oliver Brookes and Christopher Hogwood, counter-tenor, viols player and harpsichordist respectively. Two years later they were joined by the lutenist, James Tyler. This consort, sometimes augmented by extra players, gave exciting and polished performances of mediaeval and Renaissance music. Sometimes criticised for making too many assumptions about how the music should be performed, these concerts most certainly lifted 'early music' off the page. Tragically, David Munrow ended his own life in 1976, but he had already brought to practical life all the recent studies into music produced before 1650 and kindled a huge interest in it.

Working in two quite different areas of music, Stephen Banfield, Elgar Professor of Music at the University from 1992 to 2003, contributed important articles and books on English art song and on Broadway musicals.

Composers

The amount of music composed within the city may surprise some readers. To take the natives first. John R. Heath (1887 - 1950), born in Birmingham, was the son of the then Birmingham University Vice-Chancellor, living for most of his life in Wales where he worked as a GP. He nevertheless had works performed in the 1920s by the city orchestra. Dorothy Howell (1898-1982) was born in Handsworth and began composing at the age of nine. She entered the Royal Academy of music at the age of 15 where her composition studies were with J. B. McEwen. She was also a professional pianist. Several of her works were performed by Henry Wood, not least her symphonic poem *Lamia,* this at a Promenade concert in London in 1919. A performance of her *Three Divertissements* for orchestra was postponed because of the blitz but eventually given at the 1950 Elgar Festival in Malvern. She taught at one point at the Birmingham School of Music. She is buried close to the Elgar grave at Little Malvern. Most of her large-scale works were composed between 1919 and 1930, with small-scale pieces later.

Julius Harrison (1885-1963) whom we have already met in the chapter on Bantock, seems to have done most of his significant composition after 1949 when he retired because of deafness. His output was small but wide-ranging. Leslie Bridgewater, born in Halesowen, was very well-known in the realm of light music and he and his music were heard regularly on radio in the 1930s. He also worked at Stratford providing the music needed for the Shakespeare productions. His Piano Concerto, published in 1946, was recorded by Iris Loveridge with the London Promenade Orchestra, Bridgewater himself conducting. Herbert Lumby (1906-1987) born in Moseley, studied at the Midland Institute School of Music with Arthur Hytch, and played in the CBO for a number of years until 1944. He then taught and composed, having several works broadcast from the BBC Midland Region in the 1940s and 1950s. Several of these were performed under Rudolf Schwarz and Julius Harrison.

Christopher Edmunds (1899-1990), he who was Head of the Birmingham School of Music from 1945 to 1956, is in some ways the most considerable of Birmingham composers of his generation. Much of his music was not published, although many of his manuscripts have been deposited in the Special Collections section of the University of Birmingham's Main Library. This fact has worked against his wider recognition. Some of his chamber music is particularly fine and ought to be in the regular chamber music repertoire today. This applies not least to his fine Piano Trio in B minor. A former Birmingham Conservatoire teacher, Andrew Downes, has also a considerable amount of music to his credit, much of which has been performed. He is still very active.

Another composer with considerably less *gravitas* as to some of the music he wrote than most of the composers we are considering here, was Albert Ketèlbey. Born in Birmingham in 1875, he is known to those who do remember him as the composer of such sentimental lollipops as *In a Monastery Garden.* The sheet music version of this sold a million copies. His other most well-known piece, perhaps, was the *Intermezzo-Scene, In a Persian Market.* This was written for a pantomime producer who wanted music 'depicting an eastern scene with a camel train lasting four minutes'. (Quoted in John Sant op. cit). Ketèlbey's great versatility and musicianship enabled him to do that, and create something that was immensely popular in the light music genre into the bargain. The City of Birmingham Police Band was one of the first in the field to record this piece. There were subsequently a hundred others. Ketèlbey had studied at Trinity College of Music in London, subsequently becoming a theatre conductor and a music editor. He composed some serious orchestral pieces and chamber music, but perhaps his most valuable contribution to classical music in the long term was through the recording company, the English Columbia Graphophone Company, where he was Music Director and Advisor. In the light music field he was a tremendous success and he still has his devotees today.

Several musicians who have taught in the Birmingham University Music Department have produced good and interesting music. Victor Hely-Hutchinson, Professor of Music from 1934 to 1944, with a relatively small output, produced some amusing settings of nonsense verse by Edward Lear and Lewis Carroll. *A Carol Symphony* of his is still sometimes performed. One of Hely-Hutchinson's composition pupils was Peter Wishart (1921-1984) whose opera *Two in a Bush* was given at the Barber Institute in 1956. Peter Aston, born in Birmingham in 1938, studied at the Birmingham School of Music and York University, becoming Professor of Music at the University of East Anglia. He has produced much church music.

Mention must surely be made of three other former members of the University of Birmingham Music Department staff, namely Peter Dickinson, John Joubert and John Casken, all of whom have written works commissioned by the Feeney Trust. Peter Dickinson's *Transfiguration* was performed at Cheltenham Town Hall in 1970, John Joubert's choral and orchestral piece *Gong-tormented Sea*, was given at Birmingham Town Hall in 1982 and John Casken's *Tableaux des Troix Ages* played at the same venue in 1977. John Joubert's output is at the present moment the largest and is widely respected, but all these composers ought to be more widely known and their music much more often performed.

It is far too soon to make a judgement about the lasting value of the music produced by the composers connected with Birmingham. Only time will reveal that. In addition, a good deal of what was produced after William Glock became the BBC's Controller of Music in 1959, he who set his face against anything written in a more traditional style, meant that much of the music mentioned here has been given too little airing for a balanced assessment to be made, something only possible after several hearings. Today in 2006 the problem is different again and any kind of classical music at all faces a good deal of indifference, and even hostility, from large sections of society, whether it be more 'traditional' or very new and innovative.

Broadcasting and television

In its early days, the BBC regularly transmitted great classical music to every home in the country via its National programme. In the Regions, its own in-house choirs and orchestras were important but more controversial, since they often duplicated what was already being done in the area, even if they added to the general public's daily diet of classical music. In the nineteen thirties, forties and fifties, a National Programme and Home Service still presented a pot-pourri of everything, talks of all kinds, lunch-hour and evening classical music concerts, plays, dance bands, swing and jazz, so that everyone heard every kind of music, including classical. Classical music was also introduced to children in most schools in the land. Everyone had some exposure to it and could relate to it to some extent. Since the nineteen-sixties it has been different. Classical music has been tidied away to Radio 3, originally the Third Programme. In the 1980s a commercial classical music programme, Classic FM, was established, but it again has to be deliberately tuned into. Pop music has increasingly dominated more and more wavelengths, both BBC and independent, and it is often used as the background to every kind of programme, on radio and on television. A great deal of prominence was also given to programmes like *Top of the Pops*, with only an occasional chance to see an opera or an orchestra in action on the screen, let alone an individual performer.

On the other hand those who chose the classical music wave-lengths had a feast of music from every period and were advised as to the LP's and CD's that they might buy. The BBC undoubtedly rescued the Henry Wood Proms in 1927 and its regional orchestras, including the BBC Midland Orchestra, gave employment to local instrumentalists. In the 1940s and 1950s, local musicians were auditioned and given broadcasts. Among these were pianists Tom Bromley, Edna Iles and Marjorie Hazlehurst, together with string players such as Lena Wood and the Element Quartet. These were local musicians being heard nationally. It may perhaps be mentioned here that Edna Iles was already nationally known, particularly for her advocacy of the music of Medtner, who himself called her the 'ablest and bravest besieger of my musical fortresses'.

In 1967, the regions of the BBC were converted into independent local radio stations. In the city, the BBC's Radio Birmingham promoted and broadcast live concerts, given by local choirs, bands, small ensembles and soloists. Independent local radio stations were also granted licences but these paid scant attention to classical music. From 1972, Radio 3 promoted a prestigious series of chamber concerts, by national and international artists, at its Pebble Mill Studios, just opened. As with live local radio concerts, the public was admitted free of charge, causing some consternation among local chamber music societies who feared they would be undercut. Matters were certainly not improved for them. In August 1981, Anthony Cross wrote as follows in the *Musical Times*: 'The BBC contribution to Midlands music is modest. Several CBSO concerts are transmitted annually on the national network (Radio 3) but the BBC's active promotion of music locally is largely confined to a celebrity chamber music series, using artists from outside the region and essentially duplicating what the local chamber music society has been doing for years. The local BBC station which once transmitted a good deal of music-making, encouraging both performers and composers alike, now does virtually nothing'. Even this Pebble Mill enterprise has come to an end since then, however, and today the situation has not changed, a situation which two former local BBC staff members of that time, Richard Butt and Barry Lankester, continue to mourn.

Critics

The most significant musical events produced by all the activities described in this chapter were regularly reviewed in the Birmingham newspapers, and particularly the *Birmingham Post*, usually the next morning. The *Post* had several reviewers who could be called on. We have already met several of them in these pages. All have endeavoured to follow the prescription for the music critic which Elgar offered in one of his Birmingham University Inaugural Lectures in 1905. Speaking for the performer, Elgar said that they did not want to be merely told that this or that was wrong; they would like to know why it was wrong, and why the critic thought it was wrong. Most of the best men of the present day told them this; and he had never known criticism to hurt or annoy if a reason was given. English criticism should be honest, fearless and reasonable.

Though it was sometimes possible to disagree with what was written by our local critics, it was clear that it was always written on the basis of wide musical knowledge and in good faith.

Chapter 29

Phase Three: Transformation - The Rattle effect

Simon Rattle. Conductor of the City of Birmingham Symphony Orchestra 1980-1998

Too early to be regarded as 'history', this chapter is a personal assessment of the effect of one remarkable young man on the city's musical life, and on the city itself.

Simon Denis Rattle was born in Liverpool in 1955 and soon showed his musical abilities which all his family, not least his sister, encouraged. His first orchestral role was as a percussionist with the National Youth and Royal Liverpool Philharmonic Orchestras. At the age of 16 he entered the Royal Academy of Music where he studied piano, percussion and conducting. Three years later he won the John Player International Conductors' Award with the result that he was appointed as Assistant Conductor of the two Bournemouth Orchestras, the Symphony Orchestra and the Sinfonietta. Prestigious appearances in London followed when he conducted the Nash Ensemble at the Queen Elizabeth Hall in 1975 and the New Philharmonia Orchestra at the Royal Festival Hall in 1976. During the three years prior to his arrival in Birmingham, Simon Rattle was associate conductor of the Royal Liverpool Philharmonic Orchestra and assistant conductor of the BBC Scottish Symphony Orchestra. We are already, at this stage, seeing evidence not only of a very exceptional conducting talent but of someone with a huge reservoir of energy and a capacity for hard work.[1]

In 1978, Simon Rattle was himself, according to his own testimony, beginning to be aware that he had the capabilities necessary to take charge of an orchestra, even if he still had vast tracts of the orchestral repertoire to learn. He knew also that he had the necessary mental and physical capacity. Birmingham's city orchestra, on the other hand, was a capable orchestra with potential for great development, given really committed leadership. The avalanche of musicality, enthusiasm, energy and commitment unleashed over them in 1980 was just what they needed.

Both conductor and orchestra therefore, needed each other In their different ways both needed a reasonable period of time to grow to their full potential. It was clear that Simon Rattle's personality, the infectious fire and energy of his own

Chapter 29 - Phase Three: Transformation - The Rattle effect

dedication to, and love of, music was very likely indeed to be sufficient to make this happen. The idea of a long-term commitment on the part of a conductor was also fairly unusual in the orchestral sphere. Barbirolli's lengthy conductorship of the Hallé Orchestra was a precedent, with the difference that Barbirolli was well-established in his career, not at the beginning of it, when he arrived in Manchester. In Simon Rattle's case, he had youth and vigour, but he still had a name to make. To a number of people at the time when his appointment to the Birmingham orchestra was being considered, it seemed that he was 'on the way up' and would take the orchestra up with him. Others were unsure, including George Jonas, Chairman of the CBSO Society, who thought it was a very great risk. The doubters were proved wrong - very wrong in fact. What also helped to reassure Simon Rattle himself was the fact that a former much trusted colleague was now the CBSO's new General Manager, namely Edward Smith, appointed in 1978 after the precipitate departure of Arthur Baker. Simon Rattle had known Ed Smith in Liverpool, where Smith had been Assistant General Manager of the Royal Liverpool Philharmonic Orchestra. Their new partnership proved to be extremely fruitful.

Above and beyond all his outstanding musical gifts, it was perhaps Simon Rattle's special charismatic qualities which helped not only to transform the orchestra into a world-class orchestra, from being just a respectable provincial one, but played a large part in changing the city's image of itself. As has already been mentioned, it had gradually dawned on the city after the second war that it had long overtaken all other cities in the United Kingdom in terms of population, except London. It was now, therefore, the Second City. This was a two-edged sword, in reality, because it carried with it the suggestion of 'second class'. The creation of a first-class city orchestra helped to instill in the corporate mind of the Council and in the minds of the citizens that it could be as good as the first anywhere. It did not have to settle for second best.

What was the effect of this 24-year-old on the orchestra and its affairs in practice? One of the most visible effects was the rise in audience numbers to an eventual 98% attendance figure for the Thursday and Saturday series of concerts in the 1985-6 season. At this point further, the pattern of concerts had been altered by Rattle, in discussion with the Marketing Manager, Julianna Szekely. There were to be 30 weekly concerts, alternating from week to week between Tuesdays and Thursdays. Concert-goers could choose the night which suited them and still be able to attend 15 concerts in a season. The Wednesday series would consist of eight monthly concerts which would offer selected repeats from the Tuesday and Thursday series. In this way the choice of concert night for audiences was widened but the orchestra's burden of work was not thereby increased. In any case, whichever night was chosen by the concert-goer, there was a lively sense of expectation among those who attended, satisfied by increasingly alert and committed performances from the players themselves. There was a shared sense of joy and discovery in the music.

Simon Rattle himself has commented on his relationship with the orchestra and the orchestra's reaction to him.

'It was only when I got there that I realised how desperate they were to work. The whole business of establishing the style was vital because that had all slipped. They wanted to be told how to do things and work at things. I remember Felix (Kok the Leader) saying that if he asked them to play things in the same part of the bow they would laugh and ask why. This was all a long struggle, but the attitude is transformed now.... For the Boulez *Rituel* we had to do a lot of sectional rehearsal, and that helped such a lot.... What I wanted to do was to conduct the pieces I knew very well, and which could develop the orchestra and me together.... One of the things we instigated in the first year was that we would have rehearsals with just the principal string players, and work on bowing and marking the parts: that hadn't been thought of as something that was important. And in spite of problems it worked'. (Quoted by Nicholas Kenyon in *Simon Rattle. The Making of a Conductor*).

One of the most striking effects of Simon Rattle's arrival in Birmingham and the orchestra's consequent progress was the remarkable rise in the number of recordings the CBSO was asked to make. By 1983, after only three years of his conductorship, the list included Janacek's *Glagolitic Mass*, piano concertos by Liszt, Saint-Saëns and Rachmaninov, with Cecile Ousset as soloist, Britten's *War Requiem*, Rachmaninov's *Symphonic Dances*, Vaughan-Williams' *On Wenlock Edge* and *Songs of Travel*, with Robert Tear and Thomas Allen respectively, and Mahler's *Das Klagende Lied*. By 1986, Messiaen's massive *Turangalila* Symphony, Mahler's Symphony no. 2, (the *Resurrection* symphony), Elgar's *Dream of Gerontius* and the symphonies of Sibelius had been added to the list of CBSO recordings.

Visits elsewhere were soon a regular part of the orchestra's schedule and a number of foreign tours were already under discussion by 1986; Simon Rattle himself, on the other hand, being invited to conduct some of the most prestigious orchestras abroad. Soon after his arrival in Birmingham he became Principal Guest Conductor of the Los Angeles Philharmonic Orchestra, and conducted a programme of twentieth century French music with the London Philharmonic, first in London and then in Paris. More significantly, it was announced in 1986 that Rattle would be undertaking his first conducting engagements with the Concertgebouw in Amsterdam and, even more significantly for the future, with the Berlin Philharmonic Orchestra.

Birmingham music-lovers and CBSO supporters hardly needed to be told by the national press about this revolution in the city's musical life. It was gratifying nevertheless to know that opinion from all over the country - and indeed abroad - welcomed, appreciated and praised what was happening. Given the struggles over string-players during most of the orchestra's previous existence, it was particularly striking to read the following review from a Paris newspaper, *Le Matin*, regarding a concert in February 1986:

Chapter 29 - Phase Three: Transformation - The Rattle effect

'...what a discovery! One knew already that Simon Rattle is one of the finest conductors of the younger generation, but now one was also to discover... that the City of Birmingham Orchestra, of which he is principal conductor, is an ensemble of international class, totally homogeneous, supple, lively and powerful. More than that, an orchestra built on solid musical foundations, shown, for example, by the tonal beauty of the string playing. I know few orchestras who could make their entry in Beethoven's Fourth Piano Concerto with such delicacy, such gentle sweetness, ...One is given the impression that the conductor is there to some real purpose, both through the long and exacting effort which alone is capable of transfiguring a symphonic ensemble and through his constant and active presence. One must henceforth regard the Birmingham Orchestra as one to be reckoned with and, without the slightest hesitation, write the name of Rattle alongside those of Ozawa, Abbado or Muti'.

One wonders if the shades of the orchestra's founders, of George Weldon and Rudolf Schwarz, who had struggled over the standard of the strings, were rejoicing in heaven and saying 'at last!'

The joint sense of purpose of both orchestra and players is also reflected in a review from nearer home, from *The Times*, about a concert in Birmingham in September 1985.

'...I am at a loss to know how Simon Rattle achieved this immediacy, this sense of the music speaking for itself, searching and finding its own tempo, its own phrasing, even its own colouring from the strings. No doubt the secret lies somewhat in the shared sensibility of conductor and orchestra working so closely in harness (and how well Rattle's stay-put policy justifies itself). But the triumph is also a personal one, dependent on Rattle's ability to be desperately and personally involved, and yet to be so on behalf of something much larger than himself'.

The references to 'long and exacting effort', to 'constant and active presence' and the use of the word 'transfiguration' in the review in *Le Matin*, exactly describe the 'Rattle effect', not just as regards the orchestra itself but also as regards Birmingham's own 'image', nationally and internationally. This is something the present writer is keen to emphasise. The international dimension had returned to Birmingham's musical life in no uncertain terms, but this time the international renown did not depend on visitors but on musicians who lived here, as did Simon Rattle himself, and who were willing to be identified with the city in the improvement and promotion of its cultural and musical welfare.

What of the music regular concert-goers were hearing? The repertoire was extremely wide-ranging. The standard symphony orchestra pieces were included but always with a new sense of discovery when conducted by Rattle himself. He also introduced pieces which were relatively new to most audiences, such as the Boulez *Rituel (in Memoriam Maderna)*, Stravinsky's *Symphonies of Wind Instruments*, Kurt Weill's

The Seven Deadly Sins and, in October 1981, Messiaen's *Turangalila Symphony* with Jeanne Loriod, Messiaen's sister-in-law, playing the ondes martenot. In contrast, the Orchestra of St. John's Smith Square brought an all-Bach programme in the following month. No-one could complain of lack of variety, and all of this was accompanied by a new and exciting sense of there being a new beginning with a rigorously-rehearsed orchestra.

The audience was challenged; by concerts which could include Webern's Six Pieces for Orchestra op. 6, Berg's Violin Concerto, (not then so well-known as now) Stravinsky's *Apollo* and, to send them home relaxed, Ravel's *Daphnis and Chloë* Suite no. 2. The orchestra was challenged; by the huge range of styles they were having to respond to, whereby they could be playing Hindemith's *Symphony for Concert Band* and Vivaldi's *The Four Seasons* in one and the same concert. This last took place in May 1988 with the late-lamented Iona Brown as director and soloist. It may be mentioned here that in an interview with Beresford King-Smith, quoted in his book *Crescendo!,* Simon Rattle himself said: 'Iona Brown, Victor Liberman, Heinz Holliger and, later on, music specialists like Nicholas Kraemer, Frans Brüggen, Nicholas McGegan - they've all been at various times part of this essential process of growth that we've all been through; what they achieved not only had its immediate effect but it had the effect of spreading vitamins throughout the whole orchestra'. The benefits of that are still being heard today in 2006 it should be added.

Simon Rattle himself was, by his own admission, also challenged by having to learn the core symphonic repertoire from the inside for the first time. This process was to come to fruition in the shape of performances, over a period of some years, of all the Brahms, Nielsen and Beethoven symphonies. At a comparatively early stage in Simon Rattle's tenure, the Brahms interpretations were criticised in some quarters as 'unclassical' even 'incorrect', but for just as many others it was an opportunity for a really fresh look at symphonies which had often been presented in a somewhat ponderous old 'Richter' tradition.

The last season in the Town Hall, which had been the orchestra's base for the previous seventy years, saw the first year of a project devised by Simon Rattle and the late Michael Vyner which they called Towards the Millennium. Each *year* of the last decade of the twentieth century would feature music from the corresponding *decade* of the century, so that the season beginning in 1990 would present works composed between 1900 and 1910. The season beginning in 1991 would contain works written between 1910 and 1920, and so on. The final season, 1999 to 2000 would of course involve music composed within the previous ten years - virtually contemporary. As part of this scheme, the 1990 to 1991 season gave audiences Sibelius' *Nightride and Sunrise*, Schoenberg's *Erwartung, Song of the Wood Dove* and Chamber Symphony no. 1, Stravinsky's ballet music *Firebird*, Webern's *Six Pieces* for orchestra, Berg's *Seven Early Songs*, with Maria Ewing as soloist, Mahler's Symphony no. 7, Rachmaninov's Third

Chapter 29 - Phase Three: Transformation - The Rattle effect

Piano Concerto, Suk's *Asrael* Symphony, Charles Ives' *The Unanswered Question* and *Central Park in the Dark* - and of course Elgar's *Dream of Gerontius*. The performance of some of these works was given by some regular visitors to Birmingham at that time, namely the London Sinfonietta, who specialised in twentieth century music and with whom Simon Rattle worked closely. They were conducted in Birmingham by Simon Rattle himself of course - further evidence of his desire to encourage the appreciation of this area of the repertoire which, as has already been pointed out, many people still found very difficult to understand and enjoy.

It is not surprising therefore that 1991 also saw the start of the young Mark-Anthony Turnage's attachment to the orchestra as Composer in Association. This residency lasted four years and produced a number of works which helped to make Turnage's musical voice familiar to a much wider audience than would have been likely otherwise. All the parties to this arrangement learned much from it, though it has to be said that Turnage's music did not please everyone; but at least it opened ears to new sounds and provided a challenge in the process of musical assessment and evaluation to everyone involved. He was succeeded in 1995 by Judith Weir and subsequently, in 2001 for three years, by Julian Anderson.

A new era

So far, all this progress and achievement had come about in spite of the deficiencies of the 160-year-old Town Hall, with its uncomfortable seats, lino-covered floors, gas-lit corridors and strange acoustics. The personality and musical achievements of Simon Rattle had overcome these very real drawbacks and, as we have seen, audience numbers had soon risen to that 98% attendance frequently achieved at the Thursday and Saturday concerts in particular. Critical comment from every quarter continued to indicate that Birmingham now had a world-class orchestra. The movements of the best players to London not only ceased but was occasionally reversed. Inevitably and painfully, the services of some players were 'dispensed with' by Rattle after some re-auditioning, in the cause of raising standards, but the new recruits, many of them very young, brought even more vitality to the proceedings. It was particularly interesting, incidentally, to see the number of young women who were now giving us some accomplished violin playing in the string section. In this connection it is rather amusing to read a letter which appeared in the *Musical Times* of 1870 asking why young ladies cannot for once be allowed to learn the violin instead of the ubiquitous piano. How things have changed!

In any case, with permanent contracts and player representation on the Council of Management now taken for granted, conditions for orchestral players in Birmingham are far more secure than in London. The Birmingham musical public now 'takes ownership' of its orchestra, to use a modern management phrase, in a way that London never can do of all the various orchestral bodies in the capital.

Simon Rattle in the recording studio.

The effect on Birmingham itself

More than all of this, however, is the change in attitude to Birmingham itself, now that Simon Rattle has given its orchestra an international reputation. To admit to anyone that one lived in Birmingham in the 1970s, for example, was to invite negative comments such as 'well, I suppose we all have to live somewhere' - very much the 'Mrs. Elton attitude' quoted in the Introduction to this book. On holiday abroad in the 1990s, let us say, in answer to enquiries about where one lived, saying that it was Birmingham was to provoke a very different reaction. The name of Simon Rattle would immediately be mentioned, along with much more positive comments about what was happening in the city generally.

There is no doubt, again, that the successful completion of Symphony Hall and its inclusion in the new International Convention Centre (ICC) was certainly spurred on by the status that Simon Rattle had gained for the city's orchestra. He was not, of course, solely responsible and he himself paid tribute to Tom Caulcott, the city's Chief Executive at that time, who was equally determined that a concert hall should be included in the plans for the ICC. King-Smith quotes Rattle as saying

Chapter 29 - Phase Three: Transformation - The Rattle effect

'Probably the main reason why the hall was built was Tom Caulcott's sheer native cunning in pretending that a hall was *not* going to be built. It was to be a Convention Centre and for a long time what we now call Symphony Hall was just known as 'Hall 2'. (Quoted by King-Smith op. cit. pp. 273-274). So successful was this subterfuge that it gave rise to some gloomy rumours on the musical grapevine at one point, to the effect that the ICC would not contain a concert hall after all. We need not have worried, thankfully.

Thus the first CBSO concert in the grand new hall took place on 12th April 1991, some 157 years after the first Town Hall Musical Festival - again, one has to say, a long wait for a city whose motto is 'Forward'! The new hall is spacious and comfortable with very good facilities, but above everything else, of course, are its very fine acoustics. These were built into the design of the hall from the start under the supervision of Artec of New York. As to its appearance, it has to be said that some find a touch of the 1930s 'Ritz cinema' about it, but it is certainly warm and cheerful with its red upholstery. In any case, it has attracted admiration from every quarter, but, as ever, nothing is ever quite perfect. The excellent acoustics might also be described as 'merciless' too. Everything is heard with great clarity and some blemishes in the playing were exposed. This was a good thing in the long run, of course, since it spurred on efforts towards even higher playing standards. What has proved to be virtually incurable is the scourge of the unrestrained cough from members of the audience who seem blissfully unaware of how insensitive they are being. This is heard with complete clarity all over the hall and a favourite time for these folk to make their contribution to the proceedings seems all too often to be in the *pianissimo* in the final bar of a particularly affecting slow movement!

The first full CBSO season at Symphony Hall offered the now-expected full range of orchestral music. On 14th November 1991, a baroque and early classical period programme, conducted by Nicholas Kraemer, included operatic arias by Handel, Suites by J. S. Bach and Rameau and a symphony by Haydn. Michael Chance was the soloist in the Handel Arias. Occasions such as these, where a smaller ensemble is used, throw the spotlight on all the players and encourage that sense of the players' awareness of individual responsibility for their own playing that is one of the characteristics of the present orchestra, as opposed to its earlier predecessors. This sense has grown steadily, slowly since 1960, but by leaps and bounds since 1980 and it now seems to be simply taken for granted.

In contrast to the baroque programme of earlier music just mentioned, three new works by Composer in Association, Mark-Anthony Turnage, were performed during the season. These were his *Momentum, Three Screaming Popes* and *Leaving*. This last, written for chorus and small ensemble was a premiere. The rest of the season featured more Towards the Millennium programmes, this time presenting works composed between 1910 and 1919. Interestingly, it did not feature Stravinsky's *Rite of Spring* on this occasion, generally regarded as one of the key seminal works of the twentieth century - not that the orchestra had not already played this of course. Stravinsky was certainly represented, however, as were Mahler, Debussy, Berg, Satie, Ives, Schreker, Nielsen, Ravel, Szymanowski - and Elgar. This clearly constitutes a very interesting historical study of varied musical styles - and new musical languages even - at that period. Regular visitors, the London Sinfonietta, under Simon Rattle's baton, played one of these Toward the Millennium concerts in March 1992. These were often revealing programmes and it represented a fairly steep learning curve for everyone concerned, conductor, players and audiences. Nevertheless, it was working and Ed Smith, the orchestra's Chief Executive at that time, comments in the the 1998-99 Prospectus as follows: 'I can't tell you how many people come up to me following concerts which have included some less well-known repertoire - and not only contemporary - with the delight of discovering something wonderful they hadn't expected to like'. No-one could say but that Birmingham's music was thriving under Simon Rattle's guidance, presented now in the fine new concert hall. Indeed this was recognised officially when Birmingham was designated UK City of Music for 1992. Rattle himself was also, of course, personally honoured over the years, finally receiving a knighthood in 1994.

Simon Rattle and the CBSO in rehearsal (photograph by Alan Wood).

The good work continued and the 1992-93 season gave us all six Nielsen symphonies, an exciting and memorable exploration for many in the audience. In the 1995-6 season, the orchestra's 75th, Simon Rattle presented all nine Beethoven symphonies. This proved a landmark for him in many ways since it established him in the eyes of those who had earlier been inclined to accuse him of only relating to the late nineteenth and twentieth century post-Romantic repertoire. The orchestra itself had recorded all nine symphonies for Chandos, with Walter Weller conducting, so that the players were already familiar with these works. Rattle's interpretation would clearly be different and in the event reviews reveal how great was his achievement. Michael White in the *Independent on Sunday* commented as follows: 'His

Chapter 29 - Phase Three: Transformation - The Rattle effect

The Audience of tomorrow: Rattle meeting children after a CBSO family concert.

readings are a strong, coherent synthesis of period sensitivity and Grand Tradition. They feel thoroughly absorbed but brilliantly alive, with an exhilarating rhythmic ardour and a crystal clarity of sound throughout the orchestra'.

In the event, the Simon Rattle–CBSO partnership lasted until the Summer of 1998, the 1997-8 season being Rattle's last in charge of the orchestra. This added up to a remarkable 18 years, all of which had seen everyone involved grow in musical understanding. Stemming from all this was the growth of those ancillary but vital activities which underpin such an organisation, especially after the move to Symphony Hall. Making the audience feel involved in all this development led to a greater emphasis on pre-concert talks, entitled *Sounds Interesting*, and in giving the subscribers and supporters in general a greater sense of commitment to and involvement in the whole exciting project. The regular quarterly fold-up news journal, *Music Stand*, was given a face-lift and transformed into a more prestigious-looking glossy magazine. Subscribers and patrons receive this automatically. Other forms of personal sponsorship were introduced, in addition to the corporate sponsorship already established - on the American model it has to be said. Individual supporters can endow a player's chair, or be a member of the Music Director's Circle or a plain Patron, all three categories involving the donation of useful sums of money of up to £1,200 a year, over and above the ticket prices of course. Public funding continues and the revenue from that in the 2004-2005 season for example included £1.8 million (Arts Council) and £1.2 million (the City). Ticket sales in Birmingham yielded £1.6 million, sponsors and patrons adding some £571,554 to the total. Engagements elsewhere, but especially abroad, brought nearly another half a million pounds. The cost of preparing for and carrying out the whole programme in that season was £5.7 million, and management and administrative costs added up to £1.1 million. The actual processes of fund-raising itself added another £271,531 to the total expenditure. If we compare that with the orchestra's initial grant of £1,200 in 1920, even allowing for inflation, we see just how far the enterprise has progressed.

It can be seen from the above 2004-2005 figures that the orchestra's fortunes have not collapsed since the departure of Simon Rattle. His successor, Sakari Oramo (the stress on *both* first syllables of his name) has proved himself up to the daunting task of following Rattle. A first-class violinist, he brings commitment, musical imagination and expressiveness of the highest order to the performances he conducts. Audiences who hear him - if smaller in number, sadly, than they were - always respond to Oramo with enthusiastic warmth and a growing respect. The only regret is that more people do not realise what they are missing. The orchestra's performance in Symphony Hall of Elgar's *Dream of Gerontius,* under Oramo, on 3rd October 2000 attracted the following description from Geoff Brown in *The Times*: 'An orchestra alive to the score's every nuance, from the Prelude's sinuous opening to the 'sullen howl' of the brass's demons, or the stab and shudder on the word 'moment' as Gerontius's soul faces God's judgement'. Oramo has been equally effective as a violinist in music in a very different style. Part of a review in this current year, 2006, by the *Birmingham Post* Music Critic, Christopher Morley, demonstrated this. 'The event saw Oramo relinquishing the podium to preside with his violin over a little orchestral gem and embellishing one of the greatest orchestral masterpieces in a way which had me, a veteran Mozartean and hard-boiled critic, on the edge of my seat with excitement'.

Sadly we now know that Oramo will relinquish his post in 2008. He will have completed ten years with the orchestra, a period in which, it is fair to say, he has most effectively achieved what might have seemed to have been the impossible task, that of following Simon Rattle. Pleasingly, both men shared the conducting at a concert at Symphony Hall in memory of George Jonas, the orchestra's Chairman from 1974 to 1992, on 19th March 2006. It is a tribute to both conductors that the playing of the orchestra continues to be in the top class.

Branches off the main stem
A number of other musical initiatives occurred which still further widened the scope of what was on offer to the Birmingham musical public. The completion of the purpose-built CBSO Centre in Berkley Street in the Summer of 1998 meant not only a permanent home for the Administration and for orchestral rehearsals, but

Sakari Oramo.

also provided a concert venue. At last members of the orchestra were able to form various ensembles for the performance of chamber music and a regular programme is mounted. Especially dear to Simon Rattle himself was the establishment already of the Birmingham Contemporary Music Group (BCMG) in 1987. This now thrives as a separate organisation working at the CBSO Centre. They have built up an admittedly specialised audience and are making a number of impressive recordings. BCMG also have an educational programme and a scheme for encouraging the sponsorship of new compositions. This is called *Sound Investment*, originally initiated by one of the orchestral players. Under the same umbrella, so to speak, are BEAST (Birmingham Electro Acoustic Sound Theatre) and some Birmingham Jazz events. BEAST was established in the early 1980s by the composer, Jonty Harrison, a member of the Music staff at the University of Birmingham. Formed in 1976, Birmingham Jazz itself has promoted up to 110 jazz events a year in various local music venues. Since 1984, there has also been a thriving International Jazz Festival in the city.

In a totally different area of music, in 1991 the then leader of the orchestra, Peter Thomas, formed the Birmingham Ensemble, mainly from members of the orchestra. This was devoted to the smaller-scale repertoire of all periods, using mainly, though not entirely, string players. Three City of Birmingham Symphony Youth Choruses

Simon Halsey (photograph by Alan Wood).

now function which give enormous pleasure and inspiration to their listeners, when they appear, with some assured and accomplished performances. The orchestra has a vigorous and imaginative education programme under its Education Manager, Keith Stubbs and, as well as visits by players to those schools which respond to the orchestra's offer to arrange these, two major Youth Concerts at Symphony Hall are presented each year.

The CBSO Chorus, founded before Simon Rattle arrived in Birmingham, had immediately won high praise. We have already met them in a previous chapter (chapter 28). In 1982, however, Simon Halsey came to take charge of the Chorus and brought to the task that same capacity to make everyone *really* work and give of their utmost that Rattle brought to the orchestra. By 1994 the Chorus had achieved independent status and is now known as the City of Birmingham Symphony

Chorus, undertaking its own independent programme, not least outside Birmingham itself, with other orchestras for example. They too attract wide critical acclaim and are in demand for recordings.

Conclusion 2006

Since its inception in 1920, the City of Birmingham Symphony Orchestra has quite clearly been at the heart of the city's musical life. The writer has called it the city's musical flagship, comparing its role to that of the Musical Festivals in the late eighteenth and nineteenth centuries. This comparison would not have been valid without an account of how, since 1980, the city orchestra has regained that international dimension that the Festivals had. The spin-offs from this growth in stature cannot now be left out of this brief concluding survey of music in Birmingham today.

A major symphony orchestra, generally regarded as world-class and giving regular concerts in the city, naturally demands a concert hall to match it, something the Town Hall did not provide. This must surely be seen as the final spur to satisfying the long-standing demands for a worthy concert hall for the city. Given that fine new concert hall at last, the hall itself demanded a fuller programme of music, and not just for economic reasons. In the event, all this provided an opportunity to mount an international season of concerts, presenting the greatest ensembles and soloists from all over the world to the citizens of Birmingham and the Midlands. Regaining the heights indeed - the Rattle effect.

The International Concerts Season at Symphony Hall is now of course a major part of Birmingham's musical life. The Director of the Hall, Andrew Jowett, who had been Director of the Warwick Arts Centre and in his early career Assistant General Manager at the Crucible Theatre in Sheffield, was responsible for this and for the artistic programming generally. This includes a wide spectrum of music, including world musics and popular music. In the classical music area he was assisted by his Special Projects Manager, Lyndon Jenkins, who came to the task with wide experience in presenting classical music, especially to radio audiences, both nationally and locally. Audience support has been fostered by the establishment of a Friends of Symphony Hall and the institution of a subscription system. Corporate sponsorship is also a vital part of this support. Since 2001, the magnificent organ, built by Klais, has been complete and is used for frequent recitals given by prestigious visitors as well as by Birmingham's own distinguished organists, including of course our City Organist, Thomas Trotter.

With Birmingham's music now at this elevated level, it was seen as not at all inappropriate for the city to be chosen as the home of a first-class ballet company. In 1990, the Royal Ballet took the bold step of moving its sister company, Sadlers Wells Royal Ballet, from London to Birmingham and renaming it Birmingham

Royal Ballet, with its main base in the city. As a consequence, the city has been able to see regular, first-class performances of ballets, under its present Artistic Director and brilliant choreographer, David Bintley. Memorable productions have included *Hobson's Choice* and *Far from the Madding Crowd*, both to very expressive, specially-composed music by Paul Reade, *The Rake's Progress* to Stravinsky's music, *The Enigma Variations* with amazingly sensitive representations of Elgar's various friends, and a *King Arthur* trilogy with music commissioned from John McCabe. All these are in addition to their spectacular and ever popular production of Tchaikovsky's *The Nutcracker*. The company also tours of course. The Ballet Orchestra is known as the Royal Ballet Sinfonia and has, also, a separate existence, giving independent concerts at Symphony Hall and other major venues and playing for ballet companies, in both cases world-wide.

Meanwhile friends whom we have already met, for example the Welsh National Opera, the Chamber Music Society, Ex Cathedra, our organists, the Birmingham Bach Choir and other long-established choirs such as the City of Birmingham Choir and, the oldest of them all, the Festival Choral Society, all continue to add to the musical feast.

So today in Birmingham every kind of music now in existence, from 'rap' to Rachmaninov, can be heard in and around the city. Musically it has everything and so far at least, Birmingham can still also enjoy a comprehensive range of music drawn from the the best of our pan-European classical music tradition, now almost a thousand years old; and all this excellently performed in pleasant surroundings. We read attractively-presented programme notes and anticipate hearing a first-class performance. The city is a centre of classical music which again draws listeners from all over the Midlands and from London, and performers from all over the world, as it did in the nineteenth century. It seems like the fulfilment of every dream Birmingham's earlier music organisers ever had in their most optimistic moments. But for how long? In the CBSO's Annual Report for 1999 to 2000, the orchestra's Chief Executive, Stephen Maddock was drawing attention to 'a severe contraction in classical recordings and the difficulty of securing worthwhile work for the orchestra outside Birmingham'.

Against this, many will no doubt point to some of the wonderful music-making being achieved by young people, not least by the CBSO's recently established Youth Orchestra. As has been said, CBSO Youth Choruses are most impressive and the CBSO itself plays well-attended concerts for young people. Other educational projects continue, apparently successfully. The Birmingham University Music Department, established in 1905 with Elgar as its first professor, is currently a highly-respected department, gaining high ratings both for its teaching and for its research projects and thus very attractive to students. To date (2006) it has produced 1500 music graduates The Department also, incidentally, still presents an excellent season of concerts, usually in the Barber Institute of Fine Art. The Birmingham Conservatoire continues its upward course under the present Principal, George Caird, doing everything it can to establish itself as a first-class training ground for performers. As an earlier chapter has indicated, this has not been an easy task, since the organisation started out with a completely different ethos and in the difficult financial and cultural climate of the twentieth century, the resources to make real change were not always forthcoming as has already been described.

And the schools?
This is the 64 thousand dollar question. There is really no argument now about the fact that Music provision in schools is very patchy indeed. Where it is good it is often very good and probably more imaginative then it used to be, but all too often it is poor, taught by a non-specialist perhaps, or altogether absent. There is all too often nothing to help young people to engage with classical music as a source of deep satisfaction and enjoyment and to counteract the all-pervasive presence of the multi-billion pound pop industry which follows us everywhere. More insidious than that, possibly, is the fact that the GCSE and A-level Music syllabuses have been 'dumbed-down', so that they no longer ask for anything like as much evidence of a candidate's real ability to cope with degree or diploma courses. There are even proposals afoot considering the removal of classical music from some A-level Music exam syllabuses altogether. At best, in Music as in other subjects, much of a first year course at university is frequently spent teaching what should have been learned at school. In other words, lower standards are being built into the system.

We need to guard the present classical musical riches we can enjoy in Birmingham and guard them fiercely. There is concern about ageing audiences, but with the educational situation outlined above, where will the new young audience members come from? Many young people no longer see classical music as at all relevant to them, and all too often nothing some of the schools do disabuses them of this idea or gives them the chance of being intelligently introduced to it in a deeper and more rewarding way. More fundamentally, certain teacher-training gurus no longer see it as the task of teachers to open up new horizons, or expose youngsters to the greatest works of thought, literature, art or music. Thus do they, in their infinite self-satisfaction, throw away a thousand years of our culture. Surely these things are part of our heritage to which *every* child has a right to be introduced.

To end on a positive note then, all of those who value classical music must actively see to it that it is not allowed to be marginalised. Let us not betray what James Kempson, Joseph Moore, William Stockley, George Halford, Neville Chamberlain, Simon Rattle and many others, have laboured to give us over the centuries. In a report on a conference held in London on 21st September 2005, entitled *A future for Classical Music in Britain?* [2] Colin Timms, our current Peyton and Barber Professor of Music at the University of Birmingham commented that 'the social and economic context is forbidding but can be changed over time'.

So it is up to us. In the one word of Birmingham's motto - Forward!

1. See biography of Simon Rattle. Appendix No.2.
2. Report of Conference on *A Future for Classical Music in Britain*. London, 21st September 2005.

Symphony Hall.

Appendix No. 1

Office holders in the musical world in Birmingham

1. **City Organists**
Thomas Munden	1834-37
George Hollins	1837-41
James Stimpson	1842-86
C. W. Perkins	1888-1923
G. D. Cunningham	1924-48
George Thalben-Ball	1948-83
Thomas Trotter	1983-

2. **Organists at St Philip's Church**
Barnabas Gunn	1715-30
William de St. Thunes	1733-1735
John Ohio Eversmann	1735-1765
Jeremiah Clarke	1765-1803
Bishop Simms	1803-29
Henry Simms	1829-71
C. J. B. Meacham	1871-88
Yates Mander	1888-98
A. G. Thompson	1898-1901
Arthur Elmore	1901-06
Edwin Stephenson	1906-14
William F. Dunnill	1914-36
Willis Grant	1936-58
Thomas Tunnard	1958-67
Roy Massey	1968-74
David Bruce-Payne	1974-78
Hubert Best	1978-85
Marcus Huxley	1986-

   The data in this section (2) should be treated with some caution where the earlier dates are concerned.

3. **Midland Institute School of Music and Birmingham School of Music Principals**

Granville Bantock	1900-34
A. K. Blackall	1934-45
Christopher Edmunds	1945-56
Steuart Wilson	1957-60
Gordon Clinton	1960-73
Louis Carus	1973-87
Roy Wales	1987-89
Kevin Thompson	1989-93
George Caird	1993-

4. **Peyton and Barber Professors of Music, University of Birmingham**

Edward Elgar	1905-08
Granville Bantock	1908-34
Victor Hely-Hutchinson	1934-44
J. A. Westrup	1944-47
Anthony Lewis	1947-68
Ivor Keys	1968-86
Basil Deane	1987-92
Colin Timms	1992-

Elgar Professor of Music

Stephen Banfield	1992-2003

5. **City of Birmingham Symphony Orchestra**

A. **Principal Conductors and Musical Directors**

Appleby Matthews	1920-24
Adrian Boult	1924-30
Leslie Heward	1930-43
George Weldon	1944-51
Rudolf Schwarz	1951-57
Andrzej Panufnik	1957-59
Adrian Boult	1959-60
Hugo Rignold	1960-68
Louis Frémaux	1969-78
Simon Rattle	1980-98
Sakari Oramo	1998-2008

B. Staff conductors

Richard Wassell	1920-23
Joseph Lewis	1924-28
Harold Gray	1932-79
Meredith Davies	1957-60
Maurice Handford	1970-74

Principal Guest Conductors

Erich Schmid	1979-83
Neeme Järvi	1983-85
Okko Kamu	1985-88
Mark Elder	1992-95

Appendix No. 2

Biographical notes on some of the people mentioned in the text 1834-1992

PAUL BEARD 1901-1986. Violinist, born in Birmingham. Followed Alex Cohen as leader of the City of Birmingham Orchestra in 1921. In 1932 he went to London as leader of the London Philharmonic Orchestra, and to the BBC Symphony Orchestra in the same capacity in 1936. He was a violin professor at the Royal College of Music.

His father, J. A. Beard, was a viola player who led the violas in Halford's Orchestra and also played in the CBO. Paul Beard himself also played the viola, and the programme of one of the orchestra's first concerts, that conducted by Elgar on 10th November 1920, reveals him leading the viola section, with his father playing in the same section. An uncle, F. W. Beard, conducted the City Choral Society.

ERIC BLOM 1888-1959. See chapter 28. Scholars and composers section.

RUTLAND BOUGHTON 1878-1960. Born in Aylesbury. Studied composition with Stanford at the Royal College of Music in London. Was on the staff of the Midland Institute School of Music from 1904 until 1911, teaching the Rudiments of Music. He also conducted the New Choral Society in Birmingham. Between 1914 and 1925, he attempted to found a 'British Bayreuth' at Glastonbury, hoping to build a permanent festival theatre there. This scheme had the support of Elgar. The theme of the operas was to be *Arthur in Britain*. His *Immortal Hour* (1914) was successful and *The Round Table, Alkestis, The Queen of Cornwall* and *The Ever-Young* also had a hearing. The Birmingham Repertory Company staged *The Immortal Hour* and in 1922 the production was taken to the Regent Theatre, London, where it had a long run. *Bethlehem,* a setting of the Coventry mystery plays was also heard at the same theatre, and *Alkestis* was given at Covent Garden by the British National Opera Company in 1924. The latter was not well-received in London, though the company took it to a number of provincial theatres.

In about 1927, Boughton left Glastonbury with his dream of a permanent theatre unfulfilled. He wrote two more Arthurian operas between 1943 and 1946. These were *Galahad* and *Avalon;* they were never performed. He wrote a relatively small number of works in other genres. His daughter, Joy Boughton, was known in London orchestral circles as a very good oboist.

WILLIAM HAVERGAL BRIAN 1876-1972. Born in Dresden, in Staffordshire, Brian was a self-taught and cruelly neglected composer. He wrote 32 symphonies and five operas, as well as some choral works, much of all this still in manuscript.

It is true that works by him were performed, between 1907 and 1921, by noted musicians such as Thomas Beecham, Julius Harrison, Dan Godfrey, Granville Bantock and Henry Wood, but these were mainly provincial events. Brian's *English Suite* for orchestra (1903-4) and his comedy overture, *Dr. Merryheart* (1911-12), were included in the Queens Hall repertoire, in London, by Henry Wood, in 1915, but these occasional opportunities were not sufficient to compensate for Brian's lack of the right social and musical connections. *Dr. Merryheart* had previously been introduced in Birmingham in 1913 by Julius Harrison. Only the genius of an Elgar could manage to overcome the sort of disadvantages Brian suffered, but even Elgar had found it extremely difficult to break through the 'London - Oxbridge - and foreign' domination of the music scene at that time.

Brian is perhaps better known to us now as a local correspondent and critic for *The Musical World* (Manchester and Hallé correspondent), also for the *Musical Times* and for *Musical Opinion,* which he worked for from 1927 to 1940, and whose deputy editor he became. He contributed to many other papers and journals - not all specialist musical ones - but his writings in *Musical Opinion* reveal a large hearted, open minded musician, able to appreciate music both new and old, both 'serious' and less serious. Some of the best of these pieces have been collected together in one volume by Malcolm MacDonald and entitled *Havergal Brian on Music.* It is listed in the bibliography and has been drawn on, on several occasions, in this book.

He lived in Birmingham between January 1916 and May 1919, successively in Alum Rock, Erdington and Edgbaston (27 Beaufort Road).

ROSINA BUCKMAN, soprano. Born in New Zealand, ca. 1885. Died in London, 1948. She came to Birmingham at the age of 16 to attend the Midland Institute School of Music. Took part in the good opera productions being presented after Bantock became Principal of the School in 1900. Had to return to New Zealand because of ill-health and consequently did not make her operatic debut until 1911, this with the Melba Grand Opera Company in Australia. She returned to England in 1913, and in 1915 became a leading soprano with the Beecham Opera Company staying with them until 1920. She sang at Covent Garden in 1922 and 1923, was a member of the British National Opera Company and went on a world tour, in the 1922-23 season, with her husband, the tenor Maurice d'Oisly. Her performances as Aida, Butterfly and Isolde were particularly admired. She later taught at the Royal Academy of Music.

FANNY DAVIES 1861-1934. Born in Guernsey, but spent her early years in Birmingham receiving piano teaching from Charles Flavell and harmony and counterpoint lessons from A. R. Gaul. Thereafter she went to the Leipzig Conservatoire and then to the Frankfurt Conservatoire where she spent two formative years under the tuition of Clara Schumann.

Fanny Davies was always in great demand both at home and in Europe. A Myra Hess of the previous generation, and possibly even more contributive, Fanny Davies was known for her masterly playing of Beethoven, as well as for her collaboration, in chamber music of the finest kind, with artists such as the violinist, Joachim, and the 'cellist, Casals. She also played the music of her contemporaries and, in addition, pieces originally written for the virginals by William Byrd. In carrying on a successful career she sought also to serve music.

The following is a review of an early recording made by her.

A PUPIL OF CLARA SCHUMANN IN SCHUMANN'S PIANO CONCERTO

Columbia: Fanny Davies, pianist with Ernst Ansermet, conducting the Royal Philharmonic Orchestra.

Fanny Davies, pupil in the first place of the Alfred A. Gaul whose portrait appears on another page, was from 1883 to 1885 a pupil of Clara Schumann's at the Frankfort Conservatory. 'She imbibed from her great teacher,' says Mr. Colles, 'all that was finest in the tradition and ideals which Mme. Schumann represented, and returned to her own country to perpetuate and extend both'.

'It was on October 17th, 1885, that she first played in England on her return from working under Schumann's wife; and ever since she has been steadily before the public. Her performance of the Schumann piano concerto is therefore not only mellowed and made perfectly consistent by more than 40 years of experience, but it is traditional and authoritative. Miss Davies brings to us the strong, quiet, fluent art of the middle of the 19th century, - Schumann, as Schumann lived in his wife's musicianship. The little intermezzo takes us into a haven of peace (the gramophone reproduction is exceedingly happy). All through the work there is a rare purity of tone, in orchestra no less than piano'.

Source: *The British Musician*. Editor. Sydney Grew. April, 1929.

SYDNEY GREW 1879-1946. Born and died in Birmingham. Studied at the Midland Institute School of Music. Writer on music, his books included:
  Our Favourite Musicians: from Stanford to Holbrooke
  Favourite Musical Performers: from John Coates to Albert Sammons
  Masters of Music: Purcell to Liszt
  Makers of Music: Singers & Instrumentalists.

A *Book of English Prosody:*
See also Chapter 28. Scholars and composers section.

GEORGE HALFORD. Born Chilvers Coton, Warwickshire, probably in 1858. Died at Kidlington, Oxford, February 1933 at the age of 74.

George Halford lived in Birmingham from 1875 until his retirement. He was taught music by his father, a good violinist, and learned to play several instruments. He was trained in Birmingham as a pianist by Swinnerton Heap. He also gained the FRCO diploma. He had been a church organist from the age of 16, first at Attleborough and then at St. Mary's and St. George's, Birmingham. He then followed Dr. Heap at St. John's, Wolverhampton – and married a Wolverhampton girl. Thereafter he went as organist to St Michael's Church, Handsworth.

In 1886 Halford became conductor of the Birmingham Choral and Orchestral Association, in 1891 he took over the Institute's Madrigal Choir from Stockley and in 1892 became a teacher of piano at the Institute School of Music, and conductor of its affiliated orchestra. He remained on the staff of the Midland Institute School of Music until 1928.

He started his orchestral concerts, officially the Birmingham Concerts Society, in 1897 and they ran for ten years. (See chapters 22 and 23). Halford's work with his orchestra in Birmingham made him widely respected and he was invited to conduct the London Symphony Orchestra at the Albert Hall and to go to direct some of the Bournemouth orchestra's concerts.

He retired to Cleeve Prior, then to Oxford, where died. He is buried at Cleeve Prior.

CHARLES SWINNERTON HEAP 1847-1900. Heap, who was born and died in Birmingham, lived most of his life here. He resided for a period of time at 22 Clarendon Road, off Hagley Road, not far from the Oratory. He attended King Edward's School and sang in the choir as a soprano at the 1858 Musical Festival. He was articled to the organist of York Minister for two years and in 1865 won the Mendelssohn scholarship to the Leipzig Conservatoire where he also spent two years. After that, he was a pupil of W. T. Best, the noted organist, in Liverpool.

From 1868, Heap worked in Birmingham, gaining a Mus. B. and Mus. D. of Cambridge University in 1870 and 1871 by means of compositions which greatly impressed the Professor, Sterndale Bennett. From then on, Heap was probably best known as a highly successful and enterprising choral conductor, taking on the Wolverhampton Festival Choral Society and conducting the 1883 and 1886 festivals there, and the North Staffordshire Festival at Hanley from 1888 to 1889. It was from this a natural progression to becoming Birmingham's Festival Choral Society conductor on Stockley's retirement in 1897.

Heap also conducted the Birmingham Philharmonic Union from 1870 until its demise in 1886 and taught at the Midland Institute School of Music from 1895 to 1896, as well as privately. (He taught George Halford q.v.)

He wrote some chamber and choral works, and played as pianist with other first class artists in chamber music concerts. His early death at the age of 43 was a great loss to Birmingham, and, occurring as it did, just before the rehearsals for the first performance of the *Dream of Gerontius*, also deprived Elgar of what would probably have been a much more successful occasion.

JOHANN HOCK 1876-1946. A Dutch 'cellist, born in Amsterdam and died in Birmingham. He played in the Concertgebouw Orchestra from 1892 to 1898. He came to Birmingham in 1898 and remained. In 1903 he became conductor of the Birmingham Orchestral Society and was a member of the Catterall Quartet from its foundation in 1911. He played in Halford's orchestra, held chamber music classes and gave 'cello and piano recitals at the Midland Institute for the students. In 1932, he formed the Birmingham Philharmonic String Orchestra. He was a very good teacher and had many pupils at the Midland Institute School of Music.

WALTER HYDE 1875-1951. See chapter 13, penultimate paragraph.

APPLEBY MATTHEWS. See chapters 23 and 27.

ALFRED MELLON 1820-67. Born and died in London. Conductor, composer, violinist. He spent his early years in Birmingham where, as a young man he played in and led the Theatre Royal Orchestra (See chapter 10). We should not forget that in the 1840s, this still involved directing and preparing the orchestra in and for, its performances. Mellon was successful at his job, and as a consequence gained a number of prestigious appointments in London. Those he had trained and worked with in Birmingham gained the respect of no less a person than Elgar, who played with some of them in Birmingham. Mellon led the ballet orchestra at Covent Garden, was director of music at the Haymarket and Adelphi Theatres, conductor of the Pyne and Harrison Opera Company (in which capacity he would revisit Birmingham) and conductor of the Musical Society and of the Mellon Promenade Concerts, begun at the Floral Hall, Covent Garden, in 1860. In 1865 he was appointed conductor of the Liverpool Philharmonic Society.

He wrote songs for plays, and he produced his opera *Victorine* at Covent Garden in 1859.

MAX MOSSEL 1871-1929. Born and died in Holland. Violinist and brother of Isaac Mossel who taught Johann Hock (q.v.). He was a precocious musician, appearing in public at the age of 7. He went to the Rotterdam School of Music and subsequently led the Arnhem Orchestra, the Concertgebouw Orchestra and the orchestra in Biarritz.

He moved to England where, from 1894 to 1929 he taught violin at the Midland Institute School of Music in Birmingham. He also taught at the Guildhall School of Music. He gave many concerts, formed and led a string quartet, but is perhaps best known in Birmingham for the excellent series of Max Mossel Concerts which he promoted in the city and also elsewhere, including Glasgow. First class programmes and first class artists were their hall-mark. See chapter 25.

ERNEST NEWMAN 1868-1959. Born William Roberts, in Lancaster, son of Seth Roberts, a master tailor. Young William Roberts moved to Liverpool on leaving school, and worked for the Bank of Liverpool. He remained in that city until 1904. He early developed an amazing knowledge of music and began writing about it, contributing articles and programme notes for Rodewald's concerts in Liverpool and for the Hallé Society. In order to keep this activity hidden from the bank, he adopted the *nom de plume* Ernest Newman, a name he decided to adopt permanently.

He married in 1894 and had a house in Grove Street, Liverpool. He wrote a successful book on Gluck and decided to give up banking for music. While in the Liverpool area he met Granville Bantock who was organising his enterprising concerts over the water, in New Brighton. This led to his invitation, in 1904, to go as a teacher of voice production (what did Charles Lunn think?) and theory to the Midland Institute School of Music. Newman hated the work and moved to Manchester in 1905 as Music Critic of the *Manchester Guardian* as it then was. Restrictions imposed by them, and a better offer from the *Birmingham Daily Post,* brought him back to Birmingham at a higher salary than with the *Guardian,* and with freedom to write whatever else he thought fit. There he remained, from 1906 to 1919, moving to *The Observer* in London in the latter year. Grief-stricken when his first wife died in 1918, after a painful illness, he later married a Birmingham opera student whom he and his first wife had befriended.

He wrote some twenty or so books, including several on Wagner, his life and his operas, also on Liszt, Hugo Wolf, Elgar, and in 1923, on Solo Singing. A substantial number of these were written during his time in Birmingham.

ADELA JUANA MARIA PATTI (ADELINA PATTI) 1843-1919. Adelina Patti was born in Madrid, of Italian parents who were both opera singers, and on tour - almost on stage - when their youngest daughter was born. She evinced a precocious vocal talent. She was born to sing, and to sing in public, and never had any 'nerves'. Her father was manager of the Italian opera in New York for a time and, from the ages of eight to twelve, Adelina sang at public concerts in America under the direction of her brother-in-law, Maurice Strakosch. Strakosch had married her elder sister Amalia. Wisely Adelina was withdrawn from public work between about 1855 and 1859 to complete musical, vocal and other studies. She studied piano with her sister, Carlotta.

In 1859, at the age of sixteen she was ready to be launched on her long and brilliant public career. She went on a short concert tour to the West Indies with Gottschalk, returned to make her New York debut as Lucia in Donizetti's *Lucia di Lammermoor*. In that, as in other roles she was highly successful. Her London début in 1861 was in *La Sonnambula* and in that year she came to the Birmingham Musical Festival, the first of her seventeen visits to the town. Thereafter she appeared regularly in London and Paris, and occasionally in Italy and America, singing about thirty roles at Covent Garden, and undertaking provincial concert tours covering England and Ireland. She was the highest-paid singer of the time, commanding a fee of 200 guineas (£210, or about £7,500 now). She lived like a queen, only for her singing, able to leave the small details of daily life to others. She is said never to have become emotional over anything, a facet of her personality reflected by a certain lack of fire in her singing and acting. The voice more than compensated for this, and is considered in more detail in chapter 11.

She created a superb retirement home, complete with theatre, at Craig-y-Nos Castle, near Brecon, in Wales. There she was visited by many illustrious people, issuing forth occasionally to give concerts in aid of charity. She gave her last concert in 1914, at the Albert Hall, in aid of the Red Cross War Fund. She was 71 years of age. She died at home, after a brief illness, at the age of 75. She was the last of the line of great *coloratura* sopranos which had included Catalani, Pasta and Grisi.

She married three times. Her first marriage, a totally mistaken enterprise, ended in divorce. Her second husband, the tenor Nicolini, died in 1898, and her third husband, Baron Cederstrom outlived her by many years, dying in 1947.

CARLOTTA PATTI 1835-89. An older sister of Adelina, Carlotta originally trained as a pianist, but turned to concert singing in which she was very successful. She was lame, however, a circumstance which precluded her from making the kind of career in opera which her sister did. She ultimately settled in Paris where she died.
She sang in Birmingham for a Percy Harrison concert in 1875.

SIMON RATTLE. Born in Liverpool in 1955 of musically gifted parents. Father, Denis, was managing director of an import-export company, but had played with the University dance band while up at Oxford. Mother, Pauline, had run a music shop in Dover, and had a great influence on her son's musical development, as did the boy's older sister, a patient assistant. Bartók and Schoenberg formed a part of his early musical diet, as well as Mahler, Walton and Shostakovich, and the future conductor came relatively late to the so-called, standard repertoire.

Piano lessons at prep school were part of early, formal music education, as was membership, as a percussionist, of the Merseyside Youth Orchestra when a teenager. He had already attended European Summer Schools for Young Musicians, from 1966. In 1967, he was elected student of the year by the Liverpool Youth Music Committee, a body sponsored by the Education Authority from the early 1950s. This led to a performance, as piano soloist, with the Liverpool Concert Orchestra. In 1970 Simon Rattle conducted his first symphony concert, one for the Liverpool Spastic Fellowship. This was an incredibly ambitious project, using the services of amateur and professional players, including some from the Royal Liverpool Philharmonic Orchestra. The venture was a musical success and it revealed, in spite of the somewhat hysterical publicity surrounding the event, Simon Rattle's true conducting talent which had to be taken seriously. Progress was only a matter of time.

Simon Rattle entered the Royal Academy of Music at the age of 16, played once for the National Youth Orchestra, did some composing and embarked on a conducting career which has involved him in work with many orchestras, starting in Liverpool with the Merseyside Youth Orchestra and the Liverpool Philharmonic Orchestra, subsequently moving onto the world scene of conducting. He is now of course accepted as a conductor of international repute. His transformation of the CBSO and his subsequent move to the Berlin Philharmonic Orchestra is detailed in the text. (chapters 27 and 29).

DOROTHY SILK 1884-1942, soprano. Born near Birmingham, died at Alvechurch, Worcestershire. Soprano. First appearance in public at the age of four. She studied at the Midland Institute School of Music and then went to Vienna for tuition. First complete London recital in London in 1920, when already 36. Sang as a soloist with the London Bach Choir in the same year and this established her reputation as an ideal singer of Bach and Schütz's music. She also sang the less familiar music of the seventeenth and eighteenth centuries, while at the same time making a profound and moving impression as Savitri in Holst's chamber opera of that name, and as the Virgin Mary in Rutland Boughton's *Bethlehem*. She had a light, charming and flexible voice.

Bibliography

Constance Bache: *Brother Musicians*. Reminiscences of Edward and Walter Bache. London, 1901.

Lady Bell (Florence Bell): *At the Works*. A study of a manufacturing town. London, 1985.

Vivian Bird: *The Priestley Riots, 1791, and the Lunar Society*. (BMI) Birmingham, 1991.

David Brock: *The Birmingham School of Music - its first century*. Birmingham, 1986 (typescript).

Michael Broome: A *Choice Collection of Twenty-Four Psalm Tunes in Four Parts*. Birmingham, 1744.

Michael Broome: A *Collection of Psalm Tunes in IV Parts*. Birmingham, 1760.

J. T. Bunce: *Birmingham Sixty Years Ago*. Compiled from notes written for the Birmingham Weekly Post, 1899, and based on personal recollections.

trans. David Cairns: *The Memoirs of Hector Berlioz*. London, 1969.

William Camden: *Britannia*. 1586.

Cornish's Birmingham Year Book, 1915-1916.

J. W. Cross: *George Eliot's Life*. London, 1885.

Lance E. Davis and Robert A. Huttenback: *Mammon and the Pursuit of Empire*. (The Political Economy of British Imperialism 1860-1912). Oxford, 1986.

A. Deakin: *History of the Birmingham Festival Choral Society*.

Frank Downes: *Around the Horn*. Birmingham, 1994.

William Dugdale: *Antiquities of Warwickshire*. 1656.

E. Edwards: *Some account of the Origin of the Musical Festivals and of James Kempson, the originator*. Birmingham, 1882 (Article in *Birmingham Institutions*. Birmingham Central Library).

English Court Music: *Records of English Court Music*. The Lord Chamberlain's Papers. Music Library, University of Birmingham).

Roger Fiske: *English Theatre Music in the Eighteenth Century*. Oxford, 1986.

Antonia Fraser: *Cromwell our Chief of Men*. London, 1973.

John Freeth: *The Political Songster* or a *Touch on the Times on Various Subjects and adapted to common tunes*. Birmingham, 1790.

Conrad Gill and Asa Briggs: *History of Birmingham*. London, 1952.

Grove: *Dictionary of Music and Musicians*. Fifth edition (Editor: Eric Blom). London, 1961.

Bibliography

Michael Hall: *'Who knows but it may continue'*. 200 years of Methodism in Quinton. Great Britain, 1984.

Margaret Handford: *The RBSA/Midland Musicians Concerts. 1968 to 1978.* Birmingham, 2001 (Copies to view in Birmingham Central Library, Local Studies Department).

Richard H. Hoppin: *Medieval Music.* USA, 1978.

William Hutton: *An History of Birmingham.* First edition, 1780. The Second Edition with considerable additions. Birmingham, 1783.

Maud Karpeles, revised Peter Kennedy: *An Introduction to English Folk Song.* Oxford, 1987.

Nicholas Kenyon: *Simon Rattle. The making of a conductor.* London, 1987.

Nicholas Kenyon: *Simon Rattle. From Birmingham to Berlin.* London, 2001.

Beresford King-Smith: *Crescendo! A history of the City of Birmingham Symphony Orchestra.* Great Britain, 1995.

J. A. Langford: A *Century of Birmingham Life* or *A Chronicle of Local Events.* 2 volumes. 1741-1841. London, 1868.

J. A. Langford: *Modern Birmingham and its Institutions.* 2 volumes 1841-71. Birmingham, 1873.

John Leland: *Itinerary in England* ca. 1533-39. Edited by J. Toulmin Smith, 1905-10.

A. L. Lloyd: *Folk Song in England.* London, 1967.

Margaret Lowe: *James Mathew and his Marvellous Flute.* (Article in *The Magazine of the Black Country.* Winter, 1991 Vol. 25 no. 1).

Lunar Society: *An Exhibition to Commemorate the Bicentenary of the Lunar Society of Birmingham* (Booklet). Birmingham Museum and Art Gallery. 13th Oct. to 27th Nov. 1966. (Introduction by Eric Robinson, Senior Lecturer in Economic History, University of Manchester).

ed. Malcolm MacDonald: *Havergal Brian on Music. Selections from his Journalism.* Volume one: *British Music.* Great Britain, 1986.

E. O. Mackerness: *Somewhere further North.* A History of Music in Sheffield. Sheffield, 1974, ed. W. Thomas Marrocco and Nicholas Sandon: *Medieval Music.* The Oxford Anthology of Music. Oxford, 1977.

Jerrold Northrop Moore: *Edward Elgar. A Creative Life.* Oxford, 1984.

William Moughton: *The Story of Birmingham's Growth Interwoven with the Growth of the Nation.*

J. H. Muirhead: *Birmingham Institutions.* Birmingham, 1911.

New Grove Dictionary of Music and Musicians. Second edition. Editor: Stanley Sadie. London, 2000.

New Oxford History of Music: Volume 11. *Early Medieval Music to 1300.* Editor: Dom Anselm Hughes. London, 1954.

Fiona M. Palmer: *The First Fifty Years. The Barber Evening Concerts and Operas.* Birmingham, 1996.

Roy Palmer: A *Ballad History of England from 1588 to the Present Day*. London, 1979.
Charles E. Pearce: *Sims Reeves*. London, 1924.
Henry Pleasants: *The Great Singers*. London, 1967.
William Poutney: A *History of the Festivals,* 1899.
    (In Manuscript. Birmingham Central Library, Archives).
Mrs. Richard Powell: *Edward Elgar. Memories of a Variation*. London, 1947.
Victor J Price: *Birmingham Theatres, Concert and Music Halls 1740-1988*. Studley, Warwicks, 1988.
Henry Raynor: A *Social History of Music: From the middle ages to Beethoven*. London, 1972.
W. H. Reed: *Elgar as I knew him*. London, 1936, re-issued 1973.
Harold Rosenthal and John Warrack: *The Concise Oxford Dictionary of Opera*. Second edition. Oxford, 1979.
Marie B. Rowlands: *The West Midlands from AD. 1000. A Regional History of England*. London, 1987.
John Sant: *Albert W. Ketèlbey 1875-1959*. Great Britain, 2000.
Percy A. Scholes: *The Mirror of Music*. London, 1947.
Victor Skipp: A *History of Greater Birmingham - down to 1830*. Birmingham, 1980.
Victor Skipp: *The Making of Victorian Birmingham*. Birmingham, 1983.
J. Sutcliffe Smith: *The Story of Music in Birmingham*. Birmingham, 1945.
W. C. Stockley: *Fifty Years of Music in Birmingham*. Birmingham, 1913.
John Stone: *Music in Birmingham. A concise History - Five Centuries*. (Article in Hinrichsen's Musical Year Book, 1945-46. London, 1946).
Stainton de B. Taylor: *Two Centuries of Music in Liverpool*. Liverpool, 1974.
Nicholas Temperley: *The Music of the English Parish Church*. Cambridge, 1979.
Chris Upton: *A History of Birmingham*. Chichester, 2004.
Victoria County History: A *History of the County of Warwick*. Volume VII, Birmingham. University of London, 1964.
Rachel E. Waterhouse: *The Birmingham and Midland Institute*. Birmingham, 1954.
Margaret Worsley: *A History of the Birmingham Philharmonic Orchestra*. Birmingham, 1999.
Percy M. Young: A *Future for English Music* and other lectures by Edward Elgar. Great Britain, 1968.
Percy M Young: *Letters to Nimrod from Edward Elgar*. London, 1965.
Percy M Young: *The English Glee*. Oxford, 1990.

Newspapers, journals

Aris's Birmingham Gazette (from 1741)	Sundry numbers
Birmingham Daily Gazette	Sundry numbers
The Musical Times	Sundry numbers

Bibliography

The British Musician and Musical News	Sundry numbers
The Midland Musician	Sundry numbers
The Birmingham Post	Sundry numbers
British Music	Vols. 19 and 20

Compact discs

Divas (Volume 1, 1906-1935)	Nimbus Records
Divas (Volume 2, 1909-1940)	Nimbus Records
Including Tetrazzini, Melba, Patti, Eva Turner, Maggie Teyte etc.	
The Great Violinists including Joachim, Sarasate, Ysaÿe	Testament

Primary Sources

1. Chantry certificates: Warwickshire. Birmingham, St. Martins. Public Record Office E 301/31, page 28.
2. At the Birmingham Central Library, Local Studies and History:
   Programmes etc. of the following:
   Amateur Harmonic Association of Birmingham. 1856-89
   Birmingham Concerts Society. (Halford's Concerts 1897-1907)
   Birmingham Festival Choral Society. 1845-1951
   Birmingham Music Meetings and Musical Festivals in aid of the General Hospital. 1768-1912
   Birmingham Schools Choral Union. 1867-78
   Harrison's Concerts. 1853-1916
   Max Mossel's Concerts. 1898-1925
   Stockley's Concerts. 1870-97
   Stratton's Concerts. 1862-98

Index

Please note: certain entries are listed in categories as for example, choirs, composers etc.

Ackté, Aino, 181
Aird-Briscoe, Mme. 289
Allt, W. Greenhouse 241
Anderton, Thomas 150
Ansermet, Ernst 252
Archives and Primary Sources
    Birmingham (various) 184, 266
Aris's Birmingham Gazette 16
Armstrong, Sheila 296
Arts Funding,
    general 127, 302-303
    National Federation of Music Societies 302
    West Midlands Arts 302
Arts promotion CEMA 286
Aston, Peter 311
Austin, Frederic 238

Bache family 147
    Constance 149
    Edward 110, 148, 149-150, 159
    Walter 142, 148-149
Backhaus, Wilhelm 142, 235
Baker, Arthur 281, 315
Baker, Janet 296, 301
Ballads, 5, 10, 40, 44
    see also Freeth, John
Ballet, Birmingham Royal 327-8
Banfield Stephen 309
Banks, Violet 234
Balfour, Margaret 304
Bantock, Granville 159, 240-245, 305
Barbirolli, John 264
Baines, Hamilton 264
Bassano, Miss 100

BBC in Birmingham 312-313
Beard family
    F. W. (Fred) 226, 227, 241
    Paul 241, 300, 334
Beecham, Thomas
    216, 218-223, 237, 284
Bellamy, Thomas 90
Bells 44
Berry, Gwen 267, 299
Billington, Mrs. Elizabeth 53-4
Bintley, David 328
Birmingham,
    Domesday Survey 2
    general history 80-81
    markets and fairs 4
    early orchestral players 89, 98
Birmingham Musical Guild 174
Birch, Charlotte 122
Blackall, Allan K 226, 305
Blom, Eric 255, 261. 308, 334
Bothe (Booth), William 8
Bond, Capell 23, 67
Borovsky, Alexander 304
Borwick, Leonard 209
Boulton, Matthew 29, 30
Boughton, Rutland 227, 229, 241, 334-5
Boulanger, Nadia 275-6
Boult, Adrian 251-5, 270, 288, 308
Boulton, Matthew 76, 82
Bowman, James 309
Bradbeer, Albert 267
Bradbury, John 303
Braham, John 52, 61-3, 90, 100
Brain, Alfred (bro. of Aubrey) 248
Brema, Marie 238
Brent, Charlotte (Mrs. Pinto) 26, 52-53
Brian, William Havergal 212, 215, 216, 335

346

Bridge, J. S. 300
Bridgewater, Leslie 310
Broadcasting from Birmingham 312
Bromley, Tom 312
Brookes, Oliver 309
Brooks, David 246, 250
    Lady Brooks 250
Broome, Michael 15-19, 154
Brown, Iona 318
Brüggen, Franz 318
Buckley, Robert 204, 247
Buckman, Rosina 335-6
Buesst, Aylmer 258
Buggins, Samuel
    as singer 66, 104
    Oratorio Choral Soc. 66, 104
Bülow, Hans von 142
Bunce, John Thackeray 161
Busoni, Ferruccio 142, 232
Butt, Clara 145-6, 236
Butt, Richard 291
Butterworth, Naomi 288

Caradori-Allen 90, 97, 102
Carpenter, Nellie 142
Carus, Louis 307
Casals, Pablo 142, 181
Casken, John 311
Catalani, Angelica 56-7
Catley, Gwen 258
Catterall, Arthur 235, 299
Cave, Alfred 257, 299
Cervetto, James 47
Chamberlain,
    Joseph 253
    Neville 220, 246, 329
Chamber Concerts
    Amati Ensemble 303
    Barber Institute Concerts 304-5
    Birmingham Chamber
    Music Society 300-1
    Birmingham Conservatoire 307
    Birmingham Ensemble 326
    Birmingham Music Guild 300
    Catterall, Arthur 299
    Cave, Alfred 299

    Chamber Music Club 300
    Cohen, Alex 299
    Grosvenor Concerts 303
    Halcyon Consort 303
    Midland Chamber Players 300
    Mossel, Max 299
    Midland Arts Fellowship 300
    RBSA/Midland Musicians Concerts
    Society 301-2
    Ridgdowne Series 300
    Stratton, Stephen Concerts 141, 173
Chantries 8
Chipp, E. 105
Choirs
    Birmingham Bach Choir 291-2, 328
    Birmingham Festival Choral
    Society 66, 107-8, 225-6, 288, 328
    Birmingham Choral Union 166, 292
    Birmingham Oratorio Choral Society 66
    Cecilian Society 135
    Chappell Society 24-5
    City of Birmingham Choir
    226-7, 289-91, 328
    City of B'ham Symphony Chorus
    (formerly CBSO Chorus) 326-7
    Choral Society of the Town 66
    Ex Cathedra 293, 328
    Matthews' Birmingham Choir 228
    Midland Musical Society 228
    Miller Johnstone Madrigal Choir 235
    Musical and Amicable Society 20-1, 66
    New Choral Society
    (Rutland Boughton) 229
    Oriana and Rubery Choirs 288
    smaller and suburban choirs 230
    visiting choirs 229
Choral and Orchestral Societies
    Amateur Harmonic Association 134
    Birmingham Choral and Orchestral
    Assoc. 166, 227-8
    Birmingham Musical Association 133, 166
    Midland Musical Society 133, 165-6, 228
Christopher, Cyril 285
Churches
    Carrs Lane 161, 164
    Edgbaston Parish Church 297

Halesowen Parish Church,
    (Churchwardens. Accounts) 9
Harborne Parish Church 297
Oratory, The 162, 297
St. Alban's 297
St. Augustine's, Edgbaston 297
St. Bartholomew's 21, 22
St. Chad's Cathedral 162, 297
St. George's, Edgbaston 297
St. Martin's 70, 71,163, 297
St. Paul's, Hockley 46, 297
St. Peter's, Wolverhampton 9
St. Philip's Cathedral 12, 164, 229, 297
Clarke, Jeremiah 39, 154
Clef Club 120
Clifford, Julian 217
Clinton, Gordon 306
Clodeshales family 7, 8
Coates, John 226, 236, 239
Coffee Houses
    Cooke's, 20-21
    Freeth's 40-43, 80
Cohen, Alex 247
Collier, Charles 176
Composers whose music was played in Birmingham grouped in paragraphs throughout the text
Composers born or resident in B'ham listed individually
Concert life in Birmingham 18C 38
Concerts, Monday Evening 'Pops' 129-133
Cooke, Arthur 247
Corder, Frederick 159
Cortot, Alfred 304
Costa, Michael 104-5, 109-116, 119
Costello, Cecilia 294
Cowen, Frederick 217
Coward, Henry 155-6, 227
Cramer family
    Franz 60, 63-4, 90, 109, 110
    J.B. 63-4
    Wilhelm 47, 50-1, 60, 63
Craxton, Harold 235
Croft, William 68
Crosby, Denis 292
Crosdil, John 64

Culp, Julia 233
Cunningham, George (G. D.) 288, 290, 298
Curioni, Signor 90
Curwen, John 155-6, 242

Davies, Fanny 142, 232, 234, 236
Davies, Meredith 269-70
Davies, Philippa 302
Dawson, George 253
Delius, Frederick 241
Dickinson, Peter 311
Dohnányi, Ernö 252
Dolmetsch, Arnold 159
Donohoe, Peter 290
Downes family
    Andrew 310
    Frank 306-7
    Herbert 300
Dunhill, Frederick 291

Early Music Festival, Birmingham 309
Edmunds, Christopher 285, 300, 305, 310
Education in Music
    CBSO Concerts for Children 248
    Competition Music Festivals 243-4
    Conservatoire, former Midland Institute School of Music and Birmingham School of Music 156-8, 240-2, 305-7
    Schools, 153-4, 307-8, 329
    Tonic Sol-fa system 154-5
    University of Birmingham 242, 304-5 328-9
Element Quartet 312
Elgar, Edward in Birmingham 195-205,
    music played by Elgar in Stockley's Orchestra 169-71
    composer at Festivals 195-99
    at University of Birmingham 200-203
    as conductor 203-4, 247
    interest in Halford's series 212
    opinions about musicians 231, 239
Elinson, Iso 304
Eliot, George 98-9
Elliott, Edwin 225
Elwes, Gervase 181
Erskine, Mr. oboist 65

Index

Facer, Thomas 227
Feeney Trust 265, 268, 273
Festivals (Birmingham Music Meetings and
    Musical Festivals)
    first oratorios in town 22-4
    Music Meetings 24-8, 46-50
    early organisation 69
    history of 69
    at St. Martin's Church 70
    social comment on 78-9
    chorus and orchestra at Town Hall 87-8
    early solo singers 90, 98
    first performances 113
    solo singers in 1864 112
    distinguished instrumentalists 142
    organisation, 1849-82 116-8, 179
    receipts 189-91
    standards of performance 192
    changing tastes 191-2
    social changes and war 192-3
Ffrangcon-Davies, David 226
Fiedler, Max 217
Fleming, Anthony 285
Fletcher, Geoffrey 298
Fletcher, Lyn 176
Fletcher, Mr. 76
Flute Society 135-6
Folk Song 43-4, 293-4
Fortune, Nigel 308-9
Forty, Gerald 264
Foster, Muriel 181, 226, 236
Freeth, John 32, 40-44
Frémaux, Louis 276-281

Gade, Niels 114
Galli-Curci, Amelita 304
Garcia family
    Manuel, senior 58
    Manuel, junior 58
    Maria (Malibran) 58-9
    Pauline (Viardot) 58, 96
Gaskell, Elizabeth 28
Gaul, A.R. 157-8
German, Edward 217
Gill, Allen 217
Glock, William 311

Glover, Sarah Ann 154-5
Goddard, Arabella 142
Godfrey, Dan 248
Goossens, Eugene 237
Goossens, Leon 248
Gounod, Charles 114-5
Grainger, Percy 142
Grant, Willis 191, 198
Gray, Harold 269-70, 275, 277, 282 289, 292, 306
Greatorex, Thomas 67-8, 109
Greef, Arthur de 142, 222
Green, Russell 292
Greene, H. Plunkett 235
Greer, Francis, 302
Grew, Sydney 308, 336-7
Griesbach, Mr. 65
Grisi, Giulia 95-6, 100, 112, 124, 126, 138
Guild of the Holy Cross 2, 7
Gunn, Barnabas 13-15, 22, 154

Halford, George 171, 206-213, 329, 337
Hall, Marie 142, 232
Hallé, Charles 140, 142
    Hallé, Lady (Wilma Norman-Neruda) 142
Halsey, Simon 326
Hambourg, Mark 142, 233
Handford, Maurice 277, 279
Hann, William 140
Harper, Thomas 97, 112
Harris, Joseph 19, 39
Harrison, Julius 241, 258, 285, 310
Harrison, Thomas and Percy 137-146
Harty, Hamilton 233. 247
Hawes, Maria B. 122
Hawkins, Mr. 90
Hayes, Catherine 125
Hazlehurst, Marjorie 312
Heap, Charles Swinnerton 159, 226, 337-8
Heath, John R. 309
Hely-Hutchinson, Victor 256, 311
Herschel, George 218, 233
Heward, Leslie 255-8, 285, 288
Hewitt, Beatrice 235
History, General 187
Hobbs, Richard 25, 26, 154
Hock, Johann 285, 300, 338

Hogwood, Christopher 309
Holliger, Heinz 318
Hollins, George 84-5, 98, 104
Holst, Henry 300
Holt (Harold Holt Concerts) 304
Horncastle, Mr. 90
Howell, Dorothy 300, 310
Howells, Herbert 292
Hutton, William 45
Huxley, Marcus 297
Hyde, Walter 238, 338
Hytch, Arthur 228, 310

Iles, Edna 254, 312
Inns, music in the 10
International Concerts at Symphony Hall 327

Jackson, Bernard 291
Jackson, Francis 298
James, Wilfred 248
Jazz in Birmingham 184, 325
Jaeger, A. J. (Nimrod) 181
Jenkins, Lyndon 327
Jennens family
    Charles 21
    John, Iron Master 21
Jeritza, Maria 304
Joachim, Joseph 140, 142, 234
Johnstone, Miller 242
Jonas, George 315, 324
Joubert, John 311
Jowett, Andrew 327
Jullien, Louis 128-9

Kelly, Michael 61
Kempson, James 15, 19, 20, 22, 24, 26, 30, 154, 329
Kennedy, Daisy 233
Kennedy, Nigel 303
Kenrick, Byng 264
Ketèlbey, Albert 310-11
Keys, Ivor C. B. 305
Knyvett family
    Charles, son. 60
    William 60, 90, 98, 104
    Mrs. (Deborah Travis) 90

Kraemer, Nicholas 318
Kreisler, Fritz 142, 304
Kubelik, Jan 142

Lablache
    Frederick (son) 95, 97, 98 100, 112
    Luigi (father) 95-6
Lancashire Women Singers 47, 66
    See also Knyvett family
Lara, Adelina de 142-4
Larley, Patrick 289
Ledsham, Ian 309
Lehane, Maureen 296
Lehmann, Liza 304
Leider, Frieda 304
Leipsig, St. Thomas's Church 291
Lewis, Anthony 296, 305
Liberman, Victor 318
Lill, John 303
Lind, Jenny 127
Lindley, J. 51
Lindley, Robert 51, 64, 90, 98
Liszt, Franz - in Birmingham 122-3
Liverpool Philharmonic Hall 256
Lloyd, Stephen 264
Lockey, Charles 102-3
Loder, John David 90
Longbridge Motor Works 280
Lowenstein, Gunilla 303
Lucombe, Emma 126
    (Mrs. Sims Reeves)
Lumby, Herbert 310
Lunar Society 29-30
Lunn, Charles 151-2, 159, 238
Lunn, Kirkby 239
Lunt, Rev. F. 305
Lyn, Harry van der 300
McCormack, John 181
McGegan, Nicholas 318
Mackenzie, A. G. 159
MacMahon, Desmond 292
Macready
    William 73
    William Charles 73
Machin, Mr. (bass) 90
Maddock, Stephen 328

350

Index

Magazines
    Music Magazines in Birmingham 39
        (See also under Grew)
Mahon family 47
    John 65
    Mrs. Ambrose 55, 65
    Mrs. Second 55, 65
    Mrs. Salmon 55, 65
    William 65
Major, Blyth 288
Malibran, Maria (see Garcia)
Manton, G. H. 235-6
Mara, Gertrud Elizabeth 54-5
Mario, Giovanni Matteo 95, 99, 100, 112, 124, 138
Markets and Fairs (see Birmingham)
Mason, Lowell 108, 186, 192
Massey, Roy 291
Matthews, Appleby 235, 246-51, 338
Maunder, Dennis 296
Melba, Nellie 217
Mellers, Wilfred 300
Mellon, Alfred 127, 154, 338
Mendelssohn, Felix 93-7, 100-03
Midland Concert Promoters
    Assoc. 1916 (see Orchestras)
Midland Institute Music Staff 134-5, 140, 156-7, 241
Midlands Arts Centre,
    Cannon Hill Park (mac) 296
Minadieu, Madame 235
Munden, Thomas 84-5, 90, 98, 104
Moiseiwitsch, Benno 233
Moore, Joseph 50, 76-7, 82-86, 103-4, 240, 329
Morris, O'Connor 236
Morley, Christopher 302
Moscheles, Ignaz 90
Mossel, Max 159, 232, 234-6, 329
Mullings, Frank 236
Munrow, David 309
Murdoch, William 235
Musatti, Signor 97
Music Sellers and Shops 39
    Dale Forty 235-6
    Priestley and Sons 233
    Riley, Josef 304
    Sabin, later Stockley and Sabin 107
    Stockley's (Stockley and Sabin) 179, 233
Musical and Amicable Society (see Choirs)
Musicians Union 248-9, 255
Neruda, Wilma (see Hallé)
Neukomm, Chevalier Sigismund 90, 92
Newman, Ernest 241, 308, 339
Nicholls, Agnes 236, 238
Nicholson, Sydney 243, 255
North, T.W. 291, 298
Novello, Clara 90-1, 99, 112, 138

O'Donnell, Walter 285
Office Holders (Music) in Birmingham 331-3
O'Neill, Mary 309
Opera
    Barber Operas 295-6
    Beecham Opera Company 236, 238-9
    Birmingham Opera Company
        (Touring Opera) 296
    Birmingham Repertory Theatre 295
    Birmingham University Guild Operas 296
    Carl Rosa Company 236-9
    Castillano Italian and English Company 239
    Covent Garden Opera 295
    D'Oyly Carte Company 236-8
    Early Italian Opera in Birmingham 73-5
    Italian Grand Opera 124-7
    Italian Opera Company 237
    Midland Arts Centre 296
    Midland Institute Opera 239
    Midland Music Makers Grand
        Opera Company 287
    Midland Opera Company
        (Victor Fleming) 287
    Moody Manners Company 236-7
    O'Mara Company 238
    Quinlan Company 239
    Turner Opera Company 237
    Welsh National Opera Company 294-5
Oramo, Sakari 257, 285, 324
Orchestras players 89, 98, 215-6
Orchestras in Birmingham
    (NOTE: CBO/CBSO listed at the end
        of this section)
    Academy of St. Philip's 288

Appleby Matthews Orchestra 223
BBC Midland Light Orchestra 287
BBC Midland Orchestra 285, 287, 312
Beecham Orchestra 222-3, 284
Beecham Orchestral Concerts 222-3
Birmingham Chamber Orchestra 285
Birmingham Concerts Society 216-7
Birmingham Orchestral Concerts
    Society 217-8
Birmingham Schools Symphony
    Orchestra 288
Birmingham Sinfonietta 288
Birmingham Philharmonic Orchestra 287
Birmingham Philharmonic Society 218-9
Birmingham Symphony Orchestra 215-7
Birmingham Wireless Station Orchestra
    (Wireless Symphony Orchestra)
    252, 284
Birmingham Philharmonic String Orchestra
    285-6, 300
City of Birmingham Police Band
    214, 246, 248, 285
Edgbaston Philharmonic Orchestra 214
Hallé Orchestra 222, 267
Handsworth Orchestral Society 218
Landon Ronald Promenade Concerts 218
Midland Concert Promoters'
    Association 219-21
Midland Institute School of Music
    Orchestra 285
Midland Youth Orchestra 287
Moseley Musical Club String Orchestra 284
New Birmingham Symphony Orchestra
    222
New Midland Orchestra 286
New Philharmonic Society 221
Orchestra da Camera 287
Richard Wassell Orchestra 221-2, 284
Royal Ballet Sinfonia 328
Schools Music Services Ensembles 288
Stockley's Orchestra 167-72
City of Birmingham Symphony Orchestra
CBSO Centre and associated societies 325
City of B'ham Orch. (CBO) 246-63
City of B'ham Symphony Orch.
    (CBSO) 263-283, 314-27

Civic support 218
finances and fund-raising 249, 264, 267,
    280, 323-4
International Wind Competition 274
orchestral unrest 273-4, 280-1,
raising standards 259, 269, 317
Youth Choruses and Orchestra 326
Organ builders 9, 297
Organists
    Bothe (Booth), William 8
    at St. Philip's 13-15
    at St. Martin's 22-3, 26
    church organists 19C 162-3
    Elgar's comments on 239
    Town Hall and City organists (see under:
        Cunningham, Hollins, Munden,
        Stimpson, Perkins, Thalben-Ball,
        Trotter) Oxley, T.F.H. 298

Pachmann, Vladimir de 143, 232, 304
Paderewski, Ignaz 142
Panufnik, Andrzej 268-70
Parke family
    John 65
    William 65
Parepa, Euphrosyne 237
Parry, Hubert 114
Paton, Mary 58
Patterson, Jeremy 289
Patti, Adelina 112, 138-40
Patti, Carlotta 340
Payne, Arthur W. 217
Peasgood O.H. 298
Perkins C.W. 142, 179. 181, 227, 236, 298
Petri, Egon 143, 233
Phillips, Henry 90, 122
Piatti, Alfredo 140, 142
Pinto family
    Charlotte (Brent) 52-3
    George 68
    Thomas 26, 52, 53, 63, 68
Pleasure Gardens
    Apollo Gardens 30-2
    Vauxhall Gardens 23, 30-2
Pleyel, Madame 140
Pollack, Oscar 137, 216, 217, 218, 228, 234

Ponder, William 89
Pop Music 184, 328
Pountney, T. E. 174
Pountney, William 69-70, 95
Preachers
    Dale, Dr. (Carrs Lane) 164
    Dawson, George
Preston, Hamish 293
Probin family 15
Pugin, Augustus 162

Rachmaninov, Sergei 209-10, 304
Radford, Robert 226, 238
Raybould, Clarence 235, 241-2
Rheinhold family
    Henry Theodore 61
    Charles 61
Rattle, Simon 185, 260, 282, 314-27, 329, 340-1
Reeves, Sims 112, 118, 123-7, 138, 140
Reeves, Mrs. (Emma Lucombe) 126
Reynish, Timothy 303
Richter, Hans 175-80, 217
Rickard, Richard 157
Ridgeway, Wilfred 261, 285, 300
Ries, Louis 140
Rignold, Hugo 271-6, 278
Roberts, Clifford 235
Robinson, Christopher 291
Robinson, Derek 280
Ronald, Landon 217-8
Rose, Karl (see Carl Rosa Opera)
Rosenthal, Maurycy 181, 304
Rubini, Giovanni-Battista 122
Rubinstein, Arthur 304
Rudersdorff, Hermine 138
Russell, Bill 264
Russell, Lynda 320
Rutland, Harold 268

Safonoff, Wassilli 218
Saint, David 297
Salmon family
    see also Mahon family 47
    Felix 247
Sammons, Albert 143
Santley, Charles 112, 217

Sargent, Malcolm 258, 269
Sarasate, Pablo 142
Scharrer, Irene 143, 233, 236, 284, 304
Schiever, Ernst 234
Schmid, Erich 281
Schools
    Blue Coat School 15
Schumann, Clara 140-1
Schumann, Elisabeth 304
Schwarz, Rudolf 265-68, 317
Sharp, Cecil 243
Sheldon A. J. 227, 247
Sibelius, Jan 240
Silk, Dorothy 227, 241, 341
Simms family
    Bishop Simms 75-6
    John sen. 75-6
    Mr. 105
Simmonds, Herbert 247
Sinclair, George 226
Skidmore, Jeffrey 293
Smith, Edward 315, 322
Smith, T. Henry 284-5
Solo singers in Harrison Series 138
Spicer, Paul 292
Stainer, John 159
Staudigl, Joseph 100, 102
Stanford, Charles 102, 217
Stephens, Catherine (Kitty) 57-8
Stevens. C. J. 157
Stimpson, James 104, 119, 142
Stockhausen, Franz 90
Stockhausen, Margarete 90
Stockley, William 105-8, 110, 113, 157, 165, 167-72, 226, 240, 329
Stone, John 260-1
Storace family 47
    Nancy 61, 64
    Stephen (sen.) 64
Stratton, Stephen (see Chamber Music)
Strauss, Richard 197, 208
Stubbs, Keith 326
Supervia, Conchita 304
Sullivan, Arthur 120
Sutton, A. J. 105, 157
Szekely, Julianna 315

353

Tamburini, Antonio 95, 96, 112
Taylor, Mr. (bass) 90
Taylor, Coleridge 227, 241
Terrail, Mr. (counter-tenor) 90
Tertis, Lionel 235
Thalberg, Sigismond 123
Theatre Music
    18C 34-7
    19C 72-3, 122
Theatres as venues
    Alexandra 294
    Birmingham Repertory 295
    Hippodrome 296
    Moor Street Theatre 22
    Prince of Wales 295
    Theatre Royal 73
    The Theatre, New St. 22
Thomas, Peter 326
Tietjens, Thérèse 112
Timms, Colin 309, 330
Thalben-Ball, George 298
Tonic Sol-fa Association 156
Trotter, Thomas 298, 327
Tubb, Carrie 181
Turnage, Mark-Anthony 319, 321
Turner, Eva 237, 295
Twentieth Century
    state of music in the city 185-8
Tyler, James 309

University of Birmingham
    Barber Institute of Fine Arts 295

Valentine, Thomas 76
Vaughan, Thomas 90
Venues
    Barber Institute 295, 304-5
    Birmingham and Midland Institute 234
    Botanical Gardens 234
    CBSO Centre 303, 324
    Futurist Theatre 250
    Grand Hotel 234, 303
    Masonic Hall, New St. 234
    Prince of Wales Theatre 234
    Queen's College, Paradise St. 234
    RBSA Gallery, New St. 234

Symphony Hall 321
Town Hall 82, 179, 254-5, 319
Verbrugghen, Henri 217
Verne, Adela, 142, 241, 235
Verne, Mathilde 232
Vyner, Michael 318

Walter, Bruno 252
Wassell, Richard 227, 246-7, 284, 298
Waterhouse, John 262-4
Weichsel, Charles 90
Weldon, George 258-65, 267, 317
Weller, Walter 322
Wesley family
    Samuel, father 68
    S.S. (son) 99
West, Eira 303
Westrup, Jack 309
Whenham, John 309
White, Michael 323
Whitehill, Clarence 181
Wilhelmj, August 142
Willcocks, David 290
Willmann, Thomas 65, 98
Wilson, R.H. 181
Wilson, Steuart 305-6
Wilson-Johnson, David 302
Wishart, Peter 311
Wood, Henry 181, 215, 217-8, 288, 299, 310
Wood, Lena 299, 312
Wyck, Wilfrid van 304

Young, Percy M. 10, 200
Ysaÿe, Eugène 142